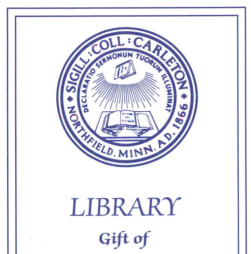

Dissenting Knowledges, Open Futures

Dissenting Knowledges, Open Futures

The Multiple Selves and Strange Destinations of Ashis Nandy

edited by
VINAY LAL

OXFORD
UNIVERSITY PRESS

OXFORD
UNIVERSITY PRESS

YMCA Library Building, Jai Singh Road, New Delhi 110001

Oxford University Press is a department of the University of Oxford. It furthers the
University's objective of excellence in research, scholarship, and education
by publishing worldwide in

Oxford   New York

Athens   Auckland   Bangkok   Bogota   Buenos Aires   Calcutta
Cape Town   Chennai   Dar es Salaam   Delhi   Florence   Hong Kong   Istanbul
Karachi   Kuala Lumpur   Madrid   Melbourne   Mexico City   Mumbai
Nairobi   Paris   Sao Paolo   Shanghai   Singapore   Taipei   Tokyo   Toronto   Warsaw

with associated companies in   Berlin   Ibadan

Oxford is a registered trade mark of Oxford University Press
in the UK and in certain other countries

Published in India
By Oxford University Press, New Delhi

ISBN   019 565 1154

Typeset by Excellent Laser Typesetters, Pitampura, Delhi 110 034
and printed by Rashtriya Printers, Delhi 110 032
Published by Manzar Khan, Oxford University Press
YMCA Library Building, Jai Singh Road, New Delhi 110 001

For Uma Nandy,
Anju,
and to the memory of
D. R. Nagaraj

Preface

In the spring of 1997, Ashis Nandy visited the University of California, Los Angeles, as the Regents' Professor. This was not his first visit to this campus; two years earlier, while he was on one of his not infrequent trips to the United States, I had arranged for him to speak to the faculty and students on Girindrasekhar Bose, India's first psychoanalyst, and the subject of a long paper in Nandy's *The Savage Freud*. In the course of that visit, Nandy also spoke to a smaller audience, mainly interested in South Asian history, the future of Indian civilization, and the prospects of pluralism, on the debacle at Ayodhya and the cultural politics of Hindu militancy. His visit generated such interest that it seemed eminently desirable to bring him back for a longer visit. No one who has any acquaintance with the Regents of the University of California, a body of largely conservative political appointees not particularly noted for their sagacity or intellectual perspicacity, would have thought it likely that Nandy, who has unsettled many an ingrained habit of thinking, would strike the Regents as an appropriate holder of a signal honour from the University of California. None the less, to my great and welcome surprise, I found that my nomination of Nandy as the Regents' Professor had succeeded, and that he was prepared to spend three weeks in Los Angeles.

It is in connection with his visit that the faculty and graduate student collective at UCLA, known as the Group for the Study of Composite Cultures, with which I have for some years been associated, decided that a special double issue of the journal *Emergences*, which from time to time had been published by the collective, would be devoted to the work of Ashis Nandy. Though Nandy has been a prominent public intellectual in India for two decades, besides being one of the principal social theorists anywhere in the world, no systematic attempt had been made to assess his work. While he has himself collected together many of his best essays in a number of books, almost an equal number of his essays remain scattered in journals that are less accessible, and many, as is indubitably common in such cases, remain unpublished. His shorter pieces have often been reprinted, sometimes with alterations, without his permission, and he has informed me that once he found a certain piece of his appearing in a Pakistani newspaper under someone else's name. A reader of his representative writings has never been put together, though reputable presses such as Routledge and Basil Blackwell have made an industry of this kind with respect to well-known Western intellectuals. There is also the consideration that the last substantive work of any kind on Indian intellectuals was done by the late Edward Shils several decades ago, and that the sociology of Indian intellectual life has not been attempted, or even gestured at, though places such as Delhi, Calcutta, and Hyderabad now appear on the circuit of the much-travelled post-colonial, Marxist, and post-structuralist thinkers in the American (and to a lesser extent British) academy. In recent years, for example, Edward Said, Frederic Jameson, and Stephen Greenblatt have visited and lectured in India, to the great delight of their numerous Indian admirers, but it is not entirely certain whether any Indian intellectual would receive the same adulation or even attention. It was less than ten years ago that a very prominent Indian historian, who presided over one of the country's premier institutions for social and historical research, remarked to me that he thought Nandy to be a romantic, whose works were taken more seriously in the West than in India. And it is only this year that a senior member of the subaltern history collective conceded to me that Nandy, at long last, had to be taken seriously in his own country, however 'outrageous' his position on a number of subjects. Thus, the *Emergences* issue on Nandy, which was released in mid-1997, can also be construed as an attempt to initiate work on Indian intellectuals, and hint at the importance of locating Nandy within the intellectual and public life of India.

I would like to thank the members of the Group for the Study of Composite Cultures for their initiative in publishing *Emergences*, and so furnishing an unusual vehicle for various projects, such as the special issue on Nandy's work, that might not otherwise have seen fruition. Every member of the collective, myself included, owes a special debt to Teshome Gabriel, Professor of Film and

Media Studies and one of the founders of the collective: his vision, generosity, and energy have made him a legendary figure on the UCLA campus. Special thanks are also owed to those members of the collective—Peter Bloom, Joyce Boss, Reinaldo Roman, and Jim Wiltgen—who contributed very substantially to the success of the double issue. A substantial portion of the present volume is a reprint of the material appearing in *Emergences*, but my introduction expands considerably upon the shorter essay in the journal. Moreover, the essays by Arif Dirlik, Frederick Buell, and Makarand Paranjape have been written especially for this book, and Nandy's Regents' lecture on the gods and goddesses of India also makes its first appearance, in its present revised version, in this volume. I am grateful to Arif Dirlik, Fred Buell, and Makarand Paranjape, and to the other contributors—Dipesh Chakrabarty, Peter Wollen, Ziauddin Sardar, and Roby Rajan—for reflecting on what the work of Nandy has meant to them and what it might mean to everyone else, and for furnishing us with those cues that make it possible to do a critical reading of the principal vectors of Nandy's thought. My greatest obligation, of course, is to Ashis Nandy, whose first, wholly characteristic, remark upon being told of this enterprise was that it was a sure sign that he was growing old, much as he felt moved by the endeavour. Ashis has been a remarkable friend and mentor over the years, and this volume is the expression of my appreciation, which is shared by a great many people and certainly by the contributors, of his profoundly democratic sensibilities, not to mention what he has done by way of opening the space in India and elsewhere for a real intellectual engagement with the principal issues of the day.

I would like to express my gratitude to Oxford University Press in Delhi, who have been Nandy's publishers for many years, for agreeing to take up this enterprise. This book is dedicated to three individuals. First, it is for Uma, who has shared Ashis's life for several decades, and never fails (at least in my presence!) to take his foibles in her stride. Her good, often sardonic, humour has made Ashis's company all the more agreeable, besides providing the first and most immediate warrant for treating him without the slightest shade of reverence. This book is also for my wife, Anju, whose tolerance for my own, not inconsiderable foibles, is greatly though not always openly appreciated. Last, but not least, it is dedicated to the memory of the late D. R. Nagaraj, whose unanticipated death in the prime of life robbed Ashis of a colleague, and Indian intellectuals and activists of one of the most probing and dissenting voices of our times.

VINAY LAL

Los Angeles
19 December 1998

Contents

Contributors   xiii

PART I

1. The Defiance of Defiance and Liberation for the
   Victims of History: Ashis Nandy in Conversation
   with Vinay Lal
   edited with an introduction and notes by Vinay Lal   3

PART II
Writings by Ashis Nandy

2. The After-Life of the Raj in Indian Academe   97

3. How I Stopped Worrying and Started Loving
   the Babus   116

4. A Report on the Present State of Health of the
   Gods and Goddesses in South Asia   127

5. Themes of State, History, and Exile in South Asian
   Politics: Modernity and The Landscape of
   Clandestine and Incommunicable Selves   151

6. The Decline in the Imagination of the Village   176

7. The Fantastic India-Pakistan Battle: Or the Future
   of the Past in South Asia   186

8. The Philosophy of Coca-Cola   201

9. The Fear of Plague: The Inner Demons of a Society   205

PART III
Critical Perspectives on Ashis Nandy

10. The A B C D (and E) of Ashis Nandy
    Ziauddin Sardar   211

11. In the Interstices of Tradition and Modernity:
    Exploring Ashis Nandy's Clandestine and
    Incommunicable Selves
    Makarand Paranjape   233

12. The Modern Indian Intellectual and the Problems
    of the Past: An Engagement with the Thoughts of
    Ashish Nandy
    Dipesh Chakrabarty   249

13. Reading Ashis Nandy: The Return of the Past;
    or Modernity with a Vengeance
    Arif Dirlik   260

14. Evasions of the Postmodern Desire
    Roby Rajan   287

15. Ashis Nandy and Globalist Discourse
    Frederick Buell   309

16. Cricket and Modernity
    Peter Wollen   334

    Selected Bibliography, 1979–98, of the Writings of
    Ashis Nandy
    Compiled by Vinay Lal   345

Notes on Contributors

FREDERICK BUELL is Professor of English at Queens College, New York. He is the author of several books of poetry, most recently *Full Summer* (Wesleyan), and several books of cultural criticism, most recently *National Culture and the New Global System* (1994).

DIPESH CHAKRABARTY is Professor in the Departments of History and South Asian Languages and Civilizations at the University of Chicago, and a founding member of the Subaltern Studies collective. He is the author of *Rethinking Working-Class History: Bengal, 1890–1940* (1989) and papers on a wide array of subjects, including colonial history, Marxism, post-modernism, and the politics of history.

ARIF DIRLIK is Professor of History at Duke University, where he specializes in modern China. His most recent works include *Postmodernism and China* (co-edited), *Critical Perspectives on Mao Zedong's Thought* (co-edited), *The Postcolonial Aura: Third World Criticism in the Age of Global Capitalism*, *After the Revolution: Waking to Global Capitalism*, and *Schools Into Fields and Factories: Anarchists, the Guomindang, and the National Labour University in Shanghai, 1927–32* (with Ming Chan). He is currently a fellow at the Netherlands Institute for Advanced Studies.

VINAY LAL is Assistant Professor of History at the University of California, Los Angeles. He is the author of *South Asian Cultural Studies: A Bibliography* (1996), and editor of an ethnography from the colonial period, *The History of Railway Thieves* (new edition, 1996). His papers on popular Indian cinema, the Indian diaspora, Gandhi, the cultural politics of sexuality, the history of colonial India, American politics, and various other subjects have appeared in nearly three dozen periodicals.

ASHIS NANDY is Senior Fellow of the Centre for the Study of Developing Societies, Delhi, and Chair of the Committee for

Cultural Choices and Global Futures. He is renowned internationally as a cultural critic, social theorist, and political psychologist, and his books include *The Intimate Enemy: Loss and Recovery of Self under Colonialism* (1982), *Traditions, Tyranny, and Utopias: Essays in the Politics of Awareness* (1987), *The Savage Freud and Other Essays on Possible and Retrievable Selves* (1995), and *Alternative Sciences* (new edn, 1995).

MAKARAND PARANJAPE is Associate Professor in the Department of Humanities and Social Sciences at the Indian Institute of Technology. He has published several novels and volumes of poetry in English, and he writes widely on Indian literature and criticism, modern Indian thinkers, and twentieth-century theory. His most books include *Decolonization and Development: Hind Svaraj Revisioned* (1993, with a foreword by Ashis Nandy), *The Narrator: A Novel* (1995), and *Nativism: Essays in Criticism* (1997, edited).

ROBY RAJAN is Professor in the School of Business at the University of Wisconsin, Parkside. His previous contributions have appeared in *The Journal of Development Studies, Third World Quarterly, Operations Research Empirical Economics, The International Economic Review, Cato Journal, Alternatives,* and *Rethinking Marxism.*

ZIAUDDIN SARDAR is a free-lance writer, critic, broadcaster, and intellectual, based in London, and formerly a Visiting Professor of Science Policy at Middlesex University. He is the editor of *Futures*, and the author and co-author of numerous books on Islam, science, and cultural politics. His most recent publications include *Distorted Imagination: Lessons from the Rushdie Affair* (1990), *Barbaric Others: A Manifesto on Western Racism* (1993), *Muhammad for Beginners* (1994), *Cyberfutures: Culture and Politics on the Information Superhighway* (1996), *Cultural Studies for Beginners* (1997), and *Postmodernism and the Other: The New Imperialism of Western Culture* (1998).

PETER WOLLEN is Professor in the School of Film and T. V. at UCLA. His books include *Signs and Meaning in the Cinema* (1972), *Raiding the Icebox: Reflections on Twentieth-Century Culture* (1993), and *Howard Hawks, American Artist* (1996).

Part I

Part 1

The Defiance of Defiance and Liberation for the Victims of History: Ashis Nandy in Conversation with Vinay Lal

Edited with an Introduction and
Note by Vinay Lal

For nearly two decades now, Ashis Nandy has been a striking figure on the Indian intellectual scene. Nandy is a Senior Fellow and former Director of the Centre for the Study of Developing Societies, New Delhi, and Chairman of the Committee for Cultural Choices and Global Futures, which derives some of its memberships from the Centre. These formal designations, however, do not as much as hint at his extraordinary place in the public life of India as a writer, thinker, public intellectual, human rights activist, and mentor to innumerable young men and women. His influence, moreover, extends far beyond India and the neighbouring South Asian countries to which he has been a regular visitor. He has played a critical role in alerting Indian intellectuals to the fact, which comes as a great surprise to many of India's metropolitan elites, that there is a world beyond India and the West, in establishing activist links between countries in the southern part of the world, and in initiating an intellectual dialogue between India and other Third-World nations. Nandy has also striven to forge a close relationship with such of those Western scholars and intellectuals who constitute a dissident minority in their own cultures. He has been admitted into the fraternity of great 'post-colonial theorists', though he himself would have little use for such a strikingly inapt form of recognition; and much of his work also stands at the forefront of what is today termed 'cultural studies' in the Western academy, though he may well disavow that not unambiguous recognition as well. Other readers and intellectuals, who are readily prepared to acknowledge the destructive legacy of colonialism and its forms of knowledge, are aware that Nandy's voice is among those which have helped to conscientize the West and make it cognizant of its own suppressed traditions of knowledge and dissent. In introducing one of his works, *Traditions, Tyranny, and Utopias: Essays in the Politics of Awareness* (Oxford, 1987), the well-known and controversial French intellectual, Roger Garaudy, noted that Nandy had delineated the 'central and vital debate of our times', that between 'an "alternative perspective" and "modern oppression".' Though Nandy has received more than the usual honours and accolades that intellectuals and academics of his attainments can expect, and though he sits on the editorial board of a dozen influential international journals, from *Psychoanalytic Review* and *Review of International Political Economy* to *Public Cultural* and *Futures*, his work with numerous human rights bodies, NGOs, and other organizations and intellectual collectives points to his wide public presence, fortunately extending far beyond the academy.

Nandy is the author of seven books, the co-author of three other books, and the editor of yet four others; he also remains among a handful of prominent Indian writers, other than those whose medium is an Indian language, who have made it a matter of principle to have their works first published in India, in his case mainly by Oxford University Press, Delhi. The decision to publish first in India is not an empty gesture, a mere retreat into nativism or cultural nationalism, since Nandy, as shall become apparent, has endeavoured to work towards the creation of alternative information orders and knowledge systems. Though he would be quite averse to the characterization of Western publishing as a wholly imperialistic enterprise, Nandy is fully cognizant of how reading communities are shaped, the extraordinary importance often attached in India and elsewhere in the developing world to works of mediocrity emanating from the West, and the ignorance in which Indian writers, intellectuals, and activists often live of the achievements of their peers in other South Asian countries. Consequently, Nandy's writings have appeared in influential periodicals as much as those which are obscure, local, or known only to particular constituencies, and this too is indicative of his politics of knowledge. He does not care to write only for those journals which are deemed 'prestigious'. Besides the books, Nandy has published several dozen other papers which have not been pulled together into collections of essays.

The mere enumeration of the titles of Nandy's works scarcely suggests the extraordinary array of subjects to which he has put his pen, and the manner in which he has often transformed the study among more reflective scholars of all those subjects. The book for which he is most well known in the West, *The Intimate Enemy: Loss and Recovery of Self Under Colonialism* (1982), is now acknowledged to be one of the principal studies of the psychological traumas and cultural dislocation induced by colonialism, and particularly of the manner in which it victimized not only the colonized but the colonizer as well. His recent collection of essays, *The Savage Freud and Other Essays in Possible and Retrievable Selves*, which also appeared in an American paperback edition from Princeton in 1995 after its publication in Delhi (and so signifying his entrance into Western markets), contains one essay each on popular Indian cinema and the 'art' cinema of Satyajit Ray, an essay on the first Indian psychoanalyst, a commentary on middle-class reactions to the death by *sati* of an Indian woman in 1987, a searing critique of modern medicine and its vivisectionist epistemology, a discursive consideration of the Tokyo War Crimes trial and the dissenting judgment of the Indian judge who was a member of the tribunal, and an essay on the emergence of Indian terrorism. This, on closer analysis turns out to have little in common with the monster into which it has been made by political scientists and the politicians and official functionaries that they commonly serve. *The Savage Freud* was not a disparate and randomly arranged set of essays, nor was it tied together only by a certain politics of resistant reading: here, as elsewhere, the essays were to bear all the marks of Nandy's inimitable confrontation with the Indian middle classes, his exploration of the shrinking space for mythic and non-historicist readings, and his critique of the prevailing technologies of knowledge.

If this appears to convey a fairly comprehensive idea of the array of subjects on which Nandy has written and the sheer versatility of his interests, one has also to consider that Nandy has authored a cultural and psychological biography of two famous Indian scientists, a book-length study of the game of cricket, which examines cricket as a metaphor for understanding colonial and modern sensibilities, and a book on Rabindranath Tagore and his critique of nationalism. Though the destruction of the Babri Masjid in December 1992 fuelled communal passions and riots, it occasioned from Nandy and some of his younger friends in journalism and activism an extended political and empirical account of the recent growth of Hindu nationalism, and what that might portend for the future of Indian civilization. While secular intellectuals were exhorting Indians to denounce the false attractions and comforts of faith, and professional historians were attempting to unravel the 'true' history of what the government described as the 'disputed structure', Nandy was inscribing a different history to that conflict, one more sensitive to India's cultural pasts and the intellectual, cultural, and emotional resources of its own people. Nandy has certainly not been one to veer away from the most pressing and conflict-ridden issues confronting Indian society.

Besides all this in Nandy's 'oeuvre', a word that one ought to use with hesitation in respect of a writer whose work in every respect defies ordinary expectations of scholarly bulk and conventional modalities of representation, there are innumerable essays on science, development, technology, and the state; a short but incisive and blunt book (co-authored with three other scholars) on the history of racism in the West; reflections on notable Western intellectuals like Adorno and Marcuse; and numerous essays on utopias, conceptions of childhood and adulthood, the culture of Indian politics, popular Indian cinema, Indian environmentalism, and constructions of women in Indian culture. Nandy has provided, as well, the most penetrating account we have yet seen of the politics of the assassination of Mahatma Gandhi, and he is primarily responsible for having revived, through several complex cultural and oppositional readings, the intellectual interest in Gandhi, who by the 1970s had been condemned by the Indian state and its elites to survive only in museums. Where the Gandhi that continues to be peddled by the state-appointed guardians of his legacy and the purveyors of 'Gandhian thought' in university courses appears as a solemn, pious, and revered figure who can be addressed only as Bapuji, or as the 'Father of the Nation' who delivered India from its ignoble servitude to the British, Nandy has sought to alert us to a Gandhi who was essentially hermeneutic in his outlook on life, ludic and yet severe in his relations with friends and associates, autocratic yet extraordinarily democratic, and defiant not only of the models of political conduct, but even of the traditions of political dissent. Long before the communal carnage of recent years appears to have driven even unrepentant Indian communists—for whom Gandhi had always remained the pre-eminent exemplar of the bourgeois Indian sensibility, the man whose (in Gramsci's words) 'passive revolution' thwarted what might otherwise have been some 'real' revolution into an acceptance of Gandhi's humanity and ecumenism, Nandy had pointed the way to a more enriched understanding of Gandhi's moral and intellectual framework. To read Nandy on Gandhi is to understand that it is not the purported romanticism of non-violence which we are enjoined to repudiate, but the romanticism of that which prides itself as being grounded in realpolitik. It is the hard-nosed realists, who are there to remind us, gratuitously, of the ways of despots and the iron laws of history, and for whom the only argument is that there is no better alternative than the chosen path of action (that being the litmus test of ethical conduct), from whom we have the most to fear.

In considering the vast and variegated body of work authored by Nandy, one is none the less struck by the dominance of several themes, and in this respect his corpus of writings can be grouped without much injustice under several heads. His most sustained interest has been in offering a critique of what might be termed knowledge systems. How is it, as Nandy has asked, that the notions of modernity, science, development, and instrumental rationality have come to predominate in our understanding and ordering of the modern world, and what have been the consequences of imposing, largely through the mechanisms of colonialism, nationalism (the purported opposite of colonialism), and now the nation-state, these supposedly natural categories, upon the entire world? All these ideologies have been totalizing, and as Nandy's work shows, innumerable people have been, and continue to be, sacrificed in the name of development. In his cryptic (and not so easily available) essay on 'Development and Authoritarianism: An Epitaph on Social Engineering' (1985), Nandy proposed that the Third-World countries that have rapidly 'developed', and made themselves most pliable to schemes of engineering designed to eliminate the pluralism of their traditions, have also been the most authoritarian. Indeed, developmentalism has won converts and recruits over whom even the most self-aggrandizing and nakedly adventurist forms of colonialism could not triumph, and in the remotest parts of the globe, which even the long hands of colonial powers could not reach, have fallen sway to the ideologies of development and consumerism. Nandy never joined the chorus of those voices that loudly trumpeted the achievements of the Asian tigers, mindful as he has always been of the immense psychic, cultural, and physical violence perpetrated by developmental regimes in their single-minded pursuit of 'growth'; and today, in the aftermath of the crumbling of the east and southeast Asian economies, and the phenomenal growth of unemployment and poverty in Indonesia and Thailand, his withering critique of authoritarian developmentalism appears almost prescient.

The ideology of development scarcely stands by itself, since a cluster of other ideas—the nation-state, secularism, big science, technicism—have come to predominate in our times. Nandy has attacked each of these relentlessly, and shown how they came to fruition in India, with consequences that have been largely undesirable, particularly for those sectors which were already marginalized. The Indian proponents of the nation-state system, which emerged in the aftermath of the treaty of Westphalia in 1648, have jettisoned the civilizational categories with which Indians have lived for centuries, and the cultural and political homogenization of the people has been one of their principal ambitions. To transform Indians into proper citizens, who would forgo the pluralism of their past for those hardened identities that provide easy membership in supposedly natural communities, give their assent to mega-projects of nation-building (from the Bhakra dam and the Sardar Sarovar project to the acquisition of nuclear weaponry), and acquiesce to having their lives shaped by scientists, development specialists, and other experts purportedly acting for the good of the nation, the Indian state has not been averse to radically altering the lifestyles of its subjects, whatever coercion and violence that may entail. Such violence, as the twentieth century is there to remind us, has an intrinsic relation not only to instrumental notions of rationality and the intrusion of managerialism into the modern sensibility (the violence of Nazism being the most evident example), but to the very ethos of science. Disrespectful of limits, vivisectionist in its ontology, and intolerant of competing notions of knowledge, modern science has generated its own culture of oppression and become, in Nandy's words, 'a reason of state'. Its advocates doggedly retain the belief, that even the superstitious and irrational Indian can be brought around to becoming a sign of the modern. For Nandy, however, the problem resides in rationality. While the famous American critic of psychiatry, Thomas Szasz, was predisposed to demonstrating the rationality of pathologies (a not unenviable achievement), and showing the manner in which schizophrenics constructed a world-view, Nandy tells a different and less recognized tale about the pathology of rationality itself.

One might suppose from Nandy's work, though nothing would be more erroneous, that he merely counterpoises tradition to modernity, autarchy to development, irrationality to rationality, and so on. His supposed binarism has disturbed some, though a more careful reading of his—well, intimate—meditation, *The Intimate Enemy*, would compel us to view the more nuanced and deceptively simple readings he has offered as anything but merely dichotomous: 'India is not non-West; it is India.' The predictable charge often levied against Nandy by the modernizers and the Marxists,[1] that he is merely a romantic who seeks to return India to an imagined harmonious past, has its echo in similar criticism voiced against Gandhi, who did nothing less than inaugurate the critique of modernity. As Nandy argued in his brilliant reading of

---

[1] Among these one might number Meera Nanda, Achin Vanaik, and Aijaz Ahmad. Meera Nanda has, in a recent piece, denounced Nandy for helping to initiate the critique of science, which has, she notes with great regret, apparently overtaken many thinkers and scholars even in the 'rational' West. She shouts herself hoarse over what she calls 'Nandy's law', namely that 'only those intellectuals who spoke in the categories of thought shared by the subaltern masses were to be seen as progressive, only they had the right to speak for the masses.' The unintelligible animosity of her remarks is nowhere better seen than in her description of Partha Chatterjee and Dipesh Chakrabarty as '*Self-described* postcolonial or subaltern intellectuals' (emphasis added). See her 'Reclaiming Modern Science for Third World Progressive Social Movements', *Economic and Political Weekly* (18 April 1998), pp. 915–22, esp. pp. 916, 922. This critique follows on the steps of an earlier article, where her animus was chiefly directed at Vandana Shiva: 'Is Modern Science a Western, Patriarchal Myth? A Critique of the Populist Orthodoxy', *South Asia Bulletin* 11, nos. 1–2 (1991): pp. 31–61.

'Gandhi's Cultural Critique of the West' (1981, rev. edn 1987), Gandhi was not so much opposed to technology as to technicism, that is, to the view that the problems raised by technology are best resolved by technology; as for Gandhi's alleged invocation of the hoary past, Nandy has written with great incisiveness, in *The Illegitimacy of Nationalism: Rabindranath Tagore and the Politics of Self* (1994), that Gandhi's 'defence of traditions carried the intimations of a post-modern consciousness.' The 'choice,' Nandy goes on to explain elsewhere apropos Gandhi, 'is not between a traditional technique and a modern technique; it is between different traditions of technology.'

Nandy, similarly, has been often attacked for his avowed defence of tradition, a line of argumentation that derives its grounding from nothing more than his forceful critique of modernity. But not many of his critics have understood that Nandy is more interested in traditions, which are suggestive of forms of life and other possibilities for imagining inter-personal relations, than he is in tradition, which is not merely a way of evading the present but, more ominously, a way of foreclosing the future. Besides, Nandy works from within modernity, and he deploys all the tools of modernity—not only mechanically, as with internet, computers, and other forms of communication—to shape his cultural and political vision. Though he is beholden to no discipline, the small frame of the individual, be it that of the scientist Ramanujan, the jurist Radhabinod Pal, or the writer Kipling, from which he extracts larger frameworks, is itself crafted in the workshop of modern psychology, just as his frequent resort to hard data is derived from the empiricism of the social sciences, however Indian, so to speak, his juxtapositions of that data. This is not to say that Nandy's interest in numbers owes nothing to the myriad ways in which Indians have manifested for a very long time an extraordinary engagement with numbers, or that the *puranas* have not been critical in giving Nandy an understanding of the structuring of Indian civilization. It is well to recall that, in 'Cultural Frames for Social Transformation: A Credo' (1987), Nandy described himself as a *critical traditionalist*, an idea that upholders of reified notions of tradition, which appears to be the only way that both adherents and critics of tradition are prepared to view it, would find oxymoronic. Lately, he would perhaps prefer to be known as an advocate of the view that we must be moved towards the acceptance of an ecological plurality of knowledge systems and civilizations.

The most compelling aspect of Nandy's work is that he resolutely refuses to concede oppositions, such as those of the colonizer and the colonized, of tradition and modernity, that have informed even the most radical work. Thus Nandy finds the traditional world more post-modern, more comfortable with multiple and fluid identities, than the late twentieth century. While many scholars were writing the history of nationalism as the history of resistance to colonialism, Nandy was writing of nationalism as the hyper-masculine form of colonialism. Nandy points not only to the difficulties in seeking resistance to colonialism through violence, itself a legacy of colonialism, but to the presence of the aggressor in the colonized subject, that is in oneself. As he says, in respect to the work of Fanon, with whose name his work is often linked, 'If Fanon had more confidence in his culture he would have sensed that his vision ties the victim more deeply to the culture of oppression than any collaboration can' (*Traditions, Tyranny, and Utopia*, p. 34). Though Nandy's work takes us considerably beyond Fanon, the fetishism attached to Fanon's work in the post-colonial sector of the Anglo-American academy has obviated that recognition. None the less, if today it is conceded that colonialism might, at last in the very long run, be more catastrophic for the colonizers than for the colonized, that insight owes a great deal to the work of Nandy. As he put it in *The Intimate Enemy* (1982), 'This century has shown that in every situation of organized opposition, the true antonyms are always the exclusive part versus the inclusive whole—not masculinity versus femininity but either of them versus androgyny, not the past versus the present but either of them versus the timelessness in which the past is the present and the present is the past, not the oppressor versus the oppressed but both of them versus the rationality which turns them into co-victims.' It is this style of thought, and a serious commitment to the idea of pluralism, that led Nandy to explain, in an interview with Nikos Papastergiadis ('Dialogue and the Diaspora', 1990), that 'there is nothing fundamental about fundamentalism'. The fundamentalists and their hated foes, the secularists, understand each other perfectly well: both are modernizers, proponents of the nation-state, committed practitioners of history, and advocates of the idea of nationalities and ethnicities. The

nation-state in the West was to some extent able to accommodate
the idea of culture; one might even say that the idea of culture crept
into the nation-state inadvertently. The nation-state in the non-
Western world, being a much more modern and managed idea, is
hostile to the idea of culture, an idea which is largely amorphous,
chaotic, and unmanageable. Thus Nandy finds himself an inveterate critic of the Indian nation-state, which has little tolerance for
dissent and for competing notions of loyalty, but contrariwise he
is a great admirer of Indian civilization, which has largely been a
pluralistic enterprise. His 'An anti-secularist manifesto' (1985) did
not make him popular with secular Indian intellectuals, whose
churlish response has sometimes been no better than to class
Nandy with the advocates of militant Hinduism.

One of Nandy's principal concerns, then, is with the oppressive-
ness of modern categories of knowledge. In a recent piece on 'The
Future University' (*Seminar*, January 1995), he noted quite aptly
that 'dominance is now exercised less and less through familiar
organized interests—class relations, colonialism, military-industrial
complexes,' and far more so through categories. All over the world,
people are being compelled, cajoled, and deceived into living their
lives according to dominant notions of health, medicine, well-being,
aesthetics, knowledge, science, education, and so on. In a country
like India where almost every baby was breast-fed, and where this
practice was put into considerable jeopardy after a dazzling display
of the marketing strategies of the modern corporate world, which
put tinned baby milk food on the market, it needed the intervention
of modern 'experts' and peddlers of scientific and medical knowledge to restore to illiterate and literate women those practices to
which they had always been led by nature, intuition, custom, habit,
tradition, and what Emerson once called 'mother-wit.' Or consider
the problem of terrorism. Why is it that 23,000 homicides in the
United States every year are merely a form of civil disorder, but
that 150 deaths in Northern Ireland, or 2,000 in the Punjab and
Kashmir, constitute 'terrorism'? Why are air raids launched against
civilian populations at the behest of elected bandits acts of honour,
worthy even of a Nobel Prize, while the mere hint of defiance by
non-elected bandits is construed as a betrayal of some alleged world
order, worthy of condign punishment?

They make war, and call it peace; they kill by inches and stealth,
and call it sanctions and non-violent conduct: so Horace for our

times. What is terrorism, and who gets to define it? Why is it that the violent deaths of a few at the hands of ultra-nationalists are terrorist-related deaths, but the deaths of hundreds of thousands, on account of famine or flooding induced by state policies predicated on the imagined benedictions of development, are classified as deaths from natural calamities? Who creates the taxonomies of classification, and what is their relationship not so much to knowledge but to oppression? By what contortion of language and knowledge did the terrorization of entire villages come to be known in English as 'pacification', itself derived from the Latin *pax*, peace? Here, again, Nandy's analyses and formulations take us much further along the road to an understanding of the phenomenon of terrorism than the conventional pieties of political scientists, or the conspiratorial theories of 'free' American journalism. In his articles on 'The Discreet Charms of Indian Terrorism' (1990) and 'Terrorism—Indian Style' (1993), Nandy established that Indian terrorism, at least until the mid-1980s, was a mild affair; the 'terrorists' were themselves largely unschooled youths, with little knowledge about realpolitik. However, the media and counter-terrorist experts, seeking to turn India into a 'hard' and strong nation-state, one that would be taken seriously by the West, and eager to justify increased defence and police expenditures, were only too willing to depict the 'terrorism' of young men barely able to wield guns into an enterprise purportedly conducted by professionals aided by the 'foreign hand'. The terrorist often has more humanity within him than the defence or bureaucratic expert who counsels his effective elimination. Terrorism, as Nandy has shown in his work, may owe as much to counter-terrorist experts as it does to nationalist, secessionist, or class movements. Once a category has been created, experts have to be found to make it into a lived experience and justify its continued existence.

Thus far we have seen that Nandy's work ranges over a vast terrain: his approach is at once theoretical and empirical, literary and ethnographic, civilizational and local. He is the co-author of *The Blinded Eye: 500 Years of Christopher Columbus* (1993), a searing tract on Western racism, and not everyone will take kindly to the indictment that appears without apology in its opening pages:

Over the 500 years that have passed since they commenced, the generally unhappy features of the European native, his disturbed thinking, his distorted perception and his spiritually barren cultural objectives have been replicated and duplicated mindlessly in all those places and within all those people on whom he sought to impose himself.

Elsewhere, too, he has written on Western culture and intellectual history, and various suppressed traditions of knowledge and forms of awareness within the West, which he sees as allied to traditions of knowledge and styles of thought in India and the southern hemisphere, have been of intrinsic interest to him. Though he is scarcely a historian of Britain, he is at home with the world of Victorian and Edwardian England. But South Asia is indubitably the region that he knows best, and his enormous erudition and sensibility have given us readings of Indian civilization that no one else has been able to offer. Dozens of books on cricket were unable to convey the complex *cultural politics* of cricket even remotely as well as Nandy did, through merely the first line of his book, *The Tao of Cricket: On Games of Destiny and the Destiny of Games* (Penguin, 1989): 'Cricket is an Indian game accidentally discovered by the English.' It is likewise Nandy's unravelling of the cultural politics of Gandhi's incursion into the Indian public space that has once again compelled Indian intellectuals, and people everywhere who are attempting to controvert and defy the reigning orthodoxies—which stress, for instance, the imperative to adopt development, retain deterrence as the prudent military doctrine, and acquire the military prowess that is said to invoke the respect of states—to take Gandhi seriously as the pre-eminent moral and intellectual voice of our age. What is lasting about Gandhi, among other things, is his reordering of sexual hierarchies and his devaluation of masculinity, and his critique linking the violence of modernity with the nation-state. It was Gandhi who demonstrated that the moral life can only be led in the slum of politics, or that the most successful form of resistance to colonialism might well be, paradoxically, disengagement. Gandhi dared to defy the models of defiance. It is with this gesture that Nandy can explain the notorious fatwa issued against Salman Rushdie, which gave the West the much-relished occasion to demonize Muslims as fanatics, as a communicative device—not as a real threat to kill, but as a form of departure from those modes of communication through which dissent is expected by Western powers to be conveyed. Dissent, much like everything else, comes packaged to us, and the West has not only insisted that its own products take precedence in the global marketplace, but that these be accepted in the packing furnished by its own agents.

In this enumeration of how the diverse strands of Nandy's work fit together, a great deal more could be said, though I shall resist that temptation, about the innumerable other subjects on which he has written. However, his other recent (co-authored) work, *Creating a Nationality: The Ramjanmabhoomi Movement and Fear of the Self* (1995), deserves at least a passing mention. Of all the problems that afflict the Indian polity today, none has been more intractable and troublesome than communalism. It is supposed that Hindus and Muslims have always been at war with each other, and that 'Hindu communities' and 'Muslim communities' are bound to exist in a relationship of unflinching and incessant hostility. But Nandy's work, which rests upon other work showing that the notions of Hindu and Muslim identity came to be frozen in relatively recent times, establishes that most people have not given up their faith in the syncretistic and pluralistic basis of Indian civilization. In the lived practices of Indian people the compulsions and imperatives of the nation-state are constantly questioned. The faith of people is more resilient than the platitudes of most secularists: that faith has indubitably room for secularism; but it is questionable whether Indian secularism today has any place for faith other than to confine it, in emulation of the colonial regime's representational practices, to the museum as a relic of a medieval mentality. The religion of the Hindutvavadis, as Nandy has argued, to the great consternation of the modernizing elements in Indian society, shares in common with secularism an intolerance towards dissenting futures. If religion is the last refuge of the scoundrel, secularism may well be the last refuge of the fundamentalist.

Nandy's work, in short, is informed (as he put it in a brochure outlining the philosophy of the Committee for Cultural Choices and Global Futures that he heads) by three concerns: 'an intellectual concern for the ecology of plural knowledge, a normative concern with cultural survival, and a political concern with the search for humane futures for the "victims of history".' Characterizing modernity as 'monolithic and cognitively coercive', and seeking to put the Enlightenment concept of progress, now stripped of much of its creative potential, into a 'pluralistic encounter with the possibilities it has suppressed', Nandy and his colleagues seek to generate knowledge that is not the product of the managerial, scientific, and secular nation-state. Nandy accordingly describes himself as a 'futurist', keen to help 'to keep options open in an institutionally closed world where the "rational" ends of all human societies seem given once and for all.'

Having said this much, it is still possible to view Nandy's accomplishments, and his place in Indian society and intellectual life, within a rather different framework. There are at least three nodal points, of which I shall make only tantalizing mention, from which his work begins to take on a distinct hue and acquire a significance that makes him, quite plainly, *sui generis*. First, Nandy cannot only not be accommodated within the trajectory of what may be called Bengali modernity, he is the principal Bengali voice of dissent from that anxiety-ridden and profoundly colonized history of Bengali intellectual engagement with the West. It was a cliché that 'what Bengal thinks today, the rest of India thinks tomorrow', and much of Indian urban intellectual life still seems to be playing out that aphorism. From Rammohan Roy, the 'father of modern India' and the initiator of the so-called Bengali renaissance, to Amartya Sen, who has now been conferred with honorary citizenship by Bangladesh and been claimed as an eternal son of the Bengali soil, Bengali scholars and intellectuals have been held captive, sometimes pathetically so, to the idea that they had only to acquire a theory of progress, create a proper nation-state (and a proper monotheistic religion to go along with it), and deploy the notions of freedom and reason as they have existed in the West since the eighteenth century, to give India the enormous face-lift it needed in the modern world, and render it respectable and decent before the community of nations. It was a Gujarati bania, emanating from a culture that had been cosmopolitan long before the Bengalis ever encountered the West, and whose adherents could carry themselves with the self-confidence of a people more finely attuned to their own past, who made the first significant dent in Bengali modernity, refusing to see in Western notions of the nation-state and theories of progress the fitting culmination of India's destiny. It is perhaps fitting that the task should now have devolved, in howsoever small a fashion, upon a Bengali intellectual such as Nandy who, while disavowing Gandhiism, has found in Gandhi a torch-bearer for a different, more pluralistic and less encumbered, future.

Secondly, it would not be too much to describe Nandy as the principal exponent, if not the originator, of *modern Indian criticism*. Anyone with even the most cursory familiarity with Hindu, Buddhist, and Jaina texts is well aware of the fact that there was an intensely analytical and exegetical tradition in pre-modern India, but criticism as it is practised today is distinctly Western in its origins, having arisen largely in the wake of the Enlightenment. In recent years, doubtless, many Indian scholars and critics have become important players in such endeavours as post-colonial theory, subaltern history, and feminist history, and critical as have been these developments in changing the contours of scholarship on colonial and modern India, we are nearly as far removed today as ever—in India and South Asia as a whole—from developing a tradition of what might be termed 'criticism'. The greater number of subaltern historians, for instance, have confined themselves to the production of scholarly works of history, however much their histories may have been inflected by readings of Foucault, Barthes, Gramsci, or Saussure, or by insurgent readings of the archives. Better history is still history, and it is well to remember both that history is a child of modernity, and perhaps not the most insightful discursive modality for capturing the Indian past and spaces. The more important consideration is that there is a certain idiom in which criticism speaks, and that there are virtually no comparable voices in India, and not merely for lack of resources and infrastructure, to such names—and the list could be prolonged at immense length—as John Berger, Primo Levi, Umberto Eco, Morris Berman, Octavio Paz, John Ralston Saul, Robert Calasso, Alberto Manguel, and even Edward Said. Their work, and the same could be said for Nandy, traverses a vast terrain, and one could scarcely think of locating these figures within a discipline; they seldom seem to recognize the authority of disciplines. Their work displays an acute but not ponderous self-reflexivity, a wide engagement with the world, an attentiveness to a canvas that can at once be large and small, and a certain kind of—shall we dare to say it—wisdom. Nandy remains the most insightful of the handful of those Indian writers—Rustom Bharucha, D. R. Nagaraj, and Shiv Viswananthan among them—who have developed a language for Indian criticism.[2]

[2] I cannot here take up the cases of such Indian intellectuals as D. D. Kosambi, Deviprasad Chattopadhyay, or A. K. Saran, or other South Asians such as Ananda Coomaraswamy, or the polymath Krishna Chaitanya, who has written gigantic works on a large number of subjects, from art history and the history of Malayalam literature to a massive five-volume tome on the

Thirdly, Nandy has made, almost uniquely, the foibles and temptations of the middle class, and commensurately a conversation with them, the centrepiece of his writing. Indian intellectuals have seldom been bothered by the middle ground, whatsoever the subject-matter under their purview. More attention has been lavished on Ritwik Ghatak, who made half a dozen feature films, than on popular Indian cinema, since no respectable scholar would want to be caught engaged in the amusements of the lower and middle classes. Marxist and 'progressive' scholars have made the sufferings of the Dalits, and the oppressions of the Brahmins and their agents, their special provenance, but the folkways of the middle classes seem to interest few people. The rituals of the Brahmins have been dissected far too often, and the descriptions of village life furnished by anthropologists have become tiresome; but the emergence of small cities and smaller towns, now numbering in the hundreds, has seldom been a subject of study, and ethnographies of these landscapes still await to be written.[3] In these matters, as in most, the middle classes have been roundly ignored, but it is with them that Nandy has entered into a long, quarrelsome, and yet affectionate conversation: they are his intimate enemy. They are the ones who, if they did not rejoice in Gandhi's assassination, saw it as a providential blessing for a nation that needed to industrialize and move forward; they have furnished the Hindutva movement with money and the trappings of power, and who joyously celebrated India's entry into the debased nuclear club; and they are the ones who have sought to build India in the image of the West. Nandy knows their ways, he lives intimately among them; he prods them into anger, even rubs salt into their wounds; and yet, because of his resounding faith that even in the hardest proponent of the efficient nation-state there is a residue of

---

history of the social sciences. The need to be authenticated by the West was a very great consideration for both Kosambi and Chattopadhyay; indeed, they were burdened by the necessity of being 'scientific'. In the case of Saran, a radical critic of the social sciences, a peculiar and deliberately cultivated scholasticism has had the effect of removing him from the pulse of Indian intellectual life, while Chaitanya has been less interested in criticism than in scholarship. Nor can I dwell on the importance of distinguishing between 'critique' and 'criticism', however much they map overlap on occasion.

[3] There are, of course, obvious exceptions, such as Pankaj Mishra's *Butter Chicken in Ludhiana* (Delhi: Penguin Books, 1994).

an older civilization, not so well-heeled but wiser and more ecumenical in its bearings, his admonishments to the middle classes are intertwined with the touch of avuncularity.

Finally, it is no small matter that there are few intellectuals anywhere in the world who have so commanding a presence in the *public* domain as does Nandy in India. In the late twentieth century, with its highly specialized and even impenetrable domains of knowledge, the advent of the so-called information specialists, and the intrusion of big business into the affairs of the university, the public intellectual has become an anomaly, at least in the Western world. Only a few years ago, the cultural historian Russell Jacoby was to lament the passing of the public intellectual in the United States; as he was so aptly to note, the intellectual in this society has been pushed into the academy, where his most critical overtures and thoughts scarcely make a dent in the fabric of society. No public intellectual has made an iota of difference to American foreign policy, for instance, unless it be to render it more domineering, intolerant, and barbaric. In France, too, the baton has passed from the free-wheeling existentialists and czars of culture to post-structuralists ensconced in the praetorian world of the academy. The erosion of the public intellectual has elicited little attention, but this is most unfortunate and alarming, for as Nandy put it in one of his most recent pieces, 'No hegemony is complete unless the predictability of dissent is ensured, and that cannot be done unless powerful criteria are set up to decide what is authentic, sane, rational dissent and, then, these criteria are systematically institutionalized through the university system' ('Bearing Witness to the Future').

In India, however, the public intellectual has a living presence, and the most prominent thinkers and critics of the day, many of whom like Nandy are not university professors or professional scholars, write editorials for the leading daily newspapers and otherwise significantly share in the public and political life of the country. There is still a vibrant newspaper culture in the country, and it is no exaggeration to describe the urban middle classes as newspaper addicts. That makes it all the more imperative for Nandy to leave his imprint on this culture, and ensure that Indian newspapers do not, as they have everywhere else, become mere mouthpieces for conventional pieties, official jargon, and hawkish sentiments. He has not been remiss in this matter. Nandy writes frequently for *The Times of India*, the oldest and most prestigious of the English-language newspapers, and in one year alone (1995), penned such pieces as 'Popular Cinema: A Slum's Eye View of Indian Politics'. 'The Philosophy of Coca Cola' (now translated into nearly fifteen languages, and reprinted in this volume), 'Responses to Development: Dissent and Cultural Destruction', 'Culture as Resistance: Violence, Victimhood and Voice', 'Culture and Consumerism: Targeting the Lonely Individuals', and 'Violence in Our Times: In Search of Total Control.' To an active reading and thinking public in India, Nandy's name is very familiar. His sense of public obligation has kept his writings free of the jargon that not merely mars the work of other dissidents and scholars with whom he is often linked in the academy, but makes it nearly inaccessible to an audience not steeped in the rarefied theoretical formulations of scholarly writing. Nandy has also acquired a mastery over the English language that belies his pronouncement in *The Intimate Enemy*, about English being a foreign language to him. As I have remarked to him on more than one occasion, his inimitable gift for titles—'The Intimate Enemy', 'The Savage Freud', 'The Secret Politics of Our Desires'—should alone ensure that people will be trekking over to his office in north Delhi for some time to come.

The fluidness of Nandy's intellectual world, his command over a vast body of literature, Indian and Western, and the remarkable acumen of his writings equally draw him to our attention. His controversial remarks on secularism and sati, or on the continuing colonization of modern Indian intellectuals, have no doubt earned him the relentless animosity of those who see themselves at the vanguard of attempts to reclaim India to the paths represented by development, science, and Marxism or (to use less teeth-clenching a term) socialism. But it would be no exaggeration to say that his work is poised to exercise an incalculable influence in the years to come, and when much of the allegedly radical critiques associated with post-structuralism, post-modernism, and post-Marxism are shown to have been largely ephemeral, Nandy's writings will still command influence. Unlike some well-known post-colonial Indian intellectuals, whose geopolitical location in the West also explains their often greater visibility, Nandy is not strictly an academic or a professional scholar; nor is his sensibility that of an university professor, compelled to work within the narrow parameters of 'disciplines', shackled by the rhetoric of 'excellence' (the only word that administrators, even at the most mediocre American

universities, insist upon using to describe their institution), and full
of the pedantism of little minds. Nandy is also, uniquely, trained
and educated at Indian institutions, and the conversational idioms
of Indian life filter through his work. Few intellectuals have done
as much as Nandy to create the conditions for a conversation
between cultures that would sensitize us to alternative futures,
dissenting knowledges, and the indivisibility of freedom. His work
is intellectually perspicacious and enduring, sensitive to questions
of culture and civilization, and rooted in the belief that knowledge
is political intervention; it is shaped by concern for the 'defeated',
and laced with a moral vision that is all too rare in our times.
Nandy magisterially and yet quietly commends himself to our
urgent attention.

[The following interview was conducted over four days between
27 August and 6 September 1994, in Ashis Nandy's office at the
Centre for the Study of Developing Societies [CSDS] , Delhi. The
conversation, excluding various interruptions, lasted for well over
six hours, and ranged over a vast array of topics, covering many
of the themes that predominate in Nandy's own writings, but a
great deal else as well. The interview has been considerably edited
and shortened, and a few quotations from Nandy's writings have
been interspersed wherever it was felt that in doing so the argument
would be considerably complicated, or sharpened. Anyone who
has a familiarity with Nandy's office at CSDS, and his mode of
engagement with visitors, must realize the immense difficulties in
sitting down over a concentrated period of time, not to mention
transcribing the conversations. Numerous people walked into
Nandy's office during our meetings, usually without an appointment, but he never turned anyone away; the air-conditioner, which
created its own din, provided much relief but often drowned out
Nandy's voice; and a chronic cough made it all the more difficult
to decipher Nandy's Bengali accent.]

VL: How did you get to where you are today? You started out
as a medical student; you then worked in the convention-bound
domains of political science and psychology. The trajectory that
you have taken seems to have carried you a considerable distance
from your early days. How would you write your own intellectual
biography?

AN: First of all, my exposure to psychology came earlier as a
part of my education; my exposure to political science came at the
Centre. Within psychology, I was already kind of straining at the

leash to find issues which would take me out of the extremely closed world in which psychologists live. Fortunately, I was trained in psychology at an institution which itself wanted to do that. I have been very lucky: its attempts to break out of conventional psychology and push psychology to its limits was itself triggered by new developments in psychoanalysis in the West: object relations theory in England, and clinical psychology in the United States, which did not seem to meet in the West. Here they did because on the one hand we had people like Erikson visiting us in Ahmedabad for a number of years; he was then doing his book on Gandhi. On the other hand, we had a long-standing relationship with the kind of work associated with Anna Freud. Between these polarities, it was still not conventional psychoanalysis, it was more, new developments in psychology. And then I began to read, and was exposed to, writers like Adorno, with his massive work on the authoritarian personality, and others of the Frankfurt School. I was already thinking of pursuing those lines, so when I had an opportunity to come to the Centre, in some sense it fulfilled my desire to understand collectivities and public life and the fate of societies like ours. Perhaps I had already sensed, though I had not formulated it at that time, that politics had become the real pace-setting system. I must have come to the conclusion that to understand culture, even to understand the changing contours of Indian personality, or changing models of Indian socialization, you had to understand something of Indian politics and the changing power structure. This Centre was in some ways a remarkable place; at that time it operated very much within a political science framework, but it was also very much in opposition to, and in dissent from, the conventional constitutionalist studies which then dominated the Indian political science scene.... Once liberalism was consolidated within political science, people could move out of it easily.

When I came to the Centre I was marginal to it, in the sense that the kind of thing I was doing, psychological biography, using biographies to talk about politics and science, was a very individual enterprise. It was not the concern of anyone else in the Centre; they were vaguely interested in it, but did not discourage it. Their main interest was the party system, comparative politics, literal politics; strangely, that was a great help to me, because I had already come to the conclusion that politics was a pace-setting force within

Indian society, in the whole of South Asia, for that matter in much of the Third World. The very fact that through these apparently ultra-positivist studies one reached and used the opinions, beliefs, attitudes, positions, political choices of the ordinary citizen—that the ordinary citizen mattered and the ordinary citizen used this choice to intervene in that society, to change the decades-old, often centuries-old social status to renegotiate terms with that society, with the most powerful groups within the community—that was the fact which stared one in the face. That was a truly educative process for me; and despite what people might say about that process, electoral studies and studies of party systems and comparative politics, in retrospect that was one role it performed and made me conscious of this voice.

VL: So what could have been a handicap turned out to be a blessing in disguise.

AN: Yes. There was a dissenting process here also.

VL: You mean a dissenting process insofar as the Centre wasn't merely collecting data about parties and electoral systems, wasn't interested in just politics in the conventional sense, but was interested in what common citizens were thinking, in the political process as a whole.

AN: We weren't doing electoral studies merely of the kind that are done at the polls; we were studying elections of the period that brought to some kind of a dynamic climax certain social processes; elections were ways of reaching these processes. But I've gone too far ahead in my story. Once I came to this Centre, I found that my interest was the psychological determinants of political behaviour. What is political legitimacy? What are the sources of legitimacy? That is the kind of thing I was interested in. I fiddled with lots of things. My doctoral dissertation was a disaster; both my guides went away, but I was none the less allowed to submit it. The thesis was basically a series of disjointed papers which could have gone into some shoddy journal of psychology; probably it had some smart statistical analysis here and there. I never published it. Once I came here and began to work on these kind of things, in the beginning I went about it academically; my earliest work was—well, competent—and it reflected some of this. I was beginning to get tired; somehow something was missing; I had published some things here and there, and had completed the collection of data for my subsequent book on *Alternative Sciences*, and had also completed a book—I didn't think much of it, though it was considered competent—called *The New Vaishyas*, but something was missing. It was more an attempt at setting up interesting puzzles and trying to solve them. I think the real break in my life came when after a decade of work here, the Emergency was announced. After one decade of work on political science, I was absolutely convinced that something like the Emergency couldn't happen in India; a number of my friends reacted similarly.

The Emergency was something which our generation did not think could be done to India and yet was done. Many shocked by it had, in their heart of hearts, always wanted something like it, to bludgeon the lazy, chaotic, cussed Indians into something more respectable—into 'proper' law-abiding citizens talking the language of the state or into a predictable proletariat moving towards a socialist utopia according to the textbooks on revolution. They were only aghast that Indira Gandhi owned up their secret desires.

'Emergency Remembered: Standing up to be Counted'
The Times of India (22 June 1995)

VL: That was a widely shared feeling, wasn't it? That it couldn't happen in India?

AN: Absolutely. Why did it happen? And I think from there onwards my writings changed. When I began to look back at what I was doing, and that meant looking back at the disciplinary culture of psychology and political science, one particular comment from Jit Singh Uberoi[4] had stuck in my mind—that all these new studies of the psychology of politics are fine, but once in a while you should do the reverse, and study the politics of psychology. He was interested in science and knowledge systems; and suddenly, in the context of the Emergency, that seemed to have an intellectual position, that comment took on a different kind of meaning. I felt that problems and issues must have priority over not only disciplines but also methods—even methodologies; the collection of election data, for instance, is a method, the philosophy of that is a methodology. Even if there were contradictions it didn't matter. A large part of my best work has been when I have felt

---

[4] Professor of Sociology at Delhi University, major Indian thinker, and a legendary teacher. His books include *Science and Culture* (Delhi: Oxford University Press, 1978) and *The Other Mind of Europe: Goethe as a Scientist* (Delhi: Oxford University Press, 1984).

that I had to do it—even if it is bad, even when everyone has said it is academically bogus, even when it had no standing in terms of disciplinary cultures or training—this work has to be done; something of what I am writing I must say. Let others debate it; the thing must be opened up. And my best writings are always of that kind. That was the real threshold. In one sense, you can ignore most of what I've done before that.

VL: Can we say that your piece on Indira Gandhi in *At the Edge of Psychology* can be said to mark the break?

AN: We can go back a bit before that. The piece on the assassination of [Mahatma] Gandhi was one of the first things I did after the Emergency. I went into Gandhi a lot because I found that modernist writers on Indian politics, even the thinkers from M. N. Roy to Nehru to the discipline-bound writers, had very little to offer. They didn't go into the breadth of issues; I went into Gandhi systematically then.

VL: Before we move into Gandhi, for that is a very large issue, I am interested in exploring further the move you have described from the psychology of politics to the politics of psychology. Though Jung had a considerable interest in India and 'Oriental wisdom', he does not appear to have excited any interest among Indian intellectuals or even psychologists. Freud, by contrast, never had even any pretence of being interested in India; in that sense he operated firmly within the parameters of Western civilization. Though educated Indians have since colonial times looked to the West for affirmation, how it is that they turned to Freud's writings, and almost altogether ignored Jung? Your own interest in Freud is well-known, and indeed the 'psychologism' of your work is sometimes adduced as a reason for not taking it seriously.

AN: Early Indian psychoanalysts met Jung: they respected him, but they were not interested in him. And some of them did tell Alan Roland that Jung didn't really understand much of Indian philosophy, but that is not a very satisfactory answer, because Freud knew even knew less of it. At least Jung had a fair guess about these larger concerns and contours but Freud didn't even know that: to him Indian philosophy was no different from various forms of primitivism, and he couldn't distinguish between Indian philosophy and Chinese philosophy. However, there was something which Freud offered to the early Indian psychoanalysts which they couldn't articulate but which I suspect informed their work. In India there had been a very long and very rich tradition of theories of consciousness and subjectivity; in Indian philosophy at least the dominant schools have consistently emphasized subjectivity, and theories of consciousness are absolutely crucial; in this kind of culture they were certainly not looking for a new theory of consciousness. They did not cognitively decide that this kind of theory of consciousness is better than the earlier ones or whatever, what they found in psychoanalysis was a theory of social criticism which at the same time was a theory of criticism in the West. Indians were looking for a theory of social criticism which had this double-edged nature. It would simultaneously be a critique of imperialism, for they were looking for something like that at that time, and one of Indian civilization—Indian culture at least—in a very radical way, for that was a project in which the Indian middle classes had been engaged for the last 150 years, certainly for 100 years. This function Freudian psychoanalysis could provide but Jung couldn't. Now I have a second reason to offer. I have used Freud because there is no doubt in my mind that though there is some creative use I could make of Jung which could be said to have a political edge, on the whole the political potentialities of Freud are much higher and much deeper than they are of Jung. Jung has many things, but he certainly doesn't have much politics. His personal life also shows that unless there is a sensitivity to politics in an age where politics has become the pace-setting system, you are pulled by storms of which you have little understanding. However sensitive might be your theory of mind, you may compromise, you don't take strong enough of a position on issues which in some sense delegitimizes your entire edifice.

VL: Jung doesn't have much of a political edge, does he?

AN: For the kind of work I wanted to do, I needed that political edge. That is true of Indian psychoanalysts, earlier and later, as well.

VL: I want to probe still further the relationship between psychoanalysis and the Indian intelligentsia. The account you have provided is very different from the relationship of psychoanalysis to the intelligentsia in both America and France. In the case of America, we know that psychoanalysis was received warmly much earlier than it was in France. But Russell Jacoby and others have argued that in America, psychoanalysis was quickly 'emasculated', that is, it lost its political edge, its possibility as a theory of social criticism. In France, on the other hand, we have to offer a different account. French intellectuals were for long averse to psychoanalysis because the retreat into the consciousness was construed as an escape from 'structures'. Something handicapped the political uses of psychoanalysis in both France and the US. Were Indian psychoanalysts, however few they may have been, similarly restrained?

AN: Indian intellectuals were not overly burdened with psychoanalysis. There were some psychoanalysts, and one might even speak of it as a cultish phenomenon, but psychoanalysis as a whole didn't have much of a social presence. One shouldn't expect it either, because India has very well-developed theories of consciousness of all kinds, constantly competing with each other. Most psychoanalysts tried to develop, at some time or the other, links between Indian theories of consciousness and psychoanalytic theories of consciousness. Now that's by way of a preliminary remark; even in the US and France, what the academics claim is not always what they do because they also have their own unconscious. I cannot, for example, see structuralist-Marxism or structuralist-radicalism, if you like, going very far without Freud; structuralism without Freud probably takes you as far as Levi-Strauss. For Althusser, and more so even for Foucault, you need Freud. What they say is secondary. If you allow me to stand structuralism on its head, and go into its structures of thought, you'll find that they may have many different kinds of judgment. Much of the radical thrust of structuralism comes from either Marx or Freud, particularly when the issue of power is brought in, and when one is not talking about the manifest, but the latent, structuring of power. When one is interested in the apparent structure of power, Freud has re-entered structuralism, whether the structuralists like it or not. As far as the American situation is concerned, while it is true that Jacoby argues that the professionalization and scientization of psychoanalysis led to its emasculation, at least to the emasculation of its radical or political thrust, I would say that if you look at the works of those psychoanalysts who have truly gone into radical psychoanalysis, they have also found it easier to load psychoanalysis with some of the burden of political analysis than they have found in other schools of thought. Freud has been revived in certain ways which I wouldn't have thought possible—within poststructuralism, for instance. You can't expect Freud to survive without Marx surviving as in the last 100 years; you can expect Freud to survive the way Marx will survive now. One of the persons who has contributed to the growth of Western consciousness—that is what Marx is now. When I say that I expect Freud to survive the way Marx will survive now, I mean something as simple as the way Hegel survives in European consciousness; Freud will survive in that fashion after 100 years. That's no mean tribute to pay to a thinker.

VL: Does that also mean that in your estimation *Civilization and Its Discontents*, a more general essay on Western civilization, will have a longer future than Freud's more 'technical' works?

AN: Yes and no. I would have liked to agree with you, as *Civilization and Its Discontents* is one of my favourite books. Personally, I have always been more deeply moved by Freud's philosophical and political essays, but I also think that even in some of his 'technical' works, where Freud himself thinks he is being technical, his impact is philosophical in a grand sense. Freud may have written *The Interpretation of Dreams* as a technical work that he might have thought was changing the science of psychology, but much more than its technical aspect, the philosophical impact of such a work will be appreciated perhaps one hundred years later.

VL: It has extraordinary literary qualities too, and is used in a great many literature or theory course. But, in any case, how would you describe the relation to Freud and Marx in your work?

AN: Frankly, I have gained very little from Marx's theories of social structure, not in the structuralist sense of structure, but in the old structuralist-functionalist sense of structure. I have never been too impressed by Marx's theory, it is too mechanistic a model; and even when I was much younger, when I was into mathematical statistics and things like that, even then it seemed to me a rather naive model. I was always deeply influenced by, and deeply aware of, Marx's theory of alienation—some of his psychological sensitivities were more obvious to a psychologist, and I would also consider Marx a major theorist of psychology, independently of his status as a thinker in economics and politics. Many of his observations and interpretations of human subjectivity I have resonated to; for a number of years, my model was quite close to that of the Frankfurt School—of Marxism or psychoanalysis, whichever way you want to think of it. I found them very useful.

VL: The Frankfurt School in its entirety, Marcuse as much as Adorno, or even the others?

AN: Mainly Adorno and Marcuse, less of Erich Fromm, very little of the others.

VL: So what works of Marx have been important to you? When I think of the corpus of your writings, Marx is visible in it only in a very amorphous sense, certainly not markedly.

AN: He wouldn't be very visible. In my recent writings , Freud is coming back, but for a long time even Freud was not very visible. And that is because I made a systematic effort not to be burdened by very large, powerful, closed systems of thought placed squarely within the Western, post-Enlightenment academic tradition. In fact, I notice that in my recent writings, I have again gone back to some of the concerns of psychoanalysis, which was not the case a decade ago.

VL: But there is a sense in which Freud, even when he is not visibly present in your works, is present in other ways. I have always thought that you had a home-grown use of Freud, you have never really carried him on your sleeve; but there are many scattered remarks in your work which remind one of Freud, even when he is not being evoked. I recall a conversation we had some times ago when you said that trivia interests you, because through it one can discern larger patterns and arguments. The whole idea of the Freudian slip, the idea in *The Pathology of Everyday Life* that little things matter the most—this is partly what I mean by the home-grown use of Freud: not nativist, but domesticated, perhaps a 'softer' use of Freud, whereas in many, more professional, works the overt use of Freud is a good deal more mechanistic and 'harder'. Your reliance on him is more intuitive and metaphorical. Would you agree with that?

AN: I would agree with you, but mind you, this came later, after a long exposure to Freud. There has been a kind of attenuation of the presence of Freud, and therefore it looks more intuitive and metaphorical. Secondly, I would like to say that even in the case of Marx, you will probably sense his presence, if you do not think as much of Marx himself, as of Adorno or Marcuse. My sense of how modern science has become a sign of violence in our times obviously owes much to Marcuse; the resort to subjectivism, and the critique of objectivism and the scientific nature, derive from Adorno. Marx after all was 'hard' with his own theories of subjectivism, being driven by a secular model; whereas these people were less burdened by such an attitude. The other thing which you often find in my work is not so much the use of metaphors from either Freud or Marx, but debates with them, whereas in some sense I will not debate many others. It gives some an undeserved intellectual prominence; whereas in the case of Marx and Freud— the former more important politically, the latter intellectually— there is a continuous running debate, because they are two persons in the pantheon of Western knowledge who have to be seriously debated, whether one admits it or not.

VL: In the beginning you described what the Centre meant to you. You've also described what Freud and Marx have meant to you. What would you describe as your other principal intellectual inspirations? I know, for example, that the work of Feyerabend meant a lot to you.

AN: The Centre, its collegiate atmosphere, and its collectivity— I cannot envision myself going in the directions I have gone without them. They formed my immediate intellectual circle. They were right there. The atmosphere in the Centre has always been collegiate and democratic and open; the freedom to explore and experiment, has been absolutely vital to the work that I do. Secondly, once I began to study the politics of psychology, heeding the advice of my friend Jit Singh Uberoi, I was naturally pushed towards more seriously exploring other African, Asian, and Latin American scholars who were writing from outside the given structures of knowledge. Often it was a back-breaking job, because many of them gave very low priority to writing itself. You tell Sunderlal Bahuguna[5] to articulate his philosophy of Chipko: despite the fact that he is one of the most articulate environmentalists in India, beyond a point you also have to participate in that venture to really get what he is saying. He cannot package it for you in the language you are accustomed to—and by that I don't mean English, but the language of knowledge that we are accustomed to. It is a very subtle exercise apart from being a back-breaking one, because their own justification for what they are doing may be entirely different from the way I will understand the consciousness which underpins what they are doing. Asghar Ali Engineer is a moving archive on ethnic violence

---

[5] Renowned environmental activist; one of the leaders of the Chipko movement, and active in the resistance movement against the construction of the Tehri dam.

in India; and he has done absolutely yeoman service to human rights organizations, besides pioneering participatory research.[6] He himself is a very serious human rights activist, but the way he theorizes his experience and knowledge is, to put it mildly, a letdown—often even pathetic. He would like to fit all his experience, activism, and knowledge in the given format, the given wisdom, of social science; whereas his own experience, activism, and knowledge allow you to stretch the margins of social knowledge in ways that he cannot even visualize.

VL: There is, however, an incongruity between the two examples you have furnished of Engineer and Bahuguna. Engineer works within the parameters of social science discourse; writing is not even Bahuguna's medium. I recall that I visited him about seven years ago at his ashram, and one of the first things he told me was, 'Vinay, *Bharat ka atman uske gaon mein hai*' ('India's soul lies in its villages'). I'm not certain that Engineer would ever say such a thing. Apart from the fact that he is an urban creature, such a remark does not fall within the structures of knowledge with which he works. We have two different problems here. Engineer may represent some of the poverty of social science discourse, but Bahuguna is altogether outside it; how does one contest this discourse from without?

AN: Bahuguna's not even interested in contesting this discourse, unless it impinges upon his life work, or upon his political or moral concerns. It is only when I read his interview with Claude Alvares[7] that I found that he was a radical critic of development; and that's because Claude put the questions to him in a certain way. Claude has his own concerns, he articulates those concerns, and he feels confident to say what he wants to say; whereas the same Sunderlal Bahuguna, at least in one or two previous interviews, has given me the impression that he favours a kind of modified, edited version of development—alternative development, sustainable development, or whatever you want to call it, but he certainly was not against development. In the interview with Claude, he takes a position, but that's partly because of Claude, who has certain

---

[6] Well-known human rights activist based in Bombay, and author of over a dozen books on Islam in Indian society, communal riots, and Indian politics.

[7] Writer, cultural critic, and environmental activist based in Goa; cofounder of the other India Press, an indigenous publishing venture; and author of significant critiques of modernity and development.

intellectual concerns: so when he asks, he formulates, and Bahuguna reacts and responds.... .

VL: So both Claude and Bahuguna partake, in a sense, of what we would call deep ecology; Engineer doesn't. I'm mindful of the fact that there is also a critique of deep ecology, and that its American supporters, in particular, are sometimes described as lovers of animals and haters of humankind. But perhaps that is not vital just now. It's true that Bahuguna's concerns are more moral, but an intellectual would also want to know how one could politically chart that position to transform it into a mode of defiance.

AN: ...If you put it exactly in those words, he wouldn't understand you. But if you put it in Gandhian terms—Gandhi considered politics to be a way of casting off evil—he'd probably agree. In the case of Engineer, it is not that he doesn't have the moral concerns, the ethical sensitivities, but he feels constrained by his own history to put it in a frame which to Sunderlal Bahuguna is an alien frame. Sunderlal doesn't have to do this, he's less burdened. Now, my first obligation to myself, but also to other academics, scholars, and intellectuals I have been associated with, particularly in the Third World, is to provide a frame of a similar sort which is less burdened, less encumbered by the paraphernalia of Western social knowledge. I would like to think of a frame where if you do not read *Political Inquiry*, you don't have to make an ideological statement that I don't read American imperialistic journals; but you can read it not unduly handicapped.

VL: So Engineer works within imperial formations, while Bahuguna employs a more indigenous idiom....

AN: In the case of Asghar Ali Engineer, it is tragic; to say that he works within imperial formations is also a half-truth. He doesn't want to, it is his intellectual socialization which has pushed him into the world where he cannot perceive—where he is not even aware of any other language in which he can articulate himself.

VL: Let me put it this way: Engineer has a great deal to unlearn, while Bahuguna perhaps doesn't.

AN: Yes, I think you have a point.

VL: The question remains: someone else, such as yourself, may provide Bahuguna's writings and teachings with a political edge that is also, in some ways, understandable within imperial formations, whereas he himself wouldn't articulate that political edge. Is that the function of the intellectual in India?

AN: Probably you have come close to what maybe I see as my function. I think the intellectual might have many functions. Sunderlal Bahuguna is also an intellectual—he is not an academic, but he is an intellectual. So then I should define myself. I have tried to provide a language where a dialogue can be established between the two. Sunderlal is not Gandhi; Gandhi could still talk in his biblical English to that very process of violence of which he felt his society was a victim and that he made sense to. The British might have had some difficulties with him, but the meaning of his action was not lost. That kind of bicultural existence is not necessarily given to anybody. To some extent Sunderlal is also bicultural; he is a major international figure in the environmental movement. But he's not intellectually as bicultural as someone like Gandhi, which is probably for the good. And why should he be? I can think of dozens of people who would disown that bicultural existence—or at least would find it irrelevant. Baba Amte is also bicultural,[8] because every Indian of that generation is; yet to him what he's doing should only make sense entirely in terms of his inner logic. He doesn't have to have two parallel sets of logic by which his world is organized. The case of an intellectual, like myself, is somewhat different. I have to negotiate these two worlds, because I don't believe that knowledge is a monopoly of the academic world. In every society, there are non-academic intellectuals who crucially shape the contours of the cultural life of that society. In some societies, at some points of time, the presence of these intellectuals may decline. I always quote the example of the United States, where the presence of intellectuals in the world of knowledge was much higher, and where it has clearly declined to the point where the intellectual world is now dominated by academics. You don't have Lewis Mumfords any more; at most you have a Susan Sontag, or Woody Allen movies, but not much more. In the fifties, when I was growing up, French intellectual life was almost dominated by non-academic intellectuals: Malraux, Camus, Sartre—these were the major presences then. Today French intellectual life has almost entirely become dominated by academic intellectuals. But that has not happened in India; it certainly has not happened in many parts of Asia, Africa, and Latin America, because there knowledge has not become that much of an organized industry.

[8] Venerated social worker and environmental activist in the Gandhian tradition.

You have to have these two, and my self-definition of an intellectual includes that element too. I would like to empower politically intellectuals who are not academics, or rather activists who are not accustomed to articulating their concerns in a language that is fully accessible to us. I would also like to have a continuous dialogue with intellectuals who are not academics because that has kept me alive...all kinds of people, all over the place....

My work on the future can be read as a political preface to the inevitable process of democratization, linking up with the language and categories of those who constitute a majority of the world. However, I am also aware that this could be a severe threat to those who want to be the voice of the voiceless and the intellectual spokespersons for the oppressed of the world. For we live in a world where the obvious has to be justified in ornate, almost baroque language of scientized social analysis or packaged in the esoteric textual analyses to be legitimate to the intellectual community.

'Bearing Witness to the Future', *Futures* 28, nos 6–7
(August–September 1996), p. 638

VL: You see yourself as questioning the mobilized industry knowledge, the imperial formations that have arisen, the parameters of social science discourse, and so on. Within any body of knowledge there is something that is taken for granted. The function of the intellectual is, to put it in a different idiom, to always contest that which is taken for granted; what is the most obvious and commonplace within a body of knowledge is precisely what needs to be interrogated. It is the known, rather than the unknown, which is the intellectual's main provenance of inquiry. Does this formulation at all describe what you're doing?

AN: Yes, but I'd like to say that many intellectuals, particularly intellectuals belonging to this part of the world, will not use the language of 'interrogating' the axioms. In fact, their aim would always be to say that if they consider the axioms to be part of eternal verities, they are merely extending them, or enriching them. That is what the great commentators, or *bhaskaras*, in India always did. They would say that I'm not doing anything new, in fact I'm saying something which is very old. This is the real meaning of such and such *sloka* [verse] or word. Usually the intellectual is less burdened by the academic frame, though to some extent in the West, the academic frame has now also informed or even 'infected' the intellectual enterprise. I cannot believe that a political scientist can talk about things without referring to some work on constitutions, or political institutions, and so on: at least he will try to have a dialogue with that. Here the intellectual is not required even to do that much because he sees these as alien. I can imagine intellectuals whose reference is not even academics in the modern sense of the term, but academics entirely in the traditional sense of the term....

VL: As expositors of texts?

AN: Yes. The man who exorcises ghosts on the banks of the Ganga in Varanasi will go to a traditional pundit, but he has no reason to be either trying to legitimize himself, or establish a dialogue, with either the modern intellectual or the modern academic—least of all the modern academic.... He has his own pundit. For the sake of simplicity, I was saying that there is a difference even between academics and intellectuals. In a society like India, even in modern India, this distinction exists. Many Indian intellectuals—Dharampal, Laxman Shastri Joshi, Girish Karnad, Ananthamurthy—are genuinely bicultural, and move in two or more worlds. This is the characteristic feature of the intellectual scene in the southern part of the world of which we have not taken adequate account. It allows you a lot of freedom, a lot of elbow room. Right within you are these multiple identities which are constantly challenging your academic sensitivities or even your sharpened intellectual sensitivities. In fact, many a time I have found that if you don't repress that voice within yourself——if you listen to it and give it a little freer play—it provides an internal critique of your own consciousness, which can be immensely creative. One of my aims would be to make the southern intellectual a little more self-confident, not only to politically empower him so that he can have that dialogue within, so that he doesn't constantly have to depend on the dialogue from outside, so to speak—which is not only outside, but partially inside. That inside—the West within—that you don't take seriously. We are constantly prone to a dialogue with the West there.

VL: ... whereas you are speaking of the dialogue with the West that is within...

AN: Yes. That West is also coloured, that West has itself in a certain way grown capable of taking into account non-Western sensitivities, and that is the most sophisticated presentation of the West that it can provide of itself. This brings us to the interesting issue: where to look for alternatives?

It is now time to turn to the second form of colonization, the one which at least six generations of the Third World have learnt to view as a prerequisite for their liberation. This colonialsim colonizes minds in addition to bodies and it releases forces within the colonized societies to alter their cultural priorities once for all. In the process, it helps generalize the concept of the modern West from a geographical and temporal entity to a psychological category. The West is now everywhere, within the West and outside; in structures and in minds.... It is also possible today to opt for a non-West which itself is a construction of the West.

The Intimate Enemy (1983), pp. xi–xii

VL: This dialogue with the West within and without: that is what the *Intimate Enemy* is about. Let me ask you a pointed question. Most people are unaware of the fact that you are a Christian. When one looks at the *Intimate Enemy*, is it at all the case that you were more sensitized to the notion of the 'other' because of your own location as a Christian, in however attenuated a form, in Indian society?

AN: I don't think in Indian society there is this kind of clear-cut separation. I once mentioned to you the example of our domestic help: here is a person who celebrated all the Hindu festivals, who appeared to be Hindu in a Christian family, but it transpired that she was a Christian by marriage. That Christianity is part of her. The philosopher and artist Jyoti Shahi once told me that in Madras the proportion of Christians is one or two per cent; but when a survey asked people who their *ishtadevataI* or personal deity was, nearly ten per cent of the people surveyed said their *ishtadevata* is Christ. It is not strange, it looks like a typically Indian thing, but it is not only Indian. Many traditional societies show the same feature. I have been struck by the number of Japanese marriages in European churches. The Japanese census says that ninety per cent of Japanese are Shintos, and eighty per cent are Buddhists! No one is shocked; they should be: religions are exclusive categories, we are told. This is common in many societies.

VL: More pluralistic societies?

AN: You are living with multiple identities, you are living many selves: it is a configurative self.

VL: In the West, living with multiple identities is considered to be problematic. Once, when the affair of the *Satanic Verses* broke out, Rushdie was asked how he lived with multiple identities, and he said the problem was living with only one. You are saying that living with multiple identities is a feature not of modernity, but of non-modern societies. There is something antecedent to modernity that has far more in common, shall we say, with post-modernism.

AN: Post-modernism is in some significant ways a direct product of Western culture, it is directly oriented to the West; it also has a project which is the direct outcome of modernity, though it calls itself post-modernism. Post-modernism cannot survive without having deep roots in modernity and the political function of modernity. The point that I am trying to make is that post-modernism is not merely the direct product of modernity, its job is to eliminate the criticisms of modernity all over the world, and to locate the citadels of this criticism in the West. So the critique is ultimately an internal critique for Western society.

VL: Besides which post-modernism—notwithstanding ACT UP, the gay and lesbian movements, and a good deal else—as a critique is located within the academy anyway....

AN: Post-modernism is never comfortable with traditions.[9] Salman Rushdie is a direct product of the post-modern vision.

VL: There is something still missing in this narrative, speaking in an academic tone, of the transition from pre-modern to post-modernism. Let me furnish an illustration. Amitav Ghosh's discussion in *In An Antique Land* of the Indian Ocean trade suggests that the numerous parties to this trade all lived by certain tacit rules: they set some limits to greed. When the Portuguese come to India, something happens; they refuse to live by these rules, one of which is that none of the parties will dominate the trade. Also, there are certain constraints that are also placed on the actors: the monsoons necessitate long periods of residence in various ports, and this leads to a culture of cosmopolitanism. He goes so far as to argue that the period from say the twelfth to the fifteenth centuries is far more cosmopolitan than the late twentieth century. What we take to be the pre-modern age is much more modern—as indicating the possibility of living in a truly pluralistic society—than our modern age. What do you think of such an argument?

AN: I'm perfectly comfortable with such an argument because it is a question of limits. It is only in a world of mega-technology

[9] For a more extended discussion of some of these considerations, see Ziauddin Sardar, *Postmodernism and the Other: The New Imperialism of Western Culture* (London: Pluto Press, 1998).

and mega-development that we can think of a totally global project. Even nineteenth-century colonization did not have it, certainly not fifteenth-century colonization. Even the modern kind of nineteenth-century colonization which the Utilitarians ended up justifying, and which some like Marx, and even Western dissenters, saw as a liberating process, even that colonization was not truly global. It has become a global project after the middle part of the twentieth century. In this increasingly global project, we don't need a sense of limits. In my concepts of politics, limits come first, and politics is the art of the possible. Even after you have established the hegemony of the market and global financial institutions all over the world, even then if there is some small place—two small villages, or a tribe with a population of less than 100 people—that is untouched, the market has to reach there. It is that which is so fearsome.

VL: And you would extend a similar argument to systems of knowledge?

AN: Yes, absolutely.

VL: In other words, let's just transpose this question of limits. The traditional Indian commentator, writing on the Gita, or the *shastras*, had a sense of limits in a way that the modern academic doesn't.

AN: Yes, even when there doesn't seem to be a sense of limits, there are implicit codes by which people live in that world. They are operating in a world of limits. The primary concern in that lifestyle was limits.

VL: So the characteristic of late modernity is that it lacks a sense of limits.

AN: We have now moved into a world of mega-technology and mega-development where we feel that history has ended, a la Foucault... .

VL: So when Gandhi says in *Hind Swaraj* (1909) that one should travel only as far as one's feet and hands take one, he is really talking of a sense of limits. Right?

AN: Yes, but we can improve on that. Even that statement has its limits. He simultaneously praises bicycles as one of the great discoveries of the modern world; there are only three elements of the modern world which he invokes, the bicycle being one of them.

VL: What are the other two?

AN: Lead and the sewing-machine. The sewing-machine is an extension of the human arm...

VL: It is a natural extension and so 'organic'.[10] But there's something else that is interesting here, because the argument about limits is usually made with reference to global capital's unceasing endeavour to always extend itself. The critique of the multinational corporation stems precisely from that circumstance. But you're arguing that it is late modernity which lacks the sense of limits, and so the critique extends to far beyond capitalism.

AN: Certainly. I have certain subjectivities in mind. Structurally there are limits, and that is what we will run up against. Nature is limited, both nature outside and human nature. You could develop a computer twenty times as powerful where you wouldn't have to use the keyboard. None the less, I very much doubt that you can take over the world as some of the Hollywood movies suggests.

VL: Anthony Giddens, in his little book on *The Consequences of Modernity*, suggests that colonialism transformed place into space. How, then, would you explain the notion of limits in relation to time and space?

AN: We are now seeing—the process has ripened—that we convert both space and time into classificatory systems...Space and time have become translatable: so a distant place, because it represents a certain kind of strangeness, becomes an indicator of rebellion against your own society. It doesn't remain that place, it is taken out of geography, and put into history, and it becomes the future state of your own society. America...is the updated version of the Chinese golden age, and India's *treta yuga*, if not *satya yuga*.... This is one part of the story. The second part of the story is that places have been deprived of their distinctiveness not because you are creating a space out of them, though that is not inconsistent. Spaces are being converted into a category. The characteristics of the place are derived not empirically from the lowest common denominator, or even the highest common denominator of these places...in the statistical sense; they are denuded of their distinctiveness because they are taken into a classificatory system and then

---

[10] However, as my sister-in-law Shikha Blaisdell reminds me, the sewing-machine may have aggravated the oppression of women confined in sweat shops.

the characteristics are derived from the classificatory system and reimposed on them. That is a two-way process. You first reincorporate them; and then in terms of your internal logic and needs, you re-exteriorize them. We have come to the stage where even India, or the former Belgian Congo, or Arabia in themselves mean nothing except as places where tourists can go; we have become a common category called 'underdeveloped' countries, or 'traditional societies', or ahistorical societies, or whatever.

VL: Which brings us again to the question of alternatives. What would be the possibility of constructing systems of knowledge which are not burdened by these processes? But perhaps you can begin by describing for me the general contours of your work, say from *Alternative Sciences* to *The Savage Freud*.

AN: Many people have told me, many friends have suggested, that I should do a brief paper outlining my theoretical position as explicitly as I can. Now that idea attracts me and also it doesn't because you would have noticed that in my work there is some kind of open-endedness; in many parts the work has an element of a projected test—people read into it what they want to read. I have met women who have said that after their husbands left them, or after their marriage was broken, for the first time they understood the nature of the relationship between themselves and their husbands, because they were colonized—I have captured something of that. One person said to me that she had been told that I am a Christian. I said, 'Yes'; she said, now I know why you could write that, only a Christian could write *The Intimate Enemy*. ... This part of the story I do not want to conclude by providing a theoretical frame which would close it, so to speak. I would, however, like to make a few things clear. One, you will notice that there is always a two-way process in my works; something is internalized, interiorized if you like to call it, if you want to use a more generalized term, because what I am saying is true not only of individuals, but also of communities, and larger aggregates; and then [there is] what is exteriorized. Often, as in the double role of the Hindi movie, you project outwards and re-interiorize in new terms, because you cannot interiorize in the first place in existing terms. You internalize and re-alter it, then you project it outwards so that you can handle it within. There are two brothers in a double role, or two sets of values within you. You are unable to handle the contradiction within, so you project them outwards as two sociological types; you allow them to negotiate terms for yourself, and then re-interiorize them as sociological characters, so you don't have to confront the painful fact that both are parts of yourself. They are actually a single entity, single unified adult, a single self so to speak. So that is one running theme.

For a major clue to the role popular films play in contemporary Indian consciousness lies in the integrative role the double has in relation to self-concepts fragmented by uprooting and deculturation.... The double here dramatizes the discontinuities introduced into Indian society by new social and political forces and simultaneously neutralizes them 'ritually', in terms of available cultural categories. So the ultra-modern, arrogant, super-competent, western-educated professional has ultimately to turn to his twin—a rustic, good-hearted, spirited but nevertheless oppressed body from the backwaters of village India—to defeat the hard-hearted smuggler or black-marketeer who in turn is a negative model of modernity and negative mix of the East and the West.

'An Intelligent Critic's Guide to Indian Cinema', in *The Savage Freud* (1995), pp. 225-7

The second running theme, if I may call it so, and it is related to the first, is that I have always worked on kind of a presumption that the conflicts one sees in society are internalized, telescoped within the person; so in some sense the person's personality reflects this larger social dynamic, and because I am by feel or by training condemned to study persons, or at least feel more confident when I study persons rather than larger aggregates, that dynamic and interaction is easier for me to disentangle and describe. I have the words for it, the language for it, and in that process I try to capture the dynamics of the larger aggregate outside. That is the second part of the story.

The third part—I think Francis Zimmerman pointed out that I do it, he said in all my work there is this element—is that I decompose what appears to me to be unitary, a molar entity, and then I recompose it, bring the elements together again in new terms. You might see that in all three points, there is the element of going out and coming in, an element of breaking and then re-making.

VL: But isn't that in general the task of reconfiguring knowledge: one takes something apart and then puts it together in a different way?

AN: Zimmerman wasn't really talking about knowledge; he was talking of something a little more specific than that. He was talking of social phenomena. I have this tendency perhaps, whether I take social phenomena horizontally or vertically, to split the phenomenon into two or three levels, and classify them as types, and then put them together. There is also, consequently, a dimensional change. Sometimes that which is vertically ordered, I would order horizontally; that which is horizontally ordered, I would order vertically.

VL: Such as?

AN: I think I could do better, but off-hand I can give you the example of Kipling. What was often seen as two parts of Kipling, I saw as hierarchicized; one part being higher and pushing the other underground. These were the two selves of Kipling. That which was seen as a kind of hypocrisy I saw as a necessary split, where one part is more oppressive than the other; similarly, more or less the same thing can be seen in the case of Satyajit Ray. The more oppressed part finds expression in the more creative work, because he has managed to negotiate the oppressive part of his self...

...Ray has partitioned his self into two neat compartments. In one he fits his classical ventures—the feature films he has made over the last three decades. In the other he fits his popular, low-brow ventures—his crime thrillers and tales of mystery, adventure, and violence.... The first category has a number of identifiable features. The most prominent of them is the centrality given to women and the use of women as windows to some of the core social problems of his society and his times.... Ray loves to tell a story in his films, not provide a political or philosophical text.... [But,] Ray's works in popular fiction are set in a nearly all-male world.... Second, Ray's popular fiction places enormous emphasis on scientific rationality, which is identified entirely with Baconian inductionism and empiricism. The stories usually posit a clear-cut division between the cognitive, on the one hand, and the affective and the normative on the other.

'Satyajit Ray's Secret Guide to Exquisite Murders: Creativity,
Social Criticism, and the Partitioning of the Self',
East-West Film Journal 4, no. 2 (1990), pp. 24–5, 27–8

VL: So do you see any problems in Zimmerman's observations about your work?

AN: No, it came back to me after many years when I was thinking of [Radha Binod] Pal.[11] I went back to this issue of the

[11] An Indian judge who sat on the Tokyo War Crimes Tribunal and delivered a dissenting opinion; Nandy's essay on him is to be found in *The Savage Freud*, pp. 53–80.

split in the Victorian consciousness and to Pal's attempt to conform to that model and yet find a way out of it; in some sense I begin with the two selves of Pal and re-configure them in some way.

VL: These three running themes would appear to describe your method for analysing a certain social phenomenon, rather than the principal subjects which have interested you for some time, such as critiques of the state, development, or rationality. Would you say something about this?

AN: I did not come to my positions of my own volition, as a deliberate act; I was gradually pushed towards them by the logic of the work, by the logic of public life in India, and by my efforts at self-transcendence. I think I have always been a little bit of an egoist, and as I did my work, I was not happy; somehow, it seemed to me that there is too great a presence of myself in my work. How could I capture something of that? It didn't come consciously; I was pushed to it. The Emergency did it, the anti-Sikh riots did it. When the anti-Sikh riots took place—as I have mentioned in my autobiographical essay in *Seminar* [and which appears in an expanded version in this volume], the whole 1946–7 carnage in Calcutta which I had seen first hand, at the ring-side so to speak, came back to me like a cinema—I was pushed by events. Some part of me said I don't care...whether academics like it or not, whether my friends consider me reactionary or not, I just don't care, I feel you have to say something.

VL: So certain events, such as the Emergency, had the effect of making you more aware than you might have been otherwise of the political nature of knowledge; not that you weren't aware...

AN: These events opened me up, pushed me outside myself...

VL: ...and provided you with, as it were, an impetus to read certain works with a different sort of political awareness.

AN: That's right. Priorities changed; I no longer cared, when I read something by a scholar, whether I went by the current wisdom or not. For example, as recently as the last two-three years, I have been very impressed with the works of the group associated with Robert Jay Lifton.[12] It is like Marcuse's work on the genocidal mentality. I've read Lifton's own work on the Nazi doctors; these

[12] See Robert Jay Lifton, *The Nazi Doctors: Medical Killing and the Psychology of Genocide* (New York: Basic Books, 1986); and Robert Jay Lifton and Eric Markusen, *The Genocidal Mentality: Nazi Holocaust and Nuclear Threat* (New York: Basic Books, 1990).

works deeply impressed me at a time when I was already worried about the situation in India—the incidents at Ayodhya had taken place. Many times I disagreed with them, very fundamentally; but there is a continuous argument in my mind with that group and I don't care whether they think my reading of the work is correct or not. I wouldn't worry if someone said that much work has been done in the American academy on Lifton's kind of political psychology, and I am giving a very odd reading to it. I wouldn't care; we have our culture, what we want to read out of the work is crucial; and when I do that, I have in mind also many of my younger friends who work in situations of violence, who are trying to study not only to fulfil their scholarly ambitions but because that gives meaning to their lives.

VL: Also at the civilizational level your argument would be the same as saying that we can read the West in ways in which it can't read itself, given that you have another civilizational basis in which you are rooted; you can read Lifton in ways which would be unavailable to Lifton's professional colleagues...

AN: That is probably true, that is the cognitive part of the argument.

VL: The biographies of certain people have been important to your work. I am thinking of the trajectory from *Alternative Sciences* to the book on Tagore. So how do you move from the psychological biography of a person to what seems to be the larger ambition that informs these works, namely the psychological biography of the nation-state—how do you move from one to the other, particularly in view of the fact that when you are looking at the person you are speaking of the 'divided self'? One of those selves is what you construe as authentic—one of the frequent invocations in your work is to Rollo May's idea of 'authentic innocence', and I'd like to have you talk about that as well—but there is then also implicitly the idea of inauthentic innocence within a person. Likewise it seems to me that there has to be the idea of an authentic self within a civilization as a whole; perhaps there is part of a civilization that is inauthentic?

AN: I wouldn't use, I think, the idea of authenticity in relation to a civilization. Civilzations have the capacity to have within them very many inauthentic constructs; I would use the idea of the authentic in relation to a culture. I don't think that the culture of narcissism was an authentic collectivism, for instance; it was collectivism all right, but not authentic collectivism; there is something in it of what Hannah Arendt called pseudo-solidarity. Civilzation has a larger architectonics, and should be able to handle an inauthentic component and live with it; I don't think there is a problem. I am sure that European civilzation would have lived happily with many inauthentic crypto-Europeans of the kind that the colonies produced; it would have taken it in its stride.

VL: So what do you mean when you say that 'each civilization must find its own authentic vision of the future and its own authenticity in future', and that 'the search for authenticity of a civilzation is always a search for the other face of the civilization, either as a hope or as a warning' (*Traditions. Tyranny, and Utopia*, pp. 54–5)? Would you elaborate on this?

AN: You cannot impose on Chinese civilization the kind of romantic vision attributed to it by many Westerners in search of an alternative; that is part of Western civilization strangely enough, though it is about Chinese civilization. Bertrand Russell's concept of China—and that is a very good example, if you read his autobiography; he did a fantastic autobiographical job on that—and Chinese civilization has very little to do with China, but it is very much a part of the history of Western civilization. It is not that China cannot live with this concept, it has lived with it; it has been forgotten so to speak, it has been taken in its stride; but the Chinese vision of the future cannot take that; there is a distinction between the two. One can give other examples of that kind; for instance, it is doubtful if the Indian vision of a good society had much to gain from the kind of Indianism which became popular in the US some two or three decades ago.... Indian music is popular in the West, there are a lot of experiments going on with it; music is still a smaller system; Indian civilization has had no stress, all these hippies coming to India, looking for an authentic civilization in India; I don't think really....

VL: But what would be the stress that Indian civilzation would feel? On the Orientalist argument, India can't experience stress, it is pictured as something of a sponge which can absorb all the spill....

AN: Not even absorb the spill, it left no stress...

VL: So a certain kind of indifference, would you say...

AN: Yes, again I would like to suggest a difference: that India, from the point of view of Indian civilization, is inauthentic; it is an inauthentic model.... An Indian, for example, moving around with the hippies and mimicking them as if he has accepted their construction of India, post-1968 India: there will be an inauthenticity about the whole thing. But the sponge argument may apply if you are thinking of Indian culture.... Indian civilization is [however] not a sponge, but a warehouse.

VL: I can see why you would think that a civilization such as that of India would be capable of living with various kinds of inauthenticities; I am still not resolved in my mind about your construction of the authentic. What is the notion of an authentic Indian civilization? How would you describe that?

AN: ...It is very difficult. In the case of an individual it is clear, in the case of culture one is less clear, in the case of a civilization it is even less clear: because civilization is basically a configurated principle, an architecture. In architecture what is authentic and inauthentic is a different kind of question; so when an architect is building a house, he must know what kind of alien style he can use along with his particular style; what he can do and get away with; there is a limit to what he can do; he cannot take something that is completely alien and get away with it, because it would stick out like a sore thumb....

VL: But that begs the question: what is 'alien'? What is the conception of the alien? Let me make myself clear by a different kind of example. What makes possible the conquest of India by the British? This question hasn't been satisfactorily answered; we have the conventional accounts which talk of Indian collaborators, the weakness of Indian military technology, the weakness of Indian social structures, the divisiveness of Indian society and the caste system, and so on. Now, one of the things that makes possible the 'conquest' is the fact that India, contrary to the European view of India perpetrated by Orientalism in the eighteenth and nineteenth centuries, is a very cosmopolitan country; Indian rulers had no reason for thinking of the British or the French as 'alien'. To a ruler in Bengal the Nawab of Mysore would have been as much, or as little, alien as the British or the French in many respects. To be cosmopolitan is to open oneself to attack: the isolationists among the American right, whose sentiments predominate even when the imperatives are internationalist, have always understood that. So far from being backward, primitive, and inward-looking, India was very cosmopolitan; which is another way of saying that there is no conception of the alien—certainly not in any reified form in India in the eighteenth century. If you are speaking of authenticity, and say we have to speak of a boundary of some sort...

AN: ...speaking of the architect, I am not saying that an element can't be alien; but it can't be alien in such a way that it destroys the unity. Many years ago Sagar Jhabvala, Ruth Jhabvala's husband and my neighbour, told me that he had given up designing houses. He told me: I am sick and tired of doing it; I have clients, who take me to dinner at a friend's house somewhere in South Delhi, and they have a balcony which is straight out of Spain. They want that in the house I am designing, though it has nothing to do with my design. Or their wives will pull combs out of their purses and say we want this colour. It is totally arbitrary.... My suspicion is that inauthenticity applies at the level of political choice but when you are talking of the civilizational level, the considerations are different. Of course, this doesn't mean that Jhabvala's design hasn't borrowed anything from anywhere.

VL: The smaller the unit, the easier it is to speak of what is authentic and what is inauthentic; in the life of a person one can make that judgment relatively easily; even in the case of a larger unit, such as Indian music, the parameters of what is authentic and inauthentic...

AN: ...the contours of what is authentic can at least be shown in a defensible way very clearly...

VL: Yes. But when one moves from music to civilization as a whole...

AN: ...it becomes much more complex.

VL: But that is exactly why I want to know how you actually move from the psychological biography of a person to the psychological biography of the nation-state—that is the larger ambition behind your writing as I see it.

AN: Well, that's a very interesting thing. Maybe I'm not able to do it, because twice or thrice I've tried to structure it that way. As a by-product of this book on nationalism, I developed a series of articles on the state. Something is there which tells me that I don't have the entire pattern of the thing; maybe that is the reason why I am not personally satisfied. Probably it isn't possible, maybe I'm being pushed to it, and I don't like it. The psychological biography of a nation-state like India would be of modern India, which has been done.... You have a point when you suggest that I was trying to capture something of modern India that is close to its heart. The moderns think that country and nation-state are the same; they want to hold on to it because they have nothing else to hold on to. Many people speak of Indian civilization as if it happens only in India. They care two hoots what the Javanese do, or what South African Indians do; or what Indians—Hindus and Muslims—in the Caribbean do; they don't care. Given the concept of civilization as world-view, if we're going to talk about Indian civilization, let's talk about the Malaysians, the Pakistanis, the Nepalese, and the Sri Lankans. Maybe I should have gone about it that way: not the psychological biography of the nation-state, but of the modern Indian, and what role the nation-state has played in his construction of the self. What kinds of meanings does he give it, and what meanings doesn't he; what he would like to see in the nation-state, and what he wouldn't like to see.

VL: But that would once again be closer to the biography of a person.

AN: That's right, and I would feel more comfortable. This would be an elaborate and indirect justification of going back to what I am more comfortable with.

VL: Would you agree at all that vis-à-vis only the West, not India, we could speak of the authentic and the inauthentic in the same relation as we do of orthodox and heterodox?

AN: No. Why speak of a civilization, even a culture—any large or creative culture—cannot survive without a very strong presence of heterodoxy. The culture of advertising, the culture of modelling can survive without heterodoxy—but not any creative larger culture. A civilization primally survives by re-prioritizing its elements, so that it can cope with challenges.

VL: That is not the same as saying that the hierarchies are re-ordered; the elements are re-arranged and re-positioned, partly to ensure survival, but the hierarchies are not necessarily reordered?

AN: That's right.

VL: So what is the sense in which you speak of authentic innocence?

The ravages of modernity are known and, since the past cannot be resurrected but only owned up, pure traditions, too, are a choice not given to us.... Ultimately, the choice is between critical modernism and critical traditionalism. It is a choice between two frames of reference and two world-views.... The critical traditionalism I have in mind is akin to Rollo May's concept of authentic innocence, as opposed to what he calls pseudo-innocence. Authentic innocence is marked by an updated sense of evil; pseudo-innocence is not, for it thrives on what psychoanalysis calls 'secondary gains' for the victim from the system.

'Cultural Frames for Social Transformation: A Credo'
Alternatives 12, no. 1 (1987), pp. 116–17

AN: Oh, that has a very clear-cut meaning in my case, and it is, as you have yourself noted, borrowed from Rollo May. The best example, which I have mentioned somewhere, is a passage in Auden that beautifully and very succinctly describes it. At the beginning of a Victorian crime thriller, there is a community, and someone in the community is a murderer or thief; his identity is not known. One person in the community has superior cognitive skills, superior rationality if you want to call it, who knows who the thief/murderer is. This person unmasks the thief or the murderer, who is then exiled from the group, eliminated...

VL: So the person with superior cognitive skills throws out the thief...

AN: ...or he is hanged or jailed. And the community re-assembles and becomes a normal community once again. But when one says it has again become a normal community one must admit that there is a difference. The earlier normality which prevailed was different. In it there was an abnormal individual, only the people did not know it: that in a community was not innocent, in the sense of the second community. That is authentic innocence. That imagery or metaphor beautifully captures a good deal. There is the innocence in which one unconsciously collaborates with one's oppressors, not as a way of saving oneself, but perhaps as a easy defensive device, perhaps as a psychopathological device; and then there is the innocence in which one truly retains the shrewdness that knowledge gives you—awareness.

VL: It is the innocence brought about from the vantage point of a superior cognition. So the second community is an instance of what you call authentic innocence. Now the question...

AN: The only thing is that the sleuth is not separate; the superior aspect of the sleuth is characteristic of the community as a whole.

VL: Does the notion of authentic innocence then presume the knowledge of evil?

AN: Absolutely. Yes, it can be seen as an updated sense of evil; I'm trying to invoke exactly the same thing. Innocence is more authentic when one has an updated sense of evil. You can cope with evil better.

VL: What if someone suggested to you that the notion of evil is characteristically un-Indian until the advent of modernity in India?

AN: Evil is there, but the concept of an absolute evil is alien to Indian civilization—and also probably to Greek civilization, if you ask me. That is a typically modern thing, and it has something to do—and for this I am grateful to Lifton and others—with the element of totalism. It is probably as an aspect of the psychology of totalism that evil is absolutized. I am not saying that before modern times evil was never absolutized, it was quite often, but there were very well-defined limits to it, even psychological and pathological breakdowns. But usually normal civilizations had some sense of limits.

VL: Do you think evil has any association with tragedy? Let me expand. I'm not certain that early Indian texts have any sense of evil as such—there is a sense of 'sin', which comes into later texts, but evil requires a different kind of ontological apparatus, which I am not sure exists.

AN: Only in the overall frame of things can we speak of evil and good. Within evil there is good too. Nobody is perfectly evil or perfectly good.... As Indian logicians would put it, there is a defiance of the law of identities: A is not not-A. Indian civilization would give something of this kind of definition: A is only primarily A, it must include something of not-A even to be A–that would be one way of putting it: A has to include something of not. A to be even fully A. You can make a similar argument that probably even someone like Gandhi would have argued that it is only specific items of modernity which are evil; it is not that all the elements of tradition are good, but one has to take an overall position.

VL: So would you say that even in the West there was no notion of absolute evil, and absolute good, until the advent of modernity and colonialism?

AN: Only if one is speaking of the Greeks. Their gods were corruptible, to some extent; good was not absolutized, and I guess evil was not absolutized either; this totalism presumes certain kinds of social changes, certain kinds of psychological states, and so on, and so forth. It is like the concept of Jews and Nazis in Germany, which is no different from the concept of greed in the modern economy, which in turn is no different from concepts of illness and disease in modern medicine. There is some element of pervasive totalism; in the book on Ayodhya, we have used Lifton's concept of the survival marginal; but we had to remodify that concept. Survival is not only the person who has survived when others have died and carries the guilt; survival is also the person who carries the memory of someone from the oppressive group who has given them the sense of protection: *that* memory also has to carry.

VL: And that's because oppressors are victims as well.

AN: Schindler is a strange phenomenon, which is why there's so much discussion on him. If there were no Schindlers, you'd have to invent Schindlers to maintain your humanity, and to continue to grant humanity to your oppressors. Traditional Indian ethics would have articulated such a view.

VL: If what characterizes modernity is a lack of limits, a certain kind of totalism, that would explain how you differentiate between forms of violence that have existed in countries such as India, and the forms of violence, highly banal and mechanistic, associated with (say) Nazism. So the ontology of the slave has room for the master but the ontology of the master refuses to grant slaves the dignity of human beings.

AN: You can reverse it and make it more modest. This would seem to suggest that Indian civilization is intrinsically superior to Western civilization, which would not be my way of looking at it; the absence of homocentrism allows Indians to think that even if he or she is not a human being, he or she has certain rights; victims have certain rights, even as part of the animal kingdom, even as a thing.

VL: Let's take a concrete example. In 1984, after the assassination of Indira Gandhi 2000 to 3000 Sikhs were killed in Delhi; large numbers of them were dragged out of their house—whether this was done by so-called organized elements who were brought in, or other disruptive elements—in point of fact they were dragged out of their homes and burnt alive. So what distinguishes this form of violence from the totalized form of violence that prevailed in concentration camps in Germany?

AN: As I've said before, that riot was to some extent an important event in my life. If you examine it closely, one or two things can be said with complete confidence. First, unlike as in Germany, in the vast majority of the cases the neighbours tried to protect the Sikhs; in fact it is not accidental—the way you are putting it almost seems accidental—that outsiders came and killed the Sikhs. The fact of the matter is that outsiders had to be brought in because the neighbours could not be mobilized against the Sikhs; in the vast majority of cases the neighbours tried to protect them, and in a few instances died doing just that. And do not forget that not only in Delhi, but even in the Punjab, in the countryside, systematic efforts were made by certain kinds of groups to precipitate Hindu-Sikh riots; despite that, in the whole of the Punjab, not a single Hindu-Sikh riot took place. It tells you something. And, finally, let us not make the mistake of thinking that Delhi is India. We are talking, when we are talking of communalism in Delhi, of some twenty odd communities, most of them recent ones: the two or three instances where the neighbours colluded, these were newcomers, recently settled, and without much of a sense of community.

VL: A similar kind of argument is usually made about cases of bride-burning as well. One thing that has been discovered, is that in a large number of cases where this has happened, people are upwardly mobile, they don't recognize the kinds of limits that were traditionally placed on dowry-giving; they come from communities that are not particularly well-settled, and in one study done of bride-burning cases in Maharashtra, they found that virtually all of the families had migrated from the Delhi or the Punjab area.

AN: Almost all of the bride-burning cases are from cities.

VL: Yes. So in the case of 2000 to 3000 Sikhs killed in Delhi in 1984, what difference does it make, from the standpoint of the victim, whether you are killed in that particular fashion, or whether you are killed in a concentration camp? From the standpoint of social dynamics it makes a difference, but from the standpoint of the victim?

AN: Probably in the case of Delhi, none. In fact, in Delhi, when the 'riot' was organized, thugs took over; it had the element of a pogrom, indeed it was a pogrom. So I wouldn't draw a very strict line between the two. Many more Sikhs would, none the less, have been killed but for the resistance of the neighbours. I'm sure that after the Babri mosque fell, riots would have taken a much heavier toll if people hadn't taken a stand against it. And if you compare this with what Eric Markusen calls spectators—he divides them into three kinds, spectators, accomplices, and perpetrators—I think there is a clear difference of style and in the number of people you find in each category.[13]

VL: Though you wanted to put it in a modest way, in the long run, from the particular way in which your analysis proceeds, it appears to me that you are ascribing a superior normative value of a kind to Indian civilization vis-a-vis the West; or let's say that you ascribe a superior normative value to certain modes of cultural accommodation.

AN: I'd agree with the second formulation. Community mores in India have not collapsed in the same sense in which they have collapsed in the West. You are not dealing with massified, atomized individuals; you are dealing with communities which are alive. I mean there can be pathologies: the 1947 partition carnage is there— one million died. One million Armenians died as well in another massacre that took place in what was certainly a traditional society. So I'm not saying there are no pathologies, and I'm not saying there cannot be outbursts of a certain kind. And for the victim it doesn't matter if you are killed efficiently with zyklon-B or whether someone comes and decapitates you. But there is a difference of some kind, I think, because this also allows you resistance, not only by the victimized, but also by parts of your group. It allows you to divide your own group: you cannot say that an entire community has turned against another. Despite all the propaganda by Hindutvavadis,[14] few Indians really believe that all Hindus have turned against Muslims. Pakistani propaganda may make some Pakistanis believe that, but they too will be of a certain kind. Most Pakistanis in their heart-of-hearts do not believe that.

VL: I was playing something of the devil's advocate, but none the less I am surprised that you should say that from the standpoint

---

[13] For snapshots of various spectators and actors involved in the destruction of the Jews, see Raul Hilberg, *Perpetrators, Victims, Bystanders: The Jewish Catastrophe 1933–1945* (New York: Harper Collins, 1992).

[14] Adherents of the Hindutva movement: Hindutva is an essentialized form of Hindu-ness, and in its recent incarnation would be allied to such causes as a Hindu state, a masculinized form of Hinduism, and so on.

of the victim it makes no difference how he or she is killed. Some civilizations bury their dead, some burn them; if I were a Christian and my kinsman has been killed, and the body has virtually disappeared, because it has been hacked into 500 pieces, or because the corpse was set on fire, and there isn't a body to bury—it would make a considerable difference, because the life of a civilization doesn't end with the life of a person.

AN: I was taking the lowest common denominator, the most moderate position; one can also say not only that it matters whether one feels that one is being killed, or is in the process of being killed, or is dying for a cause; or while killing, one is fighting for a cause, and grant that the other side also has a cause. There is a certain dignity in death also; one doesn't want to be eliminated in the way in which insects are through pesticides.

VL: Since you mentioned the partition, why do you suppose it hasn't been dealt with by Indians? If you look at something comparable—something comparable in some sense—in Europe, say the holocaust, it has generated, in the world of scholarship, a huge industry; and apart from that, the intellectual and artistic responses have been overwhelming. But we scarcely have anything on the partition.

AN: There is this difference in the quality or nature of violence. Partition was seen, as my friend Veena Das would say, as a pathological instance of sacrifice. You need a model of sacrifice to understand it; you can't comprehend it in the manner in which we talk of scientized violence, where one sets up an industry of death. So that is one difference. Secondly, I have the feeling that modern Indians thinks that partition can only be handled through history—people are now doing it, Gyan Pandey is working on partition, for instance, and I think that history is inadequate, very inadequate, particularly in our society. Historicizing the problem has its own limitations because then ultimately one will come out with something like: 'two nationalities clashed intermittently, where one went out of hand' kind of thing. There are only scattered writings about it in Bengal. The only person to whom it was an obsession...

VL: Ritwik Ghatak?

AN: ...Ritwik Ghatak would not himself have admitted that it was an obsession with him. That's very strange.

VL: Not all that strange perhaps, because as a Marxist he would have seen it from the standpoint of the nationalities question.

AN: That's a very good explanation. His expression was very spontaneous too. On the other hand, Veena Das and I found that someone like Saadat Hasan Manto[15] had captured something of the tragedy in a very major way. I agree with you that even this is an exception. I think partition survives in folk memories, very significantly; it is waiting to be studied through a study of memories of a different kind.

VL: But I'm still not certain—unlike the concentration camps, the killings in the partition did not amount to, in your words, an 'industry of death'. But why should that in itself be a reason for not having written about the partition?

AN: Because even in the West that particular form of death was not the way people were accustomed to dying; people were accustomed to dying in war...there were pogroms against Jews...

VL: ...long history of that...

AN: ...long history of that, but those were mobs attacking the Jews, even encouraged by the state or regime. Yes, but they were still not accustomed to this—and even they were shocked at the idea that one might set up a scientific state, a proper industry for death.

VL: Hadn't that already come about in World War I? Trench warfare ...

AN: Yes, but that awareness was not there. You could say that it has been captured in Richard Attenborough's 'Oh, What a Lovely War', but that is retrospectively. I don't think that in the inter-war years many people were aware or saw it in this particular fashion. Tagore understood what was happening, as I suggest in my book. What Hannah Arendt described in her book on Eichmann in Jerusalem, the banality of evil, was also a shock to most people.

VL: So if the holocaust and its experience provided a sense of shock to the West, the partition certainly did that in India. We are still left with the difference: why acute shock in one instance, generated a massive series of reflections, many no doubt pedestrian, but also many intellectual and artistic responses.

[15] Major Urdu short-story writer, who lived in Pakistan after the partition; died of alcoholism in 1954. See his collection *Kingdom's End and Other Stories*, trans. Khalid Hasan (London: Verso; Delhi: Penguin, 1987).

AN: I was trying to say that the only way that the violence of Auschwitz could be captured was through modern systems of knowledge. Butnot entirely. There may be better ways of capturing it, but that is the only way in which it has been captured.[16] Whereas there is probably an increasing awareness that if you want community life to survive, if you want certain kinds of cultural and social values to survive, you have to construct the violence of partition in a different way; and people have done that. There are the usual accounts of communal violence; but you will be surprised how many moving accounts there are of how families have survived because one Muslim friend in Pakistan helped them to come to this side: 'Sorry, I can't protect you here; go away to India, and I'll look after your property and do something about it.' From family after family I have heard this; I have asked people about this: similarly in Pakistan. I think that qualitatively the violence was different, it was seen as an aberration. I will give you an instance. Nadira Mustapha, a Pakistani journalist, is a friend of mine; her grandmother died a few years ago. As long as she lived, she used to have nightmares where she used to scream, 'The Sikhs are coming. They are killing all of us.' She had seen her own family butchered by the Sikhs. When a few days before she died, Nadira asked her, 'Grandmother, you must be very bitter about the Sikhs', she said, 'No. That was a period of madness. We had gone mad, and they also had gone mad.' You cannot say this in the context of Auschwitz or Dachau. There is a qualitative difference there. Nadira's grandmother cannot be replicated among the Jewish victims of Auschwitz.

VL: Insofar as you are speaking of an aberration...

AN: I don't care if it is empirically an aberration or not. It matters that some people have constructed it thus; it matters that even one person can say that. And she's certainly not alone; there are others I've met of that kind.

VL: Then you would surely disagree fundamentally with the continued attempts of most European and American historians

[16] Nandy and some of his colleagues on the Committee for Cultural Choices and Global Futures are engaged in a project, extending beyond India into Bangladesh and Pakistan, on 'Partition Memories'. For a short account of this project, involving in the first instance, oral histories, see Sagarika Ghose, 'The Partition Psychosis', *Outlook* (13 August 1997), pp. 92 ff. See also Ashis Nandy, Meenakshi Verma, and Aleeka, 'Freedom...and the bloodbath', *The Hindu* (25 August 1997).

to describe Nazism as an aberration within European history itself?

AN: The industrialized, scientized, technological kind of violence, Europe had tried outside Europe. In Europe, there was at most you could say trench warfare, but that was not self-conscious. Even in World War I, the killings in places like Flanders were not self-conscious exercises, as was Nazism; outside Europe it was often a self-conscious enterprise. Nazis, with Teutonic thoroughness, brought that experience to work within Europe; they applied to Europe what Europe had done outside Europe.

VL: So to make available the kind of writing on the partition that we have for the holocaust, would require that we do so through modern systems of knowledge, but you have some reservations about that...

AN: That also would be important, but that is not the whole story. Whether it would do good or not, I don't know. Maybe for the moderns it will be a self-aware thing; maybe they will learn something.

VL: So in lieu of that we can have the kind of impressionistic accounts that we've had so far.

AN: Can Nadir Mustapha's grandchildren say what Nadira's grandmother said? That would be my first question. After the history of partition has been thoroughly written, where impartially one shows both sides, then you can transcend it in a way in which Germany or England have transcended their past, with a conscious effort that in the European community we don't want any more holocausts. That is a different kind of exercise.

VL: And it may lead to a different set of problems.

AN: Yes, but once the historical score has been settled, from there one can move on. Here the logic is different, the patterning of experience is different. I would like to keep open for Nadira's grandchildren the option of saying what Nadira's grandmother said. That's all.

VL: This is an aside, but I'd like to know what you have to say. It is often said that the Germans, unlike the Japanese, have been willing to admit to their war guilt; and one of the things that testifies to this is the presence of thousands of memorials, all across Germany and Europe, in memory of the victims of the war. On that account, the Japanese, as an 'Oriental' country, have been unwilling to recognize their own war guilt. Do you think it is possible to provide an alternative reading to this account?

AN: I don't think it has ever been proven that Japanese war crimes were ever centrally managed or centrally ordered. There were war crimes, no doubt. Atrocities were widespread; all I want to say is that they didn't make an industry of it, as did the Nazis.[17] Mind you, the Japanese paid very heavily for it. Do you know that many more Japanese than Nazis were hanged? Nobody ever claimed that Japanese war crimes were as extensive or as brutal as Nazi war crimes. There is the other part of the story too: Japan was subjected to Western racism, it knew it was a victim of racism, and that too, was never acknowledged. That part of the story was entirely wiped out; so there is a reactive refusal. In the Japanese case neither of the sides have owned up to their past, and I do think that the Japanese refusal to own up to their past is partly a reaction to the refusal of the West to own up to their own past vis-à-vis Japan.

VL: But that might appear to be an attempt to exculpate them on reactive grounds...

AN: I'm not trying to exculpate them at all. I'm only trying to understand their refusal to admit to their past. Things would have been very different if the other part of the story had also been acknowledged.

The West had to acknowledge that war-time Japan wanted to beat the West at its own game, that a significant part of Japanese imperialism was only a reflection of the West's disowned self. Like Aime Cesaire, who traced Nazi racism and violence to attempts to try out within Europe what Europe's colonial experiments in the non-European world had 'legitimately' done over the centuries to its colonial subjects, Radhabinod Pal set the Japanese imperial guilt in this century in a larger global context. If the accused were guilty, so were the plaintiffs.

'The Other Within: Radhabinod Pal's Judgment of Culpability', in *The Savage Freud*, p. 79

VL: Do you think that one could furnish a more radical, different epistemological explanation that would validate the

---

[17] Some may well dispute this, pointing, for example, to the rape of Nanking, or the brutality of Japanese concentration camps. But the distinction that Nandy is making, namely that there was no central management of this brutality, and consequently it was less scientized, is what ought to be borne in mind. For a recent study, see Yuki Tanaka, *Hidden Horrors: Japanese War Crimes in World War II* (Boulder, Colorado: Westview Press, 1998).

Japanese position? I'd be prepared to argue that in the case of Germany, there is really a kind of forgetting; in other words, we have to read memorials rather differently. Far from constituting a form of remembering, they constitute a kind of forgetting. Let me offer a simple illustration. There is always a transformation in the public use of memorials. One goes to a German town, and wants to get from one place to another. A memorial becomes a geographical nexus, a geographical space for locating oneself; it is the bus stop next to the memorial that keeps it alive. The functions the memorial eventually serves are very different—there is a displacement that memorials create, and if one reads that displacement politically, these memorials are a form of forgetting rather than a form of remembering.

AN: That's beautifully said.

VL: The Japanese don't have such memorials. The reasons you've given have more to do with factual things: more Japanese were killed, Japan was itself a victim of Western racism, and so on. But there maybe a different epistemological paradigm.

AN: You're making a very significant point. In your sense, the Japanese remember more; they live the past more than do the Germans.

VL: I bring this in because I wonder if that's true of the partition, which hasn't evoked those kinds of monuments—I mean not only physically, but in terms of artistic and intellectual endeavours. Is there some kind of displacement here? Apart from the fact that the memory of the partition resides in folk memories, is there some kind of displacement? Is there a memory of the partition in other forms which have to be read differently? The Hindi film, perhaps?

AN: I was going to mention the Hindi film. There is a split in the Hindi film between the slogans of the nation-state, to which they seem to give uncritical and total allegiance on the one hand, and on the other hand is the simultaneous existence of very subtle criticisms of the ideology of the state which they project into the same films without knowing they're doing so. Maybe such a contradiction comes from survival of memories of the partition. After all, the Hindi film to a very significant extent, particularly in its present incarnations, is a product of the people who were refugees. The psychology of refugees is dominant in much of this. You also see it in journalism. Some of the most violent and blood-curdling nationalists belong to that sector; they are the victims of partition. If you read Arun Shourie, you are left in no doubt what partition has done to us. Arun Shourie, Girilal Jain, M. V. Kamath—we are not left in any doubt as to what partition has done to us.

VL: A very large number of Hindi films show families that are split or broken; the separation of brothers is a dominant motif, and you have read it as the divided self within the person. But can that also be read as a psychobiography of the tormented nation-state; there are the bifurcations that take place at the time of the partition, and perhaps individual narratives inscribe a larger narrative.

AN: Doubling actually came in earlier. Maybe it now has a different kind of meaning, may be it has acquired a different tonality. Maybe it could be a good empirical question: do the doubles created after the partition represent a different redistribution of qualities between the two brothers than the doubles in the Hindi film before partition? It is possible that things have changed.

VL: In any case you don't think that capturing the partition through historical narratives will provide us with the readings of partition—they provide us with partial readings, no doubt—we want...

AN: Let me put it this way: in a massified society, history probably can vaguely contribute to a moral framework.

VL: But India is not that yet.

AN: Not yet. I think that the patterning of memories in ways to which we are accustomed has a very strong moral component to it; because of that moral component we stick to them, probably unwilling to give them up. Probably there was this awareness among historians, artists, and social scientists that these are memories that one doesn't fiddle with. The history or social science account of that experience cannot really compete with public memory, and probably should not; now of course two generations have passed, and maybe now we shall see a different kind of awareness in this area. It's possible.

VL: So you would see history as a narrative form, a discourse, that colludes with colonialism. The entry of history into India is in tandem with the entry of modernity.

AN: Yes, it has its costs. No use in underestimating these costs. Everything has a cost; even in the world of knowledge, there is no free lunch. Everything has a cost; depends on what cost you are willing to pay.

VL: Of course history also claims a priority; it claims it is prior to ahistoricity...

AN: ...prior to alternative constructions of the past. It is not accidental that the two groups or sectors in India which are sworn to history are the Hindutvavadis and the secularists.

The old classification between the historical and ahistorical societies may not have broken down, but all large ahistorical societies now have sizeable sections of population which have become, through a process of over-correction, entirely captive to the historical mode. They not only would like to rewrite their own histories but to live up to someone else's history. It is a remarkable feature of our times that so many individuals and collectivities are willing and even eager to forego their right to design their own futures. Some societies do not any longer have a workable concept of the future. They have a past, a present and someone else's present as their future. 'The entire East', Rabindranath Tagore said more than 50 years ago, 'is attempting to take into itself a history which is not the outcome of its own living.'

'Shamans, Savages and the Wilderness: On the Audibility
of Dissent and the Future of Civilizations',
Alternatives 14 (1989), pp. 263–4

VL: Your disavowal of the historical mode shows in much of your work, but I suspect that you would be equally reluctant to have it thought of as 'theory'. So how would you describe the body of your work?

AN: I thought I would basically be a person concerned with describing life. In the process of describing life, if certain points are made, well and good. I never conceived of myself as a theoretician, though many people have begun to think of me as one; one of the reasons is that there are huge gaps both in my thinking and reading. The thinking is almost a by-product; *Traditions, Tyranny, and Utopias* is almost a by-product of *The Intimate Enemy*. As I told you once, *The Intimate Enemy* was a much longer manuscript, I cut it down to less than half its size. There are a number of things that spilled out from it.

VL: Would it be fair to say—this is an exaggerated way of putting it—that the *Traditions* book represents, as it were, the prophetic trivia that spilled out from *The Intimate Enemy*.

AN: (with a laugh) that would be a nice way of putting it. I am a thinker by default; most of the things I have thought of, I have been pushed to do so.

VL: One of your most interesting books, the one on cricket, suggests that too. The kind of arguments you make there are most congruent with your style of writing and thinking; when you say that thinking is almost a by-product, you almost negate its ascriptive apparatus. The mainstay of the book on cricket is the leaps you are willing to take, such as the wholly implied distinction between amateurs and professionals. One of the reasons why the English are more interesting colonialists is that they are amateurs, as opposed to the Germans, who are professionals.... If you were a professional thinker in that sense, the political edge to your work would be largely lost. I don't think of you as a theoretician, and I may go so far as to say that it is in the little stray line here and there that you advance a novel argument or thought. The notion of accident or chance has to come into play when one is dealing with the realm of knowledge, or else one ends up being a professional purveyor of knowledge. It is much later that I started thinking of the cricket book, rather that the *Intimate Enemy*, as your best work.

AN: The cricket book is more comprehensive. You're right, it is in some ways the book that is dearest to me. But even Penguin, who published it, think of it only as a book on cricket.

VL: It was reviewed mainly in the sports pages of newspapers.

AN: That was Penguin's concern. [A cinema journal] reviewed it, but that's because I myself sent it to them.

VL: I'm curious to know, then, which of your books you like the best? Which one are you the happiest with?

AN: Probably the Tagore book. It is very modest, direct, single-pronged; it doesn't try to be academic.

VL: A single-point theme?

AN: How nationalism can and should be constructed in this part of the world. And it has no reference to anyone except the Indians who read it, in the sense that this is one book in which I never thought of how people would react to it. I have deliberately not gone into the nuances of personalities, or the nuances of texts. It is very direct, very simple, and I would say very modest.

VL: The modesty might be a virtue, but why should its simplicity and directness be claimed as such?

AN: Because I had the courage to address groups and sectors of Indians where it will matter. Frankly, I've never been entirely satisfied with any of my books, and that is the reason why it doesn't have any frills. That is the reason I like it. I quite like *The Intimate Enemy*; I also like the new collection, *The Savage Freud*. I get a feeling from all my books that I'm trying to say something which I'm not fully able to say. In this book [on Tagore] I wasn't trying to say anything more than I've said.

VL: Which of your works is the most ambitious, and which captures best the kind of political agendas, and the notion of (alternative) futures, that you have?

AN: Probably *The Intimate Enemy*; as far as the critique of contemporaneity goes, *The Savage Freud*.

VL: There is a brochure that the Committee for Cultural Choices and Global Futures brought out which sets forth the three basic concerns of the Committee. One of them is the creation of alternative futures which enable the victims to recover their own histories—not in any vulgar sense, but in a way that makes it possible to write pluralistic histories. Would you say something more about that? What is your notion of the future?

AN: I see all constructions of the future as criticisms of the present. By virtue of the very fact that one constructs a future, one makes sure that the future will not come in the way. That input into public debate changes the nature of the public debate, changes the nature of the process which leads to the future. It is pointless to say, for instance, that George Orwell's *1984* has passed and it didn't become what he promised, because Orwell's *1984* contributed to it, very significantly; in fact I would consider it a very important book because it shaped the future. Similarly Aldous Huxley's *Brave New World* pre-empted the brave new world by being written. Some of these negative utopias have something which touch something deep in us; compared to *Brave New World*, Huxley's *Island*, which is supposed to be a positive utopia, doesn't have the same effect.

VL: Is that because fear has a greater place in the imagination of people than good? That is to say, a negative utopia evokes a certain fear as well?

AN: That may be so, but I would look at it more politically. I would say that it is easier to establish a consensus on what you don't want than on what you want. We all know we don't want

Nazism, but can we say what kind of society we want? You would have noticed that I've written on negative utopias rather than positive utopias. I've always been aware of this fact—I could never run away from the fact that negative utopias are much more potent than positive ones.

...we are better off with negatively defined utopias than with positively defined ones. A utopia which rejects technicism or the idea of mastery over nature is often a more serious affair than a utopia which recommends a specific technoeconomic or ecological solution. ... It is easier to establish communications among social criticism than to summate the values of diverse civilizations.

'Evaluating Utopias', in *Traditions, Tyranny,
and Utopias* (1987), p. 13

VL: Is there a tradition of utopian thinking in India as such?

AN: It isn't really all that different from the tradition you find in the West—utopian thinking proper started with Sir Thomas More.

VL: But then after that there is a whole series of works: think of Butler's *Erewohn*—an idea of a utopian novel, or a novel that is located in a particular utopia; the genre of the novel is more particular to the West. What is the tradition of utopian thinking in that sense...we can think of Gandhi's *Ramrajya*, and so on, but what are the utopian works of Indian culture?

AN: Both in India and China, the golden age was always located in the past. In Europe there was a difference in this respect: Eden was counterpoised against the last day of judgment. So there is a split of some kind. India has a touch of it too...

VL: But the notion of a 'golden age' is not necessarily congruent with the notion of a 'utopia'. Utopia is a form of engineering of sorts...I don't find it in any Indian works.

AN: You're right, and that kind of utopia can only come from a modern society, really speaking.

VL: Though the kind of engineering that a utopia would require is, one might say, already present in Plato's *Republic*.

AN: That's a good point.

VL: There is a series of puzzles: First, whether there is, in the sense in which you are speaking of utopias, an Indian tradition of utopian thinking. I would distinguish utopias both from the idea of 'golden age' and from—curiously you have never written on it—the idea of prophecy. One of things that has changed with the advent of modernity is the absence of prophecy; the last great prophet in Europe is Blake, and though one could speak of Freud and Marx in that vein too, the idiom in which they speak is already one that is hostile to prophecy.

AN: Anti-prophetic prophets.

VL: Indeed. I'm only trying to get at some sense of the relation between utopias, prophecy, and notions of the golden age: all these are not really congruent. So, again, what is the tradition of utopian thinking in India?

AN: Utopia as an engineerable vision of the future society is more or less, perhaps entirely, absent in pre-modern India. I think utopian thinking comes in only after modernity enters the scene.

VL: But then you're suggesting that utopias and modernity have an intrinsic relation, a necessary association; if that is so, there is a contradiction here, because Plato's *Republic* is nothing if it is not a document of social engineering with a vision of the future...

AN: Yes, I never thought of that. Now that you say so, it strikes me there is something there, but I haven't given it any thought. Probably you're right; I find your argument convincing. Perhaps something similar might have been there in Indian or Chinese thought; I do not know of it, I'll have to think about it.

VL: I might suggest that the reason why India doesn't have a tradition of utopian thinking has something to do with what you yourself say in *Traditions*. You say that 'the search for a non-oppressive society can itself sometimes become new means of oppression'. In other words, there is already present in Indian thinking some notion which is hostile to the idea of a utopian future, precisely because that utopian future is only the harbinger of something that would create yet new forms of oppression.

AN: Yes, even classical *Ramrajya* means only a good society.[18] *Ramrajya* protects oneness; the *praja* [subjects; society] need not be made up only of Hindus, it will certainly not be a Hindu *rashtra* [state; rule]. There is a contradiction between *Ramrajya* and Hindu *rashtras*, though they are perceived as similar.

VL: You had said that it is easier to construct a negative utopia, because it is easier to acquire a consensus on what one doesn't want. Then negative utopias can be said to have the same failings that

---

[18] *Ramrajya* would mean, literally, the rule of Rama, the hero of the epic *Ramayana*, and the model of a wise and judicious ruler.

characterize traditional systems of ethics, which are largely based on prescriptions as to what one shouldn't do: thou shalt not do this, thou shalt not do that....

AN: That's a most interesting point. You are suggesting that one of the reasons why negative utopias had a longer run in human affairs is because they were more congruent with traditional ethics; and it made a lot of sense to many people.

VL: That would also explain why traditional systems of ethics are not wholly adequate in situations where there isn't a predictable set of rules governing conduct, where there is a situation that is completely new, or where there are combinations of different factors which are not accounted for in a traditional system of conduct and ethics: then in fact those prescriptions don't work. Similarly that is one problem with negative utopias: once we are removed from those conditions where it is easier to gain consensus, and where the parameters are known, it would be difficult to arrive at such a consensus.

AN: I haven't thought along those lines; this is a new line that you have opened up for me. The real point I would like to add is that ultimately utopias are a way of critiquing the present, and to that extent they are a political intervention in contemporary politics. Whether it is positive or negative, whatever be the nature of the utopia, it is always some kind of political intervention in public life and public consciousness. To that extent, even those utopian studies are studies of contemporary everyday currents, and that should not be forgotten. Many people who think of utopian studies think of romantic studies, and refuse to grant future studies any dignity; they think of them as a pile of protean balloons, something only out of the imagination. They should be made aware of this sociological fact, what it's real meaning is; and it doesn't matter whether it's true or false, whether the utopian prophecy has failed or not, whether the predicted changes have come about in society or not. The predictions will almost certainly be wrong. A hundred years ago they collected predictions about the future from some of the finest minds of the nineteenth century; and the most remarkable aspect of that book, which was re-reviewed in a recent issue of a future studies journal, is that no one got it right. No one could predict air travel, though one person predicted balloon travel; no one predicted motor travel. It was thought that train travel would continue to be the fastest mode of travel. It is entirely a conservative set of scenarios that they managed to generate. I don't think that those errors tell you much. It is a different exercise to conceptualize the future in a different way: in a sense you are reconceptualizing the present in a distinctive and interesting way, and that's the role of all utopian studies.

VL: So far from being escapist or having an association with the romantic, utopian studies have a sharp political edge.

AN: People have some reservations about utopian thought. They are under the erroneous impression that future studies are mainly about projecting trends in world trade and things like that. Future studies are trying to resolve the present by looking at the future, and in the process looking at the present as well. It can be an interesting intellectual exercise.

VL: Have you ever thought of writing a history of knowledge by way of writing a history of error?

AN: That's a fascinating question, and I haven't thought of it; but the moment you mention it, it strikes me that it could be a very important exercise. That's a book waiting to be done.

VL: What inspires this suggestion is your mention of the book of predictions by important thinkers who were entirely in the wrong. More to the point, error is critical to pedagogy, but as far as I can see, there has never been a history of knowledge written by way of a history of error. I suspect you've always had something of that idea; in an analogous way, you wrote in your credo that your ambition is to write a history of poverty by writing a history of the super-rich. Would you build on that?

Following traditional wisdom, I like to believe that the story of the prince can never be told without telling the story of the pauper, and that the cause of the pauper can never be independent of the cause of the prince. My life's ambition is to write an interpretation of poverty by focussing entirely on the life-styles of the super-rich. As Frantz Fanon recognized, the suffering of the victims cannot but be the sickness of their oppressors and the inter-translatability between two sets of life-experiences is complete once the rules of translation are identified.

'Cultural Frames for Social Transformation: A Credo',
Alternatives 12, no. 1 (1987), p. 123

AN: I had this deeply Indian belief—Iris Murdoch mentions it somewhere too—that the wages of sin are the kind of person you are. I've recently argued, it is a recurrent thing, that after everything is said, it is an open question whether the slave trade, which underpinned the plantations in North America and the Caribbean, killed more blacks— despite all the cruelty, torture, all the homicidal urges of slave-drivers—or more whites by releasing into your lifestyle, into your way of life, a substance which ultimately ended up killing millions. There is a kind of balancing element, a moral trend which operates in time and space; if you break the laws of nature, the nature within you, you have to re-tool yourself in certain ways to be a proper colonial master, a slave merchant; and that task, that act, leaves its mark not only on you but on your society and the ways of thinking of that society. You come to justify that; you not only re-tool your own personality, you come to alter your public ideology, your theology and your way of life to make it more consistent. To strive for consistency is part of human nature. In the process of that consistency, you end up doing to yourself and your kind what you thought you were only doing to others. ...I have a feeling that this is a way of perceiving which in some ways protects both the dignity of the victims and does not accept or take for granted the cognitive frame of the victors and yet grants them the minimum dignity of human beings.

VL: A similar argument would be made by you about to-bacco...

AN: Yes, I mention that in my article on sugar.

The cultivation, production and popularisation of sugar which in turn owed so much to the slave trade is now repaying that blood debt with interest. My guess is that, if one takes into account both direct and indirect victimhood, including the abridgement of life and degradation of its quality, the number of people killed by sugar during this century may well turn out to be larger than the number of Africans killed on the way to America's plantations. As James Ridgeway sums up the story, 'No agricultural crop has brought such misery to the world as sugar. Sugar has ruined land from one end of the earth to the other.' There is more than poetic justice in this. There is in it the lesson that oppression always has, in the long run, proved as disastrous to the oppressors as to the victims.

'Sugar in History: An Obituary of the Humble Jaggery',
Times of India (16 July 1994)

VL: At the material level there is some disequilibrium in this equation: if you say that more of the oppressors were killed by tobacco and sugar than were the slaves, it is certainly the case, if you looked, for example, at black Americans today, that sugar is in effect the highest cause of death for them as well...

AN: I agree; this isn't a fool-proof cognitive argument.

VL: Is what you're describing something comparable to Emerson's idea of compensation in the universe? What you're describing is something of a cosmological argument.

AN: Yes, you're right, that's what I have in mind. I don't want to make a fuss about it; the costs are there, someone somewhere pays the costs. As Tagore once said, the history of Western society hasn't ended; we don't know what kind of cost ultimately we still have to pay.

VL: You recall the incident in the 1930s when there was a massive earthquake in Bihar; there had been large-scale killings of Muslims by Hindus, partly in retaliation against the killings of Hindus by Muslims in Noakhali. Gandhi said the earthquake was an act of divine retribution, and Tagore was of course appalled that the Mahatma would bring in this 'superstition' to explain...

AN: They were not Muslims, they were untouchables: the sins of untouchability...

VL: Exactly. So is what you're describing something comparable to that?

AN: Very much. In that debate, I am entirely with Gandhi in his attempt to collectivize *karma* and see it in a different light. He provides a different concept of *karma*. But I would quite accept Emerson's idea of compensation; I'm looking for frames which capture something of this. I haven't found any, except stray cases like that of Gandhi...

VL: Obviously, you don't want to locate this within a framework of rationality/irrationality; you want to locate it in a different cognitive framework. What would this cognitive framework look like?

AN: It isn't only a cognitive framework. I'm putting it cognitively, but I think it is a personological framework...

VL: Moral framework?

AN: It is moral, but it is also personological. It presumes that our morality is grounded in our biological self, there is a continuity. We choose sudden options for ourselves, which seem to go against basic human nature; and yet we pursue those alternatives because we have come to believe that they will lead us to a new secular utopia, give us secular salvation, and the very fact that one is flouting the tenets of nature means that certain kinds of psychological processes are released within one's personality. To give an example: I think the real decline in women's power in English society more or less coincided with the full-blown theories of the colonized subjects being effeminate. I'm not only speaking about the historical correlation: I'm speaking of psychological colonization to that build-up of the entire edifice of theory of effeminacy and masculinity that forced entire cultures into that framework. It is a formidable exercise: you have to do something to yourself, something to the women in your society; you have to begin to look at them differently. There also you pay the cost. I'm referring to that particular psychological process which has a reflection of course in the cognitive map which comes to arrange societies and communities in a certain point of time. But behind the cognitive map lie certain very deep emotional issues which you arrange in certain ways; you have to reconfigure your innocence in certain ways to arrive at that cognitive map.

VL: So what would be the theory of *karma* that Gandhi is employing...?

AN: Gandhi didn't really go for a theory of *karma*. There is adequate evidence to suspect that what Gandhi was trying to do was to take the concept of *karma*, which has technically by tradition entirely to do with individuals, and give it a new form—giving it a collective form. In addition to individual *karma*, there is collective *karma*. I do not agree with Tagore's criticism of it, which is only an intellectual effort. Gandhi is not a mere traditionalist: he was willing to go very far with new kinds of experiments; after all, his autobiography is called 'My Experiments with Truth'...

VL: Besides the autobiography itself is relatively a new genre in the Indian context.

AN: That also is true.

VL: Gandhi's autobiography would be one of the earliest in the Indian tradition. But let me revert to the question I had posed for you: that is, the ambition to write a history of poverty by writing about the lives of the super-rich...

AN: I haven't thought about it; we got diverted. I find it a fascinating idea. Only in places here and there have I come to do something like this in the case of persons, for instance in my treatment of Jagdish Chander Bose in *Alternative Sciences*.

VL: So would that be a way in fact of saying that within that personal ambition there is another displaced intellectual ambition of writing a history of knowledge by writing it through a history of error.

AN: It's just possible, but I haven't thought of it that way. I certainly have not consciously done it that way.... I've come close to it in the case of persons such as Kapil Bhattacharya, the first Indian environmental activist of our times. I'm basically examining why he didn't look at certain other issues, even though he was such a brilliant and sensitive man. Why didn't certain issues strike him as important? He's talking of traditional technology, traditional lifestyles—of people who consider rivers sacred—and yet he doesn't allow that awareness to intrude into his political sensibility. Can his failure to ask certain questions tell us something? But these are stray episodes, and not done very self-consciously....

VL: Would it actually be possible to write a history of that sort within the Indian context given that you also wrote another article in which you pointed out there are three languages through which one can gain some sense of native theories of oppression; these languages are central to what would be called traditional societies. One of these languages is the language of continuity: in this mode, each case of change is only a form of continuity, a special form of continuity; in the West, it is the other way around.

AN: Absolutely.

To appreciate such reinterpretations [as Gandhi's], we must learn to acknowledge or decode three languages which often hide the implicit native languages of oppression in many non-Western traditions. These are the language of continuity, the language of spiritualism and the language of self.... The language of continuity...assumes that all changes can be seen, discussed or analysed as aspects of deeper continuities.... This position is radically different from the modern Western concept of continuity as only a special case of change or as only a transient period of time which is only overtly continuous or which, if it is truly continuous, is for that reason less valuable.

'Cultural Frames for Social Transformation: A Credo', *Alternatives* 12, no. 1 (1987), p. 118

VL: If that's the case, then what would be the way one could distinguish between knowledge and error given that is itself enclosed within a language of continuity. What would be the conception of error? Error there, seems to suggest a form of heterodoxy; does the Indian tradition allow for that?

AN: I wouldn't go as far as that. This question came up in our previous conversation, in another form; I think it is an important question. Let me put it this way. It's not that we don't have a concept of error; we don't have a concept of sharp error that would allow us to talk in terms of blasphemy and apostasy. There is an accepted formulation that whatever one proposes about India, one can always find an exception to the rule; on the other hand, I would say that blasphemy and apostasy, unlike in Christianity and Islam—mind you, when I say Islam I wouldn't include South Asian Islam, which is very open—are not intelligible categories to most Indians....

VL: So when you say Islam do you mean the text-book version of Islam or do you mean...

AN: ...there is no text-book version of Islam, there are only various kinds of Islam. I am talking basically of Islam as it has been construed by Islamic scholars in the West, which is the concept of Islam that dominates—it dominates even the lives of Muslims, not all Muslims, not even a majority perhaps, but many; it certainly dominates the lives of non-Muslims; they think of Islam through the eyes of Europe.... There are traditions of Islam which have the same freedom of dissent. Shail Mayaram studied the Meos,[19] who still have non-Islamic names, but they are Muslims. The Bosnian Muslims for whom all the Muslims all over the world are crying today—Dhirubai (D. L. Sheth, a noted Indian social scientist who is a Senior Fellow at CSDS, a colleague of Nandy for over twenty-five years) has attended their Ramadan ceremonies, and he noted that in many families they took a glass of wine with the meal.... There is an engineered fear of Islam. Bosnian Muslims, much like the Meos, are now being told that they cannot live with their feet rooted in two places. The Bosnian Muslims are now told they must become Muslims in some more acceptable sense. Were the Bosnian Muslims less Muslim before? Were the Meos less Islamic before? I wouldn't agree with anyone who said that; I don't care what the Jamaat says, I think that the Islam of the Bosnians and the Meos is as Islamic as the Islam of the Malayans or anyone else....

VL: So this sense of sharp error...

AN: In the Indian context, error is of course possible; but it is very difficult to ideologize error, whatever may be its nature. In

[19] Shail Mayaram, *Resisting Regimes: Myth, Memory and the Shaping of a Muslim Identity* (New Delhi: Oxford University Press, 1997).

Islam also, ignorance and knowledge are important categories.
…but I don't think that people ideologized these categories as we
often tend to do now.…

VL: What runs through consistently in your way of looking at
these things is best seen by trying to understand your views on
violence, perhaps? You would say that forms of violence in the
West, most particularly since the early part of the twentieth
century, owe something to the managerial model; violence is
massified. It is a 'harder' kind of violence, rather than a 'softer'
kind. Certain kinds of accommodation and negotiation were
always possible in Indian society, but they have not always been
available in Western societies. So when it comes to the question
of 'error', there is as much of it among Indians as there is in the
West, but Indians can live with several forms of error.…

AN: I think we should make some further distinctions. The
question of error has a distinctly modern tone about it. In
traditional India, it is not a question of accommodation; on the
contrary, it was in the West that accommodation was possible, as
there were accommodations at one stage of time in the disputes
between Protestants and Catholics, French and Germans.

VL: What do you mean by saying that in traditional India there
was no concept of accommodation in that sense?

AN: It was a different concept, and there's no word for it; that
is why we use 'accommodation', which is somewhat misleading.
It is not that you are a Hindu, and I am a Muslim, and therefore
we accommodate each other. My Islamic way of life is incomplete
without your Hinduism, and your Hindu way of life is incomplete
without my Islam; there is a mutuality, it is something a great deal
more than accommodation.

VL: Accommodation then is something that comes from above…

AN: Accommodation is diplomatic, it comes from the subcon-
scious; we are speaking of a mutual enrichment of some kind
without ever being aware of it. The *padukan puja* that the VHP
did: all the *padukas* were built by Muslims.[20] That is the nature

---

[20] The VHP is the Vishwa Hindu Parishad, a world-wide organization that
promotes Hinduism as a creed, and that fathered the movement to 'liberate'
the *Rama Janmasthan*, which led to the destruction of the Babri Mosque in
December 1992. *Padukas* are sandals; *padukan puja* is a devotional religious
ceremony in which the feet of the deity are washed.

of the exercise I am talking about. Now someone took advantage of it, that doesn't mean that traditionally people took advantage of it as well....

VL: I take your point but I want to pursue it further to see if we can arrive at some further refinements. You are arguing that in the case of India, we are not speaking so much of forms of accommodation as they have been understood in the West, partially because (a) these forms of accommodation are not imposed from above, (b) they constitute a form of lived experience, and (c) they actually lack an element of self-consciousness.

AN: They are also not a matter of deliberate choice.

VL: Exactly: by invoking self-consciousness I was adverting to choice as well. This might be mixing metaphors: let us look at it, however, in relation to the notion of 'authentic innocence'. You've said that it has to be valorized more—in the example you had furnished, the thief is discovered, and ejected from the community. That requires both an element of self-consciousness and choice as well. But now self-consciousness is not to be valorized—rather, we must invoke an unstated and unspoken way of just living with each other.

AN: It's very difficult now to use certain words—valorization, discourse—without being aware of their more technical meanings. What I have in mind is something like the self spilling over—over its boundaries into other selves, and in turn other selves spilling over their boundaries into one's self.

VL: Let me take an example and see where you would locate it within the gamut of ideas from accommodation to mutuality. There is a story of the coming of the Parsis to India. When they first arrive, some ruler sends them a cup of milk that is overflowing, to indicate that his domains are already over-populated, and he can't accept more people. Their leader puts *shakar*, or molasses, in the hot cup of milk, and it expectedly dissolves; and he says of his people, 'We'll be like the *shakar*'.

AN: This story beautifully illustrates what I'm saying. The story may be apocryphal, but that is altogether immaterial. We do need the milk, and we do need the sugar. It's done almost without self-consciousness. That's sometimes the closest we come to articulating this concern.

VL: Yes, but who will be the sugar, and who will be the milk? In the Gandhian notion of democracy, the party that constitutes itself as the *shakar* ought to have the same privileges as the party that constitutes itself as the milk—and vice versa. The majority should be capable of thinking of itself as the minority, if they are to treat the 'real' minority well. The Gandhian view of this would allow some negotiation, but does the received version of the Parsi story allow that: the Parsis are still fixed as the minority party that must constitute itself as the sugar....

AN: Don't look at it within the framework of majority and minority, which has very little to offer. By the way, if you ask me, I'm yet to meet a Parsi in my life who really thinks that Parsis are a minority. All the Parsis I've met in my life, in their heart of hearts, believe that they are in a majority. Their number may have shrunk to a 100,000, but they say and do things, and crack jokes, that only a self-confident majority is capable of saying. Before the early 1980s, I hadn't met a Sikh who thought he was a minority. I am reasonably sure that only in the 1940s did the Muslims become aware of themselves as a minority. A majority of Muslims never thought of themselves as a minority, I am absolutely convinced. Traditionally we have not lived in an enumerative world, as Sudipta Kaviraj says;[21] we have not learned to live in an enumerative world. To some extent Indian democracy has to base itself upon an enumerative world—that's part of the problem.

VL: If one is speaking of the enumerative world, there is a regime of numbers that has come into place. Indians have always been enthralled by numbers, but of a rather different kind; they weren't understood within that mechanistic and managerial mode that begins to predominate in the 1820s—Ian Hacking's work on the history of statistics is precisely about the entry of the regime of numbers. One can have an obsession with numbers....

AN: This subject has always fascinated me a great deal. I've never been able to resolve it. ...I was fresh out of psychological training and was using this mathematized social science. Even there the contradiction was very apparent. On the one hand, Indians have this tremendous fascination with numbers, as you say they

---

[21] Indian historian and political theorist; the piece in question is 'The Imaginary Institution of India', in *Subaltern Studies VII: Writings on South Asian History and Society*, (eds), Partha Chatterjee and Gyanendra Pandey (Delhi: Oxford University Press, 1992), pp. 1–39.

are enthralled by them. For everything, they'd like to put up a number. How many people died, how many mega-battalions of soldiers died in the battle of Kurukshetra? How many children did Sagara Raja have—60,000: everything is counted. Many of the numbers are absurd. And yet this is in a society which, on the one hand, has a very long tradition of mathematical reasoning; and on the other hand, it has a very long tradition of using numbers as metaphors. This is some kind of pendulum, one oscillates between the two. Now some people are convinced that Ayodhya is more than 300,000 years old, that Rama was born there. Now they have territorialized Rama because Europeans had territorialized Jesus.

VL: That's also the whole process of the discourse of history coming into shape and becoming predominant....

AN: I've often thought about it for twenty-five years. Why do Indians have this peculiarity, it isn't only history. Being enthralled by numbers; simultaneously a mythic use of numbers, and thirdly, a refusal to use numbers....

VL: Indians are comfortable with this plurality and ambiguity, are they not?

AN: And in modern times we also have a more concretistic use of the mythic use of numbers: that's a fourth component. Numbers are fascinating in themselves. My discussion of Ramanujan has hints of that.[22] There is no element in Indian life in which numbers are not present. ...Even in today's world, most great Indian scholars have a clear bias towards mathematized ways of looking at things. The discipline which has made it entirely in India is economics. They might be giving bogus advice to political regimes, but that becomes an ideological question, and for the moment I don't want to go into that. The fact is that all economists, even the dissenters, are primarily mathematically oriented.

VL: So what accounts for that?

AN: I don't know. Is it a natural talent, or something in their socialization which allows them greater access to abstract reasoning of the kind that mathematics entails; is it...

VL: Could it have some relation to forms of religious belief and practice?

AN: Yes, certainly, one can think of that also. Some of the rituals involve enormously intricate mathematical calculations, and

[22] Srinivasa Ramanujan: Indian mathematical genius (1887–1920), discussed by Nandy in *Alternative Sciences*.

certain type of lifestyles involve that too... As I started out by saying, I haven't resolved it. ... [At this point the conversation turned
towards astrology, its relation to politics, and its pervasive place
in Indian life. Nandy noted: 'It is the limits of rationality which
are implicitly recognized by astrology; it is astrology which gives
you your sense of survival after your rationality has been exhausted'].

VL: What do these things really suggest about what is obviously
a central concern of yours, that is the notion of Indian personality?
Let's for the moment go along with what you have suggested about
astrology, that it actually reminds one of the limits of rationality;
given that, given the huge enthralment and fascination with
numbers, and a number of other things we have talked about, what
does that say about the Indian personality? What does it say—to
move to the larger political question—about notions of the Indian
self and its relationship to the other, and is this relationship
configured differently in the West?

AN: Even in the West I doubt if it was fundamentally different
in earlier times. In the West, the relationship between the self and
the other began to change in a very fundamental sense in the
aftermath of the fall of monarchical orders and the establishment
of republican states. The idea of re-tooling one's people made
demands not only of Europe itself but of the colonies. I think that
brought about stereotypes and the West's fear of the other. In their
everyday life, Western societies were not so accustomed to confronting the other as India... Now the difference is much sharper,
and even in India we are gradually moving towards... Western
conceptions of the relationship of the self to the other: the self is
a self, the other is an other, and there are boundaries: the self never
spills over the boundaries into the other, and the other self never
spills over the boundaries into your self. That is seen as a remnant,
a vestigial pathology—if not pathology, then certainly vestigial
primitivism: you don't have a developed and proper self, proper
nationalism, proper state. And this was the most distinctive part,
our strength—this is the way we defined ourselves. I doubt they
can wipe this past out; civilizations are very sturdy entities.

The real achievement of the blinded gaze of *oculus mundi* is that even
today all negotiation with Western civilization must be carried out
through the West's conventions. To secure amendment or concession, real
people have to act either as if they were the Other invented by Europe

or as if they have become part of the West. So seemingly complete is this triumph that today the Other too negotiates with its real self through the conventions of Western civilization.

The Blinded Eye: 500 Years of Christopher Columbus (1993), p. 87

VL: You're still dealing with larger entities, but what about a more concrete notion of the Indian personality itself?

AN: I could go into very great detail because that is, after all, the area in which I work, and as you are aware I have been writing on that for the last twenty-five years.... I'm recently more and more convinced that the average Indian was previously much more of a statistical artifact than he is today. If I say the average Indian, it is something mythical, a fiction—how shall I put it—an imaginary Indian who meets the statistical demands [of someone]. It's like saying that in a house where there are four people who are ten years old, and four who are eighty years old, the average will be forty-five. That's the average, but the average discusses nobody.... In my generation, you can make out from half a mile that my accent is Bengali. Supposing Nagaraj[23] and I were talking together: we would talk in English, and by listening to us you could say from my accent that I am a Bengali, and that he is from somewhere in South India. But today there are a sizable number of Indians who are Indians of a different kind. Take my daughter: you can't say from her accent that she is a Bengali, from her food preferences you cannot say which culture she comes from, and you wouldn't be able to tell that from her clothes or reading habits either. She is close to our concept of an average middle-class Indian, in a very different sense than in which I might be portrayed as an average Indian. What is that in-between accent? You would have to exercise your imagination to tell between myself and Nagaraj, what would be an Indian accent. Today that is the ground reality. You cannot say it is fictitious, that it is a statistical artifact: the average Indian is still not the majority, but he's part of a strong minority, but he is there, a very sizable presence....

VL: So how did you come to the idea of the average Indian?

[23] Prominent Kannada writer and social critic; colleague of Nandy at CSDS, Delhi, and Visiting Professor of South Asian Languages and Civilizations at the University of Chicago; died at the prime of his life, at the age of 44, in the summer of 1998.

AN: I came to that because when you ask about the Indian personality, I cannot go into the psychological details: Indian personality is nothing more than a way of framing the limits within which Indians shape their cultural and psychological world. I am outlining the Indian personality or Indian mode of personality in the classical—in the cultural-personological—studies sense of the term, though there are greater possibilities of studying that mode of personality than there were ever before.

VL: Speaking of the self, there are a great many technical problems one could begin with, one of which is that there is no adequate word in the Indian languages for 'self'. *Atman* [soul] is not self, and in fact many of the words that are used for self are often used in conjunction with another word. So my intent was to ask the following: in adverting to certain arguments about numbers, astrology, forms of violence, and so on, you are really making some larger civilizational arguments, drawn from these artifacts....

AN: Not always from choice, sometimes I am forced to take positions...

VL: But anyone familiar with your style of thinking would necessarily locate your arguments within a larger framework, given the general contours of your work. For example, with respect to many things you have written about, one could locate them in a certain way within the paradigm of 'hard' versus 'soft'.

AN: I might say in passing that while that may be not untrue, there is a strong political component even there, and it can have very direct political effect. I've always been fascinated by this issue of 'hard' versus 'soft': thus my interest in Gandhi. I'm not interested in Vinoba Bhave.[24] Why am I interested in Gandhi but not Bhave? I'm interested in Martin Luther King but not in many others.

VL: You wouldn't be interested in Vinoba Bhave because his life does not exemplify, or does not lend itself, to this dialectic between masculinity and femininity, to formulations of androgyny....

AN: That also is possible.... But I'm driving at the fact that we live in a world where it is presumed, where it is clearly and absolutely presumed, that if there is a dimension of hard and soft,

---

[24] Close disciple of Gandhi and highly influential social reformer.

the hard is the realistic, rational, pragmatic, one which yields results; soft may sometimes work, if you have a 'good' regime like the British in India, or the American democratic system which 'tolerated' Martin Luther King. The ultimate argument—not that soft is bad, or morally inferior—is that if you want to be soft in everyday life, you have to justify the 'soft', but not the 'hard'; it's exactly the same with non-violence and violence. Nobody appears to think that one should intrinsically use non-violence....

The new salience of terrorism has come at a time when a sizeable section of Indians has begun to think of India primarily as a nation-state and secondarily as a civilization having its own political language and values. This coincidence has ensured the import of concepts, styles of management and technologies of counter-terrorism from countries Indians see as 'advanced', democratic polities. Many of these concepts, styles and techniques, generated in culturally very different societies, have gradually become popular and even unassailable in modern India.

'Terrorism—Indian Style', Seminar, no, 401
(January 1993), p. 36

VL: Exactly. The onus appears to be on the proponents of non-violence to show why they should not be using violence...

AN: The basic assumption is that violence works, and non-violence doesn't, as if there was some computer that had established that with certainty. My effort is to politicize that: the civilizational arguments are almost incidental, sometimes they come about by default.

VL: But why would you say that, because your use of 'civilization' is itself political?

AN: You have a point there...if you put it that way, yes...

VL: I think somewhere you said that the history of civilization is the history of trying to become more conscious of the means of oppression that are used against one, and how one can emancipate oneself from those means of oppression. What could be a more political reading of 'civilization' than that?

AN: I was trying to make clear that it isn't only a culture argument, but that there is a clear-cut political agenda. Often I try to show—one of the few things I have done very self-consciously—that the hard is less rational, less pragmatic, often counterproductive, yet people choose it. Violence doesn't yield the results that non-violence does, but people still choose violence because there is an a-priori assumption that violence will work, non-violence will not. Very self-consciously I have done that in a number of places, and tried to show the romanticism that informs the so-called principles of real-politick. There is a point after which violence becomes an end in itself, but many of these people don't recognize it. I have seen many friends taking that slippery path in the name of rationalism, real-politick, and what not.

VL: That suggests also why Gandhi remains someone on whom one can draw upon...

AN: ...and he had the slyness of a snake also. He was a politician, he was going to make non-violence and softness work, and he did so. Martin Luther King did the same.

VL: Gandhi wasn't woolly about it, he did have political agendas.

AN: Ever since I heard it from Uma Shankar Joshi,[25] I have never forgotten that quote, which I have used more than once.

VL: Which one?

AN: Arnold Toynbee's tribute to Gandhi after he died: 'Henceforth mankind will ask its prophets, are you willing to live in the slum of politics.'...

VL: Gandhi had some conception of one world. Do you have a conception of one world, and if so, what is that conception?

AN: No, I have a concept essentially and fundamentally of plural worlds, but in communication with each other in their own way, and sometimes not even in communication. I can imagine many cultures that would be totally destroyed if you brought them into global communication with others.... Lifton's work, particularly on the survival mentality, is shot through with the awareness of the element of totalism—something in our personality that has come to the fore in this century due to technology. In the *shastras* [law books and scriptures] there are elaborate and very cruel instructions on how to treat the *mlechhas* [barbarians]. Yet I think that totalism was more metaphoric in older civilizations. ... Someone recently argued that it is a form of hypocrisy and lack of commitment to say that you want a plural world, because if you really think your concept of the ideal world is intrinsically superior to the concept of the ideal world of others, or at least better morally, then it is part of your commitment that you should have

[25] Prominent Indian intellectual and writer; one of the shapers of modern Gujarati prose.

the concept or ability of defeating those other worlds. This is very typically a product of the post-seventeenth century world where moral commitment to the vision of a desirable society intrinsically and implicitly commits you to the annihilation of, or at least battle with, other worlds. I think previously it was a more Sisyphean task: that you considered your lifestyle, your religion, your culture, your country, and your kingdom to be superior to others, and you thought it your responsibility to at least prove it to others. But you also knew that it was a futile search, that you cannot annihilate others and that you have to live with them. Your own survival depended on your recognizing that; that was the sense of limits. It is that which has given way to a new form of totalism where even if you have developed the whole world, you are not happy unless you have developed the last person living in the Andamans, because even that survival of the non-developed world in some infinitesimally small pocket makes you insecure, makes you feel that there is another source of budding dissent that may come up against the fully-controlled world you have established.... In the *Terminator*, the man goes back to the past of the rebellious defeated individuals...that is a very good indicator of things. Even defeat is not enough; the fact that these rebels are very small in number, fighting at the interstices of the new world, doesn't make you feel that you have to retain that much of diversity, that much of opposition...Now this is the ultimate.

...Coca-Cola is the ultimate symbol of the market. You can have orange juice, tea or beer without a global market. Theoretically, you can grow oranges or at least squeeze them at home. You can make your own tea or coffee or brew your own beer, if you have the patience. None of these is possible with Coca-Cola. You have to have it in some ready-made form—you need a franchise to produce it and a global market to have access to it. ... The philosophy of Coca-Cola colours many areas of life and the votaries of the philosophy would like it to inform all areas of life. They do not have to work hard for that, because the philosophy is phagocytic; it eats up other adjacent philosophies or turns them into ornamental dissents within its universe.

'Philosophy of Coca-Cola: The simple Joy of Living',
Times of India (27 August 1994)

In recent years, we have rediscovered the old saying: knowledge is power. For dominance is now exercised less and less through familiar organized interests—class relations, colonialism, military-industrial complexes, and so on. Dominance is now exercised mainly through categories. ... At one time, traditional knowledge systems looked safe; they had the allegiance of the majority. Even today, data suggest, more than three-fourth of all South Asians go to traditional healers. Yet, things have changed. Modern knowledge systems are now triumphant in our public sphere. Even in traditional societies, agronomists and dam builders are least interested in what the locals think about their grand irrigation projects and mega-dams; health planners depend almost entirely on modern medicine; and agricultural innovations are usually imposed on farmers.

'The Future University', *Seminar*, no. 425
(January 1995), pp. 95–6

VL: How would you distinguish between the *shastric* notion of the *mlechhas* and the conquistadors' notion of the other?

AN: This totalism may have been there in India in different forms, but not without a touch of futility. That is why I call it Sisyphean. You knew it wouldn't succeed; and you pretend as if it would succeed. You talked of infidels, *mlechhas, yavanas,* and how you kill them; you talked of the killing of eighteen *akshavanis* [regiments of forces] in the *Mahabharata,* of the 60,000 sons of Sagara Raja. There is something in that grandiosity that they also knew wasn't true... It's not that there wasn't any violence or sadism, that was there; there was dominance, also totalism, but that totalism was informed by a touch of futility informed by a sense of defeat. Whereas now we have the capacity of killing everyone twenty-one times over, and we can gloat over the fact that the opposition has the capacity to kill all human beings thirteen times over: something has gone wrong with us.

VL: This is the totalism of a certain kind of self-assurance.

AN: Yes. It is an achievable totalism; you know it is possible, and once in a while you have tried it. The Holocaust tells one such story; the massacre of the Armenians is something that was attempted.

VL: Two questions emerge. Do you think, then, that Gandhi had a conception of one world? That is at least the 'Quakerish' or pacifists' reading of Gandhi.

AN: You can't call it one world, that further confuses the issue. He had the concept of a normal civilization.

VL: And what is that concept?

AN: A normal civilization is a civilization where checks and counter-checks, within civilization and outside, ensure that certain limits are maintained through various concepts, such as limits on technology and knowledge. I would find it very difficult to justify cloning in terms of any of the religious world views. That is a very complex thing; is it only a question of morality, or is it a question of pragmatics too? If you by mistake are cloned, certain kinds of viruses and living organisms burst out of the laboratory, and the entire human race is doomed....

VL: Is that the sense of civilization that you speak of in most of your works?

AN: Yes. The world civilization, as my friend Satish Kumar of *Resurgence* has reminded me, carries the concept of civility and the city; culture is more modest. He thought that what I say is better expressed through the concept of culture rather than civilization. He had a point, I was quite convinced of it, and I have reduced my use of 'civilization' wherever I can. But there is an irreducible minimum where you have to fall back on 'civilizational' categories, where there is an element of checks and counter-checks, where the whole is not the parts because the parts are used in an interesting way. Someone told me that Gadamer once claimed that the real charm of Europe, its real civilizational contribution, was its diversity and cultural plurality, but that the Europeans never understood that, and they hated each others' culture and wanted to finish each other off. Something of that nature could be said about most civilizations; this plurality is built into civilizations. Culture may or may not be plural; civilizations always are. I cannot think of a monolithic civilization because it will then be a culture. Civilization is by definition a confrontation of cultures, that is the way I look at it. And it has all the strengths of a confrontation; people live mostly by culture, but sometimes they fall back on civilizations.

[There followed a very long discussion on Tagore and Gandhi, on Gandhi's endeavour to extend the agreement among Hindus and Muslims from the cultural plane to the public sphere, and on the religious and cultural unity of Indian civilization. It then veered towards Nandy's idea of dissent.]

VL: One of your books is dedicated to those who dare to defy the models of defiance. So how does one dare to defy the model of defiance?

AN: I meant something quite modest, really. I meant that the only way to be not part of the loyal opposition, the Queen's opposition on the Westminster model, is to defy the key categories of the Enlightenment. Without that you cannot make it.

No hegemony is complete unless the predictability of dissent is ensured, and that cannot be done unless powerful criteria are set up to decide what is authentic, sane, rational dissent and, then, these criteria are systematically institutionalized though the university system. This is the process that we are witnessing in the burgeoning intellectual fashion industry, inundated these days with such powerful brand names as post-modernism, post-coloniality and post-structuralism.

'Bearing Witness to the Future', *Futures* 28, nos 6–7
(August–September 1996), p. 638

VL: So Gandhi's recourse to fasting would be a defiance of the models of defiance.

AN: There can be no doubt about that. I would fully agree with that.

VL: But each act of defiance of Gandhi's sort was at the same time an attempt at communication.

AN: A two-level communication, mind you: a communication which is understood by that part of your self which has been marginalized by the Enlightenment, but not eliminated, that is your latent self; it is also a communication to the Enlightenment self where it may end up triggering a moral thing or contradiction within the Enlightenment. You must recognize both.

VL: I take your argument, but I am a bit uncertain how it would work. So let me take a more complicated example. You have somewhere a discussion on the fatwa issued against Rushdie. You point out that if Khomeini was really interested in killing Rushdie, he would never have issued a fatwa. Rushdie could have been eliminated quite easily, without the formality of a public death sentence. Rushdie was, if anything, given an opportunity to flee death. You go on to argue that the fatwa is really to be understood as a mode of communication which defies the usual modes of communication, such as diplomatic exchanges, that are expected to govern relations between states. Are you entirely comfortable with that?

AN: Yes, it doesn't mean that all modes of defiance are automatically acceptable. The range of dissent has to be widened in a certain fashion.... It doesn't mean that Khomeini's endeavour has the same meaning attached to it as the kind of defence within the Islamic world mounted by someone like Khan Abdul

Ghaffar Khan,[26] or in intellectual terms by the famous liberal theologian and theoretician, Ali Shariati. You must have this two-fold communication: but Khomeini's fatwa did not defy the internal opposition, though it did defy the Great Satan. However justifiable in other ways, however much you grant the provocation, even then you have to admit that the fatwa did not perform that role.

VL: If you say that in certain instances it would be justifiable, and in others it wouldn't, there is still the question of parameters: let me advert again to Gandhi's fasts. Gandhi was certain that a fast could be undertaken only if there was an implicit condition that by fasting you are in fact actually making it possible for the other part to respond; there has to be that possibility, an invitation to a dialogue. How does a fatwa amount to an invitation to a dialogue?

AN: Because it is communicative.

VL: There has to be some capacity within the party that is receiving the communication to understand it as such.

AN: Yes, both sides have to do so, one party cannot understand it alone. There is the factor of the market morality: it is after all a death threat which is an incentive. As if the religious good you would do is not enough, as if the very fact that you are killing an enemy of Islam and establishing your moral superiority is not enough—you have to be given an economic incentive. Don't forget that part of the story.

VL: It's not cricket any more, one might say: even cricketers need large material incentives before they'll be a sport. So let me move to the book on cricket. What were you doing in that book?

AN: I was articulating two or three things. I was first of all trying to articulate the vision of a desirable society, and how to go about it. Two, I was trying to spell out the moral framework of politics in a society like India; and three, I was trying to locate outside modernity, and modern India, something from certain modern forms of self-expression which can survive and be enriched only by being located partly outside modernity. My interest in cinema is similar, after all cinema is a Western means; others have

[26] A Pathan leader, known affectionately as the 'Frontier Gandhi', who became a close follower of Gandhi and led the non-violent movement in the North West Frontier Province; imprisoned for much of his life after 1947 by the Pakistani government.

done what I have attempted, say in the case of novel.... But in the case of cricket, which is not a self-conscious game in that way, not to that extent, it has not been done. My aim was to look at a particular genre of the open-ended products of modernity which can be partly independent of the logic of modernity; these are the cognitive counterparts of lead, the bicycle, and the sewing-machine—three elements of the modern world, that so fundamental a critic of modernity as Gandhi himself accepted as absolutely vital innovations which have enriched traditions.

Cricket is not a synecdoche in the culture of its origin; it is so only in some of the cultures which have adopted it. When a Victorian said 'It is not cricket,' he did not mean 'It is not life' nor even 'It is not society'. On the contrary, he assumed that many things which pass in politics, business or in life in general would not pass in cricket. Cricket for him was a protected domain, even if it was...often contaminated by life. If cricket with its anarchic collectivism was a synecdoche for the Victorian— that is, if cricket roughly stood for life for him—he would have ceased being himself. He might have even become a savage Asian or African.

The Tao of Cricket: On Games of Destiny and
the Destiny of Games (1989), p. 3

VL: So how do you use the argument of cricket, the life and metaphor of cricket, to explicate your vision of a desirable society?

AN: I try to show how our visions also have a political element. In our times, very crudely, the morally good is of course superior to evil, morally or aesthetically; good is superior to evil; but evil is superior at least to hypocrisy, which is evil masquerading as good. The older civilizations always believed that the ranking should be different: good, hypocrisy, and evil. Hypocrisy at least keeps the values alive for the next generation. Hypocrisy is homage to an evil-based good. Your mind and flesh may be weak; you may find the norms so rigid that you cannot follow them; but at least the norms survive and you pay respect to them for the next generation. ...Hypocrisy also has something to do with establishing communication. If you want to establish communication with your target of defiance or dissent, hypocrisy allows you that also. ...In the nineteenth century, cricket was undoubtedly a hypocritical game to very large extent. But cricket has become totally commercialized now...I think Adorno had a point which I've used in my *Traditions* book, that this so-called material interpretation tears at the mask of hypocrisy and arrives at the real

thing. It is like establishing the complicity that the police sometimes establish with the criminals; after tearing off the hypocrisy
you're left with stark materialism all the way through—there's
nothing underneath at all.

VL: So these arguments are established through your analysis
of cricket.

AN: The *Traditions, Tyranny, and Utopias* series of essays was
a by-product of the *Intimate Enemy,* more theoretical; but once I
had done that, I felt that another articulation of some of the themes
was necessary. The cricket book is a much more self-conscious
enterprise than the *Intimate Enemy.*

VL: Would you say, as an aside, that the Hindi film may
represent that older alternative you were talking about: good,
hypocrisy, evil.

AN: Absolutely. It is a vestigial dialect, as I sometimes call it,
which has survived there because of the nature of the box-office.
Three-fourths of Indians are outside modern wisdom: even Tuni-
sians, Moroccans, Fijians, Russians…too, relish the Hindi film.

VL: I hadn't thought of reading the book on cricket in relation
to some of the things you've talked about. One of the things that
stands out for me is the distinction suggested between the ethos
of the professional and the ethos of the amateur: in fact one of the
ways to read the book is not only as a commentary on modernity,
but also on colonialism. What was critical to the machinery of
colonialism in India was the ethos of the amateur in many different
ways. Many of the British histories of India were written by
amateur historians, by scholar-administrator and gentleman types.
They acquired a credibility which is extraordinary. In every respect
English colonialism is predicated on a kind of amateurism, which
accounts also for its success, as opposed to the Germans…

AN: You're very right.

VL: The Hindi film is a similar way of dealing with questions
that interest you.

AN: Yes, except in the case of the Hindi film, I would extend
myself a bit further, because it goes down lower; it is more low-
brow than cricket. The competition is even more imperfect. One
doesn't know why someone is producing a film: it may merely be
way of recycling money, because he has a lot of black or smuggled
money. It is chaos to manage it. How is this chaos managed? Indian
civilization doesn't handle chaos very well—or at least what looks

like chaos to outsiders. The film thing is an attempt to see that the chaos is not that chaotic—to extend it as chaotic has a value of its own.

VL: What do you think accounts for the longevity of the popular cinema?

AN: There is a dialectic between what is acceptable to people and the spectacular version of that acceptance. I would borrow from Roland Barthes' essay on the spectator. You cannot convince me that those who go and see American free-style wrestling don't know that it isn't a set-up. They know and don't know: it is at that level of spectacle that the inner needs of people are reconciled, the problems they are concerned with and the possible solutions....

VL: How would you give an answer to my question at the civilizational level?

AN: I don't think this is a civilizational-level question at all.

VL: I think it is.

AN: Why do you say that?

VL: I would argue that the Hindi film does not allow, in the last analysis, the possibility of a real outsider. Now there are two traditional ways in which this has been accounted for, both of which I reject. One would be the structuralist argument, the best exponent of which, with relation to India, is of course Louis Dumont. He would say that everyone is accounted for in India through the mechanism of caste—the only person who isn't is the *sannyasi*, but by virtue of the fact that he is the renouncer, there is already a place for him within the larger system. The second argument takes us back to Sanskrit literature, and alerts us to the fact that Sanskrit drama is without a tragedy: a tragedy does entail the notion of the outsider. The Hindi film doesn't allow the outsider either, but not for these two reasons. The Hindi film can have the outsider only if it abandons the cultural modes of accommodation. One of the reasons why the Hindi film has such a longevity is precisely because it doesn't allow the real outsider, and that is very close to the cultural mores with which Indians have lived. The villain is without any ontological foundation.[27]

---

[27] For a more extended discussion of these ideas, see Vinay Lal, 'The Impossibility of the outsider in the modern Hindi film', in Ashis Nandy (ed.), *The Secret Politics of Our Desires: Innocence, Culpability and Indian Popular Cinema* (Delhi: Oxford University Press, 1998), pp. 228–59.

AN: I haven't thought of this, and I'm glad you're doing this. I'm willing to be convinced of this.

VL: Would you think of comparing the Hindi film to the folktale?

AN: No, I would think of comparing it to the epics, and that too only to the *Mahabharata*. The internal contradictions, the idea that what you like today you may not like tomorrow, the idea that there is a battle between *dharma* [righteousness; the order of law] and *adharma* despite all the chaos, the concept of limits and the idea that without these limits we are doomed—even when some movies almost seem to be outside the limits, the justification is always in terms of limits. These constitute the first principles of the epic and *puranic* vision of life[28]...

VL: Now it gets interesting for me, because now you've answered it at the civilizational level, whereas I was interested in the conventions by which the Hindi film is governed. There are certain conventions which have perhaps changed a bit, but they bear a family resemblance, all the way from the 1940s down to the present day. Hindi films have a set number of characters, who exist in relation to each other in set ways: one can chart out the domain as Vladimir Propp did for the folktale.[29] For instance, one of the figures I am interested in the Hindi film is the doctor; every second Hindi film, until perhaps recently, has a doctor. But the doctor is seldom a psychiatrist. Almost never. So in this respect the Hindi film does appear to exemplify the characteristics attributed to folktales, which is not to say that it is derived from the folk idiom only, but rather, that its narrative structures are close to the folktale. At the level of narrative and conventions, the Hindi film would be close to the folktale, but at the level of its articulations it may be closer to the epics.

AN: Once again, I have to admit that I haven't thought about it that way. I'm open-minded about it. I've thought about it at the *puranic* level.

VL: How do you think of the *puranas*?

---

[28] The *puranas* are mythological texts, many in number; among the principal ones are the *Vishnu Purana* and the *Bhagvata Purana*. The Mahabharata, though an epic or *kavya*, is often numbered among the *puranas*.

[29] Russian semiologist, most famous in the English-speaking world for *Morphology of the Folktale* (1928).

AN: That's a very open-ended question. I've often thought of writing a long essay on the *Mahabharata* and the every-day use it has been put to, and what it says about this culture. There's a book by an army officer on the *Mahabharata* as a military study and another by a well-known and established psychoanalyst which shows how the *Mahabharata* can be used as a work of psycho-therapy. Half a dozen such instances show what is the nature of the enterprise.... There are very transient *puranas* and very resilient *puranas*: the *Mahabharata* is, of course, among the latter.

VL: In north India, at least in my family home, and in many other family homes that I am aware of, the *Ramayana* and the *Bhagvatam* [*Bhagvata Purana*] would be read by many of the women, but never the *Mahabharata*. Is that the same in Bengal?

AN: Your belief in north India is that reading the *Mahabharata* at home leads to family quarrels.

VL: Is that the belief in Bengal too?

AN: I have heard that people in Bengal say that, but I have never heard it at first-hand.

VL: Is it also the case that the *Mahabharata* is not as widely read?

AN: I think a lot of people read it...

VL: But even in Bengal it isn't read as a devotional work, is it?

AN: That's a point. It isn't. Probably not.

VL: So how do you suppose most Indians read it then?

AN: I think it spans both the devotional and the worldly, transcendental and this-worldly. ...In Bengal the people say that that which is not in the *Mahabharata*, is not in Bharata [India].

VL: That is a saying attributed to Vyasa himself; in any case there is a *sloka* in the Mahabharata to the effect that whatever is not found in it, does not exist.

AN: It tells you something. ... What is the status of the *Mahabharata* among your family and friends?

VL: Exactly what you have described. I asked my mother explicitly many years ago why she wouldn't read the *Mahabharata*, and she said: '*Agar Mahabharata paro, to ghar me mahabharata ho jati hai*' (If you read the *Mahabharata* at home, fights erupt within the family).

AN: Exactly the same in Bengali. I have heard many Bengalis say that others say it. There's just a possibility that it's there, there's also a possibility that it might have been a slightly late acquisition, because Bengal was not part of Brahminic culture, it became so quite late. Probably the *Mahabharata* there has a different status—it's just possible.

VL: Who would you say is the most interesting figure in the *Mahabharata*? Karna? Duryodhana?

AN: Karna is the Bengali choice *par excellence*. Every Bengali would say that.

VL: Buddhadeva Bose in his book on the *Mahabharata* also argued that. Do you share that view?

AN: I think Kunti and Draupadi, in that order.

VL: You've chosen the women, interestingly enough.

AN: I have always been struck by this epic organized around extremely powerful women characters, and the really respectable human beings are the weak persons. Bhishma. Yudhisthira. I think it tells you something about social attitudes. Think of Gandhari and Dhritrashtra: there also the same contrast. ...Men even at their best cannot transcend their weakness. Now look at the women. India has a very strong sense of matriarchy. All this talk of patriarchy has little to do with it: an anti-Third-World kind of attempt at arraigning these countries and stealing their histories to fit them with the Western construction of their past. I really mean it: it is an attempt to steal the past of the Third-World countries and fit them in the Western concept of history. They want to give us history: we will be the surrogate history.

The Other must learn to talk within itself, through its own language; for this, it must initiate a contemporary, unapologetic discourse concerning itself, unmediated through the concepts and categories imbibed in the epoch of Christopher Columbus. This involves re-learning the flexibility and dynamics of its own traditions and history.

The Blinded Eye: 500 Years of Christopher Columbus (1993), p. 89

VL: And pre-eminently that would be encroaching upon our past and imposing, in the case of the *Mahabharata*, a patriarchal structure upon it. At least in part...

AN: ...the kind of moral and cultural sensitivities which prompt us to ignore that part of the story are breath-taking and show how much of colonial creatures a lot of Indians still are.

VL: What about interpretations of the *Mahabharata* in India before the coming of the colonizers?

AN: The most interesting interpretations are those of the

regional writers. I'll give you an example from Anathamurthy[30] which I've mentioned to others. It's not the *Mahabharata* in question, it's the *Ramayana*, but it tells you something about the way interpretation works. Rama is exiled, and in Valmiki's *Ramayana*,[31] Rama asks Sita to stay back. Sita says, 'No, I'll go with you. As your devoted wife that is my duty.' And so she goes with him. But in the Kannada *Ramayana*, after giving all the standard reasons for why she should accompany him, Sita adds something which is only to be found there, 'Apart from everything else, in all other Ramayanas Sita goes with Rama to the forest. So how could I not go with you now.' What do you think of that?

---

[30] One of India's most well-established writers; major voice in Kannada literature, and President of the Sahitya Akademi, the National Academy of Literature, until recently.

[31] Valmiki's Ramayana is the Sanskrit Ramayana, from which other Ramayanas are derived, or from which they depart.

Part II

2

The After-Life of the Raj in Indian Academe[1]

Ashis Nandy

I was ten when the British left India. But they did so only technically in Calcutta. British cultural presence persisted in all walks of life. Even their physical presence did not decline. There were more British in Calcutta in the early years of independence than there had been earlier. They still dominated trade and monopolized the city's prestige clubs.

We were Bengali Christians and Calcuttans. Most of my relatives were either small-time educationists or practising doctors. My father had started life as a school teacher but, by the time we were growing up, he was a secretary of the Calcutta YMCA, an institution open to a wide cross section of the society. It attracted Christians and non-Christians, Bengalis and non-Bengalis. It was Bengali and cosmopolitan at the same time.

In this environment I came in touch with a variety of the British. They were certainly not a monolithic group, being almost as diverse as the Indians I knew. Apart from government and army officials, there were the business tycoons and box-walla, who were more numerous than those belonging to even some of the well-known Indian business communities, such as the Gujaratis and the Parsis. Only the Marwaris outnumbered the British in the business world of Calcutta.

There were also British clergy, educationists, school teachers, publishers, writers, scholars, and media persons. *The Statesman* was

[1] An earlier version of this essay was first published as 'After the Raj', *Seminar*, no. 362 (September 1989), pp. 26–31.

one of the most influential dailies in the countries then, and it was solidly British. Our teachers of chemistry and physics in the College were both Irish, and our Principal was Scots. Many of them could speak and lecture in Bengali, others could cook Bengali food, and some among them were assimilated almost entirely into the Bengali culture.

There was a fire-and-brimstone pastor in our church, Reverend Hitton, who insisted on speaking only in Bengali. That did not make him popular with us youngsters, for we dreaded his accent. We made fun of him when our elders were not around. I also remember sari-clad English friends and erstwhile teachers of my mother and aunts who visited our home. They spoke perfect Bengali and enjoyed eating Bengali food with their fingers, which the parents of some of my Indian friends could not do. Some of them felt as strongly about colonialism and imperialism as the Indians did. I also remember indigent Englishmen, even grand lunatics quite apart from the odd eccentric. In fact, the British in Calcutta were patently a slice of humanity, and contacts with them were humanizing, particularly for those who had been fiercely committed to Indian nationalism and independence. The British in Calcutta were not merely a ruling class.

The second world war sharpened this picture of diversity. I remember young English soldiers—people used to call them Tommies—looking totally lost while moving around central Calcutta. Probably they were from the countryside in Britain, and unable to adjust to the traumatic experience of war and the sudden exposure to a strange country and a city that only apparently looked familiar. They looked unnerved by the hustle and bustle of Calcutta. Previously, I had associated such reactions to the city with only Indian country bumpkins. I just could not believe that the English, looked upon as a class of rulers, could be as disoriented as our own villagers.

The British left, as the cliché goes, a unique imprint on Calcutta. The city remained very English till the end of the nineteen fifties. In no sphere was this presence more obvious than in that section of the Bengali élite that mimicked British manners and admired everything British. This mimicry and admiration cut across political ideology. No one at the time called the aping westernization. The concept of westernization—and the generalized concept of the

West which goes into it—came in after the American impact began to be felt in India. During the period I am talking about it used to be a simple case of Anglophilia. Most of the Bengalis of course denied this vehemently; they claimed that they were merely being more cosmopolitan and shedding their parochial practices.

To underline the cosmopolitan angle, some of the smarter ones did talk of France and, more rarely, of Germany. But no one spoke of the United States with much respect. I do not remember a single Bengali student of my time who wanted to go to America if he or she could get admission into Oxford or Cambridge. The latter seemed a natural choice.

It was actually a part of the same Anglicism to feign a certain anti-Americanism. Jawaharlal Nehru, being a product of a family which had risen in social stature only a generation earlier, was the proper person to take such Anglicism to its logical conclusion. Americans like John Foster Dulles (who threw fits whenever the name of Nehru and his side-kick Krishna Menon were mentioned) and Ogden Nash (the one who wrote: 'My opinion of Nehru/Is absolutely zeroo') were too dumb to appreciate the deep commitment and allegiance to the Western civilization of that generation of Indians.

Given this Anglophilia, the British presence in Calcutta seemed not merely God-given, but a cultural resource. The presence was naturally given an indigenous meaning by the Bengalis. After Durga puja, Christmas was the most important festival in Calcutta and we were told that it had been so from at least the beginning of the century. The festival was seen not only as Christian but typical cosmopolitan. People of all communities celebrated it in one way or other, even if it meant no more than going out on a jaunt to a relative's home for a holiday.

The British were accepted as a part of the Calcutta even by those who claimed to hate them. I knew political exiles who returned from the Andaman islands. They were expected to nurture a permanent hatred of the British. But even some of them looked upon the British as next-door neighbours who were greedy, devious scoundrels, rather than as strange monsters.

Yet, on the whole, the total imperial experience left a devastating effect on the Indian mind. Most destructive was the role played by the theory of progress that we had begun to borrow from

Europe in the 1830s, particularly from the British Utilitarians. In my childhood and youth, the theory was regnant in academic circles, business arts, sciences, and in sports.

The theory placed all cultures on a ladder of time. Some cultures, by definition, were advanced; others, including the Indian, were backward. The only worthwhile duty the backward were left with was to learn from the advanced, first by mimicking and then by competing. When we were growing up, we picked up these notions faithfully and accepted them as inexorable facts of life. As part of the same theory, we in turn looked upon the rural Indians, the non-Bengalis and tribes as more backward than us and, therefore, deserving the civilizing touch of the Bengali babus.

I hold the British squarely responsible for this. To justify the imperial experience, they found it necessary to push this theory of progress and it is this theory which made the British rule a part of modern imperialism. Otherwise, it would have been presumably a part of 'traditional' greed, plunder and despotism. This new hierarchy of cultures made a mess of the educational system, of indigenous forms of creativity and social criticism, and destroyed India's cultural exchanges with other civilizations, such as China, Egypt, Iran, and Turkey, which India's westernized elite began to look upon as backward. Only the cultural exchanges with the West began to seem worthwhile. This was tragic.

In retrospect, I find it difficult to accept that British Orientalists and other well-wishers of India re-discovered Indian culture and learning for the Indians. There was a cultural continuity in India which was not disrupted by military intrusions in earlier times. In the British period, for the first time, there emerged a new caste of Indians who were no longer in touch with this continuity. It was among these people that the work of British Orientalists re-awakened the sense of being Indians. Orientalism put these Indians in touch with a lost part of themselves. So the need for the re-awakening of Indians to which some British scholars, social activists and administrators contributed, was created in the first place by British imperialism itself. In this sense, too, British imperialism, being a modern kind, differed from earlier forms of colonialism. It planted and legitimized the idea of inferiority in us, not on grounds of race or skin colour only, but on grounds of secular, impersonal, scientific and evolutionary forces of history. We accepted the inferiority as a proof of our commitment to science, rationality and history. When some intellectual by-products of the colonial system began to help us fight the sense of inferiority, we accepted British intellectual leadership in that struggle, too.

I suspect that for the first time in human experience, the imperial system evolved by the British made irrelevant questions of good and evil in the sphere of political dominance. It was an imperial machine not seen in India before, or anywhere else in the world. Its organizing principle was scientific rationality. Questions of goodness and badness, of morality, probably could still be applied to the Spanish, Portuguese, and to some extent the French imperial systems.

However, the reach of the machine was not uniform in all parts of India. Experiences differed. In Gujarat, for instance, the British did not enter the interstices of Indian society. My colleague at the Centre for the Study of Developing Societies, sociologist D. L. Sheth, who is only a year older than me, saw an Englishman for the first time at close quarters when someone—I think it was David Pocock—came to teach the post-graduate classes in the Department of Sociology of the MS University of Baroda. This was around 1960. Rajni Kothari, also from Gujarat, once told me that he saw an Englishman closely for the first time while marching in a procession during the Quit India movement in 1942. That Englishman was a police officer who got down from his horse to cane the demonstrators. Kothari had been demonstrating for freedom from a people whom he had not seen at close quarters. Such experiences would have been unthinkable in the case of a Bengali babu. Interestingly, both these persons I found much less encumbered in their intellectual life than many of my Bengali friends, many of whom spent their lives dreaming of outperforming the Westerners in Western disciplines.

The intrusion of the colonial system was most intense in eastern India. The Permanent Settlement System of Lord Cornwallis produced not only political-economic but also cultural devastation. It brought into traditional land relations a new kind of impersonal negotiability and 'distant' oppression. Today, any social change in eastern UP, Bihar, West Bengal and Orissa or, for that matter, in Bangladesh must encounter the fact of this devastation and its psychological consequences. Thanks to the colonial experience, the area constitutes a distinct cultural entity which institutionally is a queer mix of the Indian and the western.

I suspect that I began to be aware of these issues only after I moved out of the Babu culture. It was about thirty years ago that I was first seriously exposed to an intellectual culture that was not Calcutta's. Thirty years is not a long time in a society's life, specially if that society has a past of three thousand odd years. But it is a long time in a person's life. In the last thirty years, enormous changes have taken place in the intellectual life of India. Many revered ideas have died; many irreverent ones have been born.

One way of locating the experience of colonialism in the life of our generation may be to look at these changes and identify some of the themes which were central to the middle-class cultures of our generation in different parts of India.

Thirty years ago I left home for the first time and became a student at Hislop College, Nagpur. I shall tell that story later. I had given up medical studies only a year ago and had taken the first unsure steps into the world of humanities and social sciences. When I gave up medicine I also had to leave Calcutta. Then, as now, one could not give up medicine or engineering in a middle-class family without everyone throwing tantrums. The middle classes are never spectacularly adventurous; they were even less so in a city of dwindling economic opportunities.

Leaving Calcutta was a painful crunch, to say the least. The city was terribly addictive. I had seen friends and relatives refusing attractive jobs and a better life to be able to stay on in Calcutta. I had seen many artists and writers develop an intense, sometimes self-destructive attachment to the city. I found that I shared their passion for the city.

A part of this passionate love rubbed off on Calcutta's distinctive intellectual ambience, a peculiar mix of the colonial and the babu. We were then sure that, but for the Londoners and the Parisians, none understood the nuances of intellectual life better than the Calcuttans. It provoked much mirth and derision when Aveek Sarkar, the proprietor of the Ananda Bazar Group, claimed a few years ago that the Calcutta Bengalis did not care for what was happening in the rest of India, being in touch with the latest trends in London and Paris. Yet, Sarkar only said what our generation of Bengalis felt, even if he did so twenty years too late, when intellectuals and artists in London and Paris were likely to find such a statement embarrassing. I am, however, sure that Sarkar is not alone; millions of middle-class Bengalis still feel that way about the capital of West Bengal. Probably Calcutta also allows you a protected, ghettoized existence which no other city does.

The Europhilia in Calcutta went with an anti-Americanism borrowed from the pre-war English gentry, and a view of India as a stage on which the Bengalis had to perform in front of a rather dumb audience. On the one hand, we were taught to pity the Americans; on other, the cow-worshipping Indians. If the former spoke an odd version of English, the later were mired in primitivism of all kinds and spoke languages which were not Bengali. Peasant leader Sharad Joshi has acquired a lot of mileage in recent years by talking of the divide between Bharat and India. The division was mother's milk to the Bengali babus. They were proudly Indian. The few who were not, usually dreamt of gate-crashing into India from Bharat twenty-four hours a day.

With this divide went a delightful set of epithets for the 'uneducated', 'uncultured'—read rural—Bengalis and the inhabitants of the nearby states, where the babus were once a part of the imperial machine but were now being displaced by the locals. The Marwaris were *Meros*, the Oriyas were *Ures*, the southerners were *Telengis*, the Uttar Pradeshis and Biharis were *Khottas*, and the Punjabis were *Painyas*. Many of the imageries have worn off, only a few have persisted. But then, it is also possible that some of them have been merely pushed into—forgive the psychologism—the Bengali unconscious. Even at this age, I am slightly wary of eating sweets made of thickened milk, *khoya*, instead of *chhana*, split milk, lest I get softened up in the brain.

Paradoxically, the historical heroes of the Bengali babus were mostly non-Bengali, though, in most cases, the heroes were considerate enough to be dead. So when we read about Rana Pratap, Tipu Sultan, Chhatrapati Shivaji, Comrade Lenin, or Bengal's own Subhas Chandra Bose, they had a certain mythical quality about them. Also, we often came to know them through their Victorian versions—Rana Pratap through Todd, Shivaji through Jadunath Sarkar, etc. There could not be a Victorian version of Stalin, who was in our youth one of Bengal's few surviving heroes, so we acquainted ourselves with his thoughts through the works of pukka English gentlemen like Rajni Palme Dutt and Christopher Caudwell. But that did not help matters much. Slowly but surely Stalin was Bengalized and, finally, he looked no different from a distant, Anglicized, but nevertheless formidable version of Jatindranath Mukherji alias Bagha Jatin or M. N. Roy. Non-Bengalis who have seen or heard Utpal Dutt on Stalin know what I mean.

Rajni Palme Dutt, by the way, was an expatriate Bengali. His cousin taught us English in Calcutta's Scottish Church College and his nephew—or was it his grand-nephew—Kalyan studied with me. Someone in the family had, I was told, asked Dutt if he would return to his motherland, now that it was free. Dutt wrote back to say, no, he was not crazy enough to return to that 'God-forsaken country.'

For a time I was like a banished child in Nagpur, lost in the central Indian wilderness, but I recovered reasonably quickly, thanks to the new freedoms I enjoyed, away from an enveloping family. Even though I had spent a few years of my childhood at Nagpur and some friends of my parents were there to complicate matters for me, they were not over-bearing. The pace of life in the city was easy and no one seemed short of time. Novelist Bhabani Bhattacharya, the author of *So Many Hungers* and *He Who Rides a Tiger*, used to live in Nagpur and he once described it as the world's friendliest city.

What pleased me most was the city's relaxed climate. It was not much of a university town, but it did not pretend to be so either. In Calcutta, I had to read many things just because in the India Coffee House you could not survive a three-minute conversation with friends who had read them. I now began to re-read books I had already read, this time for pleasure. I remember re-reading T. S. Eliot with great joy but James Joyce failed me once again. The crucial encounter, however, was with Sigmund Freud. In Calcutta's orthodox Marxist environment, I had read him with casual interest. In Nagpur, he made another kind of sense. That exposure was to change my life.

Probably it was the sharp change in my academic discipline which made it obvious to me that, whereas in the world of science the text books and the teaching were totally dominated by the

West, the attitude of most Indians to this domination was matter-of-fact. Like me, they usually neither noticed nor thought about it. They took the dominance for granted and went about their work, dreaming that in some distant future, perhaps in fifty or a hundred years, things would be different. Our elders were full of hope that, by the end of the century, the country would acquire all the paraphernalia of the advanced Western nations—from escalators to atomic power. They were not alone. Mao Zedong, being a mere peasant and not a sophisticated babu, was to express this optimism bluntly. He was to declare a few years later that China would overtake the United States in industrial capacity by the year 2000.

Many talked of the need for indigenous knowledge and *swadeshi* products, and Prime Minister Jawaharlal Nehru, whom the babus considered a great intellectual, had even a set speech on self-reliance. But this slogan of self-reliance had a limited meaning. Most academics believed that it primarily meant an Indian landscape populated by locally-made western artifacts. A few old fogies talked of a choice between labour-intensive and capital-intensive technologies but they were seen as dyed-in-the wool conservatives—mere Gandhians who had been, unfortunately, left alone by the likes of Nathuram Godse on the one hand, and the great reaper on the other. A few 'eccentrics' criticized the urban-industrial vision but we looked at them as philosophical versions of romantics like William Blake or William Wordsworth who should have been writing poetry. Those were the years of President Dwight D. Eisenhower. No question had yet arisen about the sustainability of the vision of mega-technology and development, and no one asked if permanent high growth was possible, or if the world could afford to spend 1000 billion dollars per year on defence, and so on.

The atmosphere of the social sciences was much more suffocating. Many things which remained hidden in the world of science became all too obvious in the social sciences, even to a greenhorn like me. This was because the concerns in a newly-independent country were mostly native—destitution, communal riots, entry of politics into more and more areas of life, failures of a colonial bureaucracy to live up to the new demands, corruption, and so on. But the tools of analysis and the categories used were modern and scientific, which of course meant that they were entirely imported.

Looking back, I am surprised that it did not at that time seem to flout our concept of decency. Nor did it seem to go against the tenets of nationalism so dear to us. On the contrary, it looked like it was the patriotic duty of the Indians to feel comfortable with such a transfer-of-technology model. The only serious debate was on the source of the technology. Some believed that the technology should come from the liberal West; others believed it should come from the socialist West. Each hated the other as a threat to the world's future and as paid agents of the opposition.

Even our teachers talked proudly of Indians who had made it in the international circuits and, when somebody wrote something interesting on Indian society and culture, everybody in the university setting waited to hear what the western scholars had to say about the work, before applauding it. If we did well in our class, our teachers predicted a bright future for the good students in Oxbridge or, if the teachers were not Bengalis, in an Ivy League college in the United States. This was the only future which then made sense to middle-class parents of the students of humanities and social sciences, specially since their progeny had already disappointed the parents by not being in a medical or engineering college. In the humanities, it was considered a calamity if one's child did not join economics at least in Calcutta, and a school of social work in western India. The few students who did not go by this hierarchy of disciplines were regarded as spoilt brats, born with silver-spoons in their mouths and, hence, capable of taking fashionable risks. I now suspect that the Indian middle classes began to lose some of their curiosity and sense of intellectual adventure in the fifties. Such curiosity and risk-taking was to be, then onwards, a feature of individuals rather than that of a class.

Going abroad was a big thing and I knew many friends whose parents had saved money at immense personal sacrifice to send their children for study. But it was not as yet a simple case of resident non-Indians trying hard to become non-Indians. The more nationalistic talked proudly of coming back to India and working for the downtrodden on their return from abroad. I recall that, despite the widespread awe of the West, few Indians at the time spoke of settling down in the United States or Britain as their goal in life. Except, perhaps, in the case of a few Anglo-Indians I used to know in Calcutta and a few grand eccentrics moved by the exploits of expatriate Indians in the inter-war years. The latter spoke of settling down in Paris or London in the tone of a Marc Chagall or Salvador Dali.

The colonial culture of the social sciences was underwritten by many western scholars in India—Fulbrighters and other visiting academics who ornamented the Indian universities. They took the existing academic theories of progress very seriously and carried a back-breaking civilizing mission. Strangely, though Hislop was a missionary college, I found less missionarism there than in the then-booming city of Ahmedabad to which I moved from Nagpur. After my M.A., the BM Institute in Ahmedabad gave me a training and research fellowship in clinical psychology and by that time I was a devotee of the Viennese shaman.

One characteristic of modern Ahmedabad I immediately noticed: the city's heart-throb was not Great Britain. Britain was great only to the Calcuttans, whose glorious days under the Raj were then ending. The charm of the fallen empire had already palled on the hard-boiled Ahmedabadis. To them, Washington was the new capital of the world. Ahmedabad was a pragmatic city, and by the criteria of pragmatism the United States had made it. As Oscar Wilde might have put it, good modern Ahmedabadis now went to America when they died. In the meanwhile, in a fit of this-worldly asceticism, they sent their children to America. Years afterwards, in the late 1980s, I was to discover the same attitude among the young Chinese in Beijing.

Since, however, a lot of middle-class Ahmedabadis were making a lot of money—those were boom years of the city—often this adoration for the United States led to interesting developments. For instance, most boys were sent to the United States for short periods as a preparation for a profitable business career in India, whereas the girls were sent to American universities for 'proper' studies. Till then, I had not seen such a large number of fashionable young girls, back from the United States with fashionable degrees, looking for fashionable jobs, paid or unpaid. In Calcutta, I had heard of Swiss finishing schools. In Ahmedabad, I found the city's new elite and upwardly-mobile sector using the American educational system as a huge finishing school.

Ahmedabad's other major feature was the distinct style of co-survival of the old and the new. Old Ahmedabad, Ahmedabad as a continuing city, had much less to do with cosmopolitan Ahmedabad than north Calcutta had to do with south. Till about the late sixties, I doubt if an average educated Ahmedabadi knew of the Indian Institute of Management at Ahmedabad. If he or she had heard of it, it was vague hearsay about a new institute and a big campus coming up. Yet, by that time, IIM was already one of India's most difficult institutes to get admission into.

Cosmopolitan Ahmedabad, too, knew little of old Ahmedabad. The non-Gujarati upper-middle classes talked affectionately of the old city, its elegant crafts and native craftiness, but it was the affectation of a successful brother for a clever but atavistic younger brother. Those were the days of optimistic theories of progress and everyone was certain that the old would have to be rung out, if necessary with plenty of nostalgia and a touch of coercion for the hoi polloi. The knowledgeable only wanted to make sure that the old survived as an antique piece in some respectable museum.

From the beginning, I was impressed by traditional Ahmedabad—its self-confidence, elan, its skill in handling the demands of some of the modern institutions. I had seen nothing like it in Calcutta and Nagpur. Calcutta had shown similar confidence and skill in handling some aspects of the modern knowledge systems. Ahmedabad showed no evidence of that. On the other hand, its confidence in handling modern business was enormous. It produced a sharp relief against the ruling ideology of the social sciences then, which dominated both BM and IIM. For example, I could not but notice in Ahmedabad the number of buildings built by the then-controversial architect Le Corbusier. Nobody could be more disjunctive from the traditional Gujarati concept of housing than Corbusier. Yet, by Corbusier's own admission, he was given a freer hand in the city than in his own country. I was told that at least one industrialist who commissioned Corbusier to design his house, was taken aback when the great man produced his first drawings on the back of visiting cards, but even he was supposed to have said that after spending so much money on a world-famous architect, he was not *going* to waste his own time on the subject.

All said, Ahmedabad looked to me a very civilized place. It hardly had any slums—those which existed did not look like slums to a Calcuttan—and crimes took place either in small pockets of the walled city or in textile labour colonies inhabited mainly by immigrants, away from the habitats of the city's prim upper and middle classes. Even the ruffians who supplied smuggled liquor to the thirsty cosmopolitans—Maharashtra and Gujarat were strictly dry states—were noticeably civil, a far cry from the types I had met and befriended at Nagpur. The best-known of the suppliers had still not joined politics. He did so dutifully in the eighties. The communal riots threw him up as a Muslim leader. Deprived of protection from legitimate political authorities, his community turned to him for protection and, in the process, legitimized him.

It will surprise many if I say today that Ahmedabad at that time was a city where communal violence looked the least likely. The social barriers between the Hindus and Muslims were many. But each party had a place for the other and home-brewed theories about the other. The 'other' was an other all right, but was allowed the right to the otherness. In fact, it was my Ahmedabad experience which made me first suspect that the Indian self could not be defined without its distinctive concepts of the other and the other-as-a-part-of-the-self; even when one rebelled against available cultural self-definitions, one had to aggressively borrow elements from that otherwise-disowned other. I hope I am not being too abstruse.

I shall give two instances. Once an Ahmedabadi friend of mine—a cultivated, respected professor of social science, a true connoisseur of north Indian classical music, and a liberated Brahmin—owned up in private that he liked the singing styles of only Muslim vocalists. The person given to this reverse discrimination had a perfect knowledge of the different *gharanas*; his brother and son were close to being performing classical musicians. But he had acquired his religion-based taste from an unwitting commitment to social rather than aesthetic justice. He was totally oblivious of the implications of what he was saying. Likewise, some of my other Gujarati friends—young, upper-middle-class academics—sported beards the way some of the older Muslims did, with moustaches shaved off. It was a fashion in those days. It signalled rebellion as well as cosmopolitanism. Two decades later, Bashiruddin Ahmed drew my attention to a similar process among the Punjabi Hindu, Harianvi and Garhwali drivers in Delhi whose most significant other was the Punjabi Sikh; they acquired Sikh mannerisms as an indicator of their new-found mechanical prowess.

BM Institute was an exhilarating place, what with a galaxy of gifted psychoanalysts, psychiatrists, clinical psychologists and psychiatric social workers. There were some of the big names from the international scene, too: John Sutherland, Herbert Philipson, and, later on, Erik Erikson. I remember seeing G. Morris-Carstairs there for the first time. But the real heroes were the scholarly Shib Kumar Mitra, very impressive and very handsome then; Pranab Mitra, a gifted psychiatrist whose passion was the Bengali theatre; and Kamalini Sarabhai, as attractive psychoanalyst with immense social grace and not-always-fully-justified self-confidence. Later on, these worthies were joined or substituted by colourful, intellectually superbly alert figures like Kanwal and Baljeet Mehra, B. K. Ramanujam and Prakash Desai. However, the most attractive part of the faculty was a large number of young, enthusiastic clinicians and researchers who took their work very seriously. I was lucky that they constituted the first professional peer group I ever had.

No one stayed at the BM for long. Psychiatrist Prakash Desai used to say, reversing a sentence from a well-known Aesop's fable, that he could detect pug marks of animals going out of the Institute but none that went in. The Sarabhais, who founded and ran the institute, had style and imagination. They had broken away from the traditions of philanthropy of India's business community by being superbly innovative. BM, for instance, was India's, probably the Third World's, only serious psychoanalytic research institute and clinic when I joined it. In addition, the Sarabhais were egalitarian, at least in relation to the younger faculty, and ferociously anti-feudal—a far cry from the Bengali style of institution management.

But one thing the Sarabhais did not have: the courage to break out of the technology-transfer model. Their only deviance in this respect was a bias towards England when the rest of Ahmedabad was swearing by the United States. Kamalini, who had the run of BM, suffered from the same Anglophilia. I feel guilty saying so, since Kamalini was particularly fond of me, but it became gradually clear to me that the Sarabhais, too, suffered from the fatal flaw of character of their generation—they overrated everything Western, including Indians who had succeeded in the West. It was the blindness of a generation. And it was bound to lead to a Westward exodus. There was no reason to hang on to a derivative, mimic, academic culture if the original model was available overseas. BM gradually became the refuge of the second-best.

In such an environment, the technologist-missionaries from the West were bound to thrive. Some of them were genuine stuff, willing to forego their comfortable lives for three or four years, to risk the mosquitoes, flies and the natives who populated the South Asian landscape. They took enormous care and patience to work with Indian colleagues, many of whom were fully 'unteachable,' being motivated by other less lofty interests. Norman Borlaug was the logical culmination of the Eastward movement of these new missionaries. Whether it did any good to the Indians or not, the movement brought to the dismal world of development in the nineteen sixties the romantic touch of an African safari.

However, there were quite a few ambitious academic climbers among the visiting scholars who sought to get through their Indian connection what they could not through their intellectual skills. The modern sector of Ahmedabad was the perfect grazing ground for them, because the Bania shrewdness and scepticism of Ahmedabadis collapsed when it came to anything from the West.

BM and the newly-founded Indian Institute of Management offered many interesting insights into these new academic migrants spawned by the post-war world. I specially remember the case of a programme associate at IIM who swaggered about the place as virtually a co-founder of it and as one of the most influential of its faculty. The senior faculty, which already included names like Vikram Sarabhai, Ravi Mathai and Kamla Chaudhuri, ate out of his hands and made him one of those responsible for recruiting everyone—from students to professors. It took me two years to find out that he was a graduate student at Harvard Business School. Many years afterwards, when I had come close to a number of American graduate students—warm, friendly, but also terribly insecure and self-consciously friendly with all Indians—I was often reminded of the hero of IIM, exuding self-confidence and feeling totally secure.

Two other sojourners in the country who impressed me greatly with their cool self-confidence were both representatives of foundations during the times I am describing. The first got himself appointed professor to some of the institutions to which he gave grants. So he was a professor of philosophy at Delhi University and later, some told me, a professor at the agricultural university at Pant Nagar. The other, whose status in Delhi was higher than some of the cabinet ministers, ran what could only be called an imperial foundation. He drove to his office in a buggy and the foundation during his time maintained a private plane. Under him, his foundation spent about 90 per cent of its funds on its own establishment, consultants and visiting experts. The figure is not my guess. One of his successors gave the figure after some of us had tamely guessed that it was around 60 per cent.

Not that such persons did not care for India. In many cases they retained a life-long fascination for the country. The two foundation heads I mentioned, for instance, now live out their retirement gracefully, taking a grandfatherly interest in mother India. In fact, it was their fatherly concern in those days which grated.

As for the Indians, it was still not fashionable to flamboyantly reject American money and encash that rejection in the West, and the natives were more than happy with whatever they got. Sometimes even a year's appointment at an American university sufficed; it gave unbelievable academic salience if you were in touch with the latest and the best in the land-grant universities in the Mecca of behavioural sciences.

Things are very different today. I suspect that the intellectual climate in India began to change from the early seventies. The local Maoists were the first to pluralize it. Their repertoire of invectives being what it was, they made life miserable for the high-living-and-simple-thinking liberals and the professional radicals. The liberals had already lost much of their audience and survived on slogans such as pragmatism and growth, neither of which could hope to set the heart of the young aflame. The radicals in any case were becoming fat and prosperous, and physically incapable of bouncing back when floored by the younger, more noisy Maoists. They— the professional radicals, that is—became even more hopelessly dependent on cliques within the Government of India and on the Nehru dynasty to prop them up now.

The Emergency and the suspension of civil rights during 1975–7 also turned out to be a great teacher. After it was imposed, the insensitive continued with life as if nothing had happened and the clever quickly jumped on the band wagon, correctly guessing that their support to an isolated, unpopular regime would bring them richer returns from the Indian state. The sensitive did not know what had hit them. Their text-books were no help; the empirics of life had at last caught up with them. Some of course quickly recovered and got back into their favourite ruts, but a few rethought their axioms and jettisoned parts of their known worlds.

I now suspect that we are moving towards two extremes. On the one side, the starry-eyed, panting, eroticized sycophancy towards the West has declined noticeably. The West is now more like a prosperous, next-door neighbour rather than a distant, mythical hero. Naturally, the heroic elements of westernization have diminished. No teacher in a secondary school now talks of Dr R. Ahmed—a Congress minister in B. C. Roy's time in West Bengal—who went abroad to study dentistry aboard a passenger ship, reportedly as a humble peeler of potatoes. I had to hear the story at least fifty times in my childhood. Likewise, many admirers of M. N. Roy talked more respectfully of Roy's globe-trotting cosmopolitanism and his white women than about his political and intellectual contributions to Indian society.

I not only do not see the cloying admiration for the British upper-class accent which I used to see even in my early adulthood; I am happy to find that many of my public-school-educated young friends or students cannot even recognize one when they hear it. Painfully acquired western manners—and mannerisms—which at one time went with high status in modern India, are also quickly becoming a thing of the past. No one gets goose-flesh anymore when he or she hears the word tripos or wrangler, whereas I was told early in life that Wrangler Paranjpe's wife always faithfully called him Wrangler Paranjpe. I still cannot remember Paranjpe's first name; I hope his wife did.

Also changing is the concept of fashionable life which prompted even Jawaharlal Nehru and V. K. Krishna Menon to wear Savile Row suits while being fire-eating radicals and nationalists and the idol of even *dhoti*-clad leftists. No Indian politician can now write a pot-pourri on India in Edwardian English and dare name it *The Discovery of India*. He will probably hedge his bets by calling it a rediscovery. The kind of Oxbridge accent which allowed Comrades Hiren Mukerjee and Mohit Sen to bowl over the students of Presidency College in my teens no longer cuts much ice in Indian public life.

I suspect that the decline of Brahminism and especially the decline of the Bengali babus, the Chitpavan Brahmins and, to a lesser extent, the Tamilian Brahmins as pace-setters of the Indian high-cultural scene has something to do with this change. They are still there and many of them are highly creative, too. But that creativity no longer depends on their earlier cultural hegemony. That hegemony was partly a byproduct of the immense advantages their communities had derived from their exposure to the colonial culture and it went with a built-in justification for Westernization. As a Bengali babu myself, I cannot but notice the dependence of much of the babu culture on the colonial connection. Probably in the case of Bengal, there were other long-term reasons for this easy acceptance of the West, particularly in matters of mind. I have discussed some of these reasons elsewhere. All I can add here is what I say to my Bengali friends in private—that the cultural capital of Bengal has always been outside Bengal: from Nalanda and Mithila to London, Moscow, and Beijing. Even when the community was divided, the cultural capital of West Bengal remained outside India, that of Bangladesh became Calcutta.

The Gujaratis and Punjabis who entered the modern intellectual culture later had a much more hard-boiled attitude to these things. Their entry explains, I suspect, the growing dominance of an instrumental concept of the West in India. Probably in a culture of pragmatism and absolute rationality, a defensive, totally instrumental reasoning is another road to submission. In any case, I have already said that the West's image in India is now that of a prosperous neighbour who lives at the margins of law. Knowing that he has already cornered all the resources and not left much of an opening for others, knowing that he has even the police and the judiciary in his pocket, many now feel that they have only the option to join him as junior partners in his private business or to seek residential employment with him as butlers. If while making purchases for him, they can occasionally cheat him of a few rupees or take kick-backs from others doing business with him or throw a few loaves of bread over the boundary wall to their own family, it is a bonus. They feel satiated and fulfilled.

The Indian's growing sense of competence vis-à-vis the West has come from another source which shows some continuity with the colonial culture. Many Indians have learnt to make the best out of a bad job as a partly-thought-out strategy of survival. Political scientist Anil Bhatt once told me the story of an Indian student at the University of Chicago in the seventies. Held up by two young black toughs one summer night, the Indian student, even while handing over his money and a packet of cigarettes, gave a persuasive speech about the injustice of holding up a poor black, Indian student while the whites were moving about freely in the streets of Chicago. When, moved by the peroration, one of the muggers returned half the stolen money, the Indian reminded them that he would not get any cigarettes at that time of the night. He even got back half his cigarettes.

I do not see much awe of the western culture in the Indians who settle down in the West now-a-days, either. Earlier they did not integrate only when they could not; now they do not because most of them resent the idea of merging into the mainstream. Even in the many strident radicals who have migrated to the West or packed off their children to the promised land, the concept of the West is predominantly instrumental. Perhaps that is why the number of Indian immigrants in the United States is about to reach a million, whereas in Soviet Russia, the better face of Europe according to many Indian radicals, the number remained constant at two.

It will however be terribly unfair if I do not add that, at the fringes of the academe, I also notice a growing courage to re-examine the fundamentals of the dominant theories of knowledge. Whatever else this challenge might be, it is not instrumental, for often it is counter-productive in terms of academic appointments and recognition. Not surprisingly, many of those who show such courage come from the natural sciences and the humanities. Few come from the social sciences, even fewer from the two disciplines which think they have come close to the natural sciences in precision and in formalization—economics and psychology. But they do come, and I am confident that they are the ones who will shape the Indian intellectual scene in the coming century. Perhaps, I should talk about these changes some other time.

3

How I Stopped Worrying and Started Loving the Babus*

Ashis Nandy

THE MAKING OF A BABU

Looking back, I am sometimes, surprised by my attachment to Calcutta. It is nearly thirty-five years since I lived there. All told, I have been in the city one-third of my life. Also, other cities have treated me better and, in some cases, nurtured and lionized me more. But the most formative influences on me are the culture and the past of Calcutta; my accent and the language of my thought come from Calcutta's version of Bengali; my dreams are still frequently set in the city. What can explain this hold?

I suspect it is the unique combination of the city's sense of decline, decadence and impending tragedy, and the attempts of its citizens to live with the double reality of life and art. As if that was a unique technology of survival; as if they could survive through artistic and intellectual creativity when the pathway to social creativity was blocked. As if the death-defiance of art and creative thought protected them from the ravages of life and helped them transcend the banality of everyday life. Art in Calcutta is the Bengali's last tenuous link with an imaginary world in which social intervention works.

Here perhaps lies a clue to the immense respect and love, artists, poet, writers and thinkers enjoyed in the city in our times. Intellectual and artistic life was the one domain where the citizens

* First published as 'The Remembered City', *Seminar*, no. 379 (Delhi: March 1991), pp. 43–7.

of Calcutta had still not become cynical. When later in life I moved from Calcutta, it took me years to forget that mollycoddling of those living a life of the mind. The respect I paid to intellectuals and artists was often seen by my co-students and co-workers elsewhere in India as somewhat overdone and phony. I myself came to suspect it as a new version of Brahminism. At the same time, I missed the mollycoddling in hard-boiled business cities like Bombay. It is a pity that this adoration of intellectuals has not been able to stop the decline in Calcutta's intellectual status. As the city has become more and more of a district town in creative social thinking, the hero-worship of the scholar has survived, not the culture of scholarly work. Of course, there *are* gifted social thinkers in Calcutta, but they are individuals, not parts of an atmosphere. The culture required to sustain such creative collec-tivities has been almost totally destroyed.

Both the sources of the creativity, and those of its decline, should have been patent to writers and social analysts during the early years of India's independence, but they were not. At least, we in our childhood did not see any signs of such self-awareness. The Calcuttans were still very confident, still busy importing up-to-date concepts they thought would stand the test of time. That blindness too was written into the culture of the city. One has only to read between the lines of the more sensitive writers, especially the autobiographical writings of the time, to gauge the anguish the babus were trying to articulate, but were unable to, because of the baroque imported categories they used.

There traumas shaped the mind of the Bengalis and under-pinned their social universe in our times. They were: the man-made famine of 1942, the communal carnage in Calcutta and East Bengal in 1946–7, and the partition of India which amputated two-thirds of Bengal and much of Calcutta's hinterland in 1947.

All three took place when I was a child, and the wounds inflicted by them remained raw throughout my adolescence and young adulthood. I suspect they still hurt and none can fathom the babus who have grown up in those years without confronting the psychological consequences of the three events. It has taken me years to discover the sense of unreality which surrounds many interpretations of Bengali life—from Nirad C. Chaudhuri's impres-sive if cantankerous autobiography to Ashok Mitra's elegant, once-iconoclastic *Calcutta Diary*. My suspicion is that they are somehow unable to squarely face up to the psychological impact of the three events. Even Samar Sen's memoirs, *Babu Brittanta*, which comes close to recognizing the true contours of contemporary babu consciousness, fails to take adequate note of the psychological traumata.

The famine took place when I was a toddler. I did not then live in Calcutta, except for a short stretches of time. I stayed with my younger brother and mother, then teaching in a school at Bhagalpur. Our stay at Bhagalpur was interspersed by sojourns at the homes of my two uncles or at Nagpur in Central India where my two unmarried aunts and doting grandmother lived. My father occasionally visited us. He was by that time a secretary of the Calcutta YMCA and had to stay on in the city. Everyone was happy with the arrangement, for there was then much scare about the possibility of Japanese bombing of Calcutta. Actually, only two bombs fell on the city, but the babus and the Marwaris of Calcutta were not renowned for their martial valour.

Even in distant Bhagalpur—Bhagalpur was distant then, for it took sixteen hours to go to the city from Calcutta—the famine in Bengal loomed large. Partly because we lived in a Bengali ghetto. Visitors to our home always asked for news about the famine, for my father lived at Calcutta and was expected to know. People did not trust the more hopeful news supplied by the newspapers and the government. Probably the distrust was an aftermath of the official war news supplied by the censored Indian and the British newspapers and by the then-not-so-respectable BBC; everybody suspected everything official and untamed rumours flourished. There were other reminders of the famine, too. Marriages and feasts were lack-lustre affairs, what with the guest-control order, which limited the number of guests you could invite and the kind of food you could serve. And of course, we were not allowed to waste food at home; my mother always reminded us of people dying of hunger.

The famine remained frighteningly alive for us even three or four years after it had subsided, for it weighed heavily on the minds of most people we met. Till the 1950s my maternal aunt, who had stayed back in Calcutta during the years of the famine, continued to describe in painful detail the cries of the beggars for *fan* or starch which the Bengalis, especially the affluent among them, threw away after cooking their staple cereal, parboiled rice. When we went back to Calcutta to join our father in 1944, memories of the famine were still raw and they were not allowed to die out by the cries of *fan dao ma*, 'give us some starch mother', which broke the silence of quiet afternoons in Calcutta throughout the mid-forties.

What shocked the babus the most were the beggars, mainly landless labourers who had flocked to the city from the villages. They showed no anger, none whatsoever. As if the famine was a terrible gift of fate which had to be accepted with total resignation. No grocery store or food shop—and Calcutta featured literally thousands of sweetmeat shops—was ever ransacked. There was no resistance. Skeletal, ghostly, and looking terribly tired, the poor died like so many flies, in slow motion. Even in 1944, when we moved to Calcutta, there was no dearth of epic battles between enfeebled destitutes and scavenging dogs at the dustbins of the city. These destitutes, too, looked sad or numbed, rather than angry. The content of the Bengali idea of the ultimate revolution, to be led by an enlightened, motivated vanguard pulling the masses forward by their shirt sleeves, has many sources, but this perceived passivity of victims of the famine was certainly one of them.

The passivity of the uprooted, famished peasants was matched by the heartlessness of those making money out of the war effort. The rich flouted the guest-control order with impunity and the newly rich made no effort to hide their wealth. Apocryphal stories about the prosperous, living their lives in utter contempt of the suffering around them, circulated all around us and they rang terrifyingly true. The Bengali bhadralok never had much of a tradition of austerity. They were uprooted from the mainstream Indian culture in this respect and held in contempt the very idea of austerity. They saw it either as a cover for stinginess or as a romantic ideal irrelevant to daily life. They adored the memory of Ishwarchandra Vidyasagar but, except for some lower-middle-class babus seeking to justify their low standard of living, most saw such memories as nineteenth-century morality tales.

Also, wealth in Calcutta was mostly in the hands of non-Bengalis and the urban babus who had poor social ties—and hardly any sense of community—with rural Bengal, from where the destitutes came. This made things worse. The bitterness many sensitive Bengalis felt in reaction, and the cynicism about social morality they acquired, were to become a permanent feature of the political identity and ideologies of the babus.

In the mid-fifties, when I went to live outside Bengal, I found that the memories of the famine had survived in other parts of India, too. People there still spoke of the *bhukha* (hungry) *Bangali* and associated the Bengali with a certain over-concern with food. Strangely, they found support for their stereotype of the perpetually hungry Bengali not so much by reading about or collecting money for the famine victims as by reading Bengali novelists. By far the most celebrated of these novelists was Saratchandra Chattopadhyay. Saratchandra had died in 1938, before the famine took place. But twenty years after his death, he still dominated the Indian literary scene and his depiction of Bengal was the last word on the subject for the rest of India. His model of the oral Bengali, as Sigmund Freud might have summarized the situation, was an important metaphor in our times.

Years afterwards, in the sixties, the mother of Rupa and Ela Bhat—Rupa was a close friend and professional colleague at Ahmedabad and Ela was not yet the formidable trade unionist she was to become—asked me with great curiosity in her voice, 'You are a psychologist. Tell me why in Saratchandra's novels there is so much of eating and feeding? Why do the heroines have to constantly show their love and the mothers their affection by preparing and serving food?' I suspect that the great famine of 1772, which had wiped out one-third of all Bengalis, had left its scars on the Bengali consciousness and Saratchandra faithfully reproduced that consciousness. The trauma of 1942 only reopened the wounds.

In our childhood, we did find food to be central to Bengali life. Much anxiety and a rich web of fantasies surrounded food. Marriages were usually orgies of eating; so were virtually all formal dinner invitations. And the wastage on such occasions had to be seen to be believed. But even otherwise, food was an important index of love, friendship and respect. Any visitor to the house was invariably served some food along with tea or even with a glass water. Giving only tea or a glass of water to someone thirsty was bad manners. It was a pleasant surprise when, after many years, I found out that other parts of India had easier ideas of hospitality. My wife, a Gujarati, learned the reverse of the lesson the hard way. After marriage, when she went to Calcutta and we were visiting half a dozen households a day, she was literally sick of food after the first two days. The Bengali preference for sweets, made things worse for her. She was invariably offered tea with plenty of sugar in it and once, when she was offered *lassi* and eagerly accepted the offer, it too turned out to be sweet.

Food was the source of another kind of anxiety. It was the most important carrier of diseases. Every year Calcutta had its annual visits of cholera, smallpox, dysentery and typhoid. They came like friendly demons and went away satiated after extracting their usual toll. We had to be religiously inoculated against them. Our lessons in school were interspersed every year by advices on prophylaxis, vaccination and food care. To us food was a double-edged message which had to be carefully read, lest one became its easy victim. More than four-fifths of all diseases we saw around us were water-borne and, though these diseases turned out to be fatal mostly for the plebeians, occasionally they struck nearer home. We lost school friends and even cousins.

I have even more fearsome memories of the Hindu-Muslim riots in 1946-7. By that time we had moved to Calcutta. Though I was older when the riots took place, I had almost completely forgotten them—or thought I had done so—till 1984. Walking through a devastated Sikh neighbourhood in one of west Delhi's slums, with blood caked on the pot-holed roads, memories of the earlier killings unfolded before my eyes that night, like a long forgotten documentary film.

I still remember how the slum in front of our flat on the Keshab Chandra Sen Street of Calcutta exploded on the Direct Action day called by the Muslim League in August 1946. The maid servant working at our home had reported to my mother in the morning, with some surprise in her voice, that the people in the slums were collecting sticks and knives. By the afternoon, many of the slum dwellers, used to hanging around the nearby shops, assembled on the street and began to raise slogans for Pakistan. They were led by a man I used to know as a friend of some of the servants working at the YMCA. By the evening, the beating and killing of Hindus has started. I still can see the leader, set apart by his chequered purple-blue-green *lungi*, torn vest, greying hair and *pan*-coloured teeth, beating a drum to collect the Muslim slum-dwellers in the cause of Islam. He looked a different person that day. Previously, he was a minor member of the lumpen proletariat—mousy, obsequious but friendly, when he met people like us. We used to tease him without any fear:

kan me bidi
muh me pan
ladke lenge
Pakistan

He used to smile sheepishly in response. In his new incarnation as a dutiful foot-soldier of Islam, he looked deadly. I, for one, could have never dared to repeat the couplet to him.

My father, whose life's ambition was to be a moral, practising Christian, was shattered by the scale of violence and by the hatred in the air. The first thing he did was to bring, over the rear walls of the YMCA, as many threatened Hindu families as he could. I remember the family of Rash Bihari Das, whose two youngest children were our playmates, entering our building through a back door. He was a noted professor of philosophy with the typical bearded look of a Brahmo preacher. Even under stress, he looked dignified and calm.

The smell of death was now everywhere. When after two days the Hindus began to retaliate, the horrors multiplied. Some in our family had the unique privilege of seeing from our windows an old, nearly infirm Muslim coachman being stoned to death. And I still recall the widowed mother of two young children, who had been stabbed to death close to our apartment, hysterically crying and requesting the police to shoot her dead. I still remember looking out from our second floor window at the white-saried mother and her pathetic wails. Soon the army was out, but the army's impressive route marches could not stop the assassins in each community going after the vulnerable of the other community. Those at the fringes of society never had it so good. For once they acquired a salience in their communities, as protectors and respected warriors, which they could not otherwise dream of acquiring. The poorer Muslims of Calcutta who fought for Islam and died in the *jihad* were predominantly non-Bengali. Their counterparts among the Hindus were mostly low-caste or untouchable Bengalis willing to die dutifully for the greater glory of Hinduism. The bhadralok, too, began to speak of these plebeians as 'us'. I am sure the Bagdis, Kaivartas, Ugra Kshatriyas and others of their ilk dreamt of tigers during the days of the riots.

The atmosphere in our home was, to put it mildly, tense. We children at least ate our meals, but day in and day out we saw our parents either not eating or getting up from the dining table, leaving their meals unfinished. They had lost all appetite for life. Their pain, however, had to keep company with a strange excitement which I noticed among the resident students in the YMCA hostel. The students, but for some exceptions I have not forgotten till today, were shocked by the sequence of events, but also appeared to enjoy living through such exciting, consequential times. Every one of them had his own theory of violence and had his own favourite story or rumour to share. There were Hindus and Muslims among the students and I could vaguely sense, even at that age, that their blood flowed quicker as they witnessed the gladiatorial battles from a safe distance.

Life was never the same again in Calcutta. When the gas lights in our street were lit, and the smoke from the middle-class houses gave the streets of north Calcutta its usual eerie look in the evening, there now walked strange new ghosts. We heard everyday of new limits crossed in the matter of religious violence. Hindu-Muslim riots were not unknown to Bengal and many Bengalis thought they knew all about them. But the riots this time had a new colour to them. Not only did the violence affect the middle classes directly, it patently did not carry the impress of the standard Hindu-Muslim riot at Dacca or the annual Muharrum fracas at Calcutta. The new violence had a genocidal edge and, though it gave ample scope for individual initiative and innovations, it was often clinical in its efficiency and in planning. The riots began not as an expression of anger but as a political ploy, and they were sustained by a mixture of hard-boiled strategies and street-smart, romantic heroism of the kind which the Naxalities were to later act out and to which Amitabh Bachchan was to later give voice.

After the Hindu onslaught began, my father gave refuge in the YMCA to a large number of Muslims. It was not an easy job. When the Hindus had come in, some of the Muslim residents in the YMCA had objected. A couple of them were rabid pro-Pakistanis; others thought that my father was pro-Hindu. When the Muslims came, some of the Hindu residents objected; they thought that the Muslims were getting their just desert. As if to prove his impartiality, Babu Satishchandra Nandy twice narrowly escaped death. Once when the Muslims were on the warpath; once when the Hindus were on the rampage. On one of the two occasions, it was a partisan policeman who shot at him; he thought my father was favouring the other community.

No sooner had the great Calcutta killings stopped and the memories of it begun to lose their sharpness, the carnage began in East Bengal. This time we got the news from the newspapers and from the letters and the stories of the Hindus escaping from East Bengal. As in Calcutta, the carnage went on and on, as if it had become a deadly staple for the Bengalis. In school we were constantly discussing the day's quota of violence. Outside school, I, being a Christian, was often bombarded with each community's version of the events. As usual, these versions were edged by the wildest of rumours. It was not pleasant. One thing, however, the experience did. It made me suspicious of easy constructions of religious violence for all time to come. For even about the events in my neigbourhood and the episodes I knew of first hand, there were always two sides of the story.

Our school, St Paul's on Amherst Street, had hardly any Muslim students. A few it had began to leave the school, either to go to Muslim neighbourhood schools or to stay at home till their families could move to Pakistan. I had a friend who stayed in the *imamwada* across the street. He used to often come to play with us in the evenings. Now he began to talk of migrating. One day he suddenly stopped coming. It took me weeks to find out that the family had escaped Calcutta. I was deeply hurt that my friend did not come to say goodbye to me.

I feel sorry that many of our generation of Bengalis at Calcutta were deprived of intense contacts with members of other religious groups in their formative years. They either made friends with members of other communities after entering colleges or work places, or they learnt about other communities from books. The loss was particularly tragic for the Hindu middle classes. In any case, the majority of the Bengalis were Muslims and a large part of the bhadralok community had deep links with East Bengal. The psychological divide after the great carnage cut off the community entirely from these two aspects of the Bengali experience. The rootlessness and the anomie of urban living was previously mitigated by a certain sense of community and by a frame of Bengaliness. Now, the rootlessness and the anomie were aggravated by the communal divide and by the division of Bengal.

Gradually, there grew in the younger generation of city-dwellers, right before our own eyes, a deep fear of religion and the violence it might unleash. I shared the fear and was, for many years, a hard-nosed atheist and secularist. I felt I knew what could be done in the name of religion. Only in the 1970s did I begin to rethink my secularism, influenced by the resistance offered to the new, secular, impersonal, desacralised systems of violence by their victims and by the language of faith they employed to interpret their suffering.

Some things however are irreversible; I never regained my faith. As I learnt to say subsequently, just because I developed a respect for the tenancy rights of the neighbour upstairs, it did not mean an improvement in my relationship with Him.

The third trauma was the partition of India. To most babus it seemed to be a direct result of religious bigotry and it underscored the anxieties and the panic released in them by religious violence. The Bengalis had successfully undone another partition some forty years earlier, in 1905. But this time they knew things were different. And this awareness left the babus, for once, speechless. They had quickly learnt, with obvious pride, a series of catch-words and formulae from the pre-war West and used them mechanically to make sense of the world around them. But the catch-words and formulae neither lessened the pain nor did they give them the feeling that they had understood the sources of their suffering. The partition of Bengal did not produce—and has still not produced—anything comparable to the great short stories of Saadat Hassan Manto. Writings like Nabendu Ghose's *Fierce Lane* are the best one can think of. If the famine had triggered what a not-very-bright psychoanalyst would have glibly diagnosed as heightened oral anxieties, the great killings and the partition encouraged elaborate counterphobic attempts, not always success-ful, to induce forgetting.

Those who have seen Ritwik Ghatak's films, especially *Subaranarekha, Meghe Dhaka Tara*, and *Komal Gandhar* will know what I mean. Behind the verbiage of revolution, class relations and other sundry slogans, there lay in him the anguished awareness that the ecology of the cultural, economic, and political life of the babus had collapsed with the partition of Bengal. Irretrievably so. The mixture Ghatak concocted—of self-flagellation, nostalgia, and fear of the present, masquerading as radical social critique—they all were known to us growing up in Calcutta in the forties and fifties. His genius only gave them a strange creative form on the screen, distant and yet not distant. As if he was forcing one to read one's autobiography written, uncannily, by a stranger. His cinema came closest to recognizing Bengal's real trauma and though, like many others, he sought to find pompous universalist explanations for the feelings of uprootedness, anger and breakdown of norms, his script and his camera lied less. They knew partition for what it was. His response was comparable to Manto's.

In their heart of hearts, the babus knew that, unlike as in the case of the famine and the religious violence, the partition had come to stay; nation-states were sturdy entities and so were international borders. Those who escaped from East Bengal also sensed that their dialects, life-styles and even their memories of homeland would gradually fade as they sank deeper into the melting-pot called greater Calcutta, that they were seeing nothing less than the end of a way of life. Behind all the aggressiveness of the refugees and the paeans sung to Calcutta, behind all the hatred of the hot-headed, beef-eating Mussalmans, there *was* a guilty suspicion in many that they might or should have done something that they had failed to do.

The East Bengali babus were not robust Punjabi peasants; even when they were from small towns and villages, they were more like the refugees from the city of Lahore. They had to find an acceptable meaning of the partition that would contain their vague sense of guilt and political responsibility through ornate, impersonal, social theories. Most radical and modern Lahoris I have met in life could openly lament their loss; most East Bengalis could not, without elaborate references to Hindu dominance, rural class relations, and the idiocy of village life. As I write this, I remember the title of psychoanalysts Alexander and Margarete Mitscherlich's moving account of post-Nazi German consciousness, *The Inability to Mourn.*

4

A Report on the Present State of Health of the Gods and Goddesses in South Asia[1]

Ashis Nandy

Some years ago, in the city of Bombay, a young Muslim playwright wrote and staged a play that had gods—Hindu gods and goddesses—as major characters. Such plays are not uncommon in India; some would say that they are all too common. This one also included gods and goddesses who were heroic, grand, scheming, and comical. This provoked not the audience, but Hindu nationalists, particularly the Hindu Mahasabha, for long a spent political force in Bombay, the city being dominated by a more powerful Hindu nationalist formation, the Shiv Sena.

[1] This paper began as an informal extempore presentation, and answers, to some questions raised by participants at a *samskriti shivira* (workshop on cultural studies) on gods and goddesses, organized by Ninasam, Heggodu, Karnataka, 8–15 October 1995. Subsequently, K. V. Akshara and his associates painstakingly transcribed the lecture and my exchanges with the participants for the Kannada readers. It was D. R. Nagaraj's persistent interest in the lecture that induced me to turn it into something resembling a proper paper. It was then delivered as a keynote address at the American Academy of Religion, New Orleans, 27–8 November 1996, and published in *Manushi*, March–April 1997, (99), pp. 5–19. The present revised and expanded version was delivered as the Regents' Lecture at the University of California, Los Angeles, on 1 May 1997. I am grateful to Nagaraj, U. R. Anatha Murthy, Ganesh Devi, and the intellectually extremely alert, mostly non-academic participants in the *shivira* who, through their comments and criticisms, shaped this essay in the first place.

It is doubtful if those who claimed they had been provoked were really provoked. It is more likely that they pretended to be offended and precipitated an incident to make their political presence felt. After all, such plays have been written in India since time immemorial. Vikram Savarkar of Hindu Mahasabha—a grandson of Vinayak Damodar Savarkar (1883–1966), the non-believing father of Hindu nationalism who thoughtfully gifted South Asia the concept of Hindutva—organized a demonstration in front of the theatre where the play was being staged, caught hold of the playwright, and threatened to lynch him. Ultimately, Savarkar's gang forced the writer to bow down and touch Savarkar's feet, to apologize for writing the play. The humiliation of the young playwright was complete; it was duly photographed and published in newspapers and news magazines.

Though Savarkar later claimed that Hinduism had won, for he had not allowed a Muslim to do what Muslims had not allowed Hindus to do with Islam's symbol of the sacred, at least some Hindus felt that though on that day Hindutva might have won, Hinduism had certainly lost. It had lost because a tradition at least fifteen hundred years old (things might have been different in the pre-epic days) was sought to be dismantled. During these fifteen hundred years, a crucial identifier of Hinduism—as a religion, a culture and a way of life—has been the particular style of interaction humans have with gods and goddesses. Deities in everyday Hinduism, from the heavily Brahminic to the aggressively non-Brahminic, are not entities outside everyday life, nor do they preside over life from outside, but are constituents of it. Their presence is telescoped not only into one's transcendental self but, to use Alan Roland's tripartite division, also into one's familial and individualized selves and even into one's most light-hearted, comical, naughty moments.[2] Gods are beyond and above the humans but they are, paradoxically, not outside the human fraternity.[3] You can adore or love them, you

---

[2] Alan Roland, *In Search of Self in India and Japan: Toward a Cross-Cultural Psychology* (Princeton, NJ: Princeton University Press, 1988).

[3] As a distinguished, expatriate ethnomusicologist, oblivious of the new, city-sleek 'defenders of Hinduism' has recently put it, '...the Gods and Goddesses are neither remote nor really frightening or incomprehensible, as in many other religions. Their adventures are real enough for us to empathize with them, and what makes for this feeling of reality is that they not only maintain lofty principles but also have some of our own weaknesses and

can disown or attack them, you can make them butts of your wit and sarcasm. Savarkar, not being literate in matters of faith and pitiably picking up ideas from the culture of Anglo-India to turn Hinduism into a 'proper' religion from an inchoate pagan faith, was only ensuring the humiliating defeat of Hinduism as it is known to most Hindus.

Since about the middle of the last century, perhaps beginning from the 1820s, there has been a deep embarrassment and discontent with the lived experience of Hinduism, the experience which paradoxically the young Muslim playwright, Savarkar's victim, represented. Vikram Savarkar is only the last in a series of a galaxy of people—Hindus, non-Hindus, Indians, non-Indians—who have felt uncomfortable with the over-populated Indian pantheon, its richly textured, pagan personalities, their unpredictability, variety and all too human foibles. For nearly 150 years, we have been seeing a concerted, systematic effort to either eliminate these gods and goddesses from Indian life or to tame them and make them behave. I am saying 'Indian' and not 'Hindu' life self-consciously, for these gods and goddesses not only populate the Hindu world but regularly visit and occasionally poach on territories outside it. They are not strangers outside India, either.[4] By indirectly participating in the effort to retool or gentrify them, for over one hundred years, Savarkar was only following the tradition of Baptist evangelists like William Carey and Joshua Marshman and the rationalist religious and social reformers such as Rammohun Roy and Dayanand Saraswati in nineteenth-century India, who felt that the country's main problem was its idolatry and the rather poor

---

feelings.' Nazir Ali Jairazbhoy, *Hi-Tech Shiva and Other Apocryphal Stories: An Academic Allegory* (Van Nuys, CA: Apsara Media, 1990), pp. viii–ix. See also Surabhi Sheth, 'Self and Reality', in D. L. Sheth and Ashis Nandy (eds), *The Future of Hinduism*, forthcoming.

[4] In Malaysia and Indonesia, for instance, they critically influence the mythic life of a majority of the people. Under the influence of Islamic revivalism, in Malaysia, there are now stray attempts to purify Malaysian Islam and demands that the Malaysian sultans, who constitute a ruling council, drop parts of their titles that are 'Hindu' and obvious remnants of pre-Islamic traditions. However, the sultans seem reluctant to do so, for a part of their legitimacy in a predominantly Muslim community, is linked to their ritual status. Gods and goddesses can survive in odd places.

personal quality of its gods and goddesses. These reformers wanted Indians to get rid of their superfluous deities and either live in a fully secularized, sanitized world in which rationality and scientific truth would prevail or, alternatively, set up a proper monotheistic God like the 'proper' Christians and Muslims had. Vikram Savarkar was attacking in the playwright, a part of his self no longer acceptable, but not easy to disown either.

The early attacks on the gods and goddesses by the various Hindu reform movements, from the Brahmo Samaj to the Arya Samaj, have been dutifully picked up by formations till recently at the periphery of politics in India, such as the ones centring around Hindutva. Today, overwhelmed by the experience of the Ramjanmabhumi movement and the destruction of the Babri mosque at Ayodhya, we no longer care to read the entire Hindutva literature produced over the last seventy-five years. We think we know what they have to say. If all nationalist thought is the same, as Ernest Gellner believed, Hindu nationalist thought cannot be any different, we are sure.[5] If you, however, read Hindutva literature, you will find in it a systematic, consistent, often, direct attack on Hindu gods and goddesses. Most stalwarts of Hindutva have not been interested in Hindu religion and have said so openly. Their tolerance for the rituals and myths of their faith have been even less. Many of them have come to Hindutva as a reaction to everyday, vernacular Hinduism.

This rejection is a direct product of nineteenth-century Indian modernity and its models of the ideal Hindu as a Vedantic European or, for that matter, Vedantic Muslim. That is why till recently in no *shakha* of the Rashtriya Swayam Sevak Sangh or RSS, the voluntary force that constitutes the steel frame of Hindu nationalism, there could be, by the conventions of the RSS, any icon of any deity except Bharatmata, Mother India. The Ramjanmabhumi temple is the first temple for which the RSS has shed any tear or shown any concern and that concern, to judge by their participation in worship or rituals at the temple, seems skin-deep.

In 1990–1 I had interviewed at great length the chief priest of the Ramjanmabhumi temple itself, a remarkably courageous,

---

[5] Ernest Gellner, *Nations and Nationalism* (Ithaca: Cornell University Press, 1983), p. 124.

ecumenical man of religion who was murdered soon after the mosque was demolished. He told me that during the pervious seven years of the movement in support of the temple, no major political leader of the movement had cared to worship at the temple, except one who had a *puja* done through a third party without herself visiting the temple. I may tell at this point my favourite story about the devotion to Ram of the Hindu nationalists. Once, in the course of his only visit to a RSS *shakha*, Mohandas Karamchand Gandhi looked around and found on the walls of the *shakha*, portraits of some of the famous martial heroes of Hindutva such as Shivaji and Rana Pratap. Being a devotee of Ram, Gandhi naturally asked, 'Why have you not put up a portrait of Ram also?' Those were not the days of the Ramjanmabhumi movement and the RSS leader showing him around said 'No, that we cannot do. Ram is too effeminate to serve our purpose.'

I am not going to speak about such strained styles of relating to gods and goddesses, which invites one to fight their cause without caring for them. I am going to speak about gods and goddesses who inhabit the world that we live in, sometimes as house guests, sometimes as our neighbour's headache, sometimes even as private ghosts without whom we think we can live in greater peace. Literary theorist D. R. Nagaraj accuses me of writing on these things as an outsider. 'You come to the gods and goddesses as an intellectual, academically,' he says. I have often felt like telling him that I do not want to come to them, but they force me to do so. There is an inevitable logic through which these obstreperous deities infect our life, pervade it, even invade and take it over, independently of our likes and dislikes. Like most other South Asians, belonging to a whole range of faiths, I have no choice in the matter.

For even in some persons, communities, cults, sects and religions denying gods and goddesses, relationships typical to religions with a surfeit of gods and goddesses persist. Gods and goddesses may survive as potentialities even in the most austerely monotheistic, anti-idolatrous faiths. They are not permitted into the main hall, but they are there, just outside the door, constantly threatening to enter the main hall uninvited, as in some of the best known Indonesian mosques where the entrance doors and boundary walls are guarded or manned by Hindu or Buddhist gods and goddesses. (The reverse also holds true. Some gods and goddesses do have a special symbolic place for anti-polytheism. Lord Thirupathi, the presiding deity nowadays of India's high politics, has a Muslim son-in-law whose temple is right within the Lord's campus. And Sabarimala, one of the more potent deities in South India, is also known for his Muslim friend.) Gods and goddesses are not unknown even in starkly monotheistic religions. They may not be there centre stage, but are waiting just outside the doors of consciousness. Most of the anger against *Satanic Verses* was inspired by the gratuitous insults Rushdie heaped on some of Islam's revered figures, but a part of it might also have been a response to the latent fear that the banished might return. Particularly the non-Islamic or pre-Islamic forms of consciousness which the book unwittingly invokes may or may not threaten 'mainstream' Islam, but continue to haunt many Islamic communities in those parts of the world where such forms are no longer one's distant, integrated past but, thanks to colonial constructions of 'true' Islam in the nineteenth century, often seem an immediate, destabilizing temptation in the neighbourhood. It is probably no accident that the main agitation against the *Satanic Verses* took place in Iran, Pakistan, and India, and among expatriate Indian and Pakistanis in Britain.

Shamoon Lokhandwala mentions medieval religious compositions of Western Indian Muslims that depicted Prophet Muhammad as the last of the ten *avataras* and served as the sacred texts of the Muslims.[6] But even in the more austerely monotheistic versions of Islam, gods and goddesses may survive as aspects or qualities of God, as in the ninety-nine names of Allah. Even in Judaism, despite the faith's hard monotheistic core, the dialogical relationship between God and the humans in everyday life has many of the features of pantheistic faiths. In this relationship, much sarcasm, wit, accusations of partiality and injustice, light-hearted banter and sharp criticism of the divine dispensation—of the kind that Vikram Savarkar did not relish—is usual. It is seen neither as blasphemy nor as detracting from the majesty of the divine. Such dialogues can be found in old Judaic folk tales, contemporary Jewish writers, and even in extreme conditions like recorded reactions of Jewish victims in the Nazi concentration camps.

---

[6] Shamoon T. Lokhandwala, 'Indian Islam: Composite Culture and Integration', *New Quest*, no. 50 (March–April 1985), pp. 87–101.

Theological monotheism is not foolproof protection against *theophily* or attempts to fraternize with the sacred.

In South Asia, such dialogical relationships with divinity sometimes acquire oracular grandeur. Many know the story that philosopher Ramachandra Gandhi has made famous.[7] As he tells it, the famous religious leader and social reformer Vivekananda (1863–1902), while on a visit to Kashmir, went to a temple of the goddess Kali and asked her what many self-conscious, westernized Hindus must have begun asking since the nineteenth century—why had she tolerated so much of vandalism and destruction of temples. As Vivekananda puts it, he heard in his heart the reply of the great mother goddess, 'Do you protect me or do I protect you?' Even the most fearsome deities in South Asia have, I like to believe, a double responsibility that they have to balance—they have to protect both their devotees and the humanity of their devotees. The human responses gods and goddesses give to human predicaments may also be responses to the limited human ability to give or accept human answers grounded in secular reasons or secular morality. These responses may be another kind of self-excavation represented by visions of the devotee where the questions and answers are both latent in the visionaries. In a cosmology dependent on gods and goddesses, it is a moral self-affirmation that can be simultaneously a rational argument.

A this-worldly articulation of the same process can be found in the Indian politician's perpetual fascination with astrology, palmistry, *yajnas* or sacrificial rituals, and *Tantra*. Prime Minister Indira Gandhi, for instance, undertook a series of pilgrimages during her last years (she overdid it, some spitefully say, because she lost count). I have never heard of a politician, either in her party or in the opposition, who underestimated her rational, cost-calculating, political self. Nobody believed that she would passively manage fate by depending on the good consequences of making the pilgrimages. She went to the pilgrimages, but retained her sharp, wily, ruthless political self. The issue of 'agency' in such matters is important but not simple. The heavens, though continuous with everyday life on the earth, expect nobody to be passively dependent on them. They refuse to deliver results or answers in the belief

[7] Ramchandra Gandhi, *Sita's Kitchen: A Testimony of Faith and Enquiry* (New Delhi: Eastern Wiley, 1994).

that 'agency' has been transferred to the right quarters. This compact is fully understood by all the parties involved.[8]

Nothing shows this better than the art and the science of astrology. Astrology is most popular in four sectors in South Asia: business (especially if it involves speculative ventures), spectator sports, the film world, and politics. However, I have never heard anyone claiming that the successful business persons of the region depend on astrology to solve their problems in the stock market. They do business to the best of their knowledge and understanding, *and* then take the help of astrologers, tantriks and temple priests, to negotiate terms with the gods and goddesses. As if astrology was merely another way of asking questions, they are equipped with a vague awareness that the answers might be known to one, but need to be endorsed by suprahuman specialists.[9] Thus, when after elaborate rituals and consultations with astrologers, on an average 80 per cent of the nearly 500 commercial films produced in India in a year routinely bomb at the box office, film producers or directors do not give up their belief in astrology. They blame the failure on their own imperfect reading of future and flawed ritual performances (which is another way of acknowledging one's faulty reasoning). Presumably, modernity will now make sure that psychotherapists occupy the space astrologers and priests, backed by gods and goddesses, now do. It will be in many ways a less colourful life, but that is a different story.

When gods and goddesses enter human life in South Asia, they contaminate it not in the way the modern, sophisticated, urbane believer fears they would do. Nor do they do so the way the rationalist thinks the idea of God dominates the lives of devotees. They enter human life to provide a quasi-human, sacral presence, to balance the powerful forces of desacralization in human relationships, vocations and nature. This familiarity has bred not contempt, as the Vikram Savarkars of the world suspect, but a certain self-confidence vis-à-vis the deities. Gods and humans are not distant from each other; human beings can, if they try hard enough, approximate gods. They can even aspire to be more powerful and venerable than gods. *Tapas*, penance of various kinds, and

---

[8] Ashis Nandy, *The Tao of Cricket: On Games of Destiny and the Destiny of Games* (New Delhi: Penguin, 1989), Chapter 1.

[9] This part of the story is entirely missed by those who read all recourse to astrology as the denial of free will. For a recent example, see Peter R. deSouza, 'Astrology and the Indian State', *The Times of India*, 19 July 1996.

sometimes even the benediction of one god, wisely or foolishly given, can give one superhuman, godly powers. First, spirituality is partly a gift of mortality, it is associated more with mortals than with the gods, who are usually seen to have a streak of hedonism. The persistent asceticism of Shiva is an exception rather than the rule. Second, gods can also be vulnerable and require the help of humans for fighting demons or other gods.

That is, human inferiority to gods is not absolute; no wide chasm separates the goals and motivations of the gods and that of the humans. Indeed, on some planes, the difference between immortal humans and gods becomes notional. For the classicists, this proposition is difficult to swallow because, of the seven immortals mentioned in the *puranas* (Ashvathama, Bali, Vyasa, Hanumana, Kripa, Vibhishana and Parashurama), none can, except perhaps Hanumana, claim divine status.[10] Perhaps it will be safer to say that there is a continuity between the divine and the earthly, that the chasm between gods and humans in South Asia is narrow or shifting. At times, some gods might even be less effective, potent or pious than humans.

May be that is the reason why allegiance to a deity is often personalized, why sometimes it looks like a bilateral contract or a secret intimacy between two unequal but sovereign individuals. This allegiance, a rather typical feature in this part of the globe, may have little to do with one's faith, manifestly. Anybody who knows something about the great sarod players, Alauddin Khan and Ali Akbar Khan, will also know that both have been great devotees of goddess Saraswati. Yet, they have also been simultaneously devout Muslims, and proudly so. That devotion to Islam and Islamic piety does not require them to reject their personal

---

[10] Though I have recently found out that, in Sri Lanka, there is at least one temple where Vibhishana is worshipped. Of the seven immortals (*Ashvathama BalirVyaso Hanumanscha Vibhishanah kripah Parashuramascha saptaite chiranjivinah*), Ashvathama is the best known, and, until some decades ago, one could hear claims once in a while that he had been seen still moving around with a wound on his forehead, usually in the foothills of the Himalayas. I have never been able to decipher this fondness for the hills in this tragic *puranic* character.

Notwithstanding the unenviable state of the *puranic* immortals immortality has been a major fantasy in Indian cultural life. Indian alchemy has been more concerned with the search for an elixir of life, less with the transmutation of base metals into gold.

goddess or *isthadevi* who presides over the most important area of their life, musical creativity. Aluddin Khan once composed a new *raga* called Madanmanjari. As its name indicates, the *raga* invokes Krishna and the Vaishnava culture. When someone took courage to ask the Ustad why he had used such a Hindu name, the Ustad, I am told, was surprised. 'Is it Hindu? I composed it in honour of my wife Madina Begum,' he is supposed to have said. What looked blatantly Hindu to some can seem to others a marker of Islamic devotion. The piety of neither is disturbed.

While studying the Ramjanmabhumi movement, I found a hillock at Ayodhya, venerated both by the local Hindus and Muslims. The Hindus considered it to be the discarded part of the sacred *Gandhamadan of* Ramayana, which Hanuman had foolishly carried, unable to locate the magical drug Vishalyakarani that he was told to find on the hill, for the treatment of Lakshmana's fatal war wounds. The Muslims associated the same hillock with Hazarat Shish, and considered it a remnant of Noah's ark, discarded of all places at Ayodhya, after the great deluge was over.

When gods and goddesses invade our personal life or enter it as our guests, when we give them our personal allegiance, they may or may not apparently have much to do with the generic faiths we profess. Theologian and painter Jyoti Shahi once reported a survey carried out in Madras where, according to official census, one per cent of the people are Christian. The survey found that about ten per cent of the population identified Jesus Christ as their personal god or *isthadevata*. Such data warn us not to be taken in by what some politicians acting as vendors of piety and some experts on ethnic violence tell us about the geography of faiths. The Indic civilization has been there slightly longer than the Hindutva-wallahs and the Indologists have been, and it may well survive its well-wishers. The more continuous traditions of this civilization may reassert themselves in our public life. A majority of people in South Asia know how to handle the gods and goddesses, their own and that of others. The gods and goddesses, on the other hand, not only live with each other, they also invite us to live with their plural world.

Years ago, while studying the psychological landscape of western colonialism in South Asia, I checked some nineteenth century documents on Calcutta, because Calcutta is where it all began. Not being a historian, many of the documents surprised me. For instance, the scrappy details of British households showed that they had a large retinue of servants, often including a Brahmin priest who did *puja* in the house. Many of the British houses also had small temples which the Brahmin retainers took care of. Apparently, these householders went to Church on Sundays, but found nothing inconsistent in the *puja* at home.[11] The standard reading, I guess, would be that the Indian wives or concubines of the British in India—the Suez Canal was not yet dug and most British in India had Indian spouses—required this facility. However, something else also might have been involved. For the East India Company itself owned 'shares' in at least two temples. During important religious festivals, the army band went and played at these temples and the musketeers of the Company fired volleys in the air to celebrate the occasion. In return, the Company was given a share of the donations made to the temple. It also seems that many individual British residents in India, while they proclaimed their disbelief in the special spiritual skills of the Brahmins and attacked them as charlatans, were at the same time scared stiff by the possible magical abilities of the Brahmins. At least some British householders maintained temples at their homes not because they were lapsed Christians or crypto-Hindus, but because they were afraid of the local gods and the Brahmins, and did not want to antagonize them either. It was their idea of buying an insurance policy in matters of the sacred. The apparently sharp theological distinctions between some religions may, in specific cultural contexts, observe the logic of complementary self-organization.

I have come to suspect that the theistic worlds in South Asia observe a series of principles of mediation in their relationships with each other. These mediations endorse continuity and compatibility, but also a degree of anxiety, hostility and violence, though not perhaps distance or inexplicability. Whether the protagonists are Bosnian Muslims and Serbs in East Europe, Hutus and Tutsis in Africa, or the Hindus and Muslims of South Asia, familiarity can breed contempt and venomous, genocidal passions—especially

---

[11] What arouses anxiety in modern Indians does not apparently do so in societies where the elite has not lost its cultural self-confidence. I am told that it has become fashionable in recent years for young Japanese couples to get married in picturesque European churches. They get married there according to Christian rites and the marriages are perfectly acceptable in Japan, legally and socially.

in a situation of imminent massification, threatening to negate one's cultural selfhood.

A respected Pakistani political analyst and journalist once claimed in a conversation that 'the ultimate fear in many Pakistanis is that, if they come too close to India, they would be fitted in the Hindu social order, mostly in the lower orders of the caste hierarchy.' India and Pakistan separated fifty years ago; there is hardly any Hindu left in Pakistan. Most Pakistanis have not even seen a single Hindu in their lives; they have seen Hindus only in cinemas and newsreels. Why then this anxiety? My Pakistani friend himself seemed perplexed, but insisted that there *was* this lurking fear in Pakistan that Hinduism was not something outside, but a vector within. Probably living in two complementary worlds of legends, folk tales, rituals, marriage rites, music, crafts traditions and, even, some of the same superstitions, fears, gods and demons— also has its costs. Perhaps many of the anti-idolatrous faiths in South Asia—they include many Hindu sects, too—are not merely external counterpoints to the sphere of gods and goddesses, but also constitute, with that sphere, a system of internal checks and balances. Perhaps our gods and goddesses also need such checks.

When another faith provides such an internal counterpoint, balancing principle or inhouse criticism or establishes alliances within the world inhabited by deities of other faiths, it no longer remains an alien faith or someone else's faith with whom, to conform to contemporary sensitivities, you have to open an inter-faith or inter-cultural dialogue. The dialogue already exists, waiting to be recognized or joined. Islam, for instance, by the very fact that it denies gods and goddesses, provides in South Asia a different kind of meaning-system that becomes accessible to a person who wants to defy the world of gods and goddesses while living within it. So even a threat of becoming a part of Islamic order and disowning the Hindu pantheon, by say a low-caste, oppressed Hindu, becomes a particular way of interacting with the pantheon. Islam in South Asia may mean going outside the sphere of gods and goddesses, but it may also mean renegotiating terms and conditions with one's traditional gods and goddesses. It can even mean renegotiating terms with the social status of communities deriving from a shared structure of sacredness. Many of the most famous temples of Ayodhya, the pilgrimage centre that has become a symbol of religious intolerance in South Asia today, were built with help of land grants and tax exemptions given by the Shia Nawabs of Avadh in pre-colonial days. By being patrons of Ram temples, they were making a statement both on their position vis-à-vis the Ramanandis who dominated the sacred city and the Sunnis, constituting an important component of the Muslim community there. Likewise, when B. R. Ambedkar, the Dalit leader and the writer of India's Constitution, decided to convert to Buddhism along with a sizeable section of his followers, he did so after much deliberation. It was not the standard Therawada Buddhism, with its closetful of deities that he chose, but a more austere Buddhism that, by being close to Islam and Christianity would represent a sharper disjunction with Hinduism. By his conversion, he was making a statement to the Hindu world.[12]

A more intense form of such inter-relationship is the South Asian version of multiculturism which does not remain a cultural artefact, but gets telescoped into the self of the individual. Kumar Suresh Singh's new survey of Indian communities shows that about 600 communities in India can be classified as having more than one 'religion'. (It is doubtful if these believers see themselves as having multiple religious identities; they define their Hinduism or Islam or Christianity in such a way that the symbols of sacredness of another faith acquire specific theological, cultural and familial status.) Thus, there are more than 100 communities that are both Hindu and Christian; at least 70 communities that are both Hindu and Sikh; or Sikh and Muslim. Sant Fateh Singh, who died for the cause of Khalistan, was a convert from Islam and a part of his family, I am told, remains Muslim, exactly as a part of the family of Guru Nanak, the founder of Sikhism, remains Hindu. L. K. Advani, a leader of what is reputed to be one of the world's largest fundamentalist formations, is probably the only one of his ilk to have publicly proclaimed that, in his personal religious sensitivities, he is closer to Sikhism than to his own faith, Hinduism. M. A. Jinnah, the founder of Pakistan, which separated from India on grounds of religion, belonged to a Muslim community that to many 'thorough-bred' Muslims still looks more Hindu than many Hindu communities. In all these instances, I am not talking of

---

[12] That ultimately things did not go the way Ambedkar thought they would go, and he himself had to end up as a part of the Buddhist-Hindu pantheon of the Dalits, is, of course, a different story.

recent converts retaining traces of their older faiths; I am speaking of identities that appear to be simultaneously Hindu and Muslim, culturally *and* theologically.

Shail Mayaram has worked on the Meos, one of the largest Muslim communities living near the city of Delhi in eastern Rajasthan, though many residents of Delhi may not have even heard of them.[13] The Meos trace their ancestry from the Mahabharathic clans and also often have Mahabharathic names. But they are also Muslims, devout Muslims. It is only now, after being victims of a series of communal riots since the days of Partition, that they have begun to feel that they can no longer live in two houses, that they will now have to choose, and some of them have chosen to be Muslim in the sense in which the Tabligh and the Jamaat-e-Islami define Islam. Apart from their own tradition of Islam, that is the only other Islam available to them in contemporary India. Similarly, in the re-conversion programmes being run by the Vishwa Hindu Parishad clandestinely, the aim is to introduce the non-Hindus into the Hindu fold as so many low-status, mimics of a shallow, neo-Brahminic Hinduism, because that is the only Hinduism the evangelists themselves know. This is a modern tragedy which we have not yet sensed and it affects hundreds of communities all over the region today: Muslims, Hindus, Christians, Sikhs, Buddhists. I think India will be poorer if this rich, intricate tapestry of faiths gets destroyed through neglect or shrinks into six or seven standard, mutually exclusive faiths because, in the contemporary world, only such standard faiths enjoy respectability and political clout. It will simultaneously impoverish Hinduism, Islam and the other South Asian faiths.

I have said at the beginning that South Asian gods and goddesses, like their Hellenic counterparts, can sometimes be found on the wrong side of morality or law. The *puranas* and the *upakathas* are full of instances of how loyalty to, and instrumental use of, certain gods and goddesses can destroy a person or a community. The *vamachari* tradition is old in South Asia, and there are deities who have a special relationship with deviant social groups. Years ago, while studying the nineteenth-century epidemic of sati in Bengal,

[13] Shail Mayaram, *Resisting Regimes: Myth, Memory and the Shaping of a Muslim Identity* (New Delhi: Oxford University Press, 1997); and 'Representing the Hindu-Muslim Civilisational Encounter: The Mahabharata of Community of Muslims', Jaipur: Institute of Development Studies, 1996.

I found out that the popular public worship of Kali (*sarvajanin puja*) became an important socio-religious festival in Eastern India only towards the end of the eighteenth century. Previously Kali—the fierce, violent, dark goddess of popular imagination—had been primarily the goddess of marginal groups such as robbers and thieves and some incarnations of her were even associated with certain dangerous diseases.[14] These gave her an ambivalent status. Now, along with Durga, she precipitated out as one of Bengal's two presiding deities, benevolent even if treacherously or violently so, from the great traditional mother goddess of the region, Chandi. After the great famine of 1772 killed off one-third of the population of Bengal and the colonial political economy produced large-scale cultural dislocations, Kali continued to be the chosen goddess of the marginal groups (becoming, for instance, the personal goddess of the newly-emerging sect of thugs ravaging the countryside and pilgrimage routes) but also acquired a modern connection as the chosen deity of the anomic, culturally uprooted, urban, upwardly mobile upper castes in greater Calcutta and areas heavily influenced by the British presence, where a new political economy and urban culture were ensuring the collapse of traditional social norms. Durga became a more benevolent incarnation of Chandi and gradually emerged as the most important deity in Bengal. This changing cartography of gods and goddesses, who can be benevolent but are also associated with the extra-social, the amoral and the criminal, gives an altogether different set of insights into cultural changes by profiling the anxieties, fears and hopes of a society that neither a desiccated, formal study of theology and structures of high culture yield, nor can any focus on the more formal, better known deities bare. The trivial can often be a surer pathway to cultural insights.

To give another example, in 1994, during the last episode of plague in India, I discovered that, while there were goddesses for

---

[14] Some folk tales presume Olaichandi, for instance, to be a thinly disguised incarnation of Kali, who presided over cholera. Her Islamic edition was Olaibibi. Often, in a village or town, if Olaibibi was seen as more potent, the Hindus also went to her and vice versa, exactly as many Muslims in Dhaka go to the Dhakeshwari temple for specific forms of protection or blessings. Dhakeshwari, some believe, still protects one from serious accidents and few among them want to take the risk of testing out the truth of that, not even in an Islamic society.

cholera and smallpox in large parts of India, there was no goddess for plague except in Karnataka. I wondered why this goddess, 'Pilague-amma', found a congenial abode only in that state and why she had that Anglicized name, as if she was a newcomer to the Indian scene. Could it be that plague was a pestilence that did not arouse crippling anxieties in most parts of India? Could it be a pestilence with which most Indians did not have to psychologically struggle, except perhaps in the Western coastal towns in contact with merchant ships coming from West Asia and Europe—Mangalore, Cochin, Calicut, Goa, Bombay and Surat. I do not know. Perhaps there *are* goddesses corresponding to 'Pilague-amma' in southern Gujarat and in Konkan; only I have not had the privilege of their *darshan* yet. Once again, the geography of a popular religion gives one a clue as to why plague in India has not triggered the imageries and passions it has invoked in Europe since medieval times and why Indians have never fathomed the anxieties the incidences of plague in their country aroused in some other parts of the world.

This brings us to a central feature of South Asian concepts of divinity: the intimate relationship between the gods and the goddesses, on the one hand, and the demons, *rakshasas* and ogres, on the other. The *suras* and the *asuras*, the *adityas* and the *daityas*, the *devas* and the *danavas*, are all dialectically interrelated; the gods and goddesses cannot survive or be imagined—they are not even complete—without their counterpoints among the demonic.

The divine pantheon—populated by the good and the bad, the targets of right-handed worship and those associated with left-handedness, *vamachar*—is part of a larger cosmic order. The gods and goddesses are integrally related to the anti-gods or demons. No theory of violence, no metaphysics of evil in this part of the world is complete unless it takes into account this dialectic. The fuzzy boundaries of South Asian concepts of evil, the temporal and spatial limitations of the concept of *papa* (which distinguish it from the more 'intense' Judaeo-Christian concept of sin, which is more sharply defined but, paradoxically, transcends space and time more easily) and the tolerance of diverse moral universes can be read as reflecting the inextricability of the ideas of the good, the divine and the godly from that of the evil, the desacralised and the ungodly. Appropriately, the mother of the gods and goddesses in mythic India, Aditi, is a sister of the mother of the demons, Diti, and in

story after story there is an intricate, personalized, ambivalent
relationship between gods and demons. Even Ravana, the fearsome
Brahmarakshasa, the worst kind of *rakshasa*, is intertwined with
Rama in the cosmic order as two approaches to the same divinity.
The approaches are separated by circumstances and in death this
contradiction is resolved. By dying in the hands of Rama, an
incarnation of Vishnu, Ravana reaches his personal god, Vishnu.[15]
The capacity of the great Indian thinkers, writers, and painters to
sometimes turn gods into villains, and demons into heroes, and
even the capacity of the less Sanskritized sectors to erect a temple
to someone as ungodly as Duryodhana or as demonic as Hidimba,
carries a message. Those who worship at such temples do not
worship at temples of evil. They are not part of a cabal or a secret
society, nurturing secret ambitions that they feel can be fulfilled
through some ritualized version of satanism, though that too is not
unknown in India. Rather, the worshippers seem to have an
alternative concept of divinity where Duryodhana also partakes of
the divinity which, in the more gentrified, respectable versions of
the Mahabharata, his more popular cousins seem to monopolize.

Such permeable borders between gods and demons, between the
definitions of what is sacred in everyday life and what is not, are
one of the major sources of social tolerance and of the tacit
awareness that the evil you exclude from yourself cannot be
entirely projected outwards. For such outwardly projectable sense
of the evil remains only apparently outside, at a safe distance from
the self. Indeed, the godliness you define and the ungodliness you
do not want to define but you are still forced to acknowledge, are
ordered hierarchically within, as two sets of potentialities. They
equip one with culturally distinctive theories of violence and
oppression. Last year, a political activist, a committed and successful activist, was telling me how he had started life as a Leftist; and
there was a touch of both pain and wisdom in his voice when he
said to me, 'Now, I have been in this game for twenty years. I am

[15] So Michael Madhusudan Dutt's (1824–73) great act of rebellion, his epic
Megnadbadh Kavya which makes a hero out of Ravana and a villain out of
Rama, as in some of the earlier dissenting pre-modern Ramayanas, was after
all not that disjunctive with the original as Dutt might have thought. I think
I now know why, despite being taught, like all Bengalis, to hero-worship Dutt,
I could still enjoy my grandmother's conventional version of Ramayana.

convinced that confrontations do not go very far in India. We wish they went further, but the people are like that!' But people are not like that accidentally. There is a cosmology to back them up. In that cosmology, the good and the evil are differently textured and interrelated. These interrelations—particularly the moral ambiguity that can go with it—deeply offended even a compassionate observer like Albert Schweitzer who came to believe that Hindu cosmology was inferior to its western counterparts because it did not clearly separate the good and the evil. Schweitzer felt that certain forms of social intervention and altruism were just not possible from within such pagan morality.[16] May be he was right. But that limitation also ensures that some other forms of violence, certain borderlines that are easy to draw in other civilizations— between the 'monstrous', the 'naturally perverted' or 'genetically flawed' aliens and 'us'—are not easy to draw in South Asia. In the long run, all attempts to draw such conclusive, non-equivocal lines between the insiders and the outsiders, between the godly and the ungodly, between the *suras* and the *asuras,* the *adityas* and the *daityas,* the *devas* and the *danavas,* are doomed in the region. That may not be something to be ashamed of just because Schweitzer felt otherwise. Even during the fearsome communal violence during the partitioning of British India, killings were often preceded by a call from the aggressors to the victims to change faith and the refusal by the victims to do so. To get the thrust of my argument, please try to imagine the SS offering the Jewish concentration camp victims the option to convert to Christianity and escape death.

Can this interpretation be read as only an instance of cultural nationalism or camouflaged ethnocentrism? 'Why have all the avataras *been born in India, no where else?*', a sceptic once asked me aggressively. Answers to such questions can only be as clear or vague as a culture insists on giving. In Hinduism, there *are* roughly 330 million gods and some of their *avataras* might have been born elsewhere in the world. At least one important one, I know, was born in Nepal. A proper census of these 330 million gods and goddesses and their countless incarnations is still waiting to be done.

[16] Alert Schweitzer, *Indian Thought and its Development* (New York: Beacon, 1959).

Less crudely, such questions are partly answered everyday by things like the city of Ayodhya, in Thailand. The Thai Ayodhya is not only sacred, it is unlikely that the Thais will concede it to be a copy, exactly as Tamilians are unlikely to concede that Madurai is only a derivative of Mathura. Once however you historicize Rama, once you locate his birthplace at a particular Ayodhya at a particular point of time, either to territorialize his claim to a temple or to oppose it, you automatically deny or diminish the sacredness of the other Ayodhya and, while you may serve the purposes of those who view Rama as a national leader, a historical figure and a culture hero, you cannot sustain his status as a god who, as a god, has to exist *today*. If Rama *is*, only then is he Rama. If Rama *was*, he is no Rama. That is the paradox in which one gets caught when one accepts the language of either the Hindutva-hawkers or the secular fundamentalists.

There is a question that Nagaraj raises, that of Brahminic versus non-Brahminic deities and their status relations.[17] It is closely related to an issue M. N. Srinivas discussed more than thirty years ago, though as a problem of ethnographic versus textual reality. For he had noticed in his work that it was not unusual to find out that the learned often attributed a set of qualities to a deity that others would not; that even for Sanskritic deities, the qualities associated with them in the vedas and the Puranas were not relevant in the field.[18] As Nirmal Kumar Bose pointed out years ago, south Asia has a stratarchy of gods, based on the caste system. This allows a different kind of politics of cultures, perhaps even some play in matters of spirituality. For the stratarchy seems to have a few identifiable features. First, the higher the status of a deity, the less directly helpful and relevant in everyday life he or she usually is.[19] Thus, Indra, the King of gods, has a high status in the pantheon, but his potency as a god relevant to our day-to-day existence or survival is not particularly high, not at least in

---

[17] D. R. Nagaraj, Comments made on this paper at the *Samskriti Shivira*, Ninasam, Heggodu, October 1995.

[18] M. N. Srinivas, 'A Brief Note on Ayyappa, the South Indian Deity', in K. M. Kapadia, (ed.), *Professor Ghurye Felicitation Volume* (Bombay: Popular Book Depot, 1900), pp. 238–43.

[19] This also seems to indirectly emerge from Veena Das, 'The Mythological Film and its Framework of Meaning: An Analysis of Jai Santoshi Ma', *India International Centre Quarterly* 9, no. 1 (1981), pp. 43–56.

our times. Likewise with Brahma, the creator of the universe and the seniormost in the pantheon. The Hindu temple within the precincts of most Buddhist temples in Sri Lanka are a corollary to the same principle. The devotees see the Buddhist divinity as too austere and other-worldly; for everyday purposes, they prefer to deal with the more amenable, lower-ranked Hindu deities. On one plane, the stratarchy distantiates between the Brahminic and the non-Brahminic, between the greater Sanskritic and the vernacular or local; at another, it brings together and balances the Buddhist and the Hindu.[20]

On the other hand, one's manifest loyalty to a deity, by itself, does not tell much about the powers one imputes to the deity. Thirty-five years ago, when I went to Ahmedabad to join a psycho-analytic research centre and clinic, I found most of the patients who came to the clinic to be upper-caste Gujarati Vaishnavas. Ahmedabad itself was then an identifiably Vaishnava city, a sharp contrast to my native Calcutta. My teacher, psychoanalyst Shiv Kumar Mitra, soon pointed out to me, however, that the Vaishnava style overlay a clear *Shakto* substratum, with its usual bevy of powerful mother god-desses. When confronted with serious illness or financial crisis in the family, most residents of Ahmedabad rushed to these goddesses. Popular temples in normal times were not necessarily the same as temple popular at times of crisis, as if the Ahmedabadis were discriminating enough to recognize that the goddesses could be not only more powerful than the gods, but also be a corrective to the discrepancy between the secular and sacred   status of women.

Similar corrections are represented by gods who are more powerful as children than as adults. Krishna the king in the *Mahabharata* is a god all right, but not a god of the same stature as is the child-god Balakrishna of the Bhagavata. Just as the status of the temple of Bhadarkali at Ahmedabad tells us something about the status of women in Gujarati society, the status of Balakrishna is a statement on the status of childhood in India.[21]

---

[20] Appropriately enough, Simhala chauvinists have begun to interpret this expression of mutuality as an instance of contamination of Buddhism by Hinduism.

[21] Interested readers may look up Ashis Nandy, *The Intimate Enemy: Loss and Recovery of Self Under Colonialism* (New Delhi: Oxford University Press, 1983); 'Politics of Childhood', in *Traditions, Tryanny and Utopia: Essays in the Politics of Awareness* (New Delhi: Oxford University Press, 1987), pp. 56–76.

Likewise, Rama as a raja has one set of devotees; Rama as an *avatara* of Vishnu has others. When doing field work at Ayodhya in 1991–2, I was surprised to find a section of the priests there convinced that the Ramjanmabhumi movement was a Shaivite plot to take over the pilgrimage centre. With the whole of India on fire on the Ramjanmabhumi issue, some priests insisted that what we were witnessing was a political ploy not to defeat the Muslims, but the Vaishnavas. A few of them openly expressed their displeasure that the leaders of the movement, especially the firebrand Shaivite *sannyasins* like Uma Bharati and Ritambhara, talked of Rama primarily as a king, not as a devotee of Vishnu.

If there are checks and balances *within* the pantheon in terms of power, interpersonal relations, status, morality and following, there are human checks against gods and goddesses, too. Not only in the form of pious men, women and children with unblemished records of penance whose spiritual powers make gods tremble, but also in the form of heroic, epic, if flawed figures and ordinary, humble folk who take position against mighty gods on moral grounds. Karna's defiance of fate and his disarming by Indra, Chand Saudagar's defiance of goddess Chandi and her jealous revenge against him and his family, are instances. Parents in Mithila even today reportedly refuse to allow their daughters to marry someone from Ayodhya, however eligible the prospective bride-groom, because of the ill-treatment to which Sita was subjected by Rama and the residents of Ayodhya. The practice has lasted for centuries and may outlast the Hindu nationalist politicians shouting themselves hoarse about Rama being a national hero or affirming the unity and homogeneity of the Hindu nation. I am sure there are a few devotees of Rama who support the Ramjanmabhumi movement and vote for the Hindu nationalists in elections, yet would not like their daughters to marry someone from Ayodhya. Is this refusal only comic folk superstition, or is there in this obstinacy an embedded comment on the limits of the spiritual and moral status of Rama or, for that matter, gods and goddesses in general? Do we have access to the complexity of such discriminations and loyalties?

Finally, the matter of birth and death of gods and goddesses. Now gods and goddesses are regularly born in South Asia.[22] But

---

[22] Veena Das gives, in her essay on 'Jai Santoshi Ma', a fascinating account of the birth of a god sired be commercial cinema. Such entry into the pantheon

they also die frequently, despite their theoretical immortality. They die not of illness or accidents but of forgetfulness or deliberate erasure. These are not disease that are uniquely South Asian; they are becoming epidemic the world over. Iconoclasm has killed fewer gods than erasure or reconfiguration of memory have done. Certainly, evangelical Christianity between the sixteenth and the nineteenth century could not, despite its best efforts, manage to finish off the gods and goddesses—coming from a Christian family, I know how much my family lived with them, while aggressively denying that they lived with them. And mine is not an atypical Christian family.[23] My father's Christ, in retrospect, was remarkably Vaishnava. U. R. Ananthamurthy maybe right when he talks of the European Christian onslaught on Hinduism in colonial times, an onslaught that prompted Gandhi to make his witty remark that Christianity was a good religion before it went to Europe. However, official Christianity need not be the last word on Christianity. There are Christian sects and denominations that have made systematic *theological* deals with vernacular concepts of divinity. At a pinch, most religions probably know how to live with each other; probably it is the turn of some of the religious to re-learn how to live with each other.

While gods and goddesses *are* mainly responsible to their devotees, not to outsiders scrutinizing them 'scientifically,' even for such outsiders they often faithfully hold in trust, on behalf of the future generations, parts of the selves the devotees disown and would like to jettison. Gods and goddesses do get born, they live and die, but that birth, life and death record not only what they are, but also what we are. The historian of religion, Michio Araki, once said in a conversation that the pre-modern Japan we now know, is not the Japan that encountered the West for the first time.

---

can even be quite enduring. Only a few weeks ago, writing this paper, I chanced upon a temple at Madangir, New Delhi, which claimed to be an ancient Santoshi Ma temple, *Prachin Santoshi Mata Mandir*.

[23] Probably gods have another kind of incarnation, not captured in any *avatara* theory. As we well know, many of the European Christian saints, in their Latin American incarnations, bear today clear imprints of pre-Christian Aztec deities. Even the figure of Christ has been transformed into a Meso-American one, far removed from the standardized figure of Christ in European Christendom.

Araki's argument seemed to be that Japan only theoretically escaped colonization, for it has always lived with fears of being colonized and that fear has forced it to redefine even its traditions. Today, when we speak of original Japanese culture or state as entities bearing a particular relationship with modern technology and the urban-industrial vision, we miss out crucial aspects of Japan as it was, before it saw in its neighbourhood two great civilizations, India and China, getting colonized. Araki adds, that clues to what Japan was before the western encounter and before it retooled its self-definition, cannot be found in Japanese history because, over the last two hundred years, Japan's history too has been reconceptualized. Such clues can be found only in Japanese popular religion; for it has preserved another Japan.

It is a pity that I am not a believer and that I have come to gods and goddesses through politics, mainly politics of knowledge. But for that same reason, I am all too aware that the world of gods and goddesses of people like you and me will not die soon. For our gods and goddesses, like Vivekananda's Kali, can take care of themselves. On the other hand, I cannot but be aware that there are other worlds of gods and goddesses which were being systematically wiped out. These gods and goddesses are exiting the world stage silently, without any fanfare, lament or scholarly obituary.

Some years ago, I studied the first environmental activist of India, Kapil Bhattacharjea (1904–89), who opposed the Damodar Valley Corporation, the multi-purpose project of dams, hydel plants and irrigation systems modelled on the TVA. I arrived at the usual story—that when the DVC was built in the 1950s and 1960s, hundreds of thousands of people were uprooted, a majority of them tribals. They were given paltry compensation and told to go and settle elsewhere. And as usually happened during those tumultuous times in a newly-born nation-state pathetically trying to catch up with the West, these displaced people went and quietly settled down elsewhere, lost touch with their own culture, inherited skills and environmental sensitivities (the ecology of resettlement area being usually different). Mostly belonging to the non-monetized section of the Indian economy, they also quickly spent the money they received as compensation on alcohol and fictitious land deals. Soon they became like any other uprooted community, migrant labourers working in small industrial units or landless agricultural labourers.[24] They were some of the earliest members of that growing community—an estimated fifty million Indians uprooted by various megaprojects of development over the last fifty years. This is more than three times the number of people displaced during the Partition riots. People have not forgotten the sixteen million displaced by Partition but they have certainly forgotten these 50 million. A large proportion of those displaced are tribals and Dalits; one-third of our entire tribal population has been uprooted in the last fifty years and 15 per cent of our tribes have been fully uprooted.[25] The gods and goddesses of these vanishing communities, facing silently and invisibly, threats of extinction, are the ones who have made me aware of a divine species who, unlike Vivekananda's Kali, require something in addition to devotion. There are also the gods and goddesses of communities whom, after centuries of oppression, the communities themselves have begun to undervalue or forget (so that they can redefine themselves as only a culture-less group of oppressed poor, operating from a clean cultural slate).[26] I believe that these gods and goddesses—as biographies of threatened cultures, as symbols of their resilience and resistance against the juggernaut of mega-development—deserve something more than standard, rationalist, dismissive ethnographies or archaeologies. We owe something not only to them and their humble devotees but also to our own moral selves. For no intervention in society, politics and culture becomes moral by virtue of the fact that we cannot at the moment think of any alternative to it.

[24] Ashis Nandy, 'The Range and Limits of Dissent: Kapil Bhattacharjea's Critique of the DVC', presented at the Conference on the Greening of Economics, Bellagio, 2–6 August 1993. To be published in Frédérique Apffel Marglin, (ed.), *People Count*, forthcoming.

[25] Smitu Kothari estimates that of the 60 million aboriginal tribals in India belonging to some 212 tribes, 15 per cent have been displaced by development projects. Smitu Kothari, 'Theorising Culture, Nature and Democracy in India' (Delhi: Lokayan, 1993), *ms.*

[26] Many Dalit communities in contemporary India are good examples of such deculturation. In response, some sensitive Dalit writers have made a conscious effort to rediscover and defend Dalit cultural traditions. See, for instance, D. R. Nagaraj, 'From Political Rage to Cultural Affirmation: Notes on the Kannada Dalit Poet-Activist Siddalingaiah', *India International Centre Quarterly* 21, no. 4 (Winter 1994), pp. 15–26.

5

Themes of State, History, and Exile in South Asian Politics: Modernity and the Landscape of Clandestine and Incommunicable Selves[1]

Ashis Nandy

THE NATION-STATE

Like many other similarly placed countries in the South, India—perhaps the whole of South Asia—relates to the global political economic system and the global mass culture of our times mainly through its modern political self. When India resists these global orders, the resistance is articulated and legitimized by this self; when India opens itself up for globalization, that opening up and the zeal that goes with it, are mediated through the same self. India's modern self scans, interprets, assesses and adapts to the

[1] This essay was written for and presented at the 1996 Macalester College International Roundtable in St Paul, Minnesota (October 3–5, 1996). It also appeared in volume 4 of *Macalester International* (Spring 1997) under the title 'South Asian Politics: Modernity and the Landscape of Clandestine and Incommunicable Selves.' Macalester College's permission to print this essay is deeply appreciated. As might be obvious from the unduly large number of references to my earlier work, this paper is also an apologetic conversation with myself, to formulate more neatly an argument with which I have been grappling for long. I seek the reader's forgiveness for this self-indulgence. I am grateful to the participants of the Roundtable, particularly the discussants and the chairperson in my session, and to Rustam Singh for their comments, criticisms and suggestions.

demands of the outside world, both as an entity that processes the outside world for the consumption of the Indians and as an entity that processes the Indian experience for the outsiders. The world usually knows India as it has been constructed by the modern Indians in collaboration with specialist western scholarship on India. Orientalism is frequently a joint 'dream work' where the defences and cultural 'armour' of the West is matched by the self-representation and self-engineering of the modernizing non-West.

Because these processes tend to get telescoped into the personalities of the social actors involved, the modern Indian is usually in dialogue with himself or herself when seemingly in dialogue with the rest of the world. From social and religious reformer Rammohun Roy (1772–1833), popularly known as the father of modern India, to film-maker Satyajit Ray (1920–92), probably the last larger-than-life figure India's encounter with colonial West has produced, even the most ardent modernists have had to engage in that dialogue, often with mixed results.[2] Sometimes this dialogue has to be established, through a tremendous efforts of will, almost as an exercise in self-creation. Thus, Satyajit Ray has described in painful detail how he discovered the Indian village as an urbane, highly westernized Indian, while making a film trilogy that was to paradoxically become, for the world cinema, the last word on the Indian village. As this example itself shows, such implosive dialogues may be anguished, but they also sometimes allow enormously creative uses of living in two cultures.[3]

In politics, the most remarkable part of this dialogue with self is how little the modern Indian self is dependent on, or in conversion with, what are commonly believed to be the traditional Indian definitions of state, political authority or political leadership. Despite the immense fascination with Kautilya, within India

[2] Ashis Nandy: 'Sati: A Nineteenth Century Tale of Women, Violence and Protest,' *At the Edge of Psychology: Essays on Politics and Culture* (New Delhi: Oxford University Press, 1980), pp. 1–31; and 'Satyajit Ray's Secret Guide to Exquisite Murders,' In *The Savage Freud and Other Essays in Possible and Retrievable Selves* (New Delhi: Oxford University Press and Princeton: Princeton University Press, 1995), pp. 237–66.

[3] Ashis Nandy, 'Satyajit Ray's India,' *Deep Focus*, 1996, 6, pp. 32–8; and 'The Imagination of the Village,' Presented at the *Samskritishivira* (workshop on cultural studies), organized by Ninasam, Heggodu, Karnataka, 10–20 October 1994.

and outside, the *Arthashastra* has not manifestly influenced the contemporary Indian political self-definition. Indians have been even less influenced by the political history of ancient or medieval India and the conventions of statecraft unearthed by that history. Though large empires were run by a galaxy of Hindu, Buddhist, Muslim and Sikh dynasties, and though the histories of some of these dynasties have been grist to the mills of national and subnational chauvinism in recent times, on the whole, they too have not left any significant memory trace behind. Ashoka is a more living presence in contemporary Sri Lankan politics than in India. Though the names of the likes of Rana Pratap and Guru Govind Singh are ritually invoked by Hindu nationalist propaganda, no recent, mainstream, Indian politician has been influenced in the least by any of these worthies. Even as metaphors, these figures have been marginal to contemporary Indian public life. (The case of Shivaji is a little different, because he has become identified with regional and non-Brahminic caste pride in one region of India.) If the cadres of the Hindu nationalist parties bring up these names once in a while in the service of their moth-eaten, nineteenth-century, colonial interpretation of Hinduism, the other modern Indians rejects them as parts of a cultural baggage that deserves to be only a target of millennial social engineering.

Apart from the colonial state, the only other state that has left some memory traces behind is the Mughal empire, and that is partly because during the early years of the Raj the style of governance and the culture of politics (especially the frame of legitimacy) were recognizably Mughal in some respects and they were designed to be so.[4] Till the middle of the nineteenth century, the British in India were not only sometimes called 'Nabobs', they

---

[4] So that even today, remembering the Mughal culture remains a way of going ethnic that the heritage of the Raj defines as elegant, authentic and safe. This is another way of reading Mukul Kesavan's work on the 'Islamicate' frame of Indian popular cinema. Mukul Kesavan, 'Urdu, Awadh and the Tawaif: The Islamicate Roots of the Hindi Cinema,' in Zoya Hasan (ed.), *Forging Identities: Gender, Communities and the State* (New Delhi: Kali for Women, 1994), pp. 244-58. Following Marshall Hodgson, Kesavan distinguishes between the Islamic and Islamicate, the latter standing for 'the social and cultural complex historically associated with Islam and the Muslims, both among Muslims themselves and even when found among non-Muslims' (p. 246).

continued to rule India with one eye on the conventions of the Mughal empire, the other on European ideas of statecraft. Even the official language of the Raj was Persian for about seventy-five years. The culture of the state for a long while after that reflected not only the influence of important currents of British political thought, but also the culture that had crystallized during the first seventy-five years of the Raj. Bernard Cohn's work on the 'codification of ritual idiom' under the Raj has a tacit narrative dealing with this bifocal vision: how the British defined themselves in India and how they sought to link this self-definition to the idea of the state in the ruled. For instance, the Darbar of 1911, Cohn suggests, replicated the Mughal court rituals in many ways and sought to derive consent for the Raj by systematically invoking Indian ideas of rulership.[5] The coronation of King George V was simultaneously a Mughal coronation.

However, by the 1860s, this culture began to get marginalized and pushed further underground by an increasingly assertive, Utilitarian ideology of the state which linked up with wider demands and expectations from the state in the more articulate, politicized sections of the Indian people. It is this second concept of state that has evolved gradually into a quasi-Hegelian imagination of the state in contemporary India . The process of transformation has not been entirely linear, but it has continued to have two identifiable features. First, this image of the ideal state is still heavily dependent on nineteenth century Anglo-Saxon texts on state and its social evolutionist legacy and, second, that dependence has been defined much more by texts than the practice of statecraft in Europe. As a result, the ideal state in modern India still carries with it a touch of purism and a certain fear of clumsiness, ambiguity and the dirty imprint of life. At the same time, there is paradoxically a continuous defensive attempt to define statecraft as a dirty, hard-eyed, masculine game of *realpolitik* which Indians, especially overly idealistic, romantic Indian critics of India's external policies and nuclear and security choices, cannot fathom.

Also, during the years India's modern political identity was being formed, the only real-life experience with the state to which

---

[5] Bernard S. Cohn, 'Representing Authority in Victorian India,' in *An Anthropologist Among Historians and Other Essays* (Delhi: Oxford University Press, 1987), pp. 632–82.

the modern Indians were exposed was the imperial British-Indian state. Hence the idea of the state that dominated modern India is that of an imperial state run, naturally enough now, by westernized Indians well-versed in Anglo-Saxon theories of the state. Statecraft means for many Indians a centralized command structure; a patriarchal welfare system for the poor and the powerless; an apparatus for impartial arbitration among permanently squabbling tribes, castes, religions, language groups and regions; and for the slow and steady inculcation in the citizens, of the spirit of Baconian science. Hence also, modern Indian's almost desperate belief that he or she stands between the wolves in the global nation-state system and the vulnerable sheep in the form of the irrational, uninformed majority of the Indians.[6]

The picture does not change dramatically even when religious chauvinists begin to speak of a Hindu state. That state, too, remains quasi-Hegelian and it, too, is associated with deep fears that the ordinary Hindus would not be able to sustain it. In fact, the hatred for the Muslim among Hindu nationalists is matched only by their contempt for the Hindus. They would like to herd the Hindus, too, like cattle towards the beatitude of a well-defined nationality, hitched to national security state modelled on the nineteenth-century European concept of the state. Hindu chauvinists are plaintively waiting for a Hindu Bismarck to emerge who will forge a nineteenth-century nation-state at the fag end of the twentieth century to liberate semi-Westernized Hindus from the non-Hindus on the one hand and the infra-Hindus on the other. Even the ideology of Hindu nationalism, which is supposed to back up such a state, is pathetically dependent on European nationalism of the kind popularized by the likes of Mazzini and Herder, who wrote of culture as the soul of a people and whom many Hindu nationalists in colonial times adored, as much perhaps for their ideological fervour as for their maudlin tone.[7]

---

[6] Ashis Nandy, 'Culture, State, and the Rediscovery of Indian Politics', Rajiv Bambawale Lecture 1983 (New Delhi: Indian Institute of Technology, 1984). Also in Patrick C. Hogan and Lalita Pandit (eds), *Literary India: Comparative Studies in Aesthetics, Colonialism, and Culture* (New York: The State University of New York, 1955), pp. 255–70.

[7] For some idea of the ambivalent meaning that at least Herder has acquired in our times, see Pierre Birnbaum, 'From Multiculturalism to Nationalism', *Political Theory*, 24, no. 1, (1996) pp. 33–45.

A more clinical way of describing the situation could be to say that modern Indians have stabilized their modern self by internalizing the colonial ideology of the state they confronted in the nineteenth century. Such a self has limited space for even the new currents of political culture—especially new editions of some other lesser-known ideas associated with the state in Europe and North America which have allowed them to partially transcend the gory history of wars and conquest in recent years. The frozen concept of the state among modern Indians, includes within it not only indigenized European ideas of nationality, nationalism, progress, rationality and secularism, but even a unique concept of a desirable society built mostly on once-popular ideas of European thinkers and their Indian editions prepared by a series of Indian public figures. To give random examples, Bertrand Russell, H. G. Wells, Harold Lasky, Christopher Caudwell, and Maurice Cornforth survived much longer in the warmer, grateful climate of the tropics than in the colder, forgetful intellectual environment of Europe and North America.

Such imagination of the state includes a reactive component. Many Indians have, over the last 100 years, worked hard to establish that Indian cultures had traditionally included each of the cultural prerequisites required for the sustenance of a modern state in India—from Baconian rationality to post-Reformation secularism. Once these previously repressed or cornered themes are rediscovered and revalued, so their argument goes, whatever little contradiction between traditions and modernity and exist in India will dissolve, as has reportedly happened in countries like Japan.[8]

In this way of looking at the past, British rule was implicitly a godsent instrument to modernize India and retool the natives, and such modernization had to involve the jettisoning of the 'dysfunctional' and 'degraded' aspects of heritage as a liability. The various brands of religious and ethnic nationalists have gone one better. Their model being European nationalist thought, they have actually tried to subvert the organizational frame of the heritage and reconstruct it according to the needs of a modern nationality. If the record of the Hindu Mahasabha and the Rashtriya Swayam Sevak Sangh looks abysmal in the matter of India's freedom

---

[8] The best known effort along these lines is Deviprasad Chattopadhyay, *Lokayata: A Study in Ancient Indian Materialism* (New Delhi: People's Publishing House, 1959).

struggle, it is because Hindu nationalism discovered quite early that silence, even if it was not direct collaboration with colonial rule, paid handsome political dividends and left it free to pursue its agenda against the minorities on the one hand, and non-modern and non-modernizable Hinduism on the other. The record of Muslim nationalism in South Asia, of the kind represented by Syed Ahmad Khan in some of his incarnations, perfectly mimics that of its sworn enemies among the Hindus.[9]

All these responses probably are contextualized by the growing salience of what can only be called a historical or historicized self in Indian public life.

THE ENTERPRISE OF HISTORY

The first few generations of British administrators and English-educated Indians produced a substantial volume of historical work on India. Though historical scholarship (or at least something akin to that) was not entirely unknown to either Islamic or Hindu traditions, the history the colonial historians produced was disjunctive with the constructions of the past the South Asians knew. It was history as it was conceptualized and institutionalized by the European Enlightenment. In any event, in South Asia, history itself had never enjoyed the absolute or deep legitimacy it had in modern Europe.[10] Nor did it enjoy or seek, in its pre-modern forms, a

[9] Shan Mohammad (ed.), *Writings and Speeches of Sir Syed Ahmed Khan* (Bombay: Nachiketa, 1972). I have in mind particularly those comments of Sir Syed which reek with contempt for the 'people of low rank' and 'humble origin' (for instance, p. 208).

[10] Ashis Nandy, 'History's Forgotten Doubles,' *History and Theory*, 1995, Theme Issue 34: *World Historians and their Critics,* pp. 44–66. Recently, the argument has been ventured that there are no universal, timeless principles dividing the historical from the ahistorical societies. Kerwin Lee Klein, 'In Search of Narrative Mastery: Post-modernism and the People Without History,' *History and Theory* 34, no. 4, (1995), pp 275–98. That, however, is like saying that no culture has timeless attributes. However, cultures change and yet remain identifiably the same culture. I believe that it is likewise possible to say that while the principles of separation might change, cultures may still remain different. Perhaps the problem arises because the 'double plot' which Klein speaks of, takes into account local and global histories, but not the local meanings of global histories, when the only politically and intellectually challenging act may be to make that tripartite division so as to empower competing versions of global history and, implicity, universalism.

monopoly on interpretations of the past. Most South Asians used other ways of constructing the past; European-style history to them was a new methodology/technology of organizing memories and a new form of consciousness that seemed to negate many traditional categories of thought and much of the traditional moral universe.

It is not clear what kind of legitimacy these new histories came to enjoy in India outside the modern sector. They certainly did not remain only school and college texts; nor did they substitute other forms of memory in even the middle-class families that opted for modern education and noisily and aggressively began to lament the absence of historical memory in the Indians.[11] Though many modernized Indians thought they had shed their past and chosen to live with a truncated self that had aggressively banished the ahistorical, next to them lived other Indians, often in the same household, who led a life informed with rich but non-historical modes of constructing the past—with living myths, legends, epics and folkways. They also presumably had their own non-historical 'theories' of what the historical mode meant or did.

The passions that attached to history among the historically-minded Indians were, however, not the ones that attached to the discipline in the by-now-more-fully-historical societies. Nor was it the same as the attitude to history of those outside history. The newcomers to history implicitly saw history as a new kind of epic of a moral myth that had to be constantly reaffirmed to fight the wretched state of Indian society. Enemies of history increasingly began to look to them like enemies of the Indian people. One is tempted to venture the proposition, in the context of the experiences in recent years, that one of the main sources of Hindu and Buddhist chauvinism in South Asia lies in the repressed, extra-historical attitude to history that survives in South Asia's historical self. In Pakistan, the same dynamics have come to inform the production and distribution of official history in a consumable

[11] See Vinay Lal, 'On the Perils of Historical Thinking: The Case, Puzzling as Usual of India,' in *Journal of Commonwealth and Postcolonial Studies* 3, no. 1 (Fall 1995), pp 79–112; and 'The Discourse of History and the Crisis at Ayodhya: Reflections on the Production of Knowledge, Freedom and the Future of India,' *Emergences* 5/6, (1993–4), pp. 4–44; Nandy, 'History's Forgotten Doubles.'

form in recent decades.[12] The newly historicized South Asians have brought to history the passions they had traditionally associated with epics and legends. History, while historicizing the world, dehistoricizes itself. The passions that underlie history, therefore, remain unnegotiated and begin to use history as a massive defensive shield and a new justification for violence and expropriation. The absence of self-reflexivity in Indian historians themselves and their tendency to prioritize history over life in the name of objectivity, neither of these an uncommon trait in the global culture of history, have contributed handsomely to the new, violent uses of history in India.

The idea of history, it should be obvious from the foregoing, has linked up with not merely the new idea of the state but also its various components, especially the emerging concepts of the national state, nationalism and national security; the theory of progress as concretized in the ideas and processes of development; secularism, especially its various South Asian, Left Hegelian versions; and a distinct Baconian concept of scientific rationality brought into public life as the final justification of all the other components.[13] When modern Indians, irrespective of their ideological postures, opted for the Utilitarian—and imperial—concept of the state, they also had to own up European history as being more relevant to Indian futures than the unreliable, scrappy accounts of the past in India. They did this so systematically that some thinkers came to feel that India's history had been stolen and that the country was being forced to live on borrowed history.[14]

This emergence and acceptance of the historical self, then, got quickly intertwined with the making and unmaking of Indian pasts

---

[12] Ayesha Jalal, 'Conjuring Pakistan: History as Official Imagining,' *International Journal of Middle East Studies* 27 (1995), pp. 73–89.

[13] Some of these links have been acknowledged by historian Dipesh Chakrabarty, though he may not be that uncomfortable with history's love affair with secularism, development and modern science. Dipesh Chakrabarty, 'History as Critique and Critique of History,' *Economic and Political Weekly* (14 September 1991), pp. 2262–8.

[14] For instance, this was Rabindranath Tagore's reading of Indian nationalism. Rabindranath Tagore, *Nationalism* (1917) (reprint, Madras: Macmillan, 1985). Also, Ashis Nandy, *The Illegitimacy of Nationalism: Rabindranath Tagore and the Politics of Self* (New Delhi: Oxford University Press, 1984).

and the telescoped presence of European history in these attempts to ensure the reconstruction of India's past along historical lines. This came in two versions. Either India's historical past was made to look like a belated replication of European history or it became, as in the various Left Hegelian doctrines, all of India's past and, hence, a point of departure for all social criticism. (So that in social and political analysis, the categories and the narratives could be from the first world, while the conclusions drawn and the prescriptions offered could apply to the third world.[15] All other memories related to the past were pushed out of serious intellectual consideration in modern India and were kept open for the use of the rustic, the women, the creative artists, the illiterate, the insane and the superstitious.

The self that emerges from the crucible of history has different features from that of the self that emerges from the crucible of myths, legends and epics. In both cases the self has to cope with memories, but the historical self configures memories differently from the way the ahistorical self does.

In the first case, memories are available for scrutiny, for tests of reliability and validity. The scrutiny is usually mounted from the vantage ground of what can be called distant, dispassionate objectivity, for such objectivity is supposed to guarantee the truth value of propositions about the past. (The idea of truth used here is that of modern science, not that of the moral philosopher or cultural or 'holistic ecologist' who might leave some scope for non-material truths in his model.[16]) Memories that fail the scrutiny are in effect declared non-memories or anti-memories, and are either

---

[15] This is not merely a South Asian disease. Any serious Afro-Asian scholar who has read the ethnophobic, crypto-racist histories produced in Europe and North America by some of the most respected figures in contemporary radical thought—from H. G. Wells to E. Hobsbawm—will immediately know what I am saying. In all these works, 'agency,' social creativity and transformative politics are monopolized by the northern hemisphere, not to speak of the analytic categories that structure the works. H. G. Wells, *A Short History of the World* (1992) (London: Pelican, 1965); E. Hobsbawm, *Age of Extremes: The Short Twentieth Century, 1914–91* (New Delhi: Viking, 1995).

[16] For a brief introduction to the 'historical' battle over the disputed mosque in Ayodhya, in which both sides claim scientized history to be their ally, see Lal, 'The Discourse of History and the Crisis in Ayodhya'.

banished from history or studied clinically as rumours or stereo-types, or handed over as fantasies to artists and writers for creative use. If some individuals and groups nevertheless insist on retaining or returning to these memories *in* history, they can do so, but others, if spiteful, would call such history pseudo-history or, if they are generous, myths or fantasies. There *are* persons or communities in the modern world which insist on living with 'unreliable' and 'invalid' history.[17] These individuals and communities usually end up as case histories for psychiatrists and researchers in social pathology.

But there are other persons and groups outside the modern world who live with selves that originate and are grounded in ahistorical modes of constructing the past—in legends, myths and epics—which cannot be that easily fitted in the clinical format, even though some first-generation, over-enthusiastic psychoanalysts did try to do so at one time. Sometimes, when return to childhood and unencumbered, creative innocence become an important cultural theme (as in the late 1960s and early 1970s), such persons and groups can be seen as paragons of normality, creativity and transcendental awareness. The epithets 'primitive' and ahistorical may then begin to carry an ambivalent load in historical societies where they may occasionally provide a respite from the psychological closure the historical consciousness has come to represent.[18] Otherwise, the effort is usually to separate the historical self from its ahistorical contexts. (The ongoing debate on the personality and biography of Jesus Christ in Western Christendom, for instance, parallels similar efforts that have been going on since the middle of the nineteenth century in the case of Hindu gods and goddesses.)[19]

Configuring the historically grounded self in an ahistorical society, however, acquires a second-order complexity where such

[17] I use these two terms in the sense in which mathematical statisticians use them when assessing new psychological, political or social measures such as attitude scales or personality inventories.

[18] Post-modernism, whatever may be its other merits or demerits, can be read as the formalization of this awareness and, thus, as a successful attempt to locate the world capital of dissent in the West by appropriating the available non-western critiques of the west.

[19] Ashis Nandy, 'A Report on the Present State of Health of the Gods and Goddesses in South Asia,' Plenary address at the American Academy of Religion, New Orleans, 24 November 1996: see pp. 127–50 of this volume.

a self does not get the 'normal' consensual validation from either the community or the larger culture. Such a self has to work on limited or partial endorsement from the scraps of historical selves constructed in the modern sector, often by psychologically uprooted, atomized individuals and small sectlike professional groups. History in India is basically a modest enterprise having a limited reach, it is not the entire constructed past. It has to compete with other such constructions and can either triumph over them or lose out to them.[20]

UPROOTING AND ITS COMPENSATIONS

Nation-state and history, when wedded to an urban-industrial vision and attempts to actualize the vision through conventional development, become a potent combination. They become a complex of ideas particularly appealing to persons and groups confronting the experience of uprooting, breakdown of communities, and a sense of exile. Whether it actually does so or not, this complex is presumed to work better when it operates on the assumption of a cultural *tabula rasa*, and authenticates forms of cultural intervention that ensures the decline of communities and the reduction of the person to a fully autonomous, unencumbered individual. It is this combination which is gradually turning India and its neighbouring countries, like some other old civilizations which are trying to redress their record of victimhood by catching up with the developed societies, according to dominant contemporary ideas of success—a territory of the territorially or psychologically uprooted. The ideas of nation-state and history in this respect have begun to play new, more important political- psychological roles in South Asia.

There is nothing specially new in this situation. Most ancient societies-turned-young-nation-states are learning to live in a world dominated by the psychology and culture of exile. For some, the twentieth century has been a century of refugees.[21] Others like Hannah Arendt have identified refugees as virtually a new species

[20] Ibid. There are examples of this clash also in Ashis Nandy, *The Intimate Enemy: Loss and Recovery of Self Under Colonialism* (New Delhi: Oxford University Press, 1983).

[21] Nicholas Xenos, 'Refugees: the Modern Political Condition,' *Alternatives* 18 (1993), pp. 419–30.

of human beings who have come to symbolize the violence of our times. Refugees as contemporary symbols, however, proclaim something more than the pathologies of the global nation-state system. They also represent a state of mind, a form of psychosocial displacement that has become endemic to modernizing societies. Defined thus, most refugees do not have to cross national frontiers to become refugees and many, when they do so, are more 'pulled' by the seductive appeals of self-induced displacement than the 'push' of an oppressive or violent system.[22] It is this changed status of territoriality in human life that explains why, in immigrant societies like the United States, the metaphor of exile now looks jaded. There are some who have already begun to argue that human beings need not have a 'home' as it has been traditionally understood in large parts of the world, that the idea itself is a red herring.[23] Given the cultural hierarchy in the world, many, it seems, have become reconciled to living with a labile sense of self. Displacement and the psychology of exile are in; cultural continuities and settled communities are out; they have a touch of *ennui* associated with them.

However, in societies such as China and India, which their citizens and outsiders were both accustomed to view as relatively stable and unchanging, adjustment to the pace-setting role now given to the culture of exile is disorienting and unnerving. In India, where the metaphor of eternal India continues as an important ingredient of the public lexicon, the spread of the culture of uprootedness has produced new cultural dislocations, anxieties and social tensions. Yet, many aspects of uprooting that take place in South Asia remain invisible. We have not yet noticed, for instance,

[22] This is not to estimate the push but to recognize that voluntary emigration is only another kind of uprooting, and the difference between it and enforced emigration must not have been that pronounced in systems suffering from chronic discrimination, exploitation and the early rigours of development. The last-named ailment is painful to acknowledge, though it has been known and feared since the days when it did not have its present meaning. See Karl Polanyi, *The Great Transformation* (London: Victor Gollancz, 1945).

[23] Aviezer Tucker, 'In Search of Home,' *Journal of Applied Philosophy* 11, no. 2, pp. 181–7. 'Our actual home', Tucker argues, 'is the result of our efforts to reach our ideal home, departing from our natural home....we may change our homes often throughout life, with changes in tastes, circumstances, and emotions...' pp. 181, 183.

that the psychology of displacement is becoming a serious presence in the South Asian landscape and many elements of South Asian public life are readjusting to the culture of the uprooted. However, politicians everywhere are a superbly alert lot. They never wait for the political or social scientist to supply analysis that would guide action. The South Asian politicians have grasped the power and the reach of the culture of psychological lability. They have sensed that, even though it is the culture of a minority, it none the less offers immense political opportunities, perhaps the most important of which is the scope it offers for large-scale mobilization. South Asian politicians, therefore, have refashioned their platforms and campaigns to cater to the passions of the banished and the uprooted.

As a result, the metaphor of continuity has paradoxically acquired a strange new status in Indian public life—it has become a potent myth. This is precisely because a large proportion of Indians feel uprooted geographically, culturally and psychologically and, while living with a culture of flux, which they have accepted as a ruling culture, want small, symbolic areas of turbulence-free life of predictability and continuity. These Indians demands psychological security and cultural constancy of a kind that not even a highly stable, isolated society can provide. These demands are honed by the growing evidence of flux all around. In this respect, what the horrendous Partition riots in 1947 could not do, despite uprooting on a conservative estimate ten million people, massive urbanization and industrialization backed by development have managed to do. Many communities in India are now predominantly and, in some cases, entirely communities of the displaced. Estimates are that one-third of the entire tribal population of India, consisting of at least 200 different tribes, has been displaced.[24] That is, some tribes are now entirely tribes of refugees from their natural habitats, traditional vocations, lifestyles and life-support systems. Their deculturation and disintegration as communities are virtually complete.

Some other communities have been dramatically pushed into urban industrial life because of the loss or unsustainability of their vocations or growing social discrimination of exploitation. When

[24] Smitu Kothari, 'Theorising Culture, Nature and Democracy in India' (Delhi: Lokayan, 1993), mimeo.

India became independent, its urban population was less than 70 million. Today, though the population of urban Indians has risen by only 5 per cent to about 25 per cent, it is already around 250 million, larger than all except three countries in the world. We do not have corresponding figures for Indians who move from one language area to another, from communities to individuated urban slums, from rooted vocations to contractual jobs. Many of these first-generation urban Indians show the characteristic psychology of the uprooted and they too have begun to bend the Indian political culture to their needs. Many communities of traditional artisans, especially the Muslims and the Dalits among them, fall in this category. Also, as agriculture gets industrialized, many landless labourers and small farmers are unable to sustain their traditional vocations. They are migrating to the cities and assembling there in urban slums, which are becoming the down-market depots of the culture of exile.

In recent decades, the growing environmental emigration in the region has handsomely contributed to the growth of the culture of the slum. The economic growth and prosperity through large-scale cultivation of cash crops like sugarcane and the growing industrialization of agriculture itself has led to demands for mega-dams, diversion or monopolization of water resources, deforestation, draught or rising salinity in other parts of the region. Thus, the Farakka barrage and the destruction of the Ganges has not only led to uprooting and emigration from south-west Bangladesh to India but also from Bihar and, to a lesser extent, West Bengal to other parts of India.[25]

This is, however, an age of exile in more than one sense. Not only have many communities that looked settled till recently experienced colossal dislocation through migration, war, unbridled urbanization, and mega-development, a large part of the world is now inhabited by people who have experienced, or carry within them, memories of uprooting. Even when we nowadays talk of a global order dominated by one super power, that power represents, among other things, the power of the immigrants, the refugees, the

[25] For example, Ashok Swain, *The Environmental Trap: The Ganges Diversion, Bangladeshi Migration and Conflicts in India* (Uppsala: Department of Peace and Conflict Research, Uppsala University, 1996), Report 41.

displaced, the decultured and/or recultured. It is this culture, and the public values that can survive in a society of uprooted, which dominates the global cultural order. Few will disagree that America *is* primarily a culture of the uprooted, but fewer will admit that it is a culture of the uprooted that must deny that it is atypical; that it prefers to see itself as a model for the rest of the world, a haven where the poor, the powerless and the discarded of other lands have come and re-made their lives voluntarily and produced a culture that now makes transcultural sense. This preference is continuously endorsed by the elites of other countries, especially that of the third world, constantly talking of catching up with the United States in the distant future.

That culture of exile now seeks to remake the world in its own image. In fact, the entire post-World War II world and the second half of the twentieth century can be read as an unfolding of the politics of that effort, though the celebration of the effort had begun before the efforts had, in the inter-war years. This is no wholesale criticism of the culture of uprootedness; it is an acknowledgement that, while some of this century's greatest creative achievements might have come from uprooting, deculturation, breakdown of communities, some of the greatest pathologies of our times, too, can be traced to the sense of exile and loneliness that has haunted the modern individual. The ambience of the Weimer Republic and the cultural citadels of Europe—Paris, Vienna and London—in the inter-war years, the celebration of loneliness, exile, uncertainty and liminality in lifestyles, literature, fine arts and cinema—they did contribute to the closure of the European mind in the 1930s. To speak in terms of extremes, Pablo Picasso (1881–1973) and Albert Camus (1913–60) are the other side of the same cultural process that produced European fascism.

The self that modernity-as-exile spawns has a few specific features. In its more integrative form, it is compatible with what Robert J. Lifton calls the protean personality.[26] In its more problematic form, it tends to underwrite many of the pathologies that have been major markets of the twentieth century. It is a part

---

[26] Robert J. Lifton, *The Protean Self: Human Resilience in an Age of Fragmentation* (New York: Basic, 1993) Lifton does take into account the backlogs—the broken connection—of the protean self but, on the whole he seems reconciled to this new psychodynamics of self.

of the same story that, while the over-stretched modern self offers us a range of choices as far as self-construction and self-expression go, it cannot adequately protect our self-consistency and self-continuity. That consistency and continuity have to be sought through specialist option—psychotherapy, movements for religious or spiritual self discovery, millenialism in politics and, above all, ethno-religious chauvinism and nationalism.

India has chosen to confront its over-stretched modernity mainly through ethnic chauvinism and ultra-nationalism. Few have recognized the promise of psychological security and 'therapeutic' solace fundamentalism and ethnic conflicts have begun to offer in modernizing India. To this India, the violence outside promises to bind the violence within. Those living in this India survive on a dislocated cultural self-definition, precariously perched on a labile sense of the self and are, for that very reason, continually seeking to ground it in a sense of community that would restore a sense of cultural—and through it, personal—continuity.[27] They may not be accessible to serious political appeals or to deep analysis of public life, but they are open to populist slogans and demagoguery, especially of the type that promises new brands of communitarian pseudo-solidarity à la Hannah Arendt. In open societies, based on competitive party systems, politicians seeking to mobilize the massified sections of the citizens for electoral purposes through centralized communication machines, quickly identify these needs and deploy them in various innovative ways.[28]

In recent decades, South Asian slums, like South American and East Asian counterparts, have become the ultimate targets of mobilization by every kind of extremist groupings—from ethnic chauvinists to crime syndicates that, like the *cosa nostra*, promise the individual a community and a chance of escape from loneliness

[27] Not only in India, but in Pakistan and Bangladesh, too, a high proportion of the leaders of the ultra-nationalist, ethnic chauvinist and fundamentalist groups have a background of uprooting. This is consistent with the emergence of the South Asian diaspora as one of the main sources of support for communal and ethnic chauvinism in recent decades. Strange though this may sound, the diasporic communities are becoming the psychological and cultural counterparts of the slums in metropolitan India.

[28] Ashis Nandy, Shikha Trivedy, Shail Mayaram and Achyut Yagnik, *Creating a Nationality: The Ramjanmabhumi Movement and Fear of the Self* (New Delhi: Oxford University Press, 1995).

and massification. The 'anti-social elements', of whom political analysts and journalists in South Asia talk incessantly as the main actors in ethnic or communal violence, are merely the fringe of a large sector nearer home that the middle classes in the region would like to forget.

The clearest example of this came when the Babri Masjid was demolished. The movement leading up to the event—the biggest of its kind since Independence—had received its most active support from middle-class populations in small towns and cities; it now turned out that a majority in the demolition-squad also came from provincial backgrounds.

History was made that day, but not by metropolitan India which was relegated to the level of captive bystanders, released to deal with the repercussions of the event through either post-facto analysis or communal rioting. Provincial India had upstaged it, and in doing so had only given a small demonstration of its potential.

For, apart from demolishing the Babri Masjid and so peremptorily revising the national agenda, it was also...bringing forth a new kind of sensibility: one that could combine in itself a taste for strident politics, violent films, ostentatious architecture, lewd music, rumour-mongering newspapers and overcooked food.

...From all accounts, Indian small towns and cities had shed their earlier sleepy, half-apologetic air....[29]

These newly self-assertive citizens are generally susceptible to the appeals of various forms of nationalism that depend on centralized, mass-media-based, communications and strategies of mobilizations. India may not be a mass society, but even the process of massification has released new demands and created spaces for ideologies that promise to fill the void that breakdown of communities and 'primordialities' has created. These promises are based on packaged forms of faiths that can serve both as substitutes for faiths seemingly unable to survive in their form under globalized lifestyles, and as political ideologies particularly suited to middle class mobilization. In both incarnations, the ideologies permit a certain degree of canalization of what would otherwise be free-floating violence.

[29] Pankaj Mishra, *Butter Chicken in Ludhiana* (New Delhi: Penguin, 1995), p. 11. The 'earlier, sleepy, half-apologetic air' probably came from the wide consensus that these towns mediated between the rural and the urban, whereas they have now become the phalanx of metropolitan India, reaching into the heart of the countryside and sometimes re-entering Metropolitan India as a transmogrified version of its own agenda for the rest of the country.

But apart from its close links with the growing culture of violence, the psychology of uprootedness and exile is associated with a number of personality traits that have been much adored in the literature and folklore of development: greater individual initiative, entrepreneurship and competitiveness. Immigrants are comparatively more pushy, risk-taking and less burdened by principles of sociality and shared cultural norms in their professional and business deals.[30] The refugees created in the aftermath of the Partition, in western India, on whom there are some scrappy data, are aggressive within family and outside and their trust in the interpersonal world around them is low.[31] This aggressiveness and distrust acquire a dangerous edge because the refugees also tend to have a stronger sense of invulnerability.[32] One of the unnoticed findings of the once-popular studies of achievement motive as the engine of economic growth were the links between spatial mobility, uprootedness and higher levels of achievement motivation .[33] Indeed, to complete the picture of the contemporary ideal of the achieving person, David McClelland did invoke the imagery of Hermes in the *Homeric Hymn to Hermes,* the Hellenic god who started travelling from the day he was born.

Hermes presumably had a place to come back to, and that myth of a place of return must have been for all believers a living reality

[30] They are kinds of people described in that underrated and forgotten book, Stephen Keller, *Uprooting and Social Change: The Role of Refugees in Development* (Delhi: Manohar, 1975).

[31] Ibid.

[32] Ibid. Some South Asian readers may remember how an archetypal, new hero in Indian popular cinema stormed into public consciousness in the 1970s with exactly this combination of traits. He operated at the margins of law, sometimes outside it, but always with a tinge of nostalgia for the earlier, soft, androgynous hero that had dominated the screen for nearly fifty years. See 'Introduction: Then Popular Cinema as the Slum's Eye View of Indian Politics,' in Ashis Nandy (ed.), The *Secret Politics of Our Desires: Innocence, Culpability and Popular Cinema* (London: Zed Press and New Delhi: Oxford University Press, in press).

[33] David C. McClelland, *The Achieving Society* (Princeton: Van Nostrand, 1961). Everett E. Hagen's attempts to trace economic growth to 'displaced elites' and their psychological state of 'retreatism' can also be read as an early celebration of the culture of the uprooted as the source of a modern political economy. Everett E. Hagen, *On the Theory of Social Change* (Homewood, Ill: Dorsey, 1962).

for centuries. In contemporary times, the chances are that such an idea of return, or a place to return, has primarily a mythic status and is available mainly as a consumable fantasy. Vladimir Nabokov's Russia and Salman Rushdie's India are obvious examples.

THE MYTH OF RETURN

Perhaps the basic formulation in this paper can be now further sharpened. South Asia is now linked to the global order not merely through its modern political self but, more specifically, through historicized readings of its past and the traumata of uprootedness, both seeking in the ideology of the state and in various theories of nationalism floating around in the market, greater psychological security, and symbolic redress of cultural defeat.

However, that formulation does not say much about how the modern political self in India confronts the panoply of other selves in India or about the unequal contest among them to shape the future of India's political culture and the nature of transformative politics in the region. This brings us back to the issue of a political self that is primarily in dialogue with itself because that dialogue includes a dialogue with the world. True, that conversation with self can be defensive, for it is a conversation partly with those who have been defined either as being on the other side of a monolithic, granite wall of traditions or as masses of poor, culturally deprived, somewhat obstreperous, trainee citizens. But it is conversation none the less. The fact that it takes place has a political status of its own.

Programmatically, that conversation goes on at two planes. On one plane, the aim is to bring these others within the fold of the ideology of the Indian state. On the other plane, the aim is to set them up as 'proxy-selves', by conversing with whoever you stabilize your partly individuated, culturally uprooted self. Without these dialogical experiences, modern Indian's nineteenth-century political self will be even more in touch with the past of Europe than with its present, even more in touch with Europe's construction of India than with India as most Indians see it, or live it out.

To build a political self outside this model is to build partly outside history, science and sanity; it is to start living partly outside modern India, with those already living there as outcasts. This is a painful choice socially and even psychologically. Such a scepticism towards the mainstream culture of elite politics demands a different set of identifications, empathy and forms of psychological mobility. It involves the admission that most Indians for most of the time live in another India, and de-recognizing this forgotten majority, in an open society and in competitive democratic politics, is a sure prescription for political defeat and an even surer indicator of the precariousness of the modern self in India. This is a contradiction built into India's political self which nothing, not even the immense power of globalization and unbridled capitalism, can remove. It has to be worked through the way a psychoanalyst and his or her analysand work through a case *history* of self by 'contemporanizing history, by ahistoricizing history to access levels of consciousness that are non-historical or, as moderns would have it, pre-historical. (As in all clinical disciplines, history has to be coped with and opened up for intervention by converting diachronicity into synchronicity. Intervention on the basis of a case history is never actually in history, it is always in the present. One never redresses history, only surplus suffering at present.) Clinically, history is not a way of structuring the past, but of opening up the present and the future.[34]

These demands are throwing up different concepts of cultures in South Asia and challenging the universality of the modern self grounded in the European experience with the Enlightenment. Not from a relativistic point of view but by venturing alternative forms of cosmopolitanism and universalism.[35] They seem to challenge the Enlightenment's implicit faith that while there can be many forms of relativism, there can be only one form of universalism. These alternative forms can be destabilizing; they challenge the meaning of life of generations of Indians who, under the colonial dispensation, worked with nineteenth-century European concepts of the Indian culture and had a much more romantic and optimistic image

[34] Nandy, 'History's Forgotten Doubles'.

[35] Random examples are Vandana Shiva, *Staying Alive: Women, Ecology and Survival in India* (New Delhi: Kali for Women, 1988): Claude Alvares, *Science Development and Violence: The Twilight of Modernity* (New Delhi: Oxford University Press, 1992); Frédérique Apffel Marglin and Stephen Marglin (eds), *Dominating Knowledge: Development, Culture and Resistance* (Oxford: Clarendon Press, 1990); and *Decolonising Knowledge: From Development to Dialogue* (Oxford: Clarendon Press, 1996); Ramchandra Gandhi, *Sita's Kitchen: A Testimony of Faith and Inquiry* (New Delhi: Penguin, 1992).

of the European enterprise on the world stage.[36] These Indians see the growing demands for the renegotiation of terms between culture and modern selfhood as highly destructive. The demands seem to negate the modern social and religious reform movements that started in the 1820s and, thus, the core legitimacy of the modern nation-state and the elite who seem born to it. The fact that there has been some erosion in the cultural self-confidence of European and North American intellectual elites, and some openness to multiculturalism among them, has further unnerved modern Indians. For that, too, seems to endorse the movement of the peripheralized Indians, unexposed or hostile to the modern self, to the centre of the political stage.

As a result, exactly as the historical self in India is contextualised by the passions and interests of the non-historical modes of construction of the past, the modern self too is buffeted by pre-modern, non-modern or counter-modern categories and passions. Not merely outside, but also within. This is another stratum of political awareness which shapes modernity fundamentally without being much influenced by it.

In Werner Herzog's movie *Where the Green Ants Dream* there is a moving sequence where an old Australian aborigine, who does not speak a word of English, barges into witness box during a court trial, about to decide the land rights of Australian aborigines vis-à-vis a uranium mining company. The man begins to deliver a long speech in an incomprehensible language. The shocked judge tells the lawyer fighting the cause of the aborigines that he should restrain his client. The lawyer cannot and when he tries to communicate with the trespasser with the help of the aborigines, even they fail. It then transpires that the man in the witness box is the last surviving member of an extinct tribe and nobody in the world understands him.

This moment in the movie can be read in two ways. First, it is a moment that stresses the meaningless survival of an individual who cannot share his thoughts with anyone in the world and has

---

[36] Even someone as rooted in his culture as Rabindranath Tagore confessed to such an optimism and the disappointment that followed its betrayal by Europe's death dance in the form of two world wars. Rabindranath Tagore, *The Crisis of Civilization* (Bombay: International Book House, 1941).

to wait for a lonely death to finalize the extinction of a cultural species and a community. It is also, however, a moment that symbolizes the bankruptcy of the dominant consciousness complicit with the process of extinction, a consciousness which does not even know that it is impoverished by the death of a cultural strain or aware of the brutalization unleashed by that insensitivity. Savagery lies not where the indigenous people once stayed or are staying, nor where the dirty work of colonialism or development is done, Herzog seems to suggest, but at the cultural centres of our ideas of cosmopolitanism and impartial justice.

Herzog, who must have passed through the experiences of German reconstruction, mega-development and the Green movement, underscores these readings by a number of cinematic devices. For instance, he 'sets up the stage' by painting a totally polluted environment and a pock-marked landscape, bearing man-made scars like the victim of some terrible skin disease. Herzog also makes it clear at the beginning, who have won the battle of the worlds and who rule the world today. Only ideologically motivated lonely individuals within the system can now sometimes see through it. To do so, they have to be either someone like the ineffective but well-intentioned, innocent hero or someone morally repelled by the ruling culture, such as the eccentric anthropologist living as a recluse outside civilization or the liberal public interest lawyer. They are the ones who provide scrappy, moving but also doomed resistance or dissent.

This flimsy base of dissent in the personal morality of a few atomized individuals is matched by the loveably arcane, dissenting ideology used by the aborigines protesting uranium mining in their ancestral lands, namely their belief that uranium mining will disturb the dreams of the green ants and thus threaten the survival of the world. Herzog's brilliance ultimately convinces his audience that this belief of the aborigines deserves a future other than the psychoanalyst's couch, that it probably represents a higher order sanity and rationality and probably a new point of departure for transformative politics. Yet, the overall impression remains one of incommensurability and self-defeating kindness on the one hand, and 'inaudible' dissent on the other.

In Satyajit Ray's *Agantuk* (The Visitor), the same social problem is differently posed and handled. Ray, in his last years a newcomer to the world of environmentalism and critiques of development, seems much less aware of what he is doing politically. *Agantuk* is the story of a 'lost' uncle of a typical urban, middle class, family at Calcutta, whom the family knows mainly as an elusive, professional globe-trotter. He briefly returns, uninvited, as a suspicious stranger to his family, to upset the steady, predictable rhythm of middle-class conformism. The uncle, who turns out to be a distinguished anthropologist, has by now become a savage critic of modern civilization and its cultural stratarchies. The dramatic highpoint of the film comes when the uncle suddenly leaves and the paranoiac family finds out that he was not a crook after the family's wealth, but had actually come to will his property away to the family. The family desperately looks for its benefactor and locates him in a village of Santhals, one of the most systematically victimized communities in India's march towards modernity. The real communication between generations begins when the wife, who was always a little more open to the stranger, joins the Santhals in an uninhibited dance. This time the uncle owns her up because in her attempts to self-transcend, he locates the beginning of self-discovery and a continuation of his own critical self.

There is no devastated landscape or Tarkovsky-like invocation of the terror of soul-killing hyper-urbanity in Ray. The Santhal village, it turns out, is not very far from Calcutta and it survives in poverty, indignity and neglect, but also in simplicity and natural charm. On the other hand, the 'modern affluence' of the urban, middle-class family is not that conspicuous or consumption-intensive either. To many western and some South Asian viewers Ray's idea of affluence may even look like another less obtrusive version of poverty. There is also a vague, tacit admission in the narrative that the urban, middle class that is being depicted as conformist and myopic is, while increasingly vociferous and dominant, not the whole of India, that the class still constitutes a minority. The divide between the algorithm of urbane bourgeois life and the world of the uncle and his Santhal friends *is* sharp, but there is no frontier of incommensurability between the two. When the heroine joins the Santhals in their dance, she is not so much actualizing the dream of her uncle, as admitting a previously repressed part of herself. There is certainly no awkwardness about her spontaneity in the rest of the family either. The community in some sense has been restored, even if only symbolically.

That which is a basic incommensurability in Herzog's film becomes, thus, a problem of partitioned self in Ray's. As if Ray, otherwise a fully formed ideologue of modernity, was admitting that certain possibilities that were open only through the exercise of moral imagination in the case of Australian aborigines, were open in India through self-excavation and through the ability to 'work through' one's not-so-deep psychological defences. As if to Ray, globalization was not the end of cultures, for as globalization made inroads into the interstices of cultures, so did the politics of cultural self-affirmation and self-exploration.

Exactly as some South Sea Islanders have paid for the blessings of civilization by having syphilis, anthropologist and political activist Fred Chiu suggests, globalized capital has to pay for its expansion by facing the proliferating movements and strains of consciousness—romantic, nasty, utopian, backward-looking, given to excesses, insane. Such affirmations of cultures and identities never restore the past. For post-globalization affirmation of traditions is different from the affirmation of cultures when attacks on culture are seen as external and not as something threatening to take over one's household, children and friends and even one's most intimate moments (through standardized textbooks on parent-child relations, or by offering consumers choice of shades and textures in condoms, for instance). It is possible to argue that this new, often-insecure self affirmation brings on to the world stage, a new strain of cultures and identities which lack the easy, less-self-aware affirmation of cultures and identities when they are not threatened or when the threats to them are concrete, physical and, to that extent, external. Often the new affirmations bring out or excavate for its use traditions and cultures badly contaminated by the principles of dominance and violence that characterize the present global mass culture. The Islam that has come into play in many exiled Islamic communities—among Palestinian refugees, Pakistanis in Bradford in England, Bosnians in Bosnia or outside, or Indians in American campuses—is not the same as the Islam that is a part of everyday life in much of the Islamic world. The intellectual challenge is to identify the principal characteristics of this reactive affirmation of cultures and identities in South and South-east Asia, in the hope it will also convey something of the common human experience with the politics of cultural selfhood and with the more specific tragedy of lost or stolen memories in other parts of the world.

6

The Decline in the Imagination of the Village[1]

Ashis Nandy

I start with a bald proposition—that the imagination of the village in creative Indians and their Indian audience is collapsing. By imagination I mean creative imagination of the kind that invokes the fantasy of the 'archetypal', 'remembered' but also living Indian village in those staying in villages and others having little or no obvious connection with it. The collapse has not been total. There *are* individuals whose work disproves my thesis. Many creative Indians still come from villages, and others write creatively about them. However, they are but individuals. As a collectivity, we are in the process of losing that imagination and the bonding that imagination once established between individual creativity and its cultural acceptance or meaning. The rest of this lecture is an attempt to spell out this proposition.

I begin with Mohandas Karamchand Gandhi, for many the ultimate exponent of the cultural principles enshrined in the Indian village, whether you see them as village republics or as basic constituents of the Indian civilization or as an idealized way of life that informs the culture of Indian politics. Even when some

[1] This is a revised version of a lecture at the Workshop on Village India, in the Course on Culture Studies, Ninasam, Heggodu, Karnataka on 15–28 October 1994. I am grateful to the participants and organizers of the course, particularly M. N. Srinivas and U. R. Anantha Murthy, for the excellent discussion that followed the lecture and for their critical comments. The revised version also owes much to discussions with D. L. Sheth and D. R. Nagaraj.

criticize the village as an anachronism and a change resisting depot of popular superstitions, the locus of their criticisms is often Gandhi's vision of a future India structured around the idea and the reality of the village. It is common knowledge that Gandhi took India's freedom movement to the village, that he thought of the Indian villages as the organizing principle of Indian civilization; that he wanted to think of the future of India around what could be done to and in the Indian villages. It is as the ultimate political symbol of village India in our times that he could call Indian villages 'dung heaps'. That dismissive epithet, too, was part of his critical repertoire.

However, it is not so well known that the first time Gandhi came into direct or real-life contact with a village was when he began his political work in villages in his middle years. He was born in a city, in an urban family, as the son of a *dewan* (chief minister) of a small princely state. He was educated in a city, at the ultra-élite Rajkumar College of Rajkot, and qualified for the bar at London. He then worked in South Africa where he also lived in cities, mainly at Durban. On returning to India, too, he operated from cities. It was only on his proclaimed guru Gopalkrishna Gokhale's advice that he began to seriously explore rural India in his late forties. The impact of village life on him was deep—as if he had been preparing himself for it politically and philosophically for years. After a while, it began to look as if he came from a village, as if he had lived all his life in villages and fought for them.

Why? How did a man so thoroughly a product of the city increasingly begin to speak and even look like a deeply-entrenched villager? I have come to suspect that there was latent in Gandhi, within his very selfhood, a certain retrievable imagination of the village which he could revive when he seriously—and physically—encountered the Indian village. The village was not dead within him when he went to work in villages; he did not really have to rediscover the village or reconnect to it. The village discovered itself in him as it was already there in him as a latent possibility. That latent present was ensured through the shared ideas, writings, music, rituals, folklore, epics, and other creative works of millions of people, through the traditions of his family, friends, peer-groups, his caste, sect and immediate community. That imagination of the village had survived in him; it was only waiting to be reclaimed. When he began to work in villages, he could quickly, almost naturally, take on the role of a representative or spokesman of the Indian village. He was only apparently an outsider to the village.[2]

If Gandhi's village is Indian public life's first village, Satyajit Ray's village is cinema's first Indian village. Ray's debut film, *Pather Panchali*, is often said to be the greatest film ever made on village India. More than one critic has said that, for the world of cinema today, the Indian village is Ray's village.

It might surprise many—Ray's personal life not being well known outside Bengal—that his first genuine encounter with a village was when he started shooting *Pather Panchali*. He himself says:

> Till then I had no direct experience of what one meant when using the expression village life...we slowly developed an idea of the life described in the novel.... Consequently, I had to depend on the descriptions in the original novel. The book, however, was an encyclopedia of village life. But I also knew that I could not depend only on it; that there were many things that I would have to discover myself.[3]

Ray was born in a famous urban family, settled in Calcutta for at least three generations. The family *did* have an estate in East Bengal but, by the time he grew up, he had no access to that land. One gets the flavour of his family environment from some of its contributions to Bengal's social and cultural life: one of his uncles introduced cricket to Bengal, another was the first Indian to translate the Sherlock Holmes detective stories, and his father ran a printing press and published a famous children's magazine. It was a family known for its urbane cosmopolitanism and modern accomplishments. Naturally Ray was, and saw himself as, entirely urban. He also had his early education in what could only be called a quasi-Victorian, élite public school, from within the walls of which the Indian village must have looked very distant and misty. The closest he came to a personal encounter with villages, was when he sometimes visited villages during his student days in Shantiniketan. To the end of his life, Ray ate Bengali food with

---

[2] This retrievable imagination of the village is not the same as the timeless, fully autonomous, idyllic village that the social scientists constructed, following European travellers, colonial administrators and missionaries. See Ronald Inden, *Imagining India* (Oxford: Basil Blackwell, 1990).

[3] Satyajit Ray, *Apur Panchali* (Calcutta: Ananda, 1995), pp. 68–9.

fork and knife, even the staple rice and fish curry. During most of his early life, despite being partly educated in Shantiniketan, Ray had not heard much Indian music except Rabindrasangeet. He was brought up primarily on a diet of Western classicism. Though he had studied Bengali as part of his course work, he had no self-confidence in handling the language. Finally on graduation, when he took up a job in advertising, it was with a predictably British agency.

During this period, Ray was invited to illustrate an abridged, children's version of Bibhutibhushan Bandopadhyay's famous Bengali novel, *Pather Panchali*. Writer Sunil Gangopadhyay recounts the astonishment of publisher Dilip Gupta of Signet Press when he discovered Ray's pathetic knowledge of Bengali. Gupta apparently rebuked him for being so poor in Bengali despite being the son of Sukumar Ray, one of Bengal's greatest writers and certainly Bengal's most famous children's writer. He wanted Satyajit to get better acquainted with the literature of his mother tongue and gifted him Tarashankar Bandopadhyay's *Kavi*.[4] Whether Ray read *Kavi* or not, his work for the illustrated version of *Pather Panchali* changed his life. This book was published under the title *Aam Antir Bhepu*, beautifully illustrated by Ray. In the process, he got his introduction of Bengali literature and *Pather Panchali*. Gangopadhyay adds that, if one compares the film script with the original novel, one finds that Ray's *Pather Panchali* is based entirely on the children's version of the novel.

The question that we asked about Gandhi can be posed even more sharply in the case of Satyajit Ray: where did he get his idea of the village? Given his shallow acquaintance with rural life, why did this man's imagination of the village resonate with that of so many of his contemporaries? Was it because his spectators were not themselves that well-versed in the subtleties of village life in India? That does not sound very convincing either, for *Pather Panchali* was an immense success even among those who knew at first-hand, the village life the film depicted. I am afraid we are once again forced to suspect that the imagination of the village was not dead, either in the Indian consumers of Ray's films or, even more importantly, in Ray himself. It was there in his immediate

---

[4] Sunil Gangopadhyay, 'Priya Lekhak Satyajit Ray,' in Shyamalkanti Das (ed.), *Lekhak Satyajit Ray* (Calcutta: Shivrani, 1993), pp. 17–20.

intellectual environs and in the depth of his being, and once Ray dipped into and connected to this inner image, he could make creative sense of its formidable riches and use it creatively. The fact that he was an outsider to village India—and in some sense to India, too—did not matter.

This process may go even farther. Novelist R. K. Narayan, for instance, has located most of his stories in a small town he calls Malgudi. By now, virtually all English-speaking Indians and most of those even vaguely interested in India know the town and the stories set therein. By now, Malgudi is English literature's first Indian small town. Narayan has made it such a living reality that one is sometimes surprised to discover that maps of India do not show it. Malgudi today is more real than many real-life Indian towns. (Like the residence of Sherlock Holmes at Baker Street, London, from where even today an agency replies to letters written to Holmes by fans and prospective clients from all over the world, Malgudi deserves at least a published gazetteer and a street directory.)

In the Malgudi stories, one gets a clue as to why Gandhi and Ray could so successfully invoke the imagery of the village without having any early personal link with the reality of a village. For in these stories about a town, the village is never absent. It is a constant shadowy presence and an inescapable backdrop. Even when not mentioned in the narrative, the village shapes the author's meaning and, even, his treatment of the town. Many things happening in Malgudi cannot happen, and many of the characters in Malgudi cannot be what they are unless one presumes that there is a village nearby, or that the town is surrounded by villages. The culture of the village is telescoped into the life of the town. One of the main attractions of Malgudi, something that gives it its distinctiveness *and* representativeness, is this encroachment by an omnipresent, imaginary village. This tacit presence—once again defying a sophisticated, urbane author who lives in a city and has therefore chosen to write about urban life—gives the Malgudi stories that lively, ambivalent link with a culture so difficult to define. They make the stories typically Indian by making them stories of village India, without being about village India.

The imagination of the village in India need not link one only to the village. Access to this awareness of the village might even link one to the city in a different way. It enriches even narratives on the city, for a city can also be defined by its antonym, the village.[5] Indian society is not only rural; Indians have also lived with cities for at least three millennia. Cities like Varanasi are some of the oldest in the world. But perhaps the cultural logic of an authentic Indian city demands the presence of the imagination of the village.

I am at this point tempted to give a fourth example, but it will be a digression from the psychology of individual creativity that is my concern here. However, I should at least mention that what I am saying is not only true to sleepy, old towns like Malgudi. Some of the most evocative depictions of slums in metropolitan India also derive their power from an awareness of how the village has entered the slum, and of how the slum in the city is trying to recover, re-invoke or rediscover the village in different guises. Sometimes through the kind of selective settlement of people (so that the slum might have a preponderance of migrants from one particular caste, language group or region) or through the way the slum handles or mobilizes collective efforts or passions or reconstructs the community in an atomizing, steam-rolling metropolis. Even Bombay's commercial cinema and TV serials, which shun realistic portrayals and depend upon the appeal of 'glamorized slums', invoke unashamedly the village community. The imagery of the slum in a serial like Sayeed Mirza's *Nukkad* supplies much of the romanticism and the evocativeness of the serial. Actually what looks like a slum at first sight turns out to be, after the first few episodes, a village that has survived the seductive glitter of the city. It has simultaneously captured, within the apparent heartlessness of the slum, the ambience of a 'compassionate' village community.[6]

What is true of politics, cinema and literature is not untrue of the social sciences. If Gandhi's village is the first Indian village of

[5] The reverse also is true; the village also can be defined by its antonym. Many environmental and alternative technology movements in India work with concepts of the village that bear an inverse relationship with the urban-industrial pathologies to which the Indian city is an heir.

[6] Ashis Nandy 'Introduction: The Popular Cinema as the Slum's Eye View of Indian Politics,' in Ashis Nandy (ed.), *The Secret Politics of Our Desires: Innocence, Culpability and Indian Popular Cinema* (London: Zed Books and Delhi: Oxford University Press, 1998).

politics and Ray's that of cinema, M. N. Srinivas's village is the first Indian village of the social sciences. I shall, however, focus not on his famous texts that have shaped the image of the village for at least two generations of social scientists, but on the one which U. R. Anantha Murthy has described as M. N. Srinivas' greatest work, *The Remembered Village*. For it is so in a sense that will not make any sense to most academics, not even probably to Srinivas. Anantha Murthy, not being a social scientist, does not know that few proper social scientists will agree with his estimate. For *The Remembered Village*, according to the canons of the social sciences, is marred by the author's inability to have access to his empirical data, mistakenly burnt by an over-enthusiastic pack of radicals at Palo Alto. The social scientists believe that the book carries the mark of that tragedy.

Anantha Murthy revalues the book perhaps because he is a writer and a thinker who deals with human subjectivity. His deeper concerns force him to recognize that, all said, *The Remembered Village* can be written only by a person who has access to the imagination of the village. To put it sharply and perhaps even heartlessly, we think Srinivas is fortunate that his data got burnt and that, in this one instance, he was left with only his memories.

Even within formal social anthropology, T. N. Madan's introduction to a symposium on the book, recognizes this awareness:

What is important is... that most... think that Srinivas has succeeded in evoking the totality of village life in his account of it, that he has been able to vividly capture the human element and convey the 'feel' of Rampura to the reader. This is in contrast to his earlier major works in which we encounter no human beings, only customs and rules of social intercourse, only status structures and role occupants.... Chie Nakane suggestively compares *The Remembered Village* to a high-quality painting which, she writes, reveals more of the essence of a scene than does a photograph, by dramatizing certain elements in it. Sol Tax's tribute to *Remembered Village*... as an ethnographic work which is also a work of art is echoed by most of the reviewers.

...Some readers will, perhaps, say that *Remembered Village* belongs more with the novels of Srinivas's famous friend, R. K. Narayan. It has the same emphasis on character and on the scenic in everyday life, the same delectable sense of humour as in Narayan's well-loved novels and stories about life in Malgudi. And did not Srinivas tell us in his *Social*

Change in Modern India that the sociologist who chooses to study his own society is rather like the novelist?[7]

It is this imagination of the village we are now losing. The late Girilal Jain, for many years the editor of *The Times of India*, hated villages because he came from a village. He used to say, 'I don't want to go back to a village. Keep your Gandhi to yourself. You are from a city and that's why you can speak for a village. I was brought up in a village. I know what villages are. My ideal India doesn't have a single village.' I may not agree with that view, but I respect it. On the other hand, my friend Satyendra alias Sam Pitroda—for some years an icon and a mascot of modern, scientized India—is also from a village and actually belongs to an artisan caste. His family once had very close links with rural life. But in his calculation of future India, in his conceptualization of India, there is neither hatred nor love for the village; the village emotionally simply does not exist for him any more. In his algorithm of creative life, villages are only statistics.

Today we have reached a situation where that which was once true of individuals like Pitroda, is becoming a major identifier of our public life and public sentiments. There is no longer even the hatred Girilal Jain expressed nor the love Satyajit Ray acquired. The village now exists increasingly as a demographic and statistical datum. We now calculate our national income and say how much rural India contributes to it or brings it down. We know all about urban-rural differences in education, modern health care, and population growth. We can think of backward areas where new factories can be established or dams built so that they cease to be backward areas. We can think of creating something like a village in the heart of Delhi in Pragati Maidan or in Hauz Khas where the rich and the powerful can go and see rural India on week-ends.[8] We might even, in the one-hundred twenty-fifth anniversary year of Mohandas Karamchand Gandhi's birth, honour Srinivas as the Bhishma Pitamaha of Indian sociology, a discipline

[7] T. N. Madan, *Pathways: Approaches to the Study of Society in India* (New Delhi: Oxford University Press, 1994), p. 46, 48.

[8] Emma Tarlo, 'The Discovery and Recovery of "The Village" in Delhi: Hauz Khas 1986–1994,' Paper presented at the Thirteenth European Conference of Modern Asian Studies in Toulouse, 31 August–3 September 1994.

which in India has been an important means of understanding and, sometimes, controlling the village society. But we no longer have the village as a living presence within us. Our vision of India, our computations of the nature of the inputs we shall have to make to actualize that vision, our concept of the strategies of changing Indian society include many worthwhile elements, but all these no longer contain the imagination of a village. The village for us now is primarily a place where strange people live, where sati and untouchability are practised, where Hindu–Muslim riots have been taking place for centuries, where unless civilized people like us intervene, the inhabitants will continue to pursue the sports of homicide and robbery. Some may say it is another kind of imagination of the village. But that imagination, unlike in the examples I have given, does not lead to either any great creative effort nor does it resonate with the imagination of the village in millions of others. Today no producer of even art films will finance a project like *Pather Panchali*—in this respect the situation has not changed much from the mid-1950s when Ray's film was made—but, worse, no brilliant younger film-maker will now choose something like *Pather Panchali* for filming or, like Ray, pawn his wife's jewelry to do so.

Each one of us will have to decide whether that change in our public culture enriches or impoverishes the Indian civilization.

One last word on the discovery of the village within. Is such a discovery only a matter of creative access and self-excavation? Or is there also implicit in that discovery the concept of a mythic journey that some cannot but undertake and others can, but will not? For, after all, during the last one hundred years, the village *has* been for the urban Indian the destination of an epic journey of mind from which some have returned enriched, deepened and whole; while for many others the same journey has been a traumatic descent into a nether world of self that corrodes both physically and emotionally.[9] When it is corrosive, it is the obverse of the tragic journey from the village to the city that has been the

[9] One of the brilliant invocations of this journey is found in the short story by Premendra Mitra, 'Discovering Telenapota', trans. Rina and Pritish Nandy, in Premendra Mitra, *Snake and Other Stories* (Calcutta: Seagull, 1990), pp. 1–10.

standard marker of the hero in Indian popular cinema and, through most of the twentieth century, vernacular literature.[10]

India may live in its villages, Gandhi may insist, but it is not a peasant culture; traditionally the city has had a distinct and identifiable relationship with the village and the dyadic bond between the two has been a crucial constituent of classical plays, such as those of Vasa, and of the epics, such as the *Mahabharata*. Perhaps the city and the village are not as unrelated in India as they at first look. It was this ancient mutuality that broke down with the entry of the colonial political economy in the nineteenth century, and since then, the great Indian myth makers have been trying to rediscover it on new terms. Sometimes the reconciliation has been sought through a civic life that recapitulates the village, sometimes in a village that has been apparently renewed by the city. The search for reconciliation has always been there—as an epic search for another vision of a desirable society and another vision of a future that would not be entirely disjunctive with the past.

Perhaps the heroic dimensions of the eponymic and yet culturally rooted creativity we have dealt with here were sanctioned ultimately by the myth of an inner journey they invoked. The myth linked them to their followers, viewers and readers and grounded their own mythic stature in the culture from which they came.

---

[10] See a detailed discussion of this in Ashis Nandy, 'Notes on an Antique Death: Pramathesh Chandra Barua and the Origins of the Terribly Effeminate, Maudlin, Self-destructive Heroes of Indian Cinema,' written for the Conference on the Consumption of Popular Culture, School of Oriental and African Studies, London University, 19–21 June 1995. To be published in Chris Pinney and Rachel Dwyer (eds), *Pleasure and the Nation: The History and Politics of Popular Culture in India*, forthcoming.

7

The Fantastic India–Pakistan Battle: Or the Future of the Past in South Asia[1]

Ashis Nandy

INDIA'S PAKISTAN

When the Bangladesh war created a new state to the east of India in 1971, it ended Pakistan's unique status as a country in two parts, separated by one thousand miles of hostile India. Before the war, the late Sisir Gupta, scholar and hard-eyed Indian diplomat, used to claim that the crisis of Pakistan's identity was mirrored in the inability of Pakistani children to even draw the map of their country without drawing India. Twenty-five years after the event, Indians have now proved the cultural unity of the subcontinent by successfully redefining their country in such terms that even adult Indians cannot define India without involving Pakistan in that self-definition.

Pakistan has a history and a geography. Beyond them, shaping India's imagination of her neighbour in elemental ways, is the myth of Pakistan. This myth transcends Pakistan's empirical and geopolitical status. It cannot be subsumed under rubrics such as defence

[1] Delivered as the Keynote Address at the Symposium on Rethinking South Asia, organized by the Department of Political Science, University of Hawaii, at Honolulu on 9–10 April 1996, this paper commemorates the fiftieth anniversary of the Independence of India and Pakistan. I am grateful to D. R. Nagaraj and the participants in the symposium for their comments and suggestions.

studies, class analysis, political history, and development economics. That mythic Pakistan is not even made in Pakistan. It originates
in India and dominates India's public life, though it is also
sometimes exported or smuggled into Pakistan. When it enters
Pakistan, it becomes a deadly bond between the two countries. For
the myth is not obediently mythic; it shapes behaviour and policy.
People die and kill for it. To use a cliché, if the Pakistani state does
not conform to the myth, some Indians will certainly invent a new
nation-state to do so.

Pakistan is the name of a country to the north-west of India,
carved out of the Muslim majority provinces of British India. It
has survived for nearly fifty years, to intermittently haunt the
Indian state and army. About twenty-five years ago Pakistan
shrank to less than half its original size, when Bangladesh was born.
India played an important part in that shrinkage. But few Indians
believe that the bisection taught Pakistan any lesson or reduced its
power an iota. Pakistan, they believe, is exactly what it was when
it started life as a new nation. Most Indians, therefore, react to
Pakistan as if it was the Pakistan of 1947.

For the Indian state, therefore, Pakistan has retained its parity
and remained a genuine counter-player. Few Indian state functionaries think of Pakistan as anything but superior to India in its
ability to make mischief or subvert neighbouring states. This is no
mean achievement, given that Pakistan is one-eighth the size of
India, that even after spending nearly 6 per cent of its GDP on
defence—as compared to India's 2.5 per cent[2]—its army is about
one-third the size of the Indian army, that the country has its own
ethnic problems and separatist movements, and Pakistanis seem
more unsure about Pakistan's sustainability than Indians are about
India's.

Even for many highly educated, urbane, middle-class Indians,
what matters is that Pakistan is full of Muslims, most of them from
north-west India and belonging to the 'martial races'. India's north-
west includes Punjab and that makes it worse. Secularism is all

[2] The figures on defence expenditures are official figures and taken from
The Times of India, 31 March 1995. Unofficial figures are naturally higher.
According to the UNICEF Regional Office for South Asia, Pakistan and India
have spent 25.1 per cent and 14.4 per cent respectively of their annual budgets
on defence during 1995–6.

right, even commendable, but rationality demands that one recognizes Muslims to be hot-headed, tough, masculine, anti-democratic and prone to fundamentalism. More so if they happen to be from the north. Must one not handle them firmly to protect progress and democracy and to ensure that they get stewed in the global melting pot to become atomized, law-abiding citizens of a proper modern state?

At this plane, Pakistan is what India does not want to be; indeed, it is what India's modern élite would hate to be. This bonding in hate, fifty years after the division of India into two nation-states, is growing. As India becomes more of a modern nation-state, Pakistan for it becomes both a double and the final rejected self. The next-door neighbour now arouses deep anxieties not merely in Hindu nationalist formations like the Rashtriya Swayam Sevak Sangh, the Bharatiya Janata Party and the Shiv Sena, but also in Indian liberals and leftists. For them, too, Pakistan is the ultimate symbol of irrationality and fanaticism.

Jawaharlal Nehru, we are told, expected Pakistan to collapse within months in 1947. A theocratic state, he thought, could not survive in the contemporary world. (Pakistan always looks a theocratic state to the Indian élite, never as a nation-state created by its modernizing middle classes, working with a vague pan-Islamic fervour or an instrumental concept of Islam.) Pakistan, Nehru's reading of world history presumably went, had to be an aberration in history, brought about by a few ambitious nuts who had successfully mobilized the atavistic sentiments of a section of some South Asians. Strictly speaking, the reading is no different from that of the young historian Ayesha Jalal or the respected jurist H. M. Seervai.[3] Only Nehru believed that the stupidity and ambition were concentrated in the leaders of the Muslim League; the other two believe that these qualities were concentrated in the Indian National Congress.

Nation-states in our times, however, have been sturdy entities. In the present world system, they have a logic that transcends the naive social evolutionism of Nehru. Pakistan has survived not only as an 'unreasonably' stable nation-state, to trust the Indian policy

---

[3] Ayesha Jalal, *The Sole Spokesman: Jinnah, the Muslim League and the Demand for Pakistan* (Cambridge: Cambridge University Press, 1985); H. M. Seervai, *Partition of India*, 2nd edn (Bombay: N. M. Tripathi, 1994).

makers and the leaders of India's main political parties, it has survived to become the equal of India. Today the two national security states stand face to face, more equal that ever. For India's efforts to prove, once for all, its military superiority by exploding a 'peaceful' nuclear device in 1974, has misfired. Pakistan in its unending search for parity, has acquired nuclear capability to neutralize India's one-up-manship. This new parity, gifted to Pakistan by India's super-patriots and the international arms bazaar, is going to be a permanent fixture, neutralizing the three-to-one superiority India reportedly has in conventional arms.

Is this cultivated nuclear equality unintended? Or does the Indian nation-state, to complete its self-definition, need a powerful, hostile Pakistan as its hated but valued double? Or is the fantasized Pakistan an essential technology, for modern Indians, to complete the conversion of the Indian civilization to a standard, nineteenth-century nation-state?[4] From where has Pakistan got this magical strength to take on a country eight times its size? Do Indians secretly believe what General Yahya Khan openly claimed—that each Pakistani soldier is equal to ten Indians? Is it all a matter of American military aid and the Indian state's softness, the ignominy that Professor Gunnar Myrdal so compassionately diagnosed in the 1960s and left the Indian élite to live with?[5]

One part of the answer lies in the shared memories of Pakistan's separation from India. These memories prompt every modern Indian to mutter under his or her breath about Pakistan. 'There

---

[4] These questions have as their underside others: Does an analogous process work in the case of Islamic civilization and the Pakistani state? Is statist nationalism itself an attempt to reduce complex, rich cultural and religious experiences to manageable political realities within the standardized format of the contemporary global nation-state system? Is this attempt a product of the increasing incomprehensibility and fear of these experiences to the politically powerful modernized, massified sectors of South Asian societies? These questions may not have priority in the research agenda of the South Asian diaspora, both outside and within South Asia, but they cannot but haunt the intellectuals who live with and in South Asian realities. They know that the answers will have to be simultaneously cultural-psychological and political.

[5] Gunnar Myrdal, *The Asian Drama: Inquiry into the Poverty of Nations* (London: Penguin, 1968).

goes, but for the grace of God, India.' But with it also goes the wistful belief that they should have been a little more like the Pakistanis, at least in international relations and cricket.

That ambivalence comes from two lots of pivotal images. First, Pakistan is seen as a product of the conspiracy between India's erstwhile British rulers pursuing a 'divide and rule' policy and the religion-based parties in the region.[6] Pakistan at this plane is seen as an illegitimate child of the West. The 'killer instinct' imputed to it comes partly from this. A bastard of the West is, everything said, half-western and has to be better in wily state-craft than the natives.

That Islam is a Semitic creed and that most Pakistanis are Punjabis, feed this imagery. The West might be phobic about Islam and Pakistanis may be suspicious of the West but, for modern Indians, Pakistan cannot but remain a natural ally of the West. They love to see Islam, even South Asian Islam, as closer to European Christianity than to Hinduism. Why has every modern reform movement in Hinduism, from Brahmoism to Arya Samaj, tried to make Hinduism more Semitic and incorporate within it elements of Islam?[7] And Punjabis, as is well known on both sides of the border, are pushy, martial, avaricious, and amoral at the same time. A country full of Muslims is bad enough, but a country full of Punjabi Muslims can only be considered a conspiracy against decent politics.

---

[6] According to one estimate, actually only 16 per cent of the sub-continental Muslims voted for Pakistan. Mani Shankar Aiyer, *Pakistan Papers* (New Delhi: UBS Publishers, 1994), pp. 91–8. However, a majority of the subcontinent's westernized Muslim élite certainly sympathized with the idea.

[7] My favourite quote is from Rammohun Roy (1772–1833), by common consent the father of modern India: '...I have observed with respect to distant cousins, sprung from the same family, and living in the same district, when one branch of the family had been converted to Mussulmanism, that those of the Muhammadan branch living in a freer manner, were distinguished by greater bodily activity and capacity for exertion, than those of the other branch which had adhered to the Hindoo mode of life.' Rammohun Roy, 'Additional Queries Respecting the Condition of India', *The English Works* (Calcutta: Sadharon Brahmo Samaj, 1947), Part 3, pp. 63–8; see p. 63. For this 'deformity' Roy held Hindu vegetarianism culpable, which in turned he traced to religious prejudices and 'want of bodily exertion and industry' brought about by a hot climate and a fertile land (ibid.).

Hence the frequent inability of the Indian rulers to distinguish the Pakistani people—theoretically, misguided Indians who made a wrong choice in 1947—from the Pakistani Government, led by a series of military or, as it looks from this side of the border, theocratic regimes.[8] The Pakistani disinclination to be ruled by the army or by the *mullahs* can be taken seriously by all countries in the world except India. Hence, few Indians have seriously surveyed the political support-base of Islamic parties and formations in Pakistan, their electoral performance, and the resistance they have faced. The success of Islamic fundamentalism in Pakistan is taken for granted.

Second, Pakistan has to be a successful conspirator against India, because religion, culture and state in Pakistan are seen to constitute a symbiotic triad. The symbiosis explains, to the satisfaction of many Indians, Pakistan's fanaticism and the super-human efficiency of its state. This symbiosis has been a goal of modern Indians since the last century and they feel they have not succeeded in it, thanks to the obstinate inertia of the ordinary Hindus and the 'soft', non-martial, fuzzy-ended 'effeminacy' their religion inculcates in them.[9] Therefore, the omniscience imputed to the agencies of the Pakistani state is matched by the innocence attributed to their Indian counterparts.[10] The Pakistani Army's intelligence

---

A major cultural paradox of contemporary India is how Hindu nationalism, often considered an illegitimate child of the nineteenth-century religious reform movements, has turned against Islam, not as an alien other but as the disowned part of one's own self.

[8] The ordinary Indians seem to do better in this respect. According to the only survey in India available on the subject in *The Times of India*, in January 1996, after years of effort by the Hindu nationalist parties to blur the line between the Pakistani regime and the sub-continental Muslim communities, a majority of the respondents clearly distinguished between the Pakistani citizens and the Pakistani state.

[9] Many years ago, while working on the assassination of Mohandas Karamchand Gandhi, I found to my utter astonishment that Hindu nationalist literature was the harshest, not on Islam and the Muslims, but on the Hindus. Swami Vivekananda (1866–1902) who pleaded for a Vedantic brain and Islamic body as the stuff of his vision of the future India, was only slightly less explicit.

[10] This has its obverse in the innocence attributed to the ordinary, 'lion-hearted but dumb' Muslim masses to protect whom Pakistan is supposed to have been brought into being. More about that later.

wing, the Inter-Services Intelligence, for instance, has acquired in India a mythic stature as a villain that puts to shame the boisterous villains in the popular Bombay films. In comparison, the Indian intelligence agency, the Research and Analysis Wing, is perceived as a set of bungling, politics-afflicted innocents controlled by civilians. Everything said, the staff in the ISI are seen as trained by the CIA; those in RAW are seen as either home-spun or trained by the miserable NKVD.

The obverse of that perception is the constant demand for more masculine, tough statecraft from the Indians and pleas to match the militarization of the Pakistani society by building a garrison state in India. The fear of separatism everywhere, the tendency to see all demands for decentralization as a conspiracy against Indian unity, the panicky response to criticisms of state violence by human rights groups—they all are indicators of a concept of a state critically shaped by Pakistan. So much so that it is possible to visualize a time when the Indian state will only mirror the Pakistani-state-as-fantasized-by-the-Indian-élite.

Pakistan is many things to many people. But the mythic Pakistan I am talking about is, above all, a definer of Indianness. It is a means of self-analysis and self-intervention. If Mother India can be put on an analytic couch, the enterprising psycho-analyst who does so will not miss her schizoid personality and the mix of paranoia and admiration with which some of her selves look at each other. That one of these selves is identified with Pakistan is now part of South Asia's psychological landscape. In the dynamics of that self lie crucial clues to the nature of the Indian nation-state.

PAKISTAN'S INDIA

Pakistan's India, the image of India Pakistan lives with, is also mostly Pakistan's own. It has almost nothing to do with what India is or might have been. It tells us what Pakistan is, feels it should be, or could have been.

Pakistan's India has two selves. The source of one is the official ideology of the Pakistani state; official Pakistan likes to believe it to be the only India that counts. The other is a disowned India; even Pakistani ideologues carry it in their veins, though many of them would deny that vehemently. That disowned India is also a mythic entity that defines Pakistan's boundaries and origins, loves and hates, past and future, its very core.

The official India of Pakistan—the India that looks like a pure product of Pakistani propaganda to many—is actually a desperate defence against facing the unofficial India that Pakistanis carry within themselves. That unofficial India contaminates and subverts Pakistan every day. It subverts not in the way the many Pakistanis fear being subverted—through political deceit or treachery or through the armed might of its larger neighbour—but in the way Sigmund Freud talked of the return of the unconscious to subvert our self-image as rational, normal, sane human beings.

No wily Indian politician scheming to destroy Pakistan could do worse. For the most the clever, *dhoti*-clad Indian politician can do is to try to wreck Pakistan through inspired statecraft and military adventure, against both of which Pakistan has built excellent defences in the last fifty years. Whereas the latent India that haunts Pakistan has no devious political leader to guide its destiny and no army to back it up. It is entirely a home-made Pakistani product.

That haunting, strangely seductive India, Pakistanis cannot share with any other country; they have to fight that apparition alone. Paradoxically, they can sometimes share it with Indians, who also have now begun to live with a home-made ghost called Pakistan.

The manifest India of Pakistan—to judge by Pakistan's official ideology, main-stream historical scholarship, school and college texts, and the language of propaganda used by Pakistani media—has some clear features. I state them in the form of three propositions. First, India is led by a Westernized, highly professional, upper-caste, Hindu élite who, taking advantage of their early modernization, began to dominate the subcontinent, much before the simple, lion-hearted, Kiplinesque Gungadins—also known as the South Asian Muslims—woke up to it.[11] The élite even had,

---

[11] Syed Ahmad Khan was arguably the first one to wake up to this. See Shan Mohammad (ed.), *Writings and Speeches of Sir Syed Ahmad Khan* (Bombay: Nachiketa, 1972). For a fascinating, recent exploration of official history in Pakistan and its often-comic contradictions, see Ayesha Jalal, 'Conjuring Pakistan: History as Official Imagining', *International Journal of Middle East Studies*, 1995, 27, pp. 73–89.

the self-construction of Pakistan goes, subtly changed the rules of the game in the 1920s under the leadership of the likes of M. K. Gandhi—by introducing symbols and idiom from the Hindu world-view and by refusing to grant Muslims parity with the Hindus, which the Muslims deserved for being the subcontinent's largest minority and erstwhile rulers. It was thus that the Hindu élite ensconced in the Indian National Congress prepared the ground for the creation of Pakistan. For Pakistan, according to the underside of its official history, is the only country in the world to have come into being reluctantly—as a response to the chicanery of the Hindu élite of undivided India. An authentic anti-imperialist and an important leader of the Congress, Mohammad Ali Jinnah, saw through the game, left the party, and decided to lead the Pakistan movement. Being a Westernized professional lawyer, and a Gujarati Bania to boot, Jinnah could be a perfect foil for the other Gujarati Bania who was going places with his bogus slogans of non-violence, soul force and moral politics, his unending fasts and tiresome counter-modernism.

Defeated in its own game, the Hindu upper-caste élite gulped the idea of partition of India as a political ploy but continued to have designs on the infant Pakistani state. Not only during the 1971 war but subsequently too, India has been entirely responsible for Pakistan's ethnic problems. In addition, what the Brahminic élite could not do to the bulk of Indian Muslims in pre-partition days, it has now done to India's supine Muslim minority and, for that matter, to all other minorities.

Second, Pakistan is an Islamic state and an Islamic state should not, Pakistan believes, be preoccupied with its Indian past, pre-Islamic or otherwise. For over-concern with that past can only detract from one's Islamic heritage and the solidarity of the Muslims that constitutes the Pakistani nation-state. Pakistan's history should begin neither with the Indus valley civilization nor with the entry of Islam into India at a time when India's ruling élite was still predominantly Hindu, that is, when Islam in India was not backed by state power. Pakistan's history must begin with the West Asian invaders of India who not only gave Indian Islam a new political and military edge, but also brought along with them a huge majority of the ancestors of the South Asian Muslims. The South Asian Muslims, therefore, are basically an exogenous ruling élite who have found in Pakistan a social and political status appropriate to their true self. It is this status that India's Hindu rulers grudge. The Muslims who do not fit this self-image are irrelevant and can be safely forgotten.

Not only the distant past but much of India's anti-colonial struggle—except probably the rebellion in 1857—is irrelevant to Pakistan, for the struggle sought to bypass the Indian Muslims. Many Hindu leaders of the struggle, the ideologues of Pakistan believe, were dedicated enemies of the Muslims because they wanted to inherit the mantle of the Raj in its entirety, even though representing only the sectional interests of the Hindus.

Third, Muslims and other minorities in present-day India are not only oppressed, the leaders they have thrown up are servitors of the Hindu élite who rule India with an iron hand. Official Pakistan believes that the stridency towards Pakistan displayed by many Muslim leaders of India can be traced to their political ambitions; they want to be more loyal than the king to India's Hindu state, for reasons of personal greed or ambition.

Of course, Pakistan, the declared home of South Asian Muslims, would not like to accept all the Muslims in India, even if they were willing to migrate. For that would be the end of Pakistan.[12] On the other hand, the fact that both India and Bangladesh have as large number of Muslims as Pakistan is a statistical artifact for many Pakistanis. For them, the Muslims stay in India under duress and Bangladesh is merely an Indian concoction and a trickery of history. The Indian Muslims are poor and oppressed, though their Islam is no worse than that of Pakistan; the Bangladeshi Muslims are not only poor; they are fish-eating, Bengali-speaking, non-martial, quasi-Muslims whose numerical strength is a Malthusian artifact. Ideally, India should be officially a Hindu state and the Indian rulers should shed the pretence of running a multi-ethnic state, to justify *post facto*, the creation of Pakistan. For Pakistan still desperately craves to represent the interests of all South Asian Muslims, including the Muslims of India and Bangladesh. The size and political clout of India's Muslim community discomfits Pakistan's rulers. Because granting intrinsic legitimacy to the politics of Indian Muslims—and that of the Bangladeshi Muslims— means recognizing that Pakistan is only one among the three major

---

[12] For the last twenty-five years, Pakistan has refused to accept as immigrants even non-Bengali Muslims, ideologically fully committed to Pakistan, who have been left behind in Bangladesh.

players in the region's Muslim politics and involves seeking sanction from the Muslims of India and Bangladesh before making claims in the name of Islam in this part of the world.

Underlying these components in the official ideology of the Pakistani state—which already makes Pakistan an atypical ideological state in that it depends so heavily on India to define itself—is the unofficial culture of the Pakistani state. That unofficial culture involves India in an entirely different way.

First, Pakistan was built as a home of South Asian Muslims, against the proposal for a multi-ethnic society that looked, rightly or wrongly, to most of the subcontinent's westernized Muslim élite, like a plan to create a majoritarian nation-state dominated by the Hindus. Anti-Hindu sentiments therefore have to be an ingredient of the ideology of Pakistan. Pakistan, however, is a nation-state and, like all nation-states, uncomfortable with the demands of an ideological state. (For instance, it likes to be on good terms with Nepal. The fear of big brother India brings them together but, for both, it is not a happy exposure. Pakistanis discover a Hindu state with whom they are forced to be friendly; the Nepalese, living in the world's only Hindu kingdom, discover a peculiar ally which claims to hate a central plank of Nepal's cultural self.)

Also, thanks to the large-scale violence in 1946–7 and the separation of Bangladesh, anti-Hindu themes have increasingly become an odd, anachronistic presence in Pakistan's national ideology. Many young Pakistanis, who have not even seen many Hindus, do not find the themes evocative, despite being brought up on a steady diet of anti-Hindu texts. That only increases the stridency and bitterness in official Pakistan, for it has come to feel in recent years that the younger generation in Pakistan is not adequately patriotic or aware of the sacrifices made for Pakistan by the older generation of Pakistanis.

Second, everyone is Pakistan suspects, even those who claim otherwise, that a huge majority of the South Asian Muslims have no genuine claim to West Asian ancestry. Their forefathers were converted from Hinduism or Buddhism and their 'peripheral' Islam is not a learnt behaviour but an inherited culture.[13] The real

---

[13] Ziauddin Sardar says, '[In South Asia] All Muslims were, somewhere in the past, actually Hindus, or, at best, hybrid Hindu having one parent who

fear is of drowning in the morass called Hindu cultural order as other religions and even prophetic creeds have sometimes done or being fitted within its hierarchical order, from which Islam has often been an escape for important sections of South Asians.[14] This fear might or might not have been vaguely strengthened by certain similarities between Hinduism and pre-Islamic Arab faiths that Islam fought in its earliest years.

Third, by conceptualizing Hinduism as a negation of Islam, the Pakistani state is forced to take a position on South Asian Islam, which has interacted over the centuries with other faiths, especially Hinduism, influencing them and being influenced by them. South Asian Islam cannot but look to the ideologues of Pakistan like a deviant, half-baked form of Islam that has strayed from the straight, narrow path of 'authentic' Islam practised in West Asia. The very distinctiveness of South Asian Islam, cultural and social, is seen as its liability, as the final proof that it has been influenced by Hinduism and Buddhism. Virtually every Islamic reform movement in South and South-East Asia has vended the idea of *a* genuine Islam and the myriad tropical varieties of Islam as essentially flawed. Gradually the largest Muslim communities in the world—Indonesia, India, Bangladesh, Pakistan and Malaysia, which among themselves constitute a decisive majority of the global Islamic community—have been reclassified during the last hundred years as the abodes of peripheral Islam where dumb apprentice-believers of Islam perpetually wait to be retooled into text-book versions of Muslims.

Fearful of the egalitarian thrust of Islam and its emphasis on an unmediated relationship between the believer and divinity, this

---

was Hindu. The Muslim hatred of Hindus is actually the hatred of what they have rejected in their genealogical history. The Hindu hatred of Muslims is a direct result of this betrayal—a betrayal reinforced by the partition of India and creation of Pakistan.' Ziauddin Sardar, 'On Serpents, Inevitability and the South Asian Imagination', *Futures*, November 1992, 24(10), pp. 942-9; see p. 946.

[14] It is an indicator of the remarkable hold of the Indian caste system in the subcontinent that instead of owning up to the Hindu origins of a majority of Muslims of the subcontinent and thus emphasizing the emancipatory role of Islam, most Islamicist movements in the region have emphasized their exogenous origins and further underlined a social hierarchy within Islam which corresponds to the hierarchy within Hinduism.

particular form of reformism has also led to the development of an ornate structure of theological justifications for authoritarian regimes that ambitious despots find very soothing. Pakistan's India is an adjunct to this set of justifications. Pakistanis may not like it, but their India comes closest to the India of the Hindu nationalists. What the Pakistani élite imagine India to be, the Hindu nationalists want India to be. In the India that these dedicated enemies have co-authored, there is the same pathetic masculinity striving, the same uncritical acceptance of the principles of the modern state and nationality, the same contempt towards the ordinary citizen and ordinary believers.

There is, however, one important difference. The criteria used by official Pakistan to conjure up its India are, by the standard of the Hindu nationalists, almost entirely Hindu. Whereas the criteria used by the Hindu nationalists to define their ideal India are, as paradoxically, close to the ones the ideologues of Pakistan consider truly Islamic. Both sets include elements with which the westernized middle classes in South Asia feel at home.

Fourth, Pakistan wants India to leave it alone and accept the partition of India, but Pakistan cannot accept as genuine an India that leaves it alone and accepts partition. India, to qualify as India for Pakistanis, must interfere in and try to subvert the Pakistani state. For Pakistan needs India to be its hostile but prized audience which, after trying out all its dirty tricks, will have to admit some day that Pakistan has made it, that Pakistan is not what the Pakistanis themselves secretly suspect it to be. That acceptance by India and, by implication, the Hindus, is even more important for the ideologues of Pakistan than what the common run of Pakistani citizens think of Pakistan. For, everything said, India is the exiled self of Pakistan, by exteriorizing and territorializing which Pakistan has built its identity and it remains, fifty years after its creation, the final measure of the worth of Pakistan.

THE FUTURE OF THE PAST

This story is not concerned with history; it is concerned with the future of 'reconstructed' pasts, with the myths that frame the fate of South Asia as it enters the twenty-first century. It is actually a story which has many of the ingredients that constitute an epic—a cast of millions, memories of wars and an exodus that have taken the toll of someone near to virtually everyone, and anger over lost or stolen patrimonies. Above all, to please literary theorist D. R. Nagaraj's concept of an epic, it has two antagonistic sides that are intimately related to each other through kinship and shared but often-disowned memories—like the Pandavas and the Kauravas in the Mahabharata. The only concession made to contemporary times is that both sides believe themselves to be the wronged Pandavas and the other side to be the ungodly Kauravas; yet each is convinced, as upholders of virtue, that they must retain a clandestine Kaurava self to ensure final victory of justice and truth.

Nation-states in South Asia, Ziauddin Sardar argues, are fictitious entities. Indian and Pakistani nationalism, too, is 'an artifact, a fabrication that is treated and enforced as though of the natural universe.'[15] But millions have been uprooted and much blood has already been shed for these entities. Fictions do kill in our times. What gives poignancy to that suffering is that all of it might have been a waste, though it might have consolidated two nation-states and satisfied a lost generation brought up to view the nation-state as *the* key to survival in the contemporary world.

Much of the ethnic violence—particularly the venom that has come to characterize it in India, Pakistan and Sri Lanka—has sprung not from any distance among communities or from clashing civilizations, but from proximity and fear of one's disowned selves. As in the cases of the Hutus and the Tutsis, the Bosnians and the Serbs, South Asian ethnic and religious violence, too, can be identified as a classic instance of what Sigmund Freud might have called a desperate, panicky 'turning against the self' as a means of exorcizing the feared Other. That attempted exorcism, even at the cost of self-annihilation, is becoming in South Asia the marker of a nihilistic affirmation of one's cultural selfhood. Strangely, that affirmation has come at a time when cultures are under attack not from one's neighbours, but from more impersonal forces of global cultural unification and the loss of the life-support systems that once sustained traditional identities.

This is tragic, for there are signs that the coming century may belong not to the nation-states or to public consciousness built around nation-states, but to other kinds of aggregates organized

[15] Sardar, 'On Serpents, Inevitability and the South Asian Imagination', p. 944.

around cultures and civilizations, including those previously marginalized. These aggregates will face formidable challenges from other non-state actors, such as multinational corporations and transnational economic institutions, but these corporations and institutions will have even less to do with the present order of nation-states. South Asia among all the regions of the world seems least prepared to face that situation. I remember economist Rahman Sobhan once predicting that the seven states in the region will walk like so many ghosts in the global corridors of power with none interested either in their plight or mutual bickering.

It is one of the cliches of contemporary sociology of science that, in modern science, major new discoveries or changes in cosmology are brought about not by empirical data or spectacular changes of heart in important scientists moved by reason, but by the death and retirement of the older generation of scientists. As we near the end of this particularly violent century, perhaps we should pin our hopes on an younger generation of South Asians less conditioned or brainwashed by the nineteenth-century European worldview and its obsessive preoccupation with the state. They will, I am confident, look at the organizational principles of their societies less blinkered by nineteenth-century western scholarship and rediscover that the South Asian societies are woven not around the state, but around their plural cultures and pluri-cultural identities. They will also discover, if I might use that paradoxical expression for a region that has not yet been massified, the grandeur of the humble, everyday life of their peoples and their little cultures. It is unlikely that I shall live to see that day, but I am consoled by the thought that I belong to a generation of South Asian scholars whose demise can only hasten the end of the present phase of self-hatred and attempts to live out some other culture's history.

8

The Philosophy of Coca Cola[1]

Ashis Nandy

Mr George Fernandes, who as the Minister of Industries threw Coca Cola out of India in the late 1970s, has launched a new movement against the drink. He still seems unaware that the first principle of the philosophy of Coca Cola is that it is substitutable only by another cola. For once exposed to the world of cola, life in a community never remains the same; the spectrum of human needs in it expands permanently. Everything else about Coca Cola is negotiable, but not this. A cola can never be replaced by tea, coffee, beer, wine or water. That is why, in the global scene, Coca Cola's prototypical competitor is Pepsi Cola.

Some of my friends like to flaunt their autonomy from the cola culture. They do not drink colas; they even force their children to be abstemious. Proud of their dissent from mass culture, they talk of Coca Cola the same way others talk of McDonald's and Woolworth, or red meat, hard liquor and tobacco. Their attitude to the cola drinks is a mix of contempt (towards an aspect of 'low' culture) and fear (of a caffeine-based drink 'injurious' to health).

Yet, the very fact that they have to flaunt such dissent and that their skepticism does not cover other items of useless consumption, tells us something. It tells us that Coca Cola is a world-view within which there is ample scope for diversity and dissent. Thus, when Fernandes banished Coca Cola from India, he thought he was being true to his socialism and the principle of self-reliance. Actually, he was being faithful to the philosophy of Coca Cola. For Coca Cola was duly substituted by Campa Cola, a native product, and

[1] First published in *The Times of India*, 27 August 1994.

Thumbs Up, launched by another multinational. And now, fifteen years afterwards, to spite the likes of Fernandes, Coca Cola has re-entered India triumphantly. It is even competing here with its global counter-player, Pepsi Cola, to provide the model of market competition that will supposedly be the salvation of Mother India.

It cannot be otherwise, because Coca Cola is the ultimate symbol of the market. You can have orange juice, tea or beer without a global market. Theoretically, you can grow oranges or at least squeeze them at home. You can make your own tea or coffee or brew your own beer, if you have the patience. None of these is possible with Coca Cola. You have to have it in some ready-made form—you need a franchise to produce it and a global market to have access to it.

The secret formula of Coca Cola—closely guarded by the company and an object of greedy curiosity of its competitors—also constitutes a paradigmatic puzzle of our times. Some companies have come close to the formula, to judge by the tastes of their products. Others have deliberately chosen not to duplicate it; they seek a niche for themselves in the cola market not occupied by Coca Cola. But that only deepens the mystery—the code still waiting to be cracked, the standard yet to be approximated. Local or national differences do not affect the mystery, as shown by the failure of cola drinks with a touch of cinnamon and cardamom to cater to Indian taste. Nor do levels of economic activity and political preferences. Some isolated cultures may find Coca Cola strange, some economies may not be able to sustain its production or import, and the politicians may try to 'clean' a society of its cola-philes. But remove the external compulsions and the love for Coca Cola among the moderns returns in its pure form.

Air India, which woos its Indian passengers in competition with other airlines, has understood this perfectly well. Undaunted by slogans of the self-reliance of its owner, the Government of India, the airlines has never encouraged Indian cola, not even during the heyday of bureaucratic socialism.

Coca Cola touches something deep in human existence. Like other elements of the global mass culture—pop music, denims and hamburgers—it reminds its consumer of the simple, innocent joys of living which the modern world has lost but which survive symbolically in selected artifacts of modernity. Hence both the difficulty of giving up Coca Cola and the fanaticism of those fighting it.

The philosophy of Coca Cola colours many areas of life and the votaries of the philosophy would like it to inform all areas of life. They do not have to work hard for that, because the philosophy is phagocytic; it eats up other adjacent philosophies or turns them into ornamental dissents within its universe.

One example is liberal-democratic politics. Gradually in the democracies, elections are getting depoliticized. There are increasingly media battles, with advertisement spots and droves of media experts and public relations consultants remote-controlling the battle from sidelines. The voters are given a choice between two images, both sold as alternatives to the other, while being usually the flip-sides of the other.

The candidates think the needs of the electorate are created by media experts. The experts believe that all candidates are edited versions of each other; only their public images differ. For both, the ultimate model of 'political' contests is the advertisement war among the colas, each representing inessential, artificially created needs. The aim is to ensure that the electorate, seen as a mass of consumers, do not get a chance to stop and think before deciding their own fate. The philosophy of Coca Cola insists that you never question the rules of the game, that far worse than losing is to opt out, or admit that the game bores you.

The philosophy of Coca Cola is the archetypal social philosophy of our times. Those who talk glibly of the Coca Cola culture subverting other 'superior' cultures know nothing of its appeal. Coca Cola happily grants such superiority when the market or advertisement requires it, for its appeal is nothing less than an invitation to worsen it at its own game. Japan, which can be called the Pepsi Cola of the world economy, has shown that Coca Cola can be 'defeated' if one joins the game sincerely and retools oneself to fight Coca Cola on its own terrain.

Academician Primakov, the Russian social scientist, seemed surprised in the 1980s that in Dusseldorf, McDonald's employed more people than the steel industry and Coca Cola paid more tax than Krupps. He failed to appreciate that mass culture was not only sane politics, but also rational economics, that the defiance of mass culture was already the defiance of sanity and rationality. To have the luxury of that defiance, you have to take on not merely the world of mega-consumption but also the concepts of normality and rational knowledge.

Decades ago, when as a cultural innovation, Coca Cola began its journey through the corridors of time, it allegedly included cocaine as an ingredient. If true, it shows how little the Coca Cola company understood its own product. The corporation, true to nineteenth-century capitalism, sold something addictive and injurious to health, to make the demand for its product artificially inelastic. It has no idea that it was a pioneer selling a world-view and a lifestyle, that even without an addictive ingredient, it had an addictive brew that could ensure as inelastic a demand as any bootlegger or drug peddler might want.

Mr Fernandes will not agree, but in the mass culture that has begun to engulf urban, media-exposed India, Coca Cola is already a way of thinking rather than a thought.

9

The Fear of Plague: The Inner Demons of a Society[1]

Ashis Nandy

Plague activates anxieties and images few other diseases do. Tuberculosis invokes the images of dissipation and waste, occasionally even of nineteenth-century romanticism and self-destruction. John Keats suffered from tuberculosis; so probably did Saratchandra Chattopadhyay's hero Devdas. Cancer has become associated in recent years with mindless over-consumption and the consequent revenge of nature. It is mainly seen as a disease of the rich and the powerful who have to, after getting the best of health-care, find some reason to die. Plague activates more primitive fears, particularly in Europe. There are countries in Europe that have in the past lost more than half their populations to plague. The continent as a whole has lost, at some points of time, as much as one-fourth of its inhabitants to different versions of the Black Death. That memory survives.

The primeval European fear of plague has become entwined with the fear of the Third World. There may no longer be a proper second world any more, to guide the poor and the dispossessed towards a proletarian heaven, but the Third World survives as a concept for the First World and the modern élites of Asia and Africa. In that meaning, the Third World is the abode of the third rate, where a surplus of obsolete people, living in dirt and penury, provide a fertile breeding ground for pestilences of

[1] First published in *The Times of India* as 'Fear in the Air: The Inner Demons of Society' (14 October 1994).

all kinds. Poverty is a crime and a proof of one's worldly failures and sinful ways. The ungodly are also the god-forsaken and, therefore, pestilence-prone. The best one can do is to avoid their contagion.

Albert Camus' novel, *The Plague* (1947), is set in Algeria and its white doctor-hero, working among Arab victims of plague, symbolizes a person seeking existential meaning in a battle against an epidemic that did not have a known cure when the novel was written. He acts out the philosophy of life spelt out in the author's *Le Mythe de Sisyphe* (1942). As is well known, Sisyphus was condemned by the gods to roll a stone uphill for eternity. *The Plague* is the story of a modern Sisyphus battling the random suffering of a people and, in the process, giving meaning to the otherwise meaningless.

The fear and the fantasies associated with plague, particularly in European Christendom, cannot be contained by any discovery of plague vaccines or of antibiotics effective against the disease. Most Europeans are not impressed that the mortality rate in plague has reportedly come down to below 5 per cent the world over and, in well-equipped West–European or North American hospitals, that rate cannot but be much lower. As Ingmar Bergman shows so elegantly in his *The Seventh Seal* (1956), plague is located in a melancholic, grey, mental landscape where it cohabits with ideas of sin, moral responsibility, death-defiance, repentance and expiation. That landscape remains, but has become invisible in recent centuries, thanks to the overdone festive style of modern capitalism. Europe's post-medieval prosperity promises perpetual happiness in a deathless society. Plague, which is remembered there primarily as a medieval disease, is a reminder that death does come, even in a world of plenty, dominated by mega-science and foolproof rationality packaged in super-consumption.

The fear of plague in Europe, however, is not only the fear of death. It is the fear of death that comes as the Biblical wages of sin. It carries the load of one's own past—when life was nasty, brutish, and short—projected on to the Third World. The Third World living in abject misery—because that is what the heathens deserve in God's scheme of things—is also read as Europe's past that survives and haunts the modern, desacralized Europe and its godless ways. The Third World visits Europe as plague when the

European Christendom fails to maintain its purity, of body and of mind.

Plague also gives ample scope for heroism. The knight who plays chess with Death in *The Seventh Seal* is not a mere cinematic figure. He lives in the unconscious of all Europeans. He is a crusader who has already risked his life for his faith. His decision to take on Death in plague-ridden Europe, cannot but acquire heroic proportions. Likewise, the doctor in *The Plague* battles an epidemic as the ultimate symbol of heroic resistance to the vagaries of fate. As befits an existentialist hero, he creates his morality out of essential meaninglessness.

The fear of plague in India is of a different kind. Here too, plague connotes moral waywardness and divine retribution, but the disease does not invoke the inner demons that haunt Europe. Small pox and cholera are the prototypical diseases of the tropics, without learning about which no student can graduate from a school of tropical medicine even today. Even tuberculosis has acquired a mythic status over the last hundred years in India. Plague, though it has sometimes been a great killer or *mahamari*, remains for the Indians, rightly or wrongly, an imported epidemic. It seems to thrive in cold weather, not in the torrid summers of India. Nor does it have, like Shitala and Olaichandi, any goddess or god presiding over it or the fate of its victims. It certainly does not have any distinctive, traditional ritual to go with it.

In India, as far as I know, you do not acquire mastery over plague by appeasing or establishing a contractual relationship—through a *manat or mannat*—with any particular deity. Perhaps, there is no felt need to have that sense of mastery over fate through a steady compact with divinity in the case of plague. Like malaria and unlike small pox and cholera, plague is an outsider in South Asia.

This is implicitly admitted by many Indians. Plague has been seen by them mainly as a scourge of urban India, marred by its dirty streets, mixed populations drawn from diverse often-unknown sources, unhealthy lifestyle, and crowded slums. Public hygiene and modern preventive medicine, combined with some degree of caution, are supposed to take care of plague, even when a specific plague threat exists. Hence, even during great pilgrimages like the Kumbha, efforts to inoculate the pilgrims against plague are rare; they are mostly inoculated against small pox and cholera.

Yet plague has been visiting urban India on and off to take its toll. This time Surat, and to a small extent metropolitan Bombay and Delhi, have been its main victims. I do not know how the residents of Surat explain the epidemic—as a failure in civic management, government apathy to prior warning by experts, or as the natural fate of a city that had no time to build a civic culture because it had lost its soul entirely to Mammon and chose not to look beyond commerce.

I have a fair guess what the greatest Gujarati of all times might have said on Surat's present plight. He would have almost certainly invoked his notorious theory of collective karma, the one that he had coined at the time of the Bihar earthquake in the 1920s. As we know, he blamed the earthquake on the practice of untouchability, to the utter chagrin of rational humanists like Rabindranath Tagore. Perfectly comfortable with the moral universe of pre-modern Europe, Mohandas Karamchand Gandhi would have, I am pretty sure, held the particularly cruel communal riots of Surat responsible for the outbreak of plague in the city.

Part III

Part III

10

The A B C D (and E) of
Ashis Nandy

Ziauddin Sardar

Ashis Nandy's *The Savage Freud* is dedicated to the memory of 'three Indians who symbolize the hundred-and-fifty-year-old attempt to re-engineer the Indian':

Vinayak Damodar Savarkar (1880–1965), unflinching warrior for Hindu nationalism, who spent his life trying to make the Hindu more martial, masculine, cohesive and organized; Damodar Dharmanand Kosambi (1907–60), indefatigable rationalist and progressive thinker, who never gave up his effort to make Indians more scientific, objective and historically minded; and Nirad C. Chaudhuri (b. 1897) the last of the great Edwardian modernists of India, who has always thoughtfully shared the white man's burden, especially Europe's educational responsibilities in South Asia.[1]

It would be safe to assume that Nandy himself is not in favour of re-engineering the Indian: there is nothing much wrong with the old fashioned, traditional, but somewhat world wary *Hindustani*. After all, the less than 'masculine' and 'scientific' Indian has survived centuries of colonization, decades of modernity and instrumental development—and survived with his sanity and identity intact. Even now, in the closing years of the western millennium, the *Hindustani* seems to demonstrate stubborn resilience in the face of the all-embracing embrace of postmodernism and 'globalization' and appears ever ready to preserve his or her Selfhood from

[1] Ashis Nandy, *The Savage Freud, and Other Essays on Possible and Retrievable Selves* (Delhi: Oxford University Press, 1995). See the dedication.

whatever else the twenty-first century may throw at him or her. If Nandy stands *for* anything, it is the traditional *Hindustani*; that is, some one who is much more than a mere 'Indian', a citizen of a nation-state called 'India'; someone whose Self incorporates a civilization with its own tradition, history (however defined), lifestyles and modes of knowing, being and doing.

It would be simplistic to try to understand Ashis Nandy in relation to others. For one thing, counterpoising the author of *The Intimate Enemy* with others amounts to comparing his thesis (tradition, civilization, the total Self) with their anti-thesis (nationalism, rationalism, secularism, etc.). Nandy is not amenable to this kind of (western) dualistic logic. There are three prerequisites for understanding Ashis Nandy and his thought. First: it is important to appreciate that he operates on a non-dualistic, four-fold logic where relationships of similarity and convergence are more important than cold, instrumental rationality, and the universe has more options than simply either/or duality. Second: it is necessary to understand that Nandy functions beyond (rather than outside) the established conventions of western thought. Both the man and his ideas span a different universe, a universe that includes 'the West' but only as one civilization in a multicivilizational world and then largely—and this may come as a surprise to many—as a victim. Nandy categorically locates himself with the victims of history and the casualties of an array of grand western ideas such as Science, Rationality, Development, Nation-state; but the victims of *zulm* (tyranny) in history and conceptual and ideational oppression in our time are located as much in a geographical, civilizational, intellectual and conceptual space called 'the West' as in the non-West. Nandy seeks both to unite the victims and to increase the awareness of their victimhood. Third: even though he is trained as a psychologist, Nandy has no respect for disciplinary boundaries. Indeed, to accept the disciplinary structure of modern knowledge is to accept the world-view of the West. But Nandy's scholarship is not interdisciplinary or transdisciplinary in the conventional sense; he is no 'Renaissance Man'. He is a polymath is the traditional sense; meaning he operates beyond the disciplinary structure of knowledge *and* regards all sources of knowledge—revelational as well as non-revelational, traditional as well as modern, tacit as well as objective—as equally valid *and* all methods and modes of inquiry as equally useful.

Given these traits, it is clear that Ashis Nandy's thought and scholarship is one long quest for alternatives to the dominant modes of everything! But it would be out of character if Nandy's alternatives were located within prevailing boundaries, or the search itself followed a common path.

ALTERNATIVES, ANDROGYNOUS

Nandy's first book, *Alternative Sciences: Creativity and Authenticity in Two Indian Scientists*, is dedicated to 'the Ramanujans who walk the dusty roads of India undiscovered and the Boses who almost make it but never do'.[2] The book analyses the life and work of Jagdish Chandra Bose, the Indian physicist and botanist, and Srinivasa Ramanujan, the brilliant mathematician. Bose tried to give a special Indian perspective to world science, was one of the earliest modern scientists to do interdisciplinary research, and mapped out a philosophy of science which anticipated a number of major themes in the contemporary philosophy of science. In the West, he was considered a genius and a missionary-scientist; in India, he was a national hero. Unlike Bose, Ramanujan was totally a product of traditional India. Despite the fact that he failed all his academic examinations, Ramanujan emerged as a world-class mathematician: he practised a neat, non-dualistic science that has been the forte of Indian thought since the eighth century. Through an analysis of their lives, Nandy explores how modern and traditional India tried to cope with the culture of modern science, and how their personal search for meaning personified India's search for a new self-definition.

While Bose had a total belief in science, he was concerned with the parochialism of western science and the hostility of western scientists towards India and all things Indian. He suffered, Nandy alleges, from a double bind: on the one hand, the perceived hostility of the West led him towards a growing hostility to the West; and, on the other, he felt a sense of inferiority vis-à-vis the West. He loved to have his wife and assistants sing western scientists' eulogies of his work to his visitors. Ramanujan's science relied as much on mysticism, metaphysics and astrology as it did

---

[2] Ashis Nandy, *Alternative Sciences: Creativity and Authenticity in Two Indian Scientists* (Delhi: Oxford University Press, 1995). See the dedication.

on the abstract ideas of mathematics. He developed his own philosophy of life and his mathematics formed an integrated whole with his metaphysics and astrology. Nandy shows sympathy with both scientists—indeed, he demonstrates an unconditional love towards both—but he finds both their lives as well as their perceived alternatives wanting.

So what exactly is Nandy rejecting in *Alternative Sciences?* He clearly rejects the dominant mode of western science. But he also rejects Bose's attempts to seek an alternative within western science—an Indian Science that is actually an appendage to the 'universal model' of western science. And he rejects too Ramanujan's version of traditional Indian science even though it is rooted in a folk history. Both use a strategy that uses the West as a yardstick and consider their Indianness as a negative identification. And, as such, both alternatives are derived from the western notion of what is science and strive 'to be the exact reverse of what a hypothetical model of western analysis is'.[3] Thus, for Nandy, an alternative that is genuinely an alternative cannot take the West as its reference.

So what is Nandy's alternative, alternative to? To begin with, it is an alternative to a world-view that 'believes in the absolute superiority of the human over the nonhuman and the subhuman, the masculine over the feminine, the adult over the child, the historical over the ahistorical, and the modern or progressive over the traditional or the savage' and that has its roots in 'anthropo-centric doctrines of secular salvation, in the ideologies of progress, normality and hyper-masculinity, and in theories of cumulative growth of science and technology.'[4] It is also an alternative to 'a fully homogenized, technologically controlled, absolutely hierarchized world' based on a dualistic logic of 'the modern and the primitive, the secular and the non-secular, the scientific and the unscientific, the expert and the layman, the normal and the abnormal, the developed and the underdeveloped, the vanguard and the led, the liberated and the savable.'[5]

But this alternative is not, and cannot be, an alternative to the West *per se.* For Nandy, the West is more than a geographical and temporal entity; it is a psychological category. Now the West is

[3] Ibid., p. 15.
[4] Ashis Nandy, *The Intimate Enemy: Loss and Recovery of Self Under Colonialism* (Delhi: Oxford University Press, 1983), p.x.
[5] Ibid., p.x.

everywhere: within and without the West, in thought processes and liberative actions, in colonial and neo-colonial structures and in the minds of oppressors and the oppressed—the West is part of the oppressive structure as well as in league with the victims. Thus, to be anti-West is itself tantamount to being pro-West; or in Nandy's words, 'anti-colonialism, too, could be an apologia for the colonization of minds.'[6]

Nandy's alternative then is located beyond the West/anti-West dichotomy, even beyond the indigenous constructions of modern and traditional options, in a totally different space. It lies in an entirely new construction: a 'victims' construction of the West, a West which would make sense to the non-West in terms of the non-West's experience of suffering.'[7] This construction, both of a 'victims alternative' as well as of alternative West, turns out to be a strategy for survival. Modern oppression, Nandy asserts, is unique in many respects. Unlike traditional oppression—which is an encounter between the self and the enemy, the rulers and the ruled, the believers and the infidels—modern oppression is 'a battle between dehumanized self and the objectified enemy, the technologized bureaucrat and his reified victim, pseudo-rulers and their fearsome other selves projected on to their "subjects."'[8] This is the difference between the Crusades and Auschwitz, between Hindu-Muslim riots in India and the Gulf War. And this is why, Nandy's alternative is the alternative of the victims; and whenever the oppressors make an appearance in this alternative they are revealed to be disguised victims 'at an advanced stage of psychosocial decay.'[9] The construction of their own West allows the victims to live with the alternative West 'while resisting the loving embrace of the West's dominant self.'[10]

India, then, is not the non-West. It is India and it cannot be defined in relation to the West. The ordinary Indian has no reason to seek his/her self-definition in relation to the West or to see himself/herself as a counter-player or an anti-thesis of the Western man or woman. The strain to be the opposite of the West distorts the priorities of the traditional world-view of India, dissolves the

[6] Ibid., p.xi.
[7] Ibid., p.xiii.
[8] Ibid., p.xvi.
[9] Ibid., p.xvi.
[10] Ibid., p.xiv.

holistic nature of the Indian view of humanity and its place in the universe, and destroys Indian culture's unique *Gestalt*. The search for alternatives is not a choice between East and West or between North and South: 'it is a choice—and a battle—between the Apollonian and the Dionysian *within* India and *within* the West.'[11] Even if such a distinction does not exist in an oppressive culture, Nandy asserts, 'it has to be presumed to exist by its victims for maintaining their own sanity and humanness.'[12] There is thus no need to look elsewhere for ethically sensitive and culturally-rooted alternative social knowledge for it is already partly available outside the framework of modern science and social sciences—in those who have been the 'subjects,' consumers or experimentees of these sciences.[13]

Nandy's search for alternatives beyond the Hegelian thesis/antithesis dichotomy has an interesting gender dimension. Colonial India, taking a cue from the colonizers, went through a radical shift in its gender consciousness. Traditionally, Indian thought has given greater preference to *naritva* (the essence of femininity) and *klibatva* (the essence of androgyny or hermaphroditism) in comparison to *purusatva* (the essence of masculinity). Colonial India came to perceive the notion of *naritva* and *klibatva* as dangerous pathologies that could only lead India to a negation of masculine identity. All forms of androgyny were lumped together as a dangerous anti-thesis of beneficial, undifferentiated masculinity. Nandy leans towards the traditional by carefully choosing the subjects of his inquiry. Thus Ramanujan is deliberately counterpoised against Bose because he resembled his mother and grandmother in looks and had 'a delicate and conspicuously feminine build and appearance' with 'velvety soft palms and long tapering fingers.'[14] The British mathematician, George Hardy, who gave Ramanujan the one break his genius deserved, also turns out to be a 'queer'. Most of the characters in *The Intimate Enemy*, perhaps Nandy's most influential book, have ambiguous sexualities which are deliberately played upon: Gandhi, Oscar Wilde, Kipling, C. F. Andrews (the English priest described by Gandhi as Indian at heart and a true Englishman), Aurobindo.... However, this

[11] Ibid., p. 74.
[12] Ibid., p. 74.
[13] Ibid., p.xvii.
[14] Nandy, *Alternative Sciences*, p. 100.

should not be read as an uncritical endorsement of the feminine principle. Under certain, specific conditions, Nandy argues (thinking perhaps of Mrs Indira Gandhi and Mrs Margaret Thatcher), femininity can be an indication of higher forms of masculinity.

The point here is that traditional Indian society, despite its patriarchal dimensions, does not allow gender, age and other biological differences to be transformed into principles of social stratification. On the contrary, it sees the masculine and the feminine, the infant, adult and the aged as a total continuum. The differences are acknowledged, but the boundaries are open and diffused.

BOUNDARIES, BIOGRAPHY

The dedication in *Science, Hegemony and Violence,* an anthology of essays edited by Ashis Nandy that deconstruct modern science with devastating power, reads: 'For A. K. Saran, Dharampal, Mohamed Idris who have tried to keep the future open for our generation of South Asians.'[15] Perhaps it is not widely known that Nandy is a futurist—but a futurist of a particular type. His concern, as opposed to those like Daniel Bell and Herman Kahn who would turn future studies into a closed discipline with its own priesthood, sacred texts and formal content, is to keep the boundaries of future studies and the future completely open. In their own way, the three to whom the book is dedicated have tried to do the same: A. K. Saran has spent all his intellectual energies demolishing the positivist boundaries of all Indian social science disciplines;[16] Dharampal tried to rescue the history of Indian science and education from the clutches of western and westernized historians and open it up to new interpretative possibilities,[17] and Mohamed

[15] Ashis Nandy, *Science, Hegemony and Violence: A Requiem for Modernity* (Delhi: Oxford University Press, 1990; Tokyo: The United Nations University, 1988). See the dedication.

[16] A. K. Saran is a thoroughgoing anti-positivist who is totally disdainful of all social science discourse. He is heavily influenced by Coomaraswamy as well as by marginalized western traditions, represented by such people as Marco Pollis, Simone Weil, Wittgenstein, and others. He writes in a peculiar scholastic style where footnotes often tend to be longer than the text itself.

[17] See Dharampal's classic studies, *Indian Science and Technology in the Eighteenth Century* (Delhi: 1971) and *The Beautiful Tree* (Delhi: 1983).

Idris has devoted his life to saving the environment and cultural ecology of South-east and South Asia.[18] Nandy stands for a plural future and much of his thought is concerned with the survival of cultures incompatible with western notions of modernity, science, progress, and rationality. The survival, and hence the future, of non-western cultures, he has maintained, depends on pluralizing human destiny; and future studies, in its current incoherent form, offers escape routes that history, in its current institutionalized, disciplinary form, does not.

Nandy's concern for ensuring that boundaries—of disciplines, cultures, genders, futures, alternatives—remain open and diffused, combined with his genial but aggressive stance against western grand narratives—Science, Reason, Progress, Nationalism—and his deliberate attempt to dissolve the difference between high and low art and culture, appear to locate him within the domain of post-modernism. But this location is more apparent than real. Nandy's position has some subtle and some serious differences from many of those who belong to the postmodern persuasion. Postmodernism celebrates difference but blurs the boundaries that maintain differ-ence. Under postmodernism, boundaries come crashing down. Nandy celebrates difference but not for its own sake: he wants different cultures to survive, indeed thrive, and remain different with their distinctive traits intact. Thus in his thought, boundaries are still needed so that difference can retain its difference; but one must have an open attitude to boundaries to avoid falling into the trap of 'fundamentalism', 'puritanism' and 'nationalism'. Like so many postmodern writers, Nandy does not recognize a category called 'ethnicity' which demarcates a division between 'true insid-ers' and the constructed Other, the outsider. All those people who are described as ethnic, whether in the United States—where, apart from the white Anglo–Saxons, all other communities, from the Jews to Greeks, Irish, Hispanics and Asians, are described as ethnic thus confirming their outsider status—or in India, are primordially deemed to be Others. His basic elements of analysis are culture and

[18] Mohamed Idris founded and led the Consumer Association of Penang (CAP) which is perhaps one of the most influential environmental pressure groups in the Third World. He also established the Third World Network, an information and media service on Third World issues based in Penang; and the Kuala Lumpur based Just Trust which campaigns for social justice and champions the cause of the marginalized and the oppressed.

civilization (which assumes grand narrative proportions in Nandy's writings); he wants to retain both categories as analytical tools as well as distinctive and different entities. The cultural subjects of difference, the non-Western cultures and civilizations, Nandy has argued so forcefully, must be accorded the right and the space to negotiate their own conditions of discursive control and to practise their difference as a rebellion against the hegemonic tendencies of both modernity and postmodernism. The differences and diversities in Indian culture, he writes, are often sought in the

uniqueness of certain cultural themes or in their configuration. This is not a false trail, but it does lead to some half-truths. One of them is the clear line drawn, on behalf of the Indian, between the past and the present, the native and the exogenous, and the Hindu and the non-Hindu. But... the West that is aggressive is sometimes inside; the earnest, self-declared native, too, is often an exogenous category, and the Hindu who announces himself so, is not that Hindu after all. Probably the uniqueness of Indian culture lies not so much in a unique ideology as in the society's traditional ability to live with cultural ambiguities and to use them to build psychological and even metaphysical defences against cultural invasions. Probably, the culture itself demands that a certain permeability of boundaries be maintained in one's self-image and that the self be not defined too tightly or separated mechanically from the not-self. This is the other side of the strategy of survival—the clue to India's post-colonial worldview.[19]

For non-western cultures and civilizations, as well as for Nandy, relativism cannot be absolute: it must be conditional, critical and concise—postmodernism notwithstanding.

In postmodern thought and practice, past and future implode into the present. Thus, both history and (western) utopia/dystopias become instruments of dominance and techniques of rewriting the life plan of the lesser mortals of the world. For Nandy, all politics of the past, as well as all politics of the future, are attempts to shape the present. And the search for a non-oppressive present or a just and sustainable future often ends with new modes and techniques of oppression. The past is often used to keep the non-western cultures and civilization in a vise-like grip; and it comes in useful for imposing limits on the visions of the future. The present of the non-West is often projected as the past of the West; and the future of non-West, in such a straitjacket, can only be the present of

[19] Nandy, *The Intimate Enemy*, p. 107.

the West. This linear, progressive and cumulative notion of history, a product of liberal, humanistic ideologies, is used to curb the emergence of genuine alternative worldviews, alternative visions of the future and even alternative self-definitions and self-concepts. This is why, Nandy contends, 'the peripheries of the world often feel that they are victimized not merely by partial, biased or ethnocentric history, but by the idea of history itself.[20]

How can we ensure that alternative visions of the future do not simply become steps towards the construction of new oppression? Future utopias and visions, Nandy contends, must have an in-built ability to account for their legitimate and illegitimate offspring. The oppressive actions of zealous visionaries in the name of their visions cannot be simply explained away as the actions of misguided adherents or products of misuse or deviations and false interpretations. A vision must take the responsibility of what is undertaken in its name. What this actually means is that the vision itself must have some capacity to liberate the visionaries from its own straitjacket. And, as such, it cannot claim 'a monopoly on compassion and social realism, or presume itself to hold the final key to social ethics and experience. Such a vision not only devalues all heretics and outsiders as morally and cognitively inferior, it defines them as throw-backs to an earlier stage of culture and history, fit to be judged exclusively by the norms of the vision.[21]

When Nandy uses biography and narrative as tools for cultural analysis, he deconstructs them using these criteria. In postmodernism, narrative—particularly fiction—has itself become a theory of salvation. For example, Richard Rorty argues that philosophy and theory can no longer function to ground politics and social criticism; only fiction (he is particularly partial towards Nabokov and Orwell) can give us insight into what sort of cruelty we are capable of, and awaken us to the humiliation of particular social practices.[22] In British cultural studies, biography has acquired a similar role. Our salvation lies in art, argues Fred Inglis, and 'the

---

[20] Ashis Nandy *Traditions, Tyranny, and Utopias: Essays in the Politics of Awareness* (Delhi: Oxford University Press, 1987), p. 46.

[21] Ibid., p. 11.

[22] Richard Rorty, *Philosophy and the Mirror of Nature* (Princeton: Princenton University Press, 1979).

art-form for each of our ordinary lives is, of course, biography'.[23] Thus, biography makes sense of our experiences and gives meaning to our individual lives: it teaches us how to live and how not to live. And cultural studies, particularly in its British form, is going to be the new theology that will teach the young how to think, what to feel, how to live, and what it is to be good. The assertions, writes Inglis,

arise distinctly from the structure of feeling and frame of thought which, in small corners of non-elite academies, have formed Cultural Studies. And elite or not, there is no doubt in my mind that the strong tide of interest running through a generation in the style and preoccupations of Cultural Studies however named is evidence of the subject's larger timeliness. I will risk declaring that *this is the way the best and brightest of presnt-day students in the human sciences want to learn to think and feel.* And having learned to think and feel thus, this is how they want to act and live... There is, as always, a story hidden in these assertions. It is the story of how Cultural Studies will make you good. [Italics in the original.][24]

It is beyond Nandy's intellectual constitution to be so coarse. For him, biograhy is a ground for mining psychological insights, for understanding how the Indian Self survived, or failed to survive, the onslaught of colonialism, for constructing a politics of aware-ness—not a new theology of deliverance.

But deliverance is essentially what western thought is all about, Nandy would argue. In modernity, of course, the grand narratives are essentially vehicles of salvation. Having swept all grand narratives aside, postmodern thought generates the illusion that there is nothing for us to do other than to live with the horror of meaninglessness. But both modernity and postmodern thought fall back on a single theory of salvation: the secular imagination. It is not by accident that Rorty suggests that the real goal of postmodernist thought is to de-devinize the world, to expunge all traces of religious thought,[25] and Inglis suggests 'that the study of culture, as a nature, teaches atheism'[26]—this is not a conclusion of

[23] Fred Inglis, *Cultural Studies* (Cambridge, Massachusetts: Blackwell Publishers, 1993), p. 204.

[24] Ibid., p. 229.

[25] Richard Rorty, *Contingency, Irony and Solidarity* (Cambridge: Cambridge University Press, 1989).

[26] Inglis, *Cultural Studies*, p. 231.

philosophical or cultural inquiry but a deep-seated assumption that is an essential component of dominant western consciousness. This insistence of western thought on falling back on secularism—disguised as 'liberal humanism' or 'biography' or 'cultural studies' as well as numerous other forms—has led Nandy to argue that the West and its relationship with the non-West has become deeply interwined with the problem of evil in our time. The only good that the West can see in the non-West is purely in terms of secularism. Thus, Inglis cannot see any good in Islam and is happy to dismiss it as 'angry and vengeful'.[27] He lionizes neo-orientalists like V. S. Naipaul (who is described by Nandy as 'ethnocidal') who portray the non-secularist people as puritan savages. Inglis represents the Westernized Jawaharlal Nehru as 'India' and sees in his biography the vision of what India should be because 'Nehru took the narratives embodied in the biographies of J. S. Mill and William Morris, and turned them to Indian account.'[28] The India imagined by Nehru, Inglis asserts, 'would be peaceable, independent, industrialized, united, social-democratic. It would not be Gandhi's peasant homeland with a loom in every cottage and his creaking, cranky ideas about sex, the deity, asceticism and whatnot.'[29] Yet, without Gandhi there would not be an independent India; and with Nehru we have an aggressive, warring nation state nursing Hindu nationalism and disunited communities perpetually fighting the centre for 'autonomy' or 'independence'! Grand narratives may damage your health, as Inglis suggests, but, Nandy would insist, the secular imagination underlying the dominant western thought of all varieties is pathologically demented and intrinsically, but unconsciously, part of the landscape of evil. The study of culture takes us not to atheism but towards strategies for surviving (in the case of the non-West) and curing (in the case of the West) the pathologies of the dominant, and still inherently colonial, modes of western thought. Cultural Studies must be about liberating the Western and non-Western civilizations from the suffocating embrace of the older and newer versions of ever-present colonialism.

[27] Ibid., p. 215. On neo-orientalism in general, and Naipaul in particular, see Ziauddin Sardar and Merryl Wyn Davies, *Distorted Imagination: Lessons from the Rushdie Affair* (London: Grey Seal, 1989).

[28] Ibid., p. 218.

[29] Ibid., p. 220.

COLONIALISM, CIVILIZATIONS

The dedication in *The Tao of Cricket* could not be simpler: 'To Uma'.[30] In the preface to *The Intimate Enemy*, Nandy confesses that 'without my wife Uma and my daughter Aditi I would have finished the work earlier, but it would not have been the same.'[31] The difference that wives and daughters (and sons!) make to scholarly thought and output is seldom recognized. Traditional societies do not assign different categories of thought to different sexes or to different stages of human biological growth. Men are capable of feminine thoughts, just as children can have 'adult' ideas. Wives and children, as any Sufi manual of good life will confirm, have a great deal to teach husbands and parents. But in the ideology of colonialism, thought and education flowed only one way: the aggressively masculine colonizer taught the cowardly feminine colonized subject. The subjugated non-west had nothing to teach the imperial west—particularly when its cultures were so primitive and child-like. The adult, male and virile western civilization had a responsibility to husband the weak, docile and passive cultures of the Orient.

This self-image of the colonial powers produced a counter-image in its dissenters. The conventional view holds that the only victims of colonialism were the subject cultures and societies. So colonialism is seen essentially as a political economy designed to ensure a one-way flow of goods and benefits with the non-western communities as passive and perpetual losers. But this is a vested view of colonialism propagated by colonialism itself. It suppresses the fact that the colonizers too were devoured by the ideology of colonialism: 'behind all the rhetoric of the European intelligentsia on the evils of colonialism lay their unstated faith that the gains from colonialism to Europe, to the extent that they primarily involved material products, were real, and the losses, to the extent they involved social relations and psychological states, false.'[32]

Colonialism dehumanized the colonizers as much as it brutalized the colonized. The relationship it produced between the colonizers and the colonized was akin to a family headed by an

---

[30] Ashis Nandy, *The Tao of Cricket: On Games of Destiny and the Destiny of Games* (Delhi: Penguin Books, 1989). See the dedication.

[31] Nandy, *The Intimate Enemy*, p. xx.

[32] Ibid., p. 30.

abusing husband and father: the father keeps the family together by sheer force of terror but the more he abuses the family the more he loses his own humanity, and the more the family as a whole is reduced to a groups of victims. What the European imperial powers did in the colonies bounced back to the fatherland as a new political and public culture. Colonialism transformed Britain culturally by declaring tenderness, speculation and introspection as feminine and therefore unworthy of public culture and by bringing the most brutish and masculine elements of British colonial life to the fore. It justified a restricted cultural role for women and promoted an instrumental notion of lower classes—both slightly modified versions of the colonial concept of hierarchy. Thus the calamity of colonialism for Britain was the tragedy of the women, the children, the working classes and all those placed at the bottom of the heap by a set of masculine values. Such instrumental values as punishment, discipline, productivity and subjugation, which were used in the colonies to whip the subjects into shape, were used in the fatherland to encourage new forms of institutionalized violence and ruthless social Darwinism.

In George Orwell's classic essay, 'Shooting an Elephant,' Nandy finds the most profound description of the trepidation and terror induced by colonialism in the colonizers: 'the reification of social bonds through formal, stereotyped, part-object relationships; an instrumental view of nature; created loneliness of the colonizers in the colony through a theory of cultural stratification and exclusivism; an unending search for masculinity and status before the colonized.'[33] The perception of the subject people as simple children who had to be impressed with 'conspicuous machismo' forced the colonizers into perpetual suppression of their own self for the sake of an imposed imperial identity. Over a period of time this inauthentic and generously murderous identity would be internalized. It is hardly surprising then that all the themes that can be identified with the present cultural crisis of the West are there in Orwell's essay.

The imperial powers also created a self-image for those who were being husbanded by colonialism. Inasmuch as this self-image is a dualistic opposite, it is, and remains in essence, a western

[33] Ibid., p. 40.

construction. Colonialism replaced the Eurocentric convention of portraying the Other as an incomprehensible barbarian with the pathological stereotype of the strange but predictable Oriental. He was now religious but superstitious, clever but devious, chaotically violent but effeminately cowardly. At the same time, a new discourse was developed where the basic mode of breaking out of these stereotypes was to reverse them: superstitious but spiritual, uneducated but wise, womanly but pacific. 'No colonialism could be complete,' writes Nandy, 'unless it "universalized" and enriched its ethnic stereotypes by appropriating the language of defiance of its victims. That was why the cry of the victims of colonialism was ultimately the cry to be heard in another language—unknown to the colonizer and the anti-colonial movements that he had bred and then domesticated.'[34]

The victim's language of defiance may be totally different, but the agony caused by centuries of colonialism and the experience of authoritarian imperial rule equally distorted the minds and cultures of both the imperialists and their prey. Moreover, the mutual bondage of long-term anguish generated strong justifications for this suffering from both sides of the colonial divide. The forces that unleashed and maintained this torment shape almost every aspect of our history, our contemporary lives and our imagined futures. Indeed, institutionalized suffering has acquired its own momentum and has thus become self-perpetuating.

Nandy's perspective on dealing with institutionalized torment is based on three assumptions. First, he asserts, no civilization has a monopoly on goodness and humane values. All civilizations share certain basic values and cultural traits that derive from our biological self and social experience. What is unique about a given civilization is not its values but the framework within which these values are actualized and the emphasis and priorities it assigns to these values. Thus, certain values, or traditions based on these values, may, at a given point, be receding or acquiring dominance in a civilization, but they are never solely absent or exclusively present: 'what looks like a human potentiality which ought to be

[34] Ibid., p. 70. For a more detailed discussion of the relationship between the colonizer and the colonized, see Ziauddin Sardar, Ashis Nandy and Merryl Davies, *Barbaric Others: A Manifesto on Western Racism* (London: Pluto Press, 1993).

actualized in some distant future, is often only a cornered cultural strain waiting to be renewed or rediscovered.'[35] Second,

human civilization is constantly trying to alter or expand its awareness of exploitation and oppression. Oppressions which were once outside the span of awareness are no longer so, and it is quite likely that the present awareness of suffering, too, will be found wanting and might change in the future. Who, before the socialists, had thought of class as a unit of repression? How many, before Freud, had sensed that children needed to be protected against their own parents? How many believed, before Gandhi's rebirth after the environmental crisis in the West, that modern technology, the supposed liberator of man, had become his most powerful oppressor? Our limited ethical sensitivity is not a proof of human hypocrisy; it is mostly a product of our limited cognition of the human situation. Oppression is ultimately a matter of definition, and its perception is the product of a worldview. Change the worldview, and what once seemed natural and legitimate becomes an instance of cruelty and sadism.[36]

Third, all civilizations, in as far as they are human, are imperfect, and imperfect civilizations can only produce imperfect solutions for their cultural and social imperfections. Solutions, after all, emerge from exactly the same cultural and social experience as the problem, and as such, the same thought or consciousness as well as the unthought, or unconsciousness, informs them.

What, then, are the possible boundaries of a solution? Our release from institutionalized suffering, Nandy argues, must involve both the non-West and the West. But this is not an invitation for the masculine, oppressive West to transform itself; it is the recognition that the oppressed and marginalized selves in the West need help and that they can be recognized and used as civilizational allies in the battle against institutionalized suffering. It is the non-western civilizations that must give collective representation to all suffering everywhere—the suffering of the past as well as the present to release the bondage of suffering in the future. And, as such, the non-Western civilizations have to be aware of both: the outside forces of cruelty and grief as well as the 'inner vectors' that have dislodged their true Selves. The non-Western cultures have to do much more than simply resist the West: they have to transform their cultures into cultures of resistance. And they have

---

[35] Nandy, *Traditions, Tyranny, and Utopias*, p. 21.
[36] Ibid., p. 22.

to rediscover their traditions of reinterpreting traditions to create new traditions—including new traditions of dissent.

DISSENT, DEFINITIONS

'For those who dare to defy the given models of defiance' reads the dedication in *Traditions, Tyranny and Utopias*, which is subtitled: 'Essays in the Politics of Awareness'.[37] Dissent, in Nandy's thought, is all about awareness. And any attempt at dissent must begin with two realizations. First, 'yesterday's dissent is often today's establishment and, unless resisted, becomes tomorrow's terror.'[38] Second, dissent itself has been colonized. The dissenters, the counter-players to the game of western imperialism and domination, work *within* the dominant model of universalism and *with* the dominant consciousness. Western categories and system of knowledge, argues Nandy, have been much more successful in ensuring dominance than naked political and economic power. The true power of the west lies not in its political and technological might, but in its power to define. The West defines what is freedom, history, human rights, dissent—the non-West must accept this definition. This unquestioned, and often unrecognized power of the West to define, and the game of categories the West plays with the non-West, ensures that dissent not only remains docile and confinable but serves as an illustration of its democratic spirit. Witness how easily the dominant academic culture took over 'disciplines' that began as attempts to break out of the straitjacket of conventional knowledge systems. Ecology, feminism and cultural studies have been successfully domesticated and professionalized as new specializations in the knowledge industry. Thus, by subtle but well-organized means, the dominant knowledge industry ensures that the capitals of dissent, along with the capitals of global political economy, are located in the stylish universities, think tanks and other intellectual centres of the First World. Domination is only complete when dissent can be foreseen and managed, and this cannot be done unless definitional criteria have been established to determine what is genuine and sober dissent, and these criteria have been systematically institutionalized through the

[37] Ibid., the dedication.
[38] Ibid., p. 13.

university system. This is what fashionable academic and intellectual trends, such as postmodernism, post-coloniality and poststructuralism, are designed to do. Appreciating how dissent is predicted and controlled, Nandy confesses,

> ...also explained to me some of my earlier disappointments with Western dissenters, particularly from the left. Many of them are not only eminent scholars in their own right but have brought up, with paternal concern, at least three generations of non-Western dissenting scholars, teaching them with loving care the meaning of 'true' dissent and the technology of 'authentic' radicalism. But copious tears shed for the Third World and its exploited masses, I was gradually to find out, rarely went with any respect for the Third World's own understanding of its own plight (as if that understanding had to be hidden like a family scandal from the outside world).[39]

The western ideal of cultural dissent is well presented by the story of fifteenth-century Aztec priests who were rounded up by their Spanish conquerors and given two choices: to convert or to die. The priests responded that if their gods were dead, as alleged by the Jesuit fathers, then they too would rather die. The Spanish lost no time in burning them at the stake. What would, Nandy asks, be the response of Brahmin priests if they were given the same choice? They would readily convert to Christianity; some of them would even write treatises praising the ruthless colonizers and their gods. However, their Christianity would soon reveal itself a minor variation of Hinduism. Why does the dominant culture regard the Aztec priests as models of courage and the Brahmin priests as hypocritical cowards? On one level, the answer is simple. After their last defiant act, the Aztec priests die leaving their killers to continue with their rampage and sing praises to their courage. But the Brahminic response ensures that 'unheroic cowards' are always there ready to make their presence felt when opportunity arises. The Aztec priests also set a good example, from the perspective of the dominant culture, for all dissenters to follow: die in glorified dissent.

There is also another answer. And it is this:

that the average Indian has always lived with the awareness and possibility of long-term suffering, always seen himself and protecting his deepest faith

---

[39] Ashis Nandy, 'Bearing Witness to the Future', *Futures 28*, no. 6–7 (August–September 1996), p. 638.

with the passive, 'feminine' cunning of the weak and the victimized, and surviving outer pressures by refusing to overplay his sense of autonomy and self-respect. At his heroic best, he is a *satyagrahi*, one who forges a partly-coercive weapon called *satyagraha* out of... 'perfect weakness.' In his non-heroic ordinariness, he is the archetypal survivor. Seemingly he makes all-round compromises, but he refuses to be psychologically swamped, co-opted or penetrated. Defeat, his response seems to say, is a disaster and so are the imposed ways of the victor. But worse is the loss of one's 'soul' and the internalization of one's victor, because it forces one to fight the victor according to the victor's values, within his model of dissent. Better to be a comical dissenter than to be a powerful, serious but acceptable opponent. Better to be a hated enemy, declared unworthy of any respect whatsoever, than to be a proper opponent, constantly making 'primary adjustments' to the system.[40]

By accepting a violent end to their dissent, the Aztec priests, Nandy seems to be saying, unwittingly collide with the world-view of their oppressors. In some celebrated non-western dissenters, this collusion is much more open and conscious. For example, violence has a central, cleansing role in Frantz Fanon's vision of a post-colonial society. This is why his vision, which is so alien to many Africans and Asians, has been so readily accepted in the West. Fanon argued that the oppressor is often internalized by the oppressed. So it becomes necessary for the oppressor to be confronted in violence not just to liberate oneself from his oppression but also to mark an agonizing break with a part of one's own self.[41] But, Nandy argues, if Fanon had more confidence in his culture (this is a problematic assertion as Fanon had no notion of what *his* culture was) he would have realized that his vision ties the victims more deeply to the culture of oppression than straightforward collaboration. By accepting the oppressors' principle of violence, the victims further internalize the basic values of the oppressors. And once violence is given cultural and intrinsic legitimacy, it transforms the battle between two visions and world-views into a struggle for power and resources between two groups with identical values. Thus those who are sinned against often end up sinning themselves.

The anti-violence stance, however, should not be confused with pacifism. Pacifism, like environmental consumerism, is often a

---

[40] Nandy, *The Intimate Enemy*, p. 111.
[41] Nandy, *Traditions, Tyranny, and Utopias*, p. 34.

luxury and can be a symbol of status. The rich and well-connected dodge the contaminated world of military violence more easily and skillfully. This ensures that those who are sent to fight distant wars to protect 'our national interests' are often the under-privileged and the marginalized. During the Vietnam war, for example, 'conscientious objectors' and draft dodgers were mostly well-to-do whites. Those who were shipped to fight in Vietnam were predominantly blacks and poor whites who 'neither had any respite from the system nor from their progressive, privileged fellow citizens protesting the war and feeling self-righteous.'[42] They were men who had experienced direct and institutionalized violence at home in the form of overt and latent racism, oppressive labour regulations and other discriminatory practices. The stereotyping of the 'commie' Vietcong and the genocidal behaviour of many of these soldiers is hardly surprising: 'the Vietnam war on this plane was a story of one set of victims setting upon another, on behalf of a reified, impersonal system of violence.'[43]

Beyond violence and pacifism, there is a third option: the dissenter as non-player. Here the oppressed, refusing to be a first-class citizen in the world of oppression, is neither a player nor a counter-player: he or she plays another game altogether, a game of building an alternative world where there is some hope of winning his or her humanity. And nobody plays this game better than Ashis Nandy himself.

It is a game of dissenting visions and futures. The future itself is a state of awareness. And the main aim of the game is to transform the future by changing human awareness of the future. By defining what is 'immutable' and 'universal', the West silences the visions of Other peoples and cultures to ensure the continuity of its own linear projections of the past and the present on to the future. By avoiding thinking about the future, Other cultures and societies become prisoners of the past, present and the future of Western civilization. As Thomas Szasz has declared, 'in the animal kingdom, the rule is, eat or be eaten; in the human kingdom, define or be defined.'[44] Non-Western cultures must define their own future in terms of their own categories and concepts, articulating

---

[42] Ibid., p. 31.

[43] Ibid., p. 31.

[44] Thomas Szasz, *The Second Sin* (London: Routledge and Kegan Paul, 1974), p. 20.

their visions in language that is true to their own Self even if not comprehensible 'on the other side of the global fence of academic respectability.'[45] The plurality of dissent can only be ensured if human choices are expanded by 'reconceptualizing political, social and cultural ends; by identifying emerging or previously ignored social pathologies that have to be understood, contained or transcended; by linking up the fates of different polities and societies through envisioning their common fears and hopes.'[46]

Et Cetera

Hope is perhaps the last weapon in the armoury of those who reside outside the 'civilized' world. But hope alone is not enough: 'the meek inherit the earth not by meekness alone.'[47] Nandy seeks to furnish the victims with a host of other tools that have always been there but have either been overlooked or been buried under the mental construction of internalized colonialism and modernity.

While much of Nandy's thought has been directed towards colonialism and modernity, and their disciplinary and intellectual offshoots, its hallmark has been consistency. Ashis Nandy is nothing if not totally consistent. This is not to say that he has not modified his ideas, refined and sharpened them, or that he is not aware of his own failures. For example, in the preface to the second edition of *Alternative Sciences*, he provides a critique of the book pointing out where it has failed, where he has refined his ideas and where it could be improved if he were to rewrite it. He is consistent in two senses. Firstly, he is always true to his own roots. His ideas are a distillation of the plurality of India, they emerge from examinations of all things Indian, and he tends to rely almost exclusively on Indian myths and categories for his analysis as well as Indian examples for his explanation. Anyone who has seen Nandy in action at a seminar or a conference knows that he is totally open to ideas whatever their source and is attracted by the power of ideas to move people and societies. In particular, and in line with his own position, he relishes the ideas that seek to sabotage his own position. He is ever ready to grant that his ideas

[45] Nandy, 'Bearing Witness to the Future', p. 638.
[46] Ibid., p. 637.
[47] Nandy, *The Intimate Enemy*, p. xiii.

may become irrelevant by new readings of traditional visions or by new visions with a changed perception of evil. But he measures the quality of ideas by their non-dualistic content and the import they may have on the victims of manufactured oppression. In this respect, he is a true friend of all victims—everywhere.

Secondly, he is consistent in the application of his critique and equally harsh on both the West and the non-West. Unlike the British colonial attitude to Indian culture—which, on the one hand accused the Indians of being this worldly (exceedingly shrewd, greedy, self-centred, money-minded) and on the other hand saw them as overtly other-worldly (too concerned with spirituality, mysticism and transcendence), not fit for the world of modern science and technology, statecraft and productive work—Nandy sees India as a consistent whole. He is not concerned with romanticizing Indian tradition and is as interested in the warts as in the beauty spots. As such, he is always eager to expose the folly of fossilized, suffocating tradition ('the blood-stained, oppressive heritage of a number of oriental religious ideologies') as well as tradition constructed under the impulse of modernity (so 'immaculate in the hands of their contemporary interpreters'). It is this consistency in Nandy that makes him truer to his own Self.

What more could one possibly ask from a *real* intellectual?

11

In the Interstices of Tradition and Modernity: Exploring Ashis Nandy's Clandestine and Incommunicable Selves

Makarand Paranjape

INTRODUCTION: ASHIS AND NANDY

This essay is itself split into two parts, mirroring a certain fragmentation in my approach to Ashis Nandy and his work. The first part, which is a personal appreciation of Nandy, is motivated not only by an urge to repay a debt, but by the desire to notice and applaud a presence like his in Indian academic life. The second part shifts discursive gears to critique Nandy's work by recovering what I stumbled upon quite inadvertently—a secret self which lurks beneath much of his writing. These two selves that I shall expose may be termed Ashis and Nandy respectively. I hope, however, that the two parts of the essay, which are meant respectively to reflect these two selves, together overcome, somewhat like the integrative doubles so dear to Nandy, the discontinuities that such a structure might convey.[1] My modest project here is not only

---

[1] For the idea of integrative doubles, see 'An Intelligent Critic's Guide to Indian Cinema,' in Nandy's *The Savage Freud*. My novel, *The Narrator: A Novel* (Delhi: Rupa and Co., 1995), which, incidentally, was published in the same year as Nandy's book, can be read as an extended illustration of Nandy's thesis; of course, I hadn't realized this until I read Nandy's essay much after my novel was published. This is just one more instance of how powerful and 'true'

to articulate the ambiguities and contradictions in my response to Nandy, but to uncover what I see as a schism in his life and work. In other words, I am interested in investigating the kind of 'self-representation and self-engineering'[2]—to use Nandy's words again—that go on in his work.

INSPIRING PRESENCE: THE IMPORTANCE OF BEING ASHIS

I first met Ashis-da on 20 June 1991 to give him a manuscript copy of a book I was working on. Several friends had told me that he was the best person to respond to a book like this. What amazed me when I called him up, was his eager willingness to see me. There is something about intellectuals and academics which, the more famous they get, makes them the more remote and isolated, but Ashis-da was just the opposite. He was utterly approachable, though he was probably busier than most of his peers. He thumbed through my manuscript and commented in his typical way, 'Very interesting..!' The unmistakable overlay of the Bengali accent, the broad, bearded Socratic face, and the light, dancing eyes—all these set me at ease instantly. There was nothing forbidding or formidable about him. If anything he was unassuming and disarming with a subtle sense of humour and a robust and easy laughter. Here was a man who seemed to have a special relationship with ideas; he knew each of them by name, as it were, he invited them into his mind and into his study; he introduced them to his friends and visitors; and he was actually excited by them. Clearly, Ashis-da's intellectual imagination was extremely fertile; here new ways of looking at the world jostled for space with wisdom gleaned from age-old traditions. I felt considerably reassured after our forty-minute meeting.

A few months later, when I called him up again, he said, 'Makarand, I liked your book. It's very unusual, quite refreshing.'

Nandy's ideas are; you don't realize you've been living them until he points it out.

[2] The phase occurs in the essay 'Themes of State, History, and Exile in South Asian Politics: Modernity and the Landscape of Clandestine and Incommunicable Selves', in Vinay Lal, (ed.), *Plural Worlds, Multiple Selves; Ashis Nandy and the Post-Colombian Future*, Special Issue of *Emergences*, nos. 7–8 (1995–6), p. 104.

He paused for a minute, then, in closing said very casually, almost as an afterthought, 'I asked a couple of friends to look at it—I hope you don't mind. You may hear from them soon.' I had no idea what he was hinting at until I received, quite out of the blue, a letter from Primila Lewis, then the commissioning editor of Sage Publications, expressing an interest in my book. To say that I was taken aback would be an understatement. The fact was that I was at my wit's end trying to think of which publisher to send my book to. The book itself was an attempt to rethink the idea of *Swaraj* in the present Indian context. It tried to create a neo-Gandhian space on current debates on decolonization and development. What is more, the whole of it was written in the form of a dialogue between an imaginary student and teacher, not only as a take-off on the dialogue between the Reader and the Editor in Gandhi's *Hind Swaraj*, but also as a conscious attempt to bypass, if not subvert, the dominant academic discourse. This discourse, I had long realized, denied validity or legitimacy to any form of dissent which did not meet its own specifications and terms. Who would, I wondered, countenance, let alone sponsor what was obviously my 'unripe cognition'? One had, it seemed, either to be a Gandhi, who didn't mind resorting to *The Indian Opinion*, a periodical which few Englishmen would be expected to read, or be one of the 'official' critics of the West, fed and maintained by it. So, when the letter from Sage came, I had been bracing myself for a long and frustrating engagement with the publishing profession, if not an outright rejection, in an attempt to find a taker for a project like this. The book, as it happened, had already been turned down by the Gandhi Peace Foundation, which I had first approached.

One of the things which Primila wanted, if Sage were to publish the book, was some kind of an Introduction by Nandy himself. Of course, I would have to respond to the comments of referees and to make some of the changes they might suggest. I readily agreed to the second condition, but was not sure about the first. Hesitatingly, I asked Ashis-da if he would help. Again, the alacrity with which he gave his consent was as unexpected as it was gratifying. From that point, things moved pretty fast. The comments from the referees came, the book was accepted by Sage, and, finally, Ashis-da's Foreword also came in. It was what he called a 'Trialogue', a conversation between three generations whose participants were Gandhi himself, his son Harilal, and Nandy, who stood in the place of a grandson and reclaimed the bruised and battered legacy of his putative grandfather after the reaction and rejection by the son, Harilal. I have often felt, in retrospect, that Ashis-da's masterly Foreword was the best part of my book.[3]

I have begun on this personal note not only to acknowledge, once again, my debt to Ashis-da—a debt, which is not just intellectual, but personal—but really to suggest that what he did for me was not an isolated instance of his kindness but the usual manner of his functioning. What makes Ashis-da's role in contemporary Indian academics so unique is not just the impact of his ideas, which is indeed considerable, but his personal and professional presence. He has inspired, nurtured, and launched several papers, seminars, books, and, even careers. He has encouraged and shaped scores of young minds, enabling them to develop, prosper, and flourish, even to the point of outgrowing or rejecting him. There is in him a remarkable lack of animosity towards those who disagree with him, though any normal person would consider the actions of some of these detractors to be nothing short of a betrayal. He has consistently taken unpopular positions, subjected himself to unprecedented risks, faced hostility and criticism with unfazed indifference, and consistently fought for causes he's believed in. But, what is more, he has helped create room for an authentic criticism, a middle ground, a form of dissent which requires neither the extraordinary personal courage of a Gandhi nor the knee-jerk conformity of most postcolonial academics—a space, as it were, which is neither left nor right, neither entirely traditional nor assertively modern, which can help ordinary intellectuals dare to make a meaningful intervention without compromising their dignity or self-respect.

Ashis-da, a soft-spoken, unassertive, even gentle person, may not, in himself, be a formidable personality, but the range of his intellectual interests is indeed profound and formidable. Political theory, psychology, biography, literature, cinema, urban sociology, colonialism, science and technology, governance, communalism, cricket, disarmament, global futures—there is scarcely an area of contemporary Indian culture that he has left untouched. His approach, moreover, is always innovative, interdisciplinary in a manner which is quite different from the usual connotations of

---

[3] See 'Trialogue as Foreword' to my book *Decolonization and Development: Hind Svaraj Revisioned* (New Delhi: Sage Publications, 1993) pp. 7–13.

the word. Interdisciplinarity, ordinarily, only means 'perpetrating the follies of more than one discipline in one's work,' as my friend Vinay Lal would put it. What, then, is Ashis-da's discipline? It is, in my view, the whole challenge of living in the contemporary world. To lead an authentic, meaningful, proactive, and compassionate life in a world such as ours requires an enormously complex and multifaceted wisdom, which Ashis-da's work has come to embody. That is why to say that every book of his cuts new ground is not enough; actually, he epitomizes both the need and the validity of a new academic paradigm. Lal has placed his work in the rubric of Cultural Studies, but even that has a narrowly Anglo-American ring to it. Perhaps, Nandy can best be described as a critic in the broadest sense of the word, a critic of culture, society and knowledge systems. This is not all. His work combines ideology and activism in strange and purposeful ways, thereby transcending the gulf between theory and practice.

All these factors make him an unparalleled presence and force in contemporary Indian academics. Not only is he easily the most gifted, innovative, and versatile of our social theorists, he has also exerted a great and beneficial influence on the course of India's intellectual enterprise in the last three decades. He has made a significant difference to our lives.

ESPOUSING TRADITION: NANDY'S MODERN DILEMMAS

Arguably, a good deal of the charge in, and impact of Nandy's work derives from his critique of modernity. But what makes his dissent so interesting even unique, is his ability to defy, as he himself puts it, 'the given models of defiance'.[4] For instance, Nandy fights colonialism and neo-colonialism, but not from the usual, largely Marxian positions. Instead, the fabric of his resistance seems to be cut from a different cloth—call it khadi if you like. Nandy rehabilitates Gandhi, but not from the usual moralistic, pious, or hagiographic motives; instead, he gives us a Gandhi who is sharp, savvy, contemporary, and an incorrigible gadfly, a clever, inventive, innovative, and playful Gandhi, an inveterate dissenter,

[4] This phrase, which I believe is rather obviously self-reflexive, is from Nandy's dedication in *Traditions, Tyrannies, and Utopias: Essays in the Politics of Awareness* (Delhi: Oxford University Press, 1987).

in brief, a thinking and thinker's Gandhi—a born postmodernist, almost. Again, whether it is sati or the destruction of the Babri Masjid, Nandy's outrage springs from what might best be termed the resources of tradition, not the prejudices of modernity. Similarly, whether he trains his critical sights on science or the state, Nandy seems to draw sustenance from non-modern sources. The modern condition for Nandy is a deeply flawed one, marred by great hubris and ignorance, unspeakable violence and triage; it sports islands of affluence surrounded by oceans of suffering and deprivation, a handful of victors and a legion of victims. And yet, Nandy has consistently argued against the victims turning victors, the oppressed emulating their oppressors, the downtrodden in turn, treading down on others.

This century has shown that in every situation of organized oppression the true antonyms are always the exclusive part versus the inclusive whole—not masculinity versus femininity but either versus androgyny, not the past versus the present but either of them versus the timelessness in which the past is the present and the present is the past, not the oppressor versus the oppressed but both of them versus the rationality which turns them into co-victims.[5] Consistently, Nandy advocates a third way, the way of reconciliation and compassion, of bearing witness and assuming responsibility, even of courage and self-sacrifice, to the point when both the victors and the vanquished may be transformed, seeing themselves in a new light.

In the process, like Gandhi, he has invariably espoused the cause of the rejects of development, the outcastes of modernity, the untouchables of our times—including demonized minorities, peasants and workers colonized by communalism, even the so-called terrorists, the most loathed figures in the vocabulary of the arrogant and self-serving nation state. The source of Nandy's optimism is the strength of 'living traditions' or what he calls a world view 'rooted in ancient wisdom and inherited cosmology'.[6] This, for him, is the source of the sanity of the common folk. These

---

[5] Ashis Nandy, *The Intimate Enemy. Loss and Recovery of Self Under Colonialism* (Delhi: Oxford University Press, 1983), p. 99.

[6] See Nandy, 'Cultural Frames for Social Intervention: A Personal Credo.' *Indian Philosophical Quarterly* 11, no. 4 (October 1984), p. 416; *The Intimate Enemy*, p. 100.

millions of unsung heroes and heroines, for Nandy, are the genuine protagonists of history, because it is they who exemplify the compromising Indian of 'fluid self-definition', who seeks to be not the hero, but the survivor of history. This is how the majority of the colonized, with their yielding, 'feminine,' undivided, and plural-cultural selves, saved our culture from annihilation. It is precisely such unself-conscious resistance which modernity seeks to undo and destroy. The process of modernization, then, is nothing short of a violation and disruption of this integrated self, yielding in turn, violent, fragmented, ever dissatisfied entities that seek completion and solace through violence and destruction. This, in a nutshell, is how I read Nandy's cultural psychologism, the perennial current from which he draws his intellectual nourishment, the sponsoring agency, as it were, of his theoretical expeditions.

It would, I think, be quite uncharitable to consider Nandy's valuable locutions to be nothing more than an echo of the West's own critique of itself. Such, indeed, has been the reductive accusation of some of his numerous detractors. Others have, of course, accused him of worse—intellectual hypocrisy and chicanery. My friends in the Left tend especially to be dismissive— 'Nandy is a fraud'—they say sneeringly; and, as if to clinch the point beyond argument, they add: 'he only sells abroad, not in India'. When confronted with some of these diatribes, Nandy's reaction has been characterized as much by devastating candour as by wry humour: 'The problem with the Left is that they are not democratic; the only way they can survive is by debunking and discrediting all those who disagree with them.' Besides this, the criticism is wrong: Nandy is among India's two or three best-selling academic writers, as Oxford University Press, his publishers, would testify only too readily.

Let me, therefore, abandon these tired and worn-out animadversions. Instead of attacking Nandy for not being modern or secular enough, let me interrogate him for not being traditional or spiritual enough. Secular modernity, admittedly, becomes the number one enemy in most of Nandy's work, bearing the brunt of much of his ire. At its door are laid most of our present-day ills. The breakdown of tradition social orders, the emergence of massified and deracinated elites, the cynical abuse of a semi-modern lumpen class by these elites for their own purposes—these would be some of the causes of our contemporary disorders. If so, what might seem to be the logical solution? Wouldn't it be the kind of spiritual turn that most modern Indian leaders are supposed to have taken? Not so, for Nandy. Anyone who takes that kind of turn immediately becomes suspect in Nandy's eyes, even more so if this individual seems to endorse some form of high Hinduism: 'Defiance need not always be self-conscious. It need not be always backed by the ardent murderous, moral passions in which the monotheistic faiths, and increasingly the more modern and nationalist versions of Hinduism, specialize'.[7]

In the process of creating his unique critical credo, Nandy has, without question, moved way out of his liberal, though strictly Protestant, upbringing. Coming from a family of Methodists, Nandy has not only grown out of the religion of his forefathers, but reverted to what might be termed a kind of non-denominational, non-believing 'Hinduism'. I say 'Hinduism' because I cannot call Nandy anything else—not Methodist, not Protestant, not Christian, not Muslim, not Jewish, and not secular modernist either. This makes him a kind of Hindu—sort of a convert who has lapsed back into the faith of his ancestors. I say 'faith' and not religion, because Nandy has little use for organized religion of any kind.

While Nandy cannot be considered a practising Christian, he is only distinctly uncomfortable, as I said earlier, with any overt kind of Hinduism: 'to use the term Hindu to self-define is to flout the traditional self-definition of the Hindu, and to assert aggressively one's Hinduism is to very nearly deny one's Hinduness'.[8] The very word, Hindu, for Nandy is sort of contradiction in terms. About his own identity, Nandy would say that he is not a traditionalist, but a 'critical traditionalist'.[9] That is why, for instance, he says that Gandhi interests him, but not Vinoba.[10]

Again, I suspect, that explains why he has not been enthusiastic about Pandurang Shastri Athavale's Swadhyaya movement. I

[7] Nandy, *The Intimate Enemy*, p. 98.

[8] Ibid., p. 103.

[9] Nandy, 'Cultural Frames for Social Intervention', p. 415.

[10] 'I've always been fascinated by this issue of "hard" versus "soft", thus my interest in Gandhi. I am not interested in Vinoba Bhave.' See 'Ashis Nandy in Conversation with Vinay Lal' in Lal (ed.), *Plural Worlds, Multiple Selves*, p. 63.

reckon that Nandy does not find such movements intellectually stimulating. About Swadhyaya, he told me, 'It's OK as long as Dada is around. After that it'll peter out.' It was as if he was trying to avoid coming to terms with it because it was a charismatic movement, inspired by the presence and personality of Dada, as much as by the latter's ideas. Similarly, I have perceived a distinctive discomfort in Nandy when it comes to figures like Ananda Coomaraswamy, Raja Rao, or, even, A. K. Saran. The purism of these traditionalists does not appeal to Nandy. A bit like Salman Rushdie, what inspires Nandy are hybrids, mixtures, overlaps—different kinds of impurities. As he says in his Preface to the *Intimate Enemy*, 'I have deliberately focused on the living traditions, emphasizing the dialectic between the classical, the pure and the high-status on the one hand, and the folksy, hybrid and the low-brow on the other.[11] He believes that the impurities save us because they humanize us. It is to be expected, then, that Nandy reads Gandhi in this 'impure' fashion. The Gandhi who was the ascetic, moralist, purist, faddist, and so on, is of little interest to Nandy. It is the Gandhi who was a rebel, iconoclast, reinterpreter of tradition, critic of modernity, the Gandhi who was Hindu, Muslim, Christian at the same time, who was no doubt a traditionalist, but also a radical modernizer, in short, the maverick Gandhi, who appeals to Nandy.

The difficulty, however, is that these two strands, the Great and the Little traditions, if you will, or *Marga* and *Desi*, cannot be, properly speaking separated. True, one can be played off against the other, but both together, in all their interpenetrations, constitute the *parampara* of *sanatana dharma*. I fear that Nandy's rhetoric often blurs this fact and creates binary oppositions between them. Thus, 'high' Hinduism, with its hypermasculine, semitizing, and militant tendencies becomes the villain, while the feminine, folk, culturally rooted, reasonably self-confident, living Hinduism of the masses is the saviour of Indian pluralism. In practice, however, this dangerous and distorted 'high-Hinduism' is almost impossible to find; so much so, that it seems like a creation of our intellectuals, who require a well-defined enemy. These same high-Hindus, it turns out, usually accept multiple self-definitions, worship at numerous shrines, accept Sri Ramakrishna, Sai Baba, and Gandhi,

[11] Nandy, *The Intimate Enemy*, p. xviii.

and are not known to maintain prolonged periods of rage against their favourite adversaries. The mass-hysteria and frenzy that was the precondition for the destruction of the Babri Masjid could not be sustained for long afterwards; clearly it was something alien to the Hindu psyche and artificially whipped up. This has been proven time and again by election results which show that Indians cannot be mobilized around any one divisive issue like religion, caste, or community. Even the politics of creating vote-banks must constantly adjust its hate-manufacturing engines to this fact.

Yet, while it is true that aggressive, fanatical, intolerant high-Hinduism is a shaky and unstable entity, always on the verge of lapsing back into its more amorphous, placid, and non-aggressive stable state, it is equally true that the Hindu psyche does suffer from a sense of insecurity that comes from its sense of having suffered centuries of humiliation and injury. It is this wounded psyche which needs to be healed, but finds its hurts further aggravated by what it sees as the self-deluding, intransigent minoritarianism of Muslim leadership in India. No wonder, the revivalism of the nineteenth century is seen by most Hindus as a necessary step in a process of self-recovery. To valorize Ramakrishna and Gandhi but to critique Bankim, Vivekananda, or Aurobindo does not solve the problem because most Hindus accept both sides. Yes, it is indeed possible to draw a line when it comes to Savarkar or Golwalkar, but even this line gets blurred when we discover that cultural nationalism of the latter embraces most of those who opposed it; indeed, unlike the rationalist and 'non-believing' Savarkar, Golwalkar was a 'practising' Hindu, who had received his spiritual initiation from a senior monk of the Ramakrishna order. The fact is that the overlap between Hindutva and Hinduism can be considerable; it is only a very narrow and sharp-edged version of the former which is incompatible with the latter.

I would argue that Nandy's work does not take adequate cognizance of this overlap. A book such as *Creating a Nationality: the Ramjanmabhumi Movement and the Fear of the Self*, co-authored with Shikha Trivedy, Shail Mayaram, and Achyut Yagnik, best highlights some of the difficulties in Nandy's approach.[12] The 'bad guys' are clearly identified: nationalism and communalism, broadly speaking, but more specifically, the breakdown of cultural and

---

[12] Delhi (Oxford University Press, 1995).

social ties across communities, the emergence of a modern, massified, elitist version of religion, and the ascendancy of a politicized modern and semi-modern middle class. Nandy's hatred of modernity and his deep suspicion of social and cultural elités is obvious in a book like this. But the problem is that elité religious practices have a close and complex relationship with the 'everyday faith' which Nandy eulogizes. Laying the blame for the riots at the door of secular modernity only shifts the burden of guilt. Redefining terms and boundaries does help in clarifying one's concept and beliefs, but does not necessarily make the problem go away.

Whether it is communalism or modernity, both interrelated problems of course, there is a certain hard core to them, which I fear Nandy's thought does not engage with adequately. The hard core has to do with certain struggles between incommensurables which must be resolved, at times, the bloody and difficult way. Gandhi was aware of this and did not hesitate to engage with it. He knew that there was enough ammunition of accumulated hatred and misunderstanding between the two communities to create a terrible conflagration. He knew, first-hand, how horribly violent a struggle to resolve their differences might be. That is why what he proposed was nothing short of a new faith for Hindustanis, a faith which would take Hindus and Muslims beyond the conventional boundaries of their respective religions and allow them to embrace one another on common theistic and cultural ground. This invitation was accepted only partially. Unfortunately, large sections of both Hindus and Muslims chose not to participate in Gandhi's solution. The result was the blood bath of Partition. But the struggle between the stubborn elements in both communities has not yet been resolved. It has a deadly logic which, it would seem, will be played out. It is my fear that Nandy's social and political theories evade this hard core precisely because they celebrate and exemplify a femininity and softness which are so crucial for the survival of a civilization. But, what this entails is that in place of Gandhi's purposeful and effective androgyny, we have Nandy's emasculated and ineffective theoretic.

When we move from Nandy's work to his life, some of the contradictions that I have outlined become even more evident. Nandy loves technology—that is, he loves playing with the latest gadgets, whether these are laptop computers or electronic diaries.

Similarly, he enjoys computer games and net-surfing. Moreover, there is an evident relish in his approach to certain aspects of the modern, cosmopolitan experience. At the same time, Nandy has little or no attraction to actually living a traditional life—whatever that might mean. That is, he has no tradition to speak of with which he himself can be connected, except the modern, bourgeois tradition of the Westernized Bengali elites. There is hardly anything prior to that that is a part of his life. The practice of any overt spiritual *sadhana*, too, would be alien to his personality. I cannot imagine him doing japa, or Yoga, or mediation, or going to any guru or ashram.[13] Rather, he is more comfortable discussing politics over Scotch, with a half-smoked pipe in his hand. To put it simply, there is nothing remotely traditional or spiritual about Nandy, though he constantly speaks on behalf of tradition and of what might be termed the truly religious approach to life. The fact is that Nandy is located both personally and ideologically in the realm of the secular and the modern, both of which he criticizes consistently and mercilessly. It would appear that he is allergic to the dominant versions of both modernity and secularism. To oppose them he takes recourse to tradition and its religious resources. And yet, he cannot be seen as a traditional or religious person himself.

Now, unless we find a way out of this paradox, a good deal of the work that Nandy has done will be open to question on precisely the grounds that he uses to critique modernity and secularism. If his life and work do not display a consistency and coherence, the very space that his criticism occupies will be suspect. After all, one way to characterize modernity is that it creates a dichotomy between the personal and the public, thus giving rise to ideologues, not exemplars. The traditional person, on the other hand, shows a consistency between *anubhav*, *vichar*, and *achar*—between experience, thought, and deed. That is, a traditional person's thought is consistent with his experience, and his actions are consistent with both thought and experience.[14]

[13] Even the way he uses a word like 'self-transcendence' is entirely secular. See Lal (ed.), *Plural Works, Multiple Selves*, p. 31.

[14] I owe these concepts to the late K. J. Shah, a philosopher whom Nandy also admires. For an introduction to his ideas, see 'Philosophy, Religion, Morality, Spirituality: Some Issues,' *Journal of the Indian Council of Philosophical Research* 7, no. 2 (1990), pp. 1–12.

Without clarifying Nandy's own relationship to the traditional and to the religious, the viability of his own position will be undermined.

Conclusion: Nandy's Modern Tradition

I hope to reconcile the two selves of Ashis Nandy by proposing that Nandy's redefinitions and reappropriations of tradition are fairly modern.[15] That is, Nandy's episteme is a modern one, but rather different from the predatory, dominant version. The key to Nandy's mind, in my view, is the word 'criticism.' Nandy's work is, above all, a form of criticism. It helps us rethink categories, change our perception of things, and, eventually, look at the world afresh. Criticism of this kind is very much a modern thing, a child of the European Enlightenment. It is not that critical rationality was entirely absent in traditional societies. As Nandy himself says, 'Indian thought, including many of is folk elements, can be and has been used as a critical base, because critical rationality is neither the monopoly of modern times nor that of the Greaco-Roman tradition.[16] Yet, the crucial difference is that traditional criticism was usually stereological, linked to *moksha, jnana, kevalya, nirvana,* or some such goal. Or else, it was 'practical wisdom' as in the *Panchatantra* or the *Hitopadesha*. No doubt, there is much critical discrimination in Buddhism, as there is in Sankara, Basava, Kabir, Tukaram, Vivekananda, and, of course, Gandhi. But when it comes to Nandy, it is the criticism that is appealing to him, not the spiritual idealism. If Nandy had to choose between tradition and criticism, he would, I believe, choose the latter. A tradition which has lost its ability to critique itself, for Nandy, would be no living tradition at all, certainly not a tradition worth saving. That is why sometimes I feel that it would be more

---

[15] I believe my friend, the late D. R. Nagaraj, has made a similar point in his Prologue to Nandy's *Exiled at Home* (Delhi: Oxford University Press, 1998). I haven't read the piece itself but a reference to it appears in Ramachandra Guha's tribute to Nagaraj, 'From one universe to another,' *The Hindu Literary Supplement*, 6 September 1998: x. Nagaraj asks for a 'critique of the project of modernity from those intellectual, emotional, symbolic and semiotic structures which exist beyond its reaches' (x).

[16] Nandy, 'Cultural Frames for Social Intervention', p. 415,

accurate to describe Nandy as a critical, if not crypto-modernist, than a critical traditionalist.[17.]

The fact of the matter is that Nandy doesn't conform to his own self-definitions: neither a critical traditionalist nor a critical modernist, he is something in between. As I said earlier, it is his criticism that is crucial, not his traditionalism or modernity. On deeper examination, it is even possible to make a tentative formulation of what might be termed Nandy's faith. For I believe that Nandy does have a faith of his own, a version of his own identity which takes into account the supra-rational and the supernatural. I think Nandy's faith is a type of humanism which has the following features: (i) it is sensitive to its pasts; (ii) it acknowledges both its local and civilizational heritage; (iii) and, yet, it is non-sectarian and non-ritualistic. If Nandy had his way, he would invent a new, non-denominational ritual and liturgy, even using Sanskrit if necessary, for himself and other people like him. In fact, the beginnings of this were evidenced in the wedding ceremony of his daughter, Aditi. The Sanskrit mantras, chosen by Nandy himself, were spiritual without being religious or denominational.

At this juncture, it might be fruitful to invoke another of tradition's prodigal sons, Ramachandra Gandhi. Ramubhai, who started his intellectual life as an analytical philosopher, was reclaimed to Indian philosophical traditions by the greatest mind-slayer of this century, Sri Ramanna Maharishi. Ramubhai once told me that unlike many other traditional people he does not believe that secular modernity affords no enlightened space for an individual, but, he added that that space is rather rare and difficult to occupy, and also that it is certainly not the only enlightened space that there is in human experience. I believe that Nandy's position approximates this enlightened space within the secular and the

---

[17] Nandy calls this tendency 'the modernist's dislike for modernity' which is 'a unique feature and mark of modernity'; similarly, he says 'modernity at its most creative cannot do without its opposite: anti-modernity' ('Cultural Frames', p. 412). Nandy uses the term 'critical modernists' in a rather limited sense of those who 'do not challenge the content of modern science' and 'take for granted the modern nation-state system' (ibid., 413). Certainly, Nandy isn't a critical modernist in this sense, but then, he is not an outsider to modernity either, as were Blake, Carlyle, Emerson, Thoreau, Ruskin, Tolstoy, or Gandhi, whom he mentions (ibid.).

modern. Unlike a *sanatani* Hindu, Nandy has inherited no ritual that he can continue with ease from his own Methodist background; nor, at the same time has he felt a necessity to cross over to the rituals of any other tradition. Perhaps, this is the real difference between someone like him and Ramubhai. While the latter found more than one ready-made path in his own tradition to which he could revert to, Nandy discovered that his own secular profession to be more engaging and rewarding than any traditional *sadhana*. That is why, it seems to me, he has accepted the rituals and protocols of his position as a modern academic—an intellectual street-fighter, as he sometimes calls himself. That is where his passion and penance find their raison d'être.

Ultimately, if I were to describe Nandy in a couple of words, I could call him an inverted reformist. He best belongs to the tradition of social reformers in India, but unlike those of the nineteenth and early twentieth centuries, he does not use modernity to reform tradition, but tradition to reform modernity. Like Gandhi, he believes that it is modernity that has gone too far in its violence and rapacity and that it is tradition which needs to be restored to its rightful place as a source of wisdom and sustainable lifestyles. It was Gandhi who reversed the direction of reform, but Gandhi was equally critical of both tradition and modernity and used each against the other. Nandy does little to critique tradition but instead wages war against modernity; yet, unlike Gandhi, he does not use a religious or traditional idiom to do so. Indeed I would call Nandy the Brahmo or Protestant among Hindu intellectuals. He shares a traditional, even spiritual and theistic space with the latter, but refuses to go all the way to succumbing to any prescribed rituals of *sadhana* or self-culture.

No wonder, beyond a point, Nandy's collusion with modernity is rather deceptive and misleading. As he himself says, 'what looks like Westernization is often only a means of domesticating the West, sometimes by reducing the West to the level of the comic and the trival.'[18] Nandy is a cultural hero precisely because he fights against a mighty adversary but emerges undefeated, even if not obviously triumphant. 'Seemingly he makes all-round compromise,' wrote Nandy of the average Indian in words that seem to offer a self-description, 'but he refuses to be psychologically

---

[18] Nandy, *The Intimate Enemy*, p. 108.

swamped, co-opted or penetrated'.[19] Nandy continues to receive lucrative offers from the metropolitan academy, visits abroad regularly, but refuses to leave his home, India. His career, unlike that of Gayatri Chakravorty Spivak or Homi Bhabha, is thus not a metropolitan success story, but an Indian, homespun one. Hence, his biculturalism is of an enabling, empowering kind for the Indian academy, unlike that of the others who make good abroad, only by paying the price of joining the dominant system.

Yet, however much Nandy respects traditional wisdom, his means and methods are primarily intellectual. So, though he is aware of deeper wellsprings of strength and inspiration, he does not attempt to find sustenance in them. As D. R. Nagaraj put it, Nandy has difficulties 'in getting into the symbolic and philosophical universes of Nagarjuna, Shankara, Sarhapada or even of pre-Enlightenment Christian thinkers and mystics' (quoted in Guha x). This has led me to wonder if his work has reached a plateau, if not a dead end: has his creative curve turned into an asymptote, the dreaded flattening-out after a long and exponential rise? It seems as if his project is not moving ahead or up, but spreading itself sideways or horizontally. A publication of a volume like this is itself a sign not only of a certain level of intellectual attainment, but of the achievement of a completion of thought. Perhaps, the things that have guided and inspired him so far may now be insufficient to people or produce new work of the same calibre, intensity, or profundity. Restless as he is, Nandy is sure to reinvent himself, to find fresh pastures for his foraging mind, but if he can touch what is really *sanatana* or eternal in tradition, I think even his work on alternative futures will have the kind of ripeness and potency that will promote him from the brotherhood of reformers to the fellowship of sages and boddhisattvas. The latter, for me, is the only true tradition of the human race, the only tradition, that, in the ultimate analysis, is worth belonging to.

---

[19] Ibid., p. 111.

12

The Modern Indian Intellectual and the Problem of the Past: An Engagement with the Thoughts of Ashis Nandy

Dipesh Chakrabarty

Whatever else it may mean for those who do not explicitly set out to intellectualize, embracing modernity has always posed a question to the Indian intellectual since the middle of the nineteenth century: what does one do with, or about those practices of the past which seem undesirable but which have nevertheless refused to die? Consider the undemocratic and cruel practice of caste-discrimination or the practice of sati among upper-caste Hindus in India. It is far from certain that these practices are extinct as practices even in educated milieus (sati, of course, being far, far less common than caste-discrimination). Or try and imagine the numerous instances of everyday incidents when people in the subcontinent invoke the supernatural, whether in newspaper columns on astrology or in the cause of a political movement. All academic intellectuals in India—like intellectuals in many other Third-World countries—would have grown up with some of these practices being conducted in their surroundings, if not in the heart of their own immediate families. These experiences may form the 'innocent' stuff of childhood memories. But they also may not be so innocent, after all, as when the 'supernatural' event of images of the god Ganesh drinking milk gets a political interpretation justifying a militantly Hindu and anti-Muslim political movement, or when astrology or indigenous medicine act as the excuse for sheer commercial exploitation of the needy or the poor. This experience of being a modern intellectual in an India in which undesirable practices from the past seem to help produce deformities in the modern, gives that modernity a peculiar edge. The intellectual has an ambivalent relationship to the past, whether this past is embodied in rural India or in one's older relatives. This can be seen in the problem of defining 'tradition'. Should 'tradition' include all of the past? Or should it only include those bits of the past that meet with our approval today? Should the aim of education be to educate people out of the practices that are contrary to the principles of modernity, to move them away from activities or ideas that scientific rationality, democratic politics, and modern aesthetics find disturbing if not downright repulsive?

It is only rarely that Indian intellectuals have addressed this problem in a self-conscious manner though it often erupts in what they write about the past. In the brief span of this short essay on Ashis Nandy, who, more than anybody else in India, has drawn our attention to the questions the very idea of 'tradition' poses to all modernizers/cultural critics of the subcontinent, I will endeavour to show how the question I began with—the problem of the undesirable past—configures itself in Nandy's work.

Much of Nandy's admirable and powerful critique of modernity strikes me as decisionist in spirit. By 'decisionism', I mean a disposition which allows the critic to talk about the future and the past as though there were concrete, value-laden choices or decisions to be made with regard to both. The critic is guided by his or her values as to what the most desirable, sane and wise future for humanity should be, and looks to the past as a warehouse of resources on which to draw as needed. This position is different from the revolutionary-modernist position—that of early Ambedkar, for instance, in his polemic against Gandhi about the (de)merits of caste—in which the reformer seeks to bring (a particular) history to a nullity in order to build society up from scratch. The decisionist position, on the other hand, respects the past but is not bound by it. It uses tradition but the use is guided by the critique it has developed of the present. It thus represents a peculiar freedom from history while it is respectful of the past. In discussing Gandhi—in many ways, the person who comes closest to Nandy's idea of a wise political leader—Nandy calls this 'critical tradition-alism'. Critical traditionalism, according to Nandy, is also different from uncritical adulation of past practices, a position Nandy finds illustrated in the writings of the Anglo-Sri Lankan intellectual Ananda Kentish Coomaraswamy for whom, says Nandy:

tradition remains homogeneous and undifferentiated from the point of view of man-made suffering. His defence of the charming theory of *sati*, for example, never takes into account its victims, the women who often died without the benefit of the theory. ...Such traditionalism reactively demystifies modernity to remystify traditions. ...Likewise, one may concur with Coomaraswamy that the untouchables in tradi-tional India were better off than the proletariat in the industrial societies. But this would be an empty statement to those victimized by the caste system today. When many untouchables opt for proletarianization in contemporary India, is their choice merely a function of faulty self-knowledge? ...I am afraid Coomaraswamy's traditionalism, despite being holistic by design, does not allow a creative, critical use of modernity within traditions.[1]

Nandy's positive examples are those of Gandhi and Tagore, arguably the two best products of the Indo-British cultural encoun-ter. Nandy sees Tagore's novel *Gora* as pointing to 'another kind of tradition which is reflective as well as self-critical, which does not reject or bypass the experience of modernity but encapsulates or digests it.' Gandhi, he names as someone who 'represented this concept of critical traditionalism aggressively.'[2]

Clearly, then, people who have accused Nandy of practising some kind of atavistic indigenism have read him wrong. His position is indeed different from that of the revolutionary mod-ernizer but it is also different from that of a so-called nativist. A critical traditionalist is critical of post-Enlightenment rationalism as an overall guide to living though s/he does not reject science in toto:

The critical traditionalism I am talking about does not have to see modern science as alien to it, even though it may see it as alienating....Such traditionalism uncompromisingly criticizes isolation and the over-concern with objectivity, but it never denies the creative possibilities of

---

[1] Ashis Nandy, 'Science, Authoritarianism and Culture' in his *Traditions, Tyranny and Utopia: Essays in the Politics of Awareness* (Delhi: 1987), p. 121.
[2] Ibid., p. 124. Nandy complicates the issue in a later essay, see p. 153.

limited objectivity. Ultimately, intelligence and knowledge are poor—in fact, dangerous—substitutes for intellect and wisdom.[3]

This limited appreciation of objectivity leads to a theory of resisting enslavement to the discipline of history. 'Liberation from the fear of childhood,' writes Nandy in critiquing modern conceptions of life-stories of humans, 'is also liberation from the more subtly institutionalized ethnocentrism towards past times.' By 'ethnocentrism' he means the process whereby, in the name of objectivity, the historian mobilizes voices from the past for fighting projects that are modern and contemporary. What makes the enterprise 'ethnocentric' for Nandy is the fact that these voices, unlike the native informants of the anthropologist, cannot talk back or argue with the historian: 'Elsewhere, I have discussed the absolute and total subjection of the subjects of history, who can neither rebel against the present times nor contest the present interpretations of the past.'[4]

The point receives elaboration in an essay on Gandhi:

Critics of objectification have not often noticed that the subjects of 'scientific history' are subjects irrevocably and permanently. ...there can be no transference, no real dialogue, perceived mutuality or continuity between the historian and his subjects from the subjects' point of view. The historian's subjects are, after all, mostly dead. ...One wonders if some vague awareness of this asymmetry between the subjects and the objects, and between the knowers and the known, prompted Gandhi to reject history as a guide to moral action and derive such guidance from his reading of texts and myths. ...Gandhi, like Blake and Thoreau before him, defied this new fatalism [the idea of historical laws—D. C.] of our times.[5]

Myth for history, tradition for modernity, wisdom and intellect for science and intelligence—Nandy's choices are clear. But they are, in my sense, decisionist. They do not share the same ground with the Marxist or liberal revolutionary. They may even sound conservative (in the good sense of the term). But one would be mistaken in seeing Nandy as anything but a modern intellectual. For decisionism, even of his kind, entails the same kind of heroic

---

[3] Ibid., p. 125.
[4] 'Reconstructing Childhood' in ibid., pp. 73–4.
[5] 'From Outside the Imperium' in ibid., pp. 147–8.

self-invention that has characterized the modern in Europe.[6] The theme of choice, albeit backed by up by the notion of wisdom rather than that of scientific objectivity, and in particular the continual construction in his writings of an object called 'the future,' an object without which Nandy's critique of Western modernity would have no meaning, tell us that we are listening to an intellectual who takes his bearings in the world from concerns that are unmistakably modern.

I want to suggest that what makes Nandy's critique of modernity truly interesting and powerful is a particular tension that sometimes breaks surface in his writings. It is a tension between the decisionist, heroic strand and other possible positions with regard to the past. These other positions are not subject to the binary of historical law (modern fatalism) vs. mythopoeic fables. Nor do they offer us immediate choices about how to live, mainly because these are positions which do not assume complete transparency of the object of investigation, whatever the object may be—society, culture, tradition. In these positions, one gives up the assumption that more research or intelligence will help us dispel the opacity in the object itself. The warmth of respect does not clear the mist here any more than does the light of scientific reason. It is at these points that Nandy's sensitivities cease to suggest solutions such as 'critical traditionalism' and become instead an invitation to deepen our questions. I say this in a spirit of gratitude for it is, unfortunately, a rare moment in current Indian scholarship when an intellectual, instead of rushing to suggest that solutions would be just around the corner if only we would listen to the right-minded analysis, actually allows the question to become deeper and more complex.

I see such a moment emerging in an essay that Nandy wrote in the course of the debate in India on sati after Roop Kanwar, a young woman from the village of Deorala near Jaipur in Rajasthan, killed herself by becoming a sati in 1987.[7] These debates—some of them between Nandy and secular liberals/feminists from Delhi—were heated exchanges in which labels were

[6] My reference here is obviously to Foucault's well-known discussion, in his essay 'What is Enlightenment?', of Baudelaire's essay, 'The Painting of Modern Life'.

[7] 'Sati in Kali Yuga' in Ashis Nandy, *The Savage Freud and Other Essays on Possible and Retrievable Selves* (New Jersey: 1995), pp. 32–52.

traded on all sides, labels that sought both to classify and abuse at the same time. Thus Nandy called his opponents 'Anglophile, psychologically uprooted Indians'; they retaliated by writing about 'attempts, usually from anti-Marxist, neo-Gandhian positions, to re-establish the difference between us and them (the west) by taking a stand against the values of the Enlightenment (reason, science, progress) using a rhetoric of anti-colonial indigenism. ...'[8] Nandy himself mentions—with justifiable relish—some of the criticism his essay received on publication: 'It was read as directly supporting sati and some, not knowing that I was not a Hindu, even found in it indicators of Hindu fanaticism.'[9] These labels are unhelpful. We have to argue against Nandy that no Indian, however Anglo-phile they may be, is thereby rendered into an instance of a 'culturally uprooted' person for Anglophilia exists in India as a phenomenon of contemporary Indian culture. It is, culturally, as legitimate as any form of orthopraxy. Similarly, it is patently absurd to suggest that Nandy could have been by any means abetting the practice of sati. Even the few quotes from his writings that I have used in this short essay would make clear how unfair that charge is.

For me, the interesting moment in Nandy's reflections on sati comes when he recognizes that it was possible for modern South Asian intellectuals like Rabindranath Tagore, Abanindranath Tagore or Ananda Coomaraswamy to be appreciative of the values that the practice, in its idealized representations, was meant to embody in the past while (as in the case of the Tagore family) fighting against the practice in one's own times. This is grist to Nandy's mill of 'critical traditionalism'—his injunction that once modernity has arrived and has inserted everybody in historical time, one should approach the past myths respectfully and use them to fight historical battles for a more just society. He writes:

This differentiation between sati in mythical time and sati in historical time, between sati as an event (*ghatana*) and sati as a system (*pratha*), between the authentic sati and its inauthentic offspring, between those who respect it and those who organize it in our times, is not my

[8] Nandy, ibid., p. 47; Kumkum Sangari quoted in Rajeswari Sunder Rajan, *Real and Imagined Women: Gender, Culture and Postcolonialism* (London and New York: 1993), p. 7.
[9] Nandy, '*Sati*,' p. 41, n. 15.

contribution to the understanding of the rite. These distinctions were already implicit, for instance, in the writings of Rabindranath Tagore, who was an aggressive opponent of sati as practised in contemporary times, yet respectful towards the ideas behind it.[10]

At first sight, this may look like a vindication of Nandy's strategy of critical traditionalism. Yet the essay is interesting because the strategy actually breaks down in some other parts of it. Why is a tradition entitled to respect even when one does not agree with it? Its popularity is no clear answer. Any strategist-politician in a political system where numbers matter has to reckon with that which is genuinely popular. But this does not mean that the popular practice is respectable. One can perform, effectively but instrumentally, the language of respect in order to mobilize the 'masses'. Or one can practice the anthropologist's language of politeness which, in effect, says to the native, 'yes, I respect your beliefs but they are not mine.' This respect is shallow and, as we know, is often replaced by arrogance when the proverbial crunch comes. Some of Nandy's answers to the question as to why the tradition of sati is to be respected are couched in terms of the desire not to be alienated: 'What does one do with the faith of millions of Indians that the soil that received the divided body of Sati constitutes the sacred land of India?' Once again, there seems to be no reason why a minority-position, which is the only place from where reformers can begin, has to be described as alienated. One can understand and yet genuinely disagree. If the answer is in terms of a humanist plea for respect for different life-forms, then it is not clear how that answer would suit the strategy of 'critical tradition-alism' for it has to be remembered that the aim of this strategy is eventually to build a more just society—as Nandy explains repeatedly in his book *Traditions, Tyranny and Utopias*—and there is no guarantee that the life-form one respects will truly bend itself to such a project.

Nandy recognizes a problem here but the recognition is not explicit yet. His critique of the violence of the extreme modernizers is persuasive. Yet the ground for the respectful attitude which he recommends towards tradition is not clear when we are confronted with a cultural monstrosity such as sati. Because he does not yet explicitly confront the problem that the past has produced

[10] Ibid., pp. 40–1.

at this point for his problematic—how to combine a respectful attitude towards tradition with the search for the principles for a more just society—the dilemma breaks out into a plethora of practical, policy-related questions in Nandy's essay. Commenting on the ambiguities and impracticalities contained in a bill recently passed in the Indian parliament—with assistance from feminists— banning any kind of 'glorification' of sati, Nandy launches into a series of powerful but rhetorical questions:

[H]ow far can or should glorification of sati go? ...Does the new law mean that children will not read about or admire Queen Padmini's self-chosen death in medieval times? Does it mean that that part of the Mahabharata which describes Madri's sati will· now be censored? What about Rabindranath Tagore's awe-inspiring, respectful depiction of *sati* and Abanindranath Tagore's brilliant invocation of the courage, idealism, and tragedy of sati in medieval Rajasthan? Do we proscribe their works too...? What about Kabir...who constantly uses the 'impulse to sati' as an image of surrendering one's ego to God [?].... Does one ban the celebration of Durga Puja or, for that matter, Kalidasa's *Kumarasambhava*, thought both celebrate the goddess who committed *sati*? Do we follow the logic of the two young activists who were keen to get the Ramayana declared unconstitutional...? ...That these questions may not in the future remain merely theoretical or hypothetical is made obvious by the fact that the Indian History Congress felt obliged to adopt a statement critical of the TV Ramayana in its 1988 convention.[11]

Behind these questions lies a larger issue: how does a modern intellectual think about the way a culture may have elaborated a series of values for itself from practices of cruelty and violence? Sati is one example, blood-feud could be another. Here I am deliberately avoiding Nandy's more practical formulation of the question: 'what does one do?' and asking instead 'how does one think?' Doers will have to answer their questions practically, in terms of the specific historical opportunities available to them, and that is why the options of a Tagore or Coomaraswamy may not be available to us (though this is no reason for not considering their examples carefully). Besides, my location in the US would make the practical question somewhat pretentious for me to consider. But as an academic-intellectual from India, I can join Nandy and his colleagues in the shared project of thinking about India.

[11] Ibid., pp. 38–9.

In answering this question, I take my cue from a perceptive remark of Nandy's. 'Every culture,' he says, 'has a dark side':

Sati in the *kali yuga* is an actualization of some of the possibilities inherent in the darker side of India's traditional culture, even if this actualization has been made possible by the forces of modernity impinging on and seeking to subvert the culture. After all, the tradition of sati exists only in some cultures, not in all; the kind of pathological self-expression displayed by some cultures in South Asia is not found in other parts of the world.[12]

Nandy's use of the word 'dark' is obviously related to his use of the word 'pathology.' I grant him that use though I will note that it is 'normal' for human beings both to contract diseases and to seek cures (that is, to seek restoration to some kind of a normal, though not necessarily normalized, body). One might think of cultures in similar terms. Whether modern or not, cultures will have pathological sides, just as Nandy argues, and some of the choice may be between pathologies. But let me read the word 'dark' in its more literal sense. Dark is where light cannot pass, it is that which cannot be illuminated. There are parts of society that remain opaque to the theoretical gaze of the modern. Why a culture will seize on a particular practice—especially a practice of cruelty and/or violence—and elaborate a lot of its own themes around it, is a question that cannot be answered by the social sciences. It is also in this literal sense, it seems to me, that cultures have a dark side; we cannot see into them, not everywhere.

In saying this, then, I oppose the liberal modernists whose investigative methods not only treat the investigator as transparent but also assume that society itself is such a transparent object that they can look into its heart and find an explanatory key (in class, patriarchy, technology). My point is that societies at best are translucent. Beyond a point theory cannot see. And where theory cannot see is where we live only practically. (None of this denies the heuristic value of class, patriarchy or technology in social analysis. But the clarity of the model is not the same as the clarity in the object of which the model stands.)

But this position also obliges me to modify Nandy's strategy of 'critical traditionalism' in one important respect. I do not entirely see into society; hence I cannot use tradition in a completely

---

[12] Ibid., p. 49.

voluntarist or decisionist manner. To the extent that I am self-consciously modern, Nandy's strategy—and in some respects even the strategies of his opponents (one has to remember that the debate as such is not with Marx or Gandhi nor always between them)—may provide an ethic of living and for working for a more acceptable future. But the past also comes to me in ways that I cannot see or figure out—or can do so sometimes only retrospectively—for it comes to me as taste, as embodied memories, as cultural training of the senses, as reflexes, as things I do not even sometimes know I carry. It has the capacity, in other words, to take me by surprise and to overwhelm and shock me. Faced with this, I cease to be the self-inventing hero of modern life. As happens in the relationship between humans and language, I am to some extent a tool in the hands of past and traditions, they speak through me even before I have chosen them critically or approached them with respect. That is why, it seems to me, that in addition to the feeling of respect for traditions, fear and anxiety would have to be the other affects with which the modern intellectual—modernity here implying a capacity to create the future as an object of deliberate planning—relates to the past. One never knows with any degree of certitude that a sati will never happen again or that an ugly communal riot will never again break out. It is out of this anxiety that the desire arises in the breast of the political revolutionary to scrap the past, to start from scratch, to create, as they say, the 'new' man. Out of the same fear may even arise the attitude of respect. But pasts retain, as Derrida says, a power to haunt.[13] They are a play of the visible and the invisible; they partially resist discursivity in the same way that pain resists language. My theory then always somewhat gropes and, as in all cases of speculation, takes a leap in the dark. And where theory cannot see, I can only live practically and the future ceases to exist as an object of analytic consideration (while it can always be the subject of poetic utterance). Decisions, which have this factor of darkness built into them, cannot therefore be based on any ground of certainty that would justify the infliction of suffering on others in the name of progress. This is the burden of Nandy's critique of modernity and

---

[13] Jacques Derrida, *Specters of Marx: The State of the Debt, the Work of Mourning, and the New International* (trans.), Peggy Kamuf (New York and London: 1994).

with it I concur. At the same time, I would argue that an acknowledgment of the opacity of the world makes critical traditionalism less voluntarist than I found it on my first few readings of Nandy. A commitment to a future that we want to work out in advance at least in principle, makes us anxious about the past in ways that are peculiar to the modern. As moderns, we may therefore want to defy the past and reduce it to zero. That, as I have said, is the path of the revolutionary and it is open to much of Nandy's critique. Alternatively, we may want to respect the past and relate critically, as Nandy so superbly explains, to tradition. The problem with this choice, it seems to me, is that it overstates the autonomy we have with respect to the past. To live with a limited sense of autonomy is to accept pragmatism as a principle of living.

13

Reading Ashis Nandy: The Return of the Past; Or Modernity with a Vengeance

Arif Dirlik

The discussion below very likely reads as one big question, rather than an answer to anything. When I was asked to contribute to a volume on Ashis Nandy, I was both gratified and hesitant. I have been an admirer of Nandy's work, which has helped me articulate intellectual and political issues in my own work. A contribution such as this one provides an occasion for acknowledging a debt, as well as confronting some of those issues directly.

There was hesitation as well, a product partly of a built-in resistance to a tendency of our times to render critical intellectuals into iconic celebrities, with detrimental consequences for intellectual life. More importantly in this case, I am aware that Nandy's work has been quite controversial within the immediate Indian context. For someone like myself who is an outsider to Indian intellectual and political life, such an undertaking seems little different from venturing into a mine-field without a reliable mine detector. What makes the risk worth taking is the relevance of what Nandy has to say beyond Indian intellectual borders. I am especially interested here in the triangular relationship between science, history and developmentalism that informs much of his writing.

Against the grain of Nandy's anti-historicism, I find it important to historicize his work and its impact. In his Preface to *The Intimate Enemy*, Nandy writes of the unease with the knowledge-systems underlying theories of progress that,

This awareness has not made everyone give up his theory of progress but it has given confidence to a few to look askance at the old universalism within which the earlier critiques of colonialism were offered. It is now possible for some to combine fundamental social criticism with a defence of non-modern cultures and traditions. It is possible to speak of the plurality of critical traditions and a human rationality. At long last we seem to have recognized that neither is Descartes the last word on reason nor is Marx that on the critical spirit.[1]

The statement may have something to tell us about the conditions of possibility of Nandy's speech: the 'confidence' that has been enabled by the discrediting of, or loss of faith in, the 'old universalisms'. The 'universalisms' that Nandy has in mind are quite evidently Eurocentric universals, including those that informed earlier *radical* critiques of colonialism. This recognition may enable us to evaluate what Nandy has to offer critically in its crucial insights as well as its limitations. To this end, I would like to place Nandy's thinking within the context of two contradictory intellectual tendencies of our times, that are also products of the retreat of the 'old universalisms': a postcolonialism that nourishes off a new universalism under the guise of diasporic globalization, and a contrary tendency to ethnocentrism in the reassertion of alternative civilizational values submerged earlier under the flood of Eurocentric modernity. For all their contradictoriness, these two tendencies both point to a return of the past, not in the negation of modernity but in its complication; for this contemporary turn to suppressed pasts, while it may be conceived as a reaction to modernity, also represents its triumph.

From Frantz Fanon to Ashis Nandy

Nandy's training as a psychologist, and the importance of psychology to the way he frames problems of colonialism and modernity, immediately recall to mind that other psychologist,[2] Frantz

[1] Ashis Nandy, *The Intimate Enemy: Loss and Recovery of Self Under Colonialism* (Delhi: Oxford University Press, 1983), p. x. This essay was written during my residence as a fellow at the Netherlands Institute for Advanced Studies in the Humanities and the Social Sciences. For comments and encouragement, I would like to thank Vinay Bahl, Reinhart Koselleck, Vinay Lal, Harbans Mukhia, Roxann Prazniak and Jowen Tung.

[2] The fact that Fanon was a psychoanalyst does not have any bearing on this discussion.

Fanon, whose writings left a deep imprint on an earlier, revolutionary age, the disappearance of which is one of the fundamental conditions of our own. It is not possible here to engage in a close comparison of two texts such as *The Intimate Enemy* and Fanon's *Black Skin White Masks*[3] which offer many interesting parallels. Both texts practise what Nandy calls a 'cultural psychology' of colonialism, although it may be revealing that Fanon refers to his undertaking also as 'sociodiagnosis'.[4] Central to both texts is the colonial subject, the colonized as well as the colonizer, and the psychic damage both suffer as a result of colonialism. Both texts are intended to 'decolonize' the colonial subject, although Fanon more often uses the term 'disalienation', as he is intensely preoccupied with the alienation of black men and women not only from their own subjectivities but also from, to use a term of Marx's, their 'species-being'. Central to both analyses are issues of class and sexuality in colonial relations of domination and resistance. Colonialism created a new class of cultural hybrids, the 'babus', to use the term from the Indian context, alienated from their own cultures in their feelings of superiority toward their societies, and yet despised by the colonialists with whom they strove to identify. It also introduced or exacerbated gender antagonisms. The 'feminization' of the colonized by the colonizer was to find a response on the part of the colonized male in an unhealthy stress on assertions of sexual potency, dichotomizing gender relations in society.

These issues are central to contemporary postcolonial criticism; how they are framed and dealt with go a long way toward locating not only individual intellectual and political positions, but also historical transformations in attitudes toward colonialism and its legacies. Fanon's own legacy has been the subject of debate, occasioned by efforts to appropriate his analyses of the colonial encounter for postcolonialism of a post-structuralist bent.[5] My goal

[3] Frantz Fanon, *Black Skin White Masks* (trans.), Charles L. Markmann (London: Macgibbon and Kee, 1968). French original published in 1952. Hereafter, *BSWM.*

[4] For 'cultural psychology,' see Ashis Nandy, *At the Edge of Psychology: Essays in Politics and Culture* (Delhi: Oxford University Press, 1993), p.vii. For 'sociodiagnosis', see, *BSWM*, p. 13.

[5] For a critical discussion see, Henry Louis Gates, Jr., 'Critical Fanonism', *Critical Inquiry*, 17 (Spring 1991): pp. 457–70.

in invoking the parallels between the two texts by Fanon and Nandy is not to assimilate the one to the other, but to get at the differences between them, which may be even more significant than that which their texts share in common. The thematic parallels between *The Intimate Enemy* and *Black Skin White Masks* are overshadowed by the different ways in which the two authors handle the themes. These differences are magnified further if we juxtapose two other texts that are not just diagnostic, but point to solutions to the problems created by colonialism: *The Wretched of the Earth* and *Traditions, Tyranny, and Utopias*.[6]

These differences at one level point to the different milieu within which these works were produced. Fanon's Caribbean and Africa are a long way in the problems they present from Nandy's India. As my intention here is not to engage in an intellectual history of the two thinkers, but rather to evaluate how they handle the problems of colonialism and domination, I am more interested in what Nandy's works reveal about the distance of our times from the context within which Fanon's works were produced and received. Even the ways in which we conceive spatial distances have their temporality. An earlier age, which found significant meaning in a term such as 'Third World', and in a theory with universal claims such as Marxism, could ignore the distance of India from Africa. That neither Third World nor Marxism commands such significance any more is a gauge of temporal distance. These distancings may also help us locate Nandy historically both with regard to an earlier problematic of liberation from the colonial, and contemporary postcolonial re-phrasings of the problem.[7] If Fanon

---

[6] Frantz Fanon, *The Wretched of the Earth*, (trans.), Constance Farrington (New York: Penguin Books, 1977), first published in French in 1961, and, Ashis Nandy, *Traditions, Tyranny, and Utopias: Essays in the Politics of Awareness* (Delhi: Oxford University Press, 1987).

[7] A note is in order here that is of both methodological and political significance. Henry Louis Gates cautions against rendering Fanon into a 'type', that deprives him of his historicity, his contradictions, and his own problematic relationship to his audiences and readers (ibid., pp. 459, 468–9). The point is well-taken. Inserting Fanon into the narratives of revolution of his time or postcolonial narratives of a later time no doubt violates his historical specificity. On the other hand, Fanon did address broad questions of revolutionary change beyond specific problems of race, and intra-racial difference, and the appeal of his texts did not stop at the boundaries provided

now sounds like a voice from the past, what he had to say still offers a way to evaluate our own voices critically.

FANON AND NANDY IN POSTCOLONIAL PERSPECTIVES

There is no better place to start in enunciating these differences than an evaluation Nandy has offered of Fanon's answer to the problem of colonialism. What he has to say is worth quoting at some length because of the number of problems it touches upon, as well as his own perception of his differences from Fanon:

...Despite all the indignity and oppression they have faced, many defeated cultures refuse to draw a clear line between the victor and the defeated, the oppressor and the oppressed, the rulers and the ruled...Drawing upon the non-dualist traditions of their religions, myths and folkways, these cultures try to set some vague, half-effective limits on the objectification of living beings and on the violence which flows from it. They try to protect the faith—increasingly lost to the modern world—that the border-lines of evil can never be clearly defined, that there is always a continuity between the aggressor and his victim, and that liberation from oppressive structures outside has at the same time to mean freedom from an oppressive part of one's own self... The cleansing role Frantz Fanon grants to violence in his vision of a post-colonial society sounds so alien to many Africans and Asians mainly because it is insensitive to this cultural resistance. Fanon admits the internalization of the oppressor. But he calls for an exorcism in which the ghost outside has to be finally confronted in violence, for it carries the burden of the ghost within. The outer violence, Fanon suggests, is the only means of making a painful break with a part of one's own self. If Fanon had more confidence in his culture he would have sensed that his vision ties the victim more deeply to the culture of oppression than any collaboration can. Cultural accep-tance of the major technique of oppression in our times, organized violence, cannot but further socialize the victims to the basic values of

by the colour line. We should be able, on the basis of textual evidence, to distinguish what he said, how it was received at his time, and how it is received presently in different quarters. Much the same may be said, of course, about Nandy, who focuses on specifically Indian questions, and yet also speaks to broader problems of the age. One distinction is important, as the discussion below should reveal: Nandy, as a reader of Fanon, in part responds to Fanon, and Fanon's analysis of the problem of liberation.

their oppressors...Perhaps if Fanon had lived longer, he would have come to admit that in his method of exorcism lies a partial answer to two vital questions about the search for liberation in our times, namely, why dictatorships of the proletariat never end and why revolutions always devour their children.[8]

I am not concerned here with the adequacy of this reading of Fanon on the issue of violence, but rather with what it has to tell us about Nandy. A careful reading of the last two chapters of Fanon's *Black Skin White Masks* suggests considerable ambivalence on the issue of violence. This early text, which Gates describes as Fanon's 'most overtly psychoanalytic book,'[9] is the preferred text for postcolonial interpretations of Fanon, which seek to find in Fanon an ambivalence similar to that in postcolonial criticism over the relationship of the colonized to the colonizer. On the other hand, an affirmative discussion of violence opens up Fanon's later book, *The Wretched of the Earth*, where Fanon describes the colonial world as 'a Manichean world,' from which there is no escape except through violence. Not surprisingly, *The Wretched of the Earth*, does not easily permit a postcolonial reading of Fanon that would erase the relentless opposition between the colonizer and the colonized.[10] While Nandy cites both of these texts in the footnote to the passage above, it seems that he gives priority to *The Wretched of the Earth* in his evaluation of what Fanon has to say about violence. Unlike in other postcolonial interpretations, in other words, he seeks a distance from, not an appropriation of, Fanon.[11]

[8] Ashis Nandy, 'Towards A Third World Utopia,' in *Traditions, Tyranny, and Utopias*: 20–55, pp. 33–4.

[9] Gates, 'Critical Fanonism', p. 470, fn.

[10] *The Wretched of the Earth*, pp. 31–40, for the Manichean world. See Gates, pp. 458–60, for postcolonial readings of Fanon. For a critique, that affirms Fanon's Manichaenism see, Abdul R. Jan Mohamed, 'The Economy of Manichean Allegory: The Function of Racial Difference in Colonialist Literature,' *Critical Inquiry* 12 (Autumn 1985): 59–87, pp. 59–60.

[11] Likewise, in his Preface to *The Intimate Enemy*, Nandy writes of Fanon: 'Let us not forget that the most violent denunciation of the West produced by Fanon is written in the elegant style of a Jean-Paul Sartre. The West has not merely produced modern colonialism, it informs most interpretations of colonialism.' In this case, however, he also bridges his distance from Fanon somewhat by adding that, 'it colours even this interpretation of interpretation' (p. xii).

The distancing is not just ideological, it is also temporal, as is implicit in his observation that 'if Fanon had lived longer', he would have seen revolutions for what they are, which is clearer to us from *our* vantage point in time.

This double distance—from past revolutionary responses to colonialism and contemporary efforts to erase the revolutionary past by subsuming those responses in new postcolonial narratives— offers one way to place Nandy intellectually and politically. Strangely enough, while Nandy's evaluation of Fanon may differ from that in postcolonial criticism, the premises that inform his evaluation share much in common with the latter. As far as I am aware, Nandy has only a tenuous relationship to fellow Indian intellectuals who have done much to propagate postcolonial criticism abroad.[12] The Centre for the Study of Developing Societies, of which he has been Fellow and Director, addresses questions of quite a different nature than those in postcolonial criticism, and draws on a Gandhian legacy to challenge modernity, including a postcolonial modernity.

I will say more on these issues below. The differences in Nandy's critique of colonialism from that in postcolonial criticism should not lead us to ignore that the two critiques are contemporaries, that for all their differences they also may share commonalities which distinguish what they have to say about colonialism from past responses to it—and ultimately suggest a broader range to postcolonial criticism than is allowed for in Euro-American conceptions of it informed by diasporic intellectuals. The most obvious commonality may be that both critiques are post-revolutionary, in the sense both of 'after-' and 'anti-'. This is quite explicit in the case of Nandy. It may also be seen without much effort in postcolonial criticism, which in its repudiation of metanarratives, or fixed identities, also militates against revolutionary possibilities by denying the structural and subjective conditions of revolution. When Nandy writes that 'conventional anti-colonialism, too, could be an apologia for the colonization of minds,' he might easily be

---

[12] The only reference to postcolonial intellectuals that I have been able to locate is one to Dipesh Chakrabarty and Gyan Prakash on history, where Nandy refers admiringly to their questionings of history while also observing that they do not go far enough in their critiques. See, Ashis Nandy, 'History's Forgotten Doubles,' *History and Theory* 34.2 (1995): 44–66, pp. 52–3.

speaking as a 'postcolonial critic'.[13] The repudiation or the appropriation of Fanon, while quite antithetical in interpretation, nevertheless converge in their denial of revolution as a means to liberation from colonialism.

Secondly, Nandy is at one with much of postcolonial criticism in his emphasis on colonialism as a cultural or a pychological entity. This, of course, was the case also with Fanon, who was one of the first Third World intellectuals to make a powerful case that liberation from oppressive structures requires also freedom from the self shaped by colonial domination; that decolonization as a political act is inseparable from psychological and cultural decolonization. Fanon also argued, as do Nandy and postcolonial critics, that this cultural and psychological colonialism shaped the colonizer as much as the colonized. This is what has enabled the assimilation of his analyses to postcolonial narratives.

On the other hand, the way in which Fanon understood this process of psychological/cultural decolonization distinguishes him from these later interpretations in two significant ways. No reader of *Black Skin White Masks* can escape the impression of the tragedy of the colonized subject, who has been deprived not only of cultural affinities to the society of origin, or the society of the colonizer which she/he mimics, but totally of his and her humanity. Fanon, of course, is speaking not just of colonial oppression, but of a racially motivated colonialism, which has reduced the black person to a biological minimum. The tragedy of the violence he proceeds to affirm in *The Wretched of the Earth* follows from this prior tragedy, where the restoration of selfhood may be achieved only by turning that violence against the colonizer. Fanon's works are written in the trope of tragedy.

By contrast, when Nandy refers to 'colonialism as a shared culture,[14] the relationship that he has in mind is a significantly more negotiable one. Much as Homi Bhabha speaks of a 'colonial subject' that includes both the colonizer and the colonized, Nandy

---

[13] *The Intimate Enemy*, p.xi. For a further discussion of 'post-revolutionary' in the periodization of the contemporary, see Arif Dirlik, 'Postcolonial or Postrevolutionary? The Problem of History in Postcolonial Criticism,' in A. Dirlik, *The Postcolonial Aura: Third World Criticism in the Age of Global Capitalism* (Boulder, CO: Westview Press, 1997).

[14] *The Intimate Enemy*, p. 2.

speaks of 'continuity between the oppressor and the oppressed';[15] his, too, is the language of 'hybridity' and 'interface' against the 'dichotomies' of which Fanon speaks. Where the Europeanization of the black intellectual appears in Fanon's work in terms of a zero-sum relationship (the more white, the less black), Nandy's babu is 'grudgingly recognized as an interface who processes the West on behalf of his society and reduces it to a digestible bolus. Both his comical and dangerous selves protect his society against the White Sahib.'[16] For Nandy, it is in the end the oppressed who have the better deal, as they are able to contain the colonial encounter more successfully than the colonized:

This is the underside of non-modern India's ethnic universalism. It is a universalism which takes into account the colonial experience, including the immense suffering colonialism brought, and builds out of it a maturer, more contemporary, more self-critical version of Indian traditions. It is a universalism which sees the Westernized India as a subtradition which, in spite of its pathology and its tragi-comic core, is a 'digested' form of another civilization that had once gate-crashed into India. India *has* tried to capture the differentia of the West within its own cultural domain, not merely on the basis of a view of the West as politically intrusive or as culturally inferior, but as a subculture meaningful in itself and important, though not all-important, in the Indian context. This is what I meant when I said that Kipling, when he wanted to be Western, could not be both Western and Indian, whereas the everyday Indian, even when he remains only Indian, is both Indian and Western.[17]

Fanon's attentiveness to questions of political economy is a second distinguishing feature of his approach to the question of colonial domination, which may be deeply psychological, but is embedded in the structures of political economy. Nandy shares with postcolonial criticism a tendency to culturalism, to a displacement and relocation of colonialism to the realm of culture. As we shall see below, his emphasis on forms of knowledge in the colonization of the world leads him to rather radical questions about the nature and consequences of modernity, but there are also certain fundamental questions that are raised by the relative absence of attention to questions of political economy in his work. Postcolonialism's avoidance of political economy is rationalized

[15] Ibid., p. 39.
[16] Ibid., p. xv.
[17] Ibid., pp 75–6.

by the repudiation of metanarratives and foundations, which Nandy does not share. It is all the more remarkable then that Nandy, no less than postcolonial critics, should give relatively little notice to the importance Fanon assigns to questions of 'land and bread'.[18] Two out of the six chapters in *The Wretched of the Earth* are devoted to questions of political economy and class in anti-colonial struggles for liberation, which in the end shape Fanon's attitude toward revolution as a revolution not just against colonial-ism, but also as an internal class struggle. Nandy in his turn does speak of a relationship between internal and external colonialism, and he shares with Fanon an emphasis on 'folkways' (the culture of the masses) as the reservoir of cultural resources that have not been invaded by colonial culture, and indispensable as such to any struggle for liberation from colonialism. But here too the emphasis is largely on colonialism and liberation as cultural and psychologi-cal problems. As he puts it, 'the political economy of colonization is of course important, but the crudity and inanity of colonialism are principally expressed in the sphere of psychology and, to the extent the variables used to describe states of mind under colonial-ism have themselves become politicized since the entry of modern colonialism on the world scene, in the sphere of political psychol-ogy.[19] And when he writes of the village in India, presumably the ultimate location for native cultural resources, he is concerned less with the concrete than with the imagined village.[20] In this version of colonialism, the 'modern West' itself appears not just as a geographical or a temporal but as a 'psychological category'.[21]

[18] *The Wretched of the Earth*, p. 34, where Fanon writes that 'for a colonized people the most essential value, because the most concrete, is first and foremost the land; the land which will bring them bread and, above all, dignity.'

[19] *The Intimate Enemy*, p. 2.

[20] See the remarkable essay, remarkable both for its imaginativeness and for its presentation of the village as a problem in imagination, 'The Decline in the Imagination of the Village,' in this volume. I should note here that my discussion here is based entirely on the place of political economy in Nandy's own texts. The Centre for the Study of Developing Societies is very much concerned with issues of political economy, albeit in a direction quite different from Fanon's Marxist-inspired approach. Nandy's approach, if viewed in terms of a division of labour within the Centre, would appear differently than I read it here. Still, it suggests problems which I will take up below.

[21] Ibid., p. xi.

Nandy writes that 'colonialism minus a civilizational mission is no colonialism at all'.[22] The statement is indicative of his approach to colonialism, as well as the distance that separates contemporary critiques of colonialism from those that prevailed just a generation earlier.

Nowhere is Nandy's distance from Fanon more apparent than over the question of history. His reference in the passage above to Fanon's 'insensitivity' to resistance to colonialism of native cultures is an interesting understatement that says as much about Nandy as it does about Fanon. As I shall take up Nandy's own ideas of history and culture below, there is little need to elaborate on this question here, except to point out that Fanon and Nandy share some similarities in their repudiation of civilizational or national pasts rewritten to compensate for the 'lack' of 'manliness' or civilization indicated by the colonial conquest, which merely deepens colonial hegemony. But beyond this they part ways in very revealing ways. Fanon's is a radical rejection of the past, which places the burden for the creation of history and culture on the revolutionary struggle itself.[23] The history thus to be created is a history which is universal:

I am a man, and what I have to recapture is the whole past of the world....Every time a man has contributed to the victory of the dignity of the spirit, every time a man has said no to an attempt to subjugate his fellows, I have felt solidarity with his act. In no way should I derive my basic purpose from the past of peoples of colour. In no way should I dedicate myself to the revival of an unjustly unrecognized Negro civilization. I will not make myself the man of any past. I do not want to exalt the past at the expense of my present and my future.[24]

Against this universalist humanism which negates the past in order to ground the future in a revolutionary vision, that may be most striking in a contemporary perspective for its Eurocentric premises, Nandy proposes alternative universalisms embodied in different cultural traditions. His affirmation of different civilizational pasts distinguishes his vision not only from a revolutionary vision such as Fanon's, but also abolishes what affinity he may have to contemporary postcolonialist arguments. Where in the postcolonial

[22] Ibid., p. 11.
[23] *The Wretched of the Earth*, Chapter 4; *BSWM*, Chapter 8.
[24] *BSWM*, p. 226.

argument, different pasts return only to lose their authenticities in new, hybrid, rephrasings, Nandy's utilizes hybridities produced by the colonial encounter as means to the rediscovery and recovery of authentic pasts. This, in turn, points to a different, contradictory, affinity with contemporary reassertions of alternative civilizational ideals.

NANDY'S WORK IN THE PERSPECTIVE OF CONTEMPORARY ETHNOCENTRIC REVIVALS

Ours is not only an age of postcolonialist erasure of differences in the name of difference, it is also an age of the reassertion of differences with a vengeance. From Islamic and Hindu reassertions of cultural pasts to the Confucian revival of East Asia to Samuel Huntington's new geopolitics based on civilizations, there is a widespread reassertion of cultural or civilizational authenticities even as authenticity is called into question in Euro-American postmodern or postcolonial circles. Authenticity may be lodged in nations, ethnicities or civilizations, or it may be lodged in entities as diverse as diasporas and indigenous localisms, but these locations all contribute to the same end: the fragmentation of the world even as slogans of globalization increasingly decorate the roosts of academia—which, ironically, celebrate such fragmentation as a sign of globalization. The fragmentation of politics and culture most importantly calls into question the knowability of the world as knowledge itself is ethnicized, or even biologized.

This may be the 'condition of postmodernity' that is most relevant from a global perspective. Or we may describe it as 'modernity with a vengeance'. Huntington is correct to point out in his celebrated (and notorious) essays that rather than erase 'traditions', modernization has strengthened them—by empowering the very identities that it endangered.[25] The rapid economic development of East Asian societies during the last two decades has empowered the 'Confucian revival' in those societies.[26] Islamic fundamentalists as much as American evangelicals rationalize what

[25] Samuel P. Huntington, 'The Clash of Civilizations?' *Foreign Affairs* (Summer 1992), pp. 22–49.

[26] Arif Dirlik, 'Confucius in the Borderlands: Global Capitalism and the Reinvention of Confucianism,' *Boundary* 2, 22.3 (Fall 1995), pp. 229–73.

they offer in the languages of modernity. Nandy himself writes of his own source of inspiration that, 'Gandhi, despite being a counter-modernist, re-emerged for the moderns as a major critic of modernity whose defence of traditions carried the intimations of a post-modern consciousness.'[27] His own reading of Indian civilization contributes to a contemporary postmodernity by strongly asserting an Indian presence in the contemporary world, but he parts ways quickly with contemporary ethnocentrism, by bringing to the idea of Indianness his own postmodern consciousness.

Nandy's challenges to the 'old universalisms' are informed by a conviction that colonialism and modernization, far from erasing India's pasts, have enabled the construction of 'a maturer, more contemporary, more self-critical version of Indian traditions'.[28] As I have noted several times above, Nandy is quite sensitive to the fact that an anti-colonialist re-writing of native pasts may well replicate the premises of colonialism and Orientalism, as he believes was the case with efforts in India to discover masculinity or national consciousness in the past, which rendered 'the golden age of Hinduism... [into] an ancient version of the modern West.[29] Against such efforts he counterpoises what he calls 'critical traditionalism', which requires an effort to 'take a critical look at Indian traditions, evaluate the nature of the Western impact on them, and update Indian culture without disturbing its authenticity.[30] The statement is one that is likely to grate on postcolonial ears in its affirmation of 'authenticity'. And there is an apparent contradiction between a tradition that is subject to constant revision ('invention?'), and yet manages somehow to retain its authenticity. Nandy's resolution of the problem, I think, distinguishes him from ethnocentrists in India and elsewhere, overcomes the nationalist chauvinism that characterizes much of contemporary nativist revivalism, and opens up critically creative ways of thinking modernity in relation to the past. It is also possible that

[27] Ashis Nandy, *The Illegitimacy of Nationalism: Rabindranath Tagore and the Politics of Self* (Delhi: Oxford University Press, 1994), p. 2.

[28] *The Intimate Enemy*, p. 75.

[29] Ibid., p. 26.

[30] Ibid., p. xvii, for 'critical traditionalism', and p. 27, for the quotation. I am taking the liberty here of interpreting what Nandy means by 'critical traditionalism', since he does not offer a definition in his initial reference.

the same resolution in the end defeats his efforts to salvage the Indian past.

First, the 'traditions' that Nandy defends are the traditions of a civilization, which he distinguishes from and sets against the nation-state. Nandy is resolutely anti-nationalist. Like Partha Chatterjee, he sees in the nationalist appropriation of the past a replication of Orientalism, and he perhaps goes beyond Chatterjee in viewing the nation-state's efforts to homogenize national culture as a form of 'internal colonialism'.[31] As he writes in the preface to his study of Tagore and nationalism, 'I hope that young Indians confronting and perhaps resisting the violent emergence of a steamrolling modern nation-state in their country will discover in this essay an useful construction of the past.[32] A historical survey of Nandy's publications suggests that the concern with nationalism has come to overshadow in recent years the concern with colonialism. Rather than an obstacle to national unity, Nandy's recent writings suggest, communal conflict in India may be a product of 'the concept of a "mainstream national culture" that is fearful of diversities, intolerant of dissent unless it is cast in the language of the mainstream, and panicky about any self-assertion or search for autonomy by ethnic groups.'[33] As he (and his collaborators) write in a study of the Ramjanmabhumi Movement,

South Asia has always been a salad bowl of cultures. For long it has avoided—to the exasperation of modern nationalists and statists of the right and the left—the American-style melting pot model and its individualistic assumptions and anti-communitarian bias. In a salad, the ingredients retain their distinctiveness, but each ingredient transcends its individuality through the presence of others. In a melting pot, primordial identities are supposed to melt. Those that do not are expected to survive as coagulates

[31] '...the rhetoric of progress uses the fact of internal colonialism to subvert the cultures of societies subject to external colonialism and... internal colonialism in turn uses the fact of external threat to legitimize and perpetuate itself,' *The Intimate Enemy*, p. xii. See, also, Partha Chatterjee, *Nationalist Thought and the Colonial World: A Derivative Discourse?* (Atlantic Heights, NJ: ZED Books, 1986).

[32] Ashis Nandy, *The Illegitimacy of Nationalism: Rabindranath Tagore and the Politics of Self.*

[33] Ashis Nandy, Shikha Trivedy, Shail Mayaram and Achyut Yagnik, *Creating a Nationality: The Ramjanmabhumi Movement and Fear of the Self* (Delhi: Oxford University Press, 1995), p. 19.

and are called nationalities or minorities; they are expected to dissolve in the long run. Much of the recent violence in South Asia can be traced to the systematic efforts being made to impose the melting pot-model upon time-worn Indian realities.[34]

It should be apparent from these critiques of nationalism, secondly, that ironic as it may seem, for Nandy, the core values of Indian civilization rest on the repudiation of an authentic Indianness. He writes of a nineteenth-century predecessor, Iswarchandra Vidyasagar, that,

He refused to use the imagery of a golden age of the Hindus from which contemporary Hindus had allegedly fallen, he refused to be psychologically tied to the history of non-Hindu rule of India, he resisted reading Hinduism as a 'proper religion' in the Islamic or Western sense, he rejected the ideologies of masculinity and adulthood, and he refused to settle scores with the West by creating a nation of super-Hindus or by defending Hinduism as an all-perfect antidote to Western cultural encroachment. His was an effort to protect not the formal structure of Hinduism but its spirit, as an open, anarchic federation of sub-cultures and textual authorities which allowed new readings and internal criticisms.[35]

This reading of the Indian past pervades Nandy's texts. Nandy's affirmation of an authentic Indian culture resists ethnocentric containment as it is presented throughout in an ironic mode: 'Only in recent times have the Hindus begun to describe themselves as Hindus. Thus, the very expression has a built-in contradiction: to use the term Hindu to self-define is to flout the traditional self-definition of the Hindu, and to assert aggressively one's Hinduism is to very nearly deny one's Hinduness.'[36] He writes in the closing pages of *The Intimate Enemy*, in terms that almost repudiate his affirmations of an authentic Indian civilization earlier in the book, that,

The differentia of Indian culture has often been sought by social analysts, including this writer, in the uniqueness of certain cultural themes or in their configuration. This is not a false trail, but it does lead to some

---

[34] Ibid., p. vi. See also D. L. Sheth and Ashis Nandy (eds), *The Multiverse of Democracy* (New Delhi: Sage Publications, 1996), where the contributors (mostly critics of modernity from abroad) discuss the ways in which the modern nation-state contributes to the curtailment of diversity and democracy.

[35] *The Intimate Enemy*, p. 28.

[36] Ibid., p. 103

half-truths. One of them is the clear line drawn, on behalf of the Indian, between the past and the present, the native and the exogenous, and the Hindu and the non-Hindu. But, as I have suggested, the West that is aggressive is sometimes inside; the earnest, self-declared native, too, is often an exogenous category, and the Hindu who announces himself so, is not Hindu after all. Probably the uniqueness of Indian culture lies not so much in a unique ideology as in the society's traditional ability to live with cultural ambiguities and to use them to build psychological and even metaphysical defences against cultural invasions. Probably, the culture itself demands that a certain permeability of boundaries be maintained in one's self-image and that the self be not defined too tightly or separated mechanically from the not-self.[37]

An unsympathetic reader could easily dismiss this self-main-tained ironic stance as sheer befuddlement. To this reader, Nandy overcomes this befuddlement by carrying his critique to another critical level—to the dehistoricization of Indian civilization, not in the manner of Orientalist dehistoricization, but by taking it outside of history. His inspiration here is Gandhi, whose 'specific orientation to myth became a more general orientation to public consciousness. Public consciousness was not seen as a causal product of history but as related to history non-causally through memories and anti-memories. If for the West the present was a special case of an unfolding history, for Gandhi as a representative of traditional India history was a special case of an all-embracing permanent present, waiting to be interpreted and reinterpreted.'[38] Nandy attributes to Gandhi an 'anti-historical assumption that, because they faithfully contain history, because they are contem-porary and, unlike history, are amendable to intervention, myths are the essence of a culture, history being at best superfluous and at worst misleading. Gandhi implicitly assumed that history...was one-way traffic, a set of myths about past time...built up as independent variables which limit human options and pre-empt human futures....Myths, on the other hand, consciously acknowl-edged as the core of a culture...widen instead of restricting human choice.' Nandy's own conclusion is that 'the affirmation of ahistoricity is an affirmation of the dignity and autonomy of non-modern peoples.[39] He writes elsewhere that,

[37] Ibid., p. 107
[38] Ibid., p. 57
[39] Ibid., p. 59

The rejection of history to protect self-esteem and ensure survival is often a response to the structure of cognition history presumes. The more scientific a history, the more oppressive it tends to be in the experimental laboratory called the third world. It is scientific history which has allowed the idea of social intervention to be cannibalized by the ideal of social engineering at the peripheries of the world. For the moderns, history has always been the unfolding of a theory of progress, a serialized expression of a telos which, by definition, cannot be shared by communities on the lower rungs of the ladder of history. Even the histories of oppression and the historical theories of liberation postulate stages of growth which, instead of widening the victims' options, reduce them...The ethnocentrism of the anthropologist can be corrected; he is segregated from his subject only socially and, some day, his subjects can talk back. The ethnocentrism towards the past mostly goes unchallenged. The dead do not rebel, nor can they speak out. So the subjecthood of the subjects of history is absolute, and the demand for a real or scientific history is the demand for a continuity between subjecthood in history and subjection in the present. The corollary to the refusal to accept the primacy of history is the refusal to chain the future to the past. This refusal is a special attitude to human potentialities, an alternative form of utopianism that has survived till now as a language alien to, and subversive of, every theory which in the name of liberation circumscribes and makes predictable the spirit of human rebelliousness.[40]

Contemporary ethnocentrisms for the most part insist on drawing boundaries between nations, ethnicities and civilizations that are so firm that it becomes meaningless to speak of communication across boundaries. National and civilizational characteristics are likewise projected deep into the past so as to render history into an alibi for the divisions of the present. Interestingly, in the case of Nandy, the insistence on civilizational authenticity serves as the means to a new universalism that ends up breaking down the very boundaries with which he starts his argument. Indeed, in his refusal to allow the past to serve as a hindrance to the imagination of the future, he is not very far from Fanon's present-mindedness which refuses to locate in the past the burden for creating the future. Ironically, for all his refusal to rely on the past, Fanon's writings express a much keener awareness of the burden of the past on the present; of the structures of colonial and pre-colonial pasts which need to be eliminated so that the future can be created out of the very struggles for liberation. As

[40] 'Towards a Third World Utopia,' pp. 48–9.

the statement quoted above indicates, Fanon seems to have envisioned the future thus to be created as a cosmopolitan universalism, where everybody's past would in the end be everybody else's past.

As Dipesh Chakrabarty points out, Nandy has a voluntarist (or, 'decisionist', as Chakrabarty puts it) attitude toward the past which, as a product of constant invention, allows multiple visions of the future.[41] Nandy unlike Fanon, is postcolonial and postmodern in his readings of the past, no less than his visions for the future. On the other hand, placing him against contemporary ethnocentrisms indicates that he does not easily fall in with those categories either. Against postcolonial and postmodern tendencies to dissolve cultural identities into hybridities, or whatever, he insists on authentic and even 'primordial' identities, even if those identities are located only in the myths people live by. The insistence is intended to bring into the present the voices of those who have been suppressed in history—national no less than civilizational history. What he and his colleagues wrote of South Asia as a salad bowl may be paradigmatic of the way he envisages the contemporary world: that it consists (or should consist) of ingredients that retain their individuality, but also transcend that individuality through the presence of others. Hence Fanon's cosmopolitan universalism appears in his vision of the future as a dialogue between alternative universalities:

...the search for authenticity of a civilization is always a search for the other face of the civilization, either as a hope or as a warning. The search for a civilization's utopia, too, is part of this larger quest. It needs not merely the ability to interpret and reinterpret one's own traditions, but also the ability to involve the often-recessive aspect of other civilizations as allies in one's struggle for cultural rediscovery, the willingness to become allies to other civilizations trying to discover their other faces, and the skills to give more centrality to these new readings of civilizations and civilizational concerns. This is the only form of a dialogue of cultures which can transcend the flourishing intercultural barters of our times.[42]

---

[41] Dipesh Chakrabarty, 'The Modern Indian Intellectual and the Problem of the Past: An Engagement with the Thoughts of Ashis Nandy,' in this volume.

[42] 'Towards a Third World Utopia', p. 55.

MODERNITY, ANTI-MODERNITY, NON-MODERNITY: HISTORY, SCIENCE AND DEVELOPMENT

It is difficult (and probably irrelevant) to say whether anti-modernism is a source of, or a solution to, the problems thrown up by Nandy's critiques of colonialism, nationalism, and the failure of radical visions of the past. But it is everywhere in his writing. There is nothing new about anti-modernism, which may be part and parcel of modernism. On the other hand, the manner in which it is phrased is historical in partaking of the problems of the age. To use the distinction Chatterjee has offered in his study of nationalism, if anti-modernism shares the thematic of modernism, its problematic is nevertheless derivative of concrete situations.[43] The globalization of capital since World War II, becoming evident in the 1980s, has resulted in a reconfiguration of the ways in which we think the world, blurring earlier boundaries, including boundaries between the colonizer and the colonized. It has brought forth more sharply than ever the problem of cultural homogenization, especially through the globalization of material habits as embodied in practices of consumption; it makes little sense to speak of cultural imperialism when the culturally colonized willingly embrace their colonization, which casts the whole history of colonialism in a new light. The postcolonial and post-socialist nation-state, in its depredations against its own constituents, appears less as a bulwark against colonialism than as a colonizing agent in its own right. Socialism, in its failures, appears not so much as an alternative to capitalism but as an alternative form of capitalist modernization doomed by its own internal contradictions. Globalization itself internationalizes class exploitation even as it produces a new fragmentation of the globe. In the meantime, the utopian promise of welfare and equality for all recedes ever further into the future, a future that seems less and less attainable as unbridled developmentalism erodes the very material bases of subsistence and survival. Also, our aptly re-named knowledge industries seem to be intent on covering up the global crisis rather

---

[43] Partha Chatterjee, *Nationalist Thought and the Colonial World,* Chapter 1.

than contemplating serious alternatives to the way we plunder the earth and its inhabitants, including its human inhabitants. It is difficult not to be anti-modernist in times like these.

And yet it also takes a great deal of courage to be seriously anti-modern, not the New Age or the postmodernist variety that nourishes itself off the very modernity it deplores, but the kind of anti-modernism that insists on the indispensable relevance of the non-modern if we are to be able to think our way out of the problems presented by modernity. One need not agree with everything about such an anti-modernism in order to recognize the courage involved in daring to give soft answers to hard questions, that elevates weakness over strength, promotes diversity at the cost of economic non-development, and proclaims that the promise of democracy may lie not with those who spread it around the globe with the force of arms but with those who have never heard the word.

It is not my intention here to render Ashis Nandy into an icon of anti-modernism (or, non-modernism, as he might prefer). Other names that I have called upon to similar effect in my own work include his colleague Vandana Shiva, the Amerindian scholar and historian Vine Deloria, Jr., and Subcomandante Marcos. Others could be invoked with ease. Many participate these days in the return of the non-modern.

It is important nevertheless to recognize Nandy as an eloquent voice in the contemporary critique of modernity, a voice that retains a hope in universalism even as it protests against manufactured uniformity. It is a voice that is deeply radical in its willingness to confront what are almost unconsciously accepted faiths of our times. Two of these faiths, those in history and science, are worth noting here.

I have already raised the question of history in Nandy's thinking; suffice it to say here that these days, when Eurocentrism in the writing and conceptualization of history is a major concern within and without Euro-America, Nandy's critique takes us far beyond the limited questions of who is to be included, and how, to confront history and historical thinking as a problem. The argument is deceptively simple, as perhaps a radical critique should be: History, as one more of thinking about the past, present and future, has been established in the modern world as the *only* way to think them, consigning all other ways of thinking, along with those who thought in those ways, to the realm of the non-historical. The dominance of history

is derived from the links the idea of history has established with the modern nation-state, the secular world-view, the Baconian concept of scientific rationality, nineteenth-century theories of progress, and, in recent decades, development...once exported to the non-modern world, historical consciousness has not only tended to absolutize the past in cultures that have lived with open-ended concepts of the past or depended on myths, legends, and epics to define their cultural selves, it has also made the historical world-view complicit with many new forms of violence, exploitation and satanism in our times and helped rigidify civilizational, cultural, and national boundaries.[44]

Most available criticisms of history are themselves historical. As in the case of colonial nationalism which assimilates Oriental-ism in its own self-definition, to be historical in the non-Euro-American world is to rewrite the past under the hegemony of an epistemology that has Eurocentrism built into its very structure.[45] On the other hand, from this same perspective, contemporary efforts in Euro-America to globalize history by writing everyone into it, even in all their differences, appear as little more than an effort to contain genuine difference by rendering all societies historical. Nandy concedes that 'at one time not long ago, historical consciousness had to coexist with other modes of experiencing and constructing the past even within the modern world. The conquest of the past through history was still incomplete in the late nineteenth century, as was the conquest of space through the railways....As long as the non-historical modes thrived, history remained viable as a baseline for radical social criticism. That is perhaps why the great dissenters of the nineteenth century were the most aggressively historical.[46] But such is no

[44] 'History's Forgotten Doubles,' p. 44 (abstract).

[45] This, of course, may be even more of a problem in Marxist than in liberal historiography. For a discussion, see, Arif Dirlik, 'Marxism and Chinese History: The Globalization of Marxist Historical Discourse and the Problem of Hegemony in Marxism,' *Journal of Third World Studies* 4, no. 1 (Spring 1987): pp. 151–64. As this journal is not easily accessible, the essay was also published as, 'Marxisme et Histoire Chinoise: La Globalisation Du Discourse Historique Et La Question De L'Hegemonie Dans La Reference Marxist A L'Histoire,' *Extreme-Orient Extreme-Occident*, no. 9 (August 1987), pp. 91–112.

[46] 'History's Forgotten Doubles,' p. 46.

longer the case, as the historical way has become the only way of knowing the past, when a critical epistemology has turned into a means of dominance. The point presently is not to find alternative histories, but *alternatives to history*.[47]

Similarly, where science is concerned, the question Nandy raises is not whether or not science is constructed, and therefore limited in its claims, but rather the more fundamental question that science has become the source of a new authoritarianism. The objectification of the world which legitimizes claims to scientific truth is made possible by 'the splitting of cognition and affect', that is characteristic of the pathology of 'isolation'.[48] This pathological condition, associated by some with the psychology of Fascism, is a condition of the modern world as it has been shaped by the domination of the scientific world-view: '...by the early fifties it was clear to many that fascism was a typical psychopathology of the modern world, for it merely took to logical conclusions what was central to modernity, namely the ability to partition away human cognition and pursue this cognition unbridled by emotional or moral constraints.'[49] The question, however, is not merely that of a pathology in the premises of science, but the invasion of the life-world by the scientific world-view, which will allow no competitors in the comprehension of the world:

Today, in the last decade of the century...older, tired and wiser, we can now take courage to affirm that the main civilizational problem is not with irrational, self-contradicting superstitions but with the ways of thinking associated with the modern concept of rationality...According to this world view, the irrationality of rationality in organized normal science is no longer a mere slogan. It is threatening to take over all of

---

[47] Ibid., p. 53. For further discussion of some of these problems, see, Vinay Lal, 'History and the Possibilities of Emancipation: Some Lessons from India,' *Journal of the Indian Council of Philosophical Research* (June 1996): pp. 97–137, and, Arif Dirlik, 'History Without A Centre? Reflections of Eurocentrism,' in E. Fuchs and B. Stuchtey (eds), *Historiographical Traditions and Cultural Identities in the Nineteenth and Twentieth Centuries* (Washington, DC: German Historical Institute, forthcoming).

[48] Ashis Nandy, 'Modern Science and Authoritarianism: From Objectivity to Objectification,' *Bulletin of the Science and Technology Society*, vol. 7, no. 1 (1997), pp. 8–12. This essay is a much abbreviated version of a chapter in *Traditions, Tyranny and Utopias*, pp. 95–126.

[49] Ibid., p. 9.

human life, every interstice of culture and every form of individuality. We now have scientific training in modern sports and recreations; our everyday social relations and social activism are more and more guided by pseudo-sciences like management and social work. Our future is being conceptualized and shaped by the modern witchcraft called the science of economics. In fact, the scientific study of poverty has become more important than poverty itself. If we do not love such a future, scientific child-rearing and scientific psychotherapy are ever ready to certify us as dangerous lunatics. Another set of modern witch-doctors has taken over the responsibility of making even the revolutionaries among us scientific. Even in bed, our sexual performance is now judged according to the objective criteria of some highly scientific, how-to-do-it manuals on sex.[50]

The next step of manufacturing human beings may invalidate many of these objections based on good old-fashioned humanism, but that is not the point here. Neither is the point the juxtaposition of a scientific to a humanistic world-view. The point is that, similarly to history, science as it has taken over the world has become a negation of its own critical premises:

…modern science was once a movement of dissent. It then pluralized the world of ideas…I am now suggesting that modern science, which began as a creative adjunct to the post-medieval world and as an alternative to modern authoritarianism, has itself acquired many of the psychological features of the latter. In fact, in its ability to legitimize a vivisectional posture toward all living beings and non-living nature, modern science is now moving toward acquiring the absolute narcissism of a new passionless Caligula.[51]

It may be noteworthy that there is an ethical motivation underlying Nandy's criticism of science; to recall the sentence with which he concludes *The Intimate Enemy*: 'knowledge without ethics is not so much bad ethics as inferior knowledge.'[52]

The third corner in the triangulation of modernity is development, which is empowered by the faith in science and technology, and legitimized by a history informed by its teleology. Science and technology have been crucial to the legitimation of colonialism as a modernizing force: 'When towards the middle of the nineteenth century a proper theory of imperialism began to take shape, the

[50] Ibid., p. 10.
[51] Ibid., p. 11.
[52] *The Intimate Enemy*, p. 113.

theory used modern technology and its culture as major justifications for colonialism and its civilizing mission: Western technology
was superior because Western man and Western technological
culture were better equipped for technological achievements than
their savage counterparts.'[53] History, written in terms of various
versions of stages of development, was to serve as an alibi to this
claim, so that, if I may paraphrase, only those pasts were celebrated
which were seen as conducive to modernization and development;
and those pasts were rued which were seen as resistant to
modernity and development.[54] Developmentalism, or the ideology
of development, may be the most enduring legacy of colonialism,
that has outlasted formal colonialism:

> The problem with the idea of development is not its failure. The idea
> has succeeded beyond the dreams of its early partisans who never
> imagined that they had hit upon something whose day had come.
> Developmentalism has succeeded where western colonialism and evangeli-
> cal Christianity failed. It has established itself as one of the few genuine
> universals of our time. It has become an intimate part of every surviving
> civilization and changed the self-definitions of some of the least accessible
> societies. Development has converted even the seemingly non-
> proselytizable.[55]

I may add here in a slight revision of Nandy's sense that the
triumph of developmentalism is testimonial to the ultimate victory
of colonialism. Globalization in our day has taken over the
civilizing mission from modernization, to finish the task that
formal colonialism was unable to achieve. The ethnocentrisms that
assert themselves against Euro-American hegemony, or even against

---

[53] Ashis Nandy, 'The Traditions of Technology', in *Traditions, Tyranny and Utopias*, pp. 77–94, p. 87. The 'civilizing mission' of science and technology has been receiving increased attention in recent years. For two prominent examples, see Michael Adas, *Machines as the Measure of Man: Science, Technology and the Ideologies of Western Dominance* (Ithaca, NY: Cornell University Press, 1990), and Lewis Pyenson, *Civilizing Mission: The Exact Sciences and French Overseas Expansion* (Baltimore, MD: Johns Hopkins University Press, 1993). What distinguishes the work of Nandy and his colleagues at the Centre for the Study of Developing Societies is the critique of modernity that they base on the critique of science and technology, and their search for alternatives.

[54] Ashis Nandy, 'Development and Violence,' Working Papers, Zentrum fur europaische Studien, University of Trier, 1995, p. 2.

[55] Ibid., p. 1.

globalization, are nevertheless colonized to the extent that they legitimize themselves in terms of development; the appending of the adjective, 'alternative', to development in these cases does not really change the fact that development has become, as Gilbert Rist puts it, a 'global faith'.[56] Hence the importance to the critique of developmentalism of the non-modern, the non-scientific, and the non-historical; in other words, the indigenous. Indigenous societies around the world that showed no signs of political and economic development toward modernity were shoved out of time, as 'peoples without history', to become fair game for physical and cultural extinction. Now, in our awareness of the complicity of history in developmentalism, those societies without history, much more so than the 'civilizations' that engaged in *their* various forms of colonialism, occupy a crucial critical place in any consideration of alternatives to development—if only as paradigms, for few survive physically or culturally.[57]

CONCLUDING THOUGHTS

How to read Nandy? Some of the ideas that I have pulled out of his work have been subjects of controversy within his Indian context. His discussion of sati in terms of a native ideal of womanhood, that was perverted by the 'masculinization' of Indian society in response to colonialism, has drawn the fire of Indian

---

[56] Gilbert Rist, *The History of Development: From Western Origins to Global Faith,* (trans.), Patrick Camiller (London: Zed Books, 1997). It is interesting that with the recent crisis of 'globalization' the language of colonialism has once again returned to political discourse. Nandy has suggested, drawing on the work of Philip Aries, that developmentalist history was based on an analogy with a new conception of childhood that emerged in the seventeenth century: the child as an inferior, rather than a smaller, version of the adult (*The Intimate Enemy*, p. 14). It is interesting that as those like Mahathir Mohamed now speak of a new colonialism, his Euro-American counterparts attribute the crisis in South-East Asia to the 'immaturity' of these societies in their lack of experience with capitalism.

[57] I have elaborated on this question, and the need for distinguishing claims to authenticity of indigenous peoples from those of civilizations in, 'Postcolonial Criticism in the Perspective of Indigenous Historicism,' in Arif Dirlik, *The Postcolonial Aura: Third World Criticism in the Age of Global Capitalism* (Boulder, CO: Westview Press, 1997).

feminists and others.[58] Others have been critical of his advocacy of communitarianism (along with some of his colleagues, including Partha Chatterjee). His defence of faith against secularism has come under criticism. Still others have focused on the 'relativism' in his (and his colleagues', most prominently Vandana Shiva) discussions of science and technology that not only obscure the benefits of science, but also elevate knowledge systems that were themselves oppressive. Some like Aijaz Ahmad find in Nandy's defence of Indian traditions a cover-up of oppressive native traditions by blaming them on colonialism.[59]

As I wrote at the beginning of this discussion, it is not my intention to get involved in any of these debates. I think I appreciate the concerns of critics who view Nandy's writings from within a society that is torn by communitarian strife, where religious conflict is part of everyday politics, where the practice of *sati* continues and is condoned. The question for me is whether views such as Nandy's and those of his associates should be withheld from public debate for fear of consequences, or whether it is those very circumstances that demand the airing of such views. There is certainly a great deal of irony in the charge of 'anti-feminism' against a thinker who bemoans the 'masculinization' of Indian society, or in the suggestion that a rewriting of Indian history to stress the need for pluralism should appear as the condoning of communal violence.

I have stressed above the complexities of Nandy's thinking; complexities that may appear to the unsympathetic as contradictions: does he really repudiate history, when he concedes that history may serve critical perspectives (or even calls for 'the

[58] Ashis Nandy, 'Sati: A Nineteenth Century Tale of Women, Violence and Protest,' in Nandy, *At the Edge of Psychology: Essays in Politics and Culture* (Delhi: Oxford University Press, 1993), pp. 1–31. First published in 1980.

[59] For some of these criticisms, see Sumanta Banerjee, 'Reviewing a Debate' (Review of *Secularism and Its Critics*, (ed.), Rajeev Bhargava), *Economic and Political Weekly [EPW]* (11 July 1998): 1826–8; Meera Nanda, 'Reclaiming Modern Science for Third World Progressive Social Movements,' *EPW* (18 April 1998), pp. 915–23; Sarah Joseph, 'Politics of Contemporary Indian Communitarianism,' *EPW* (4 October 1997): 2517–23; Nivedita Menon, 'State/Gender/Community: Citizenship in Contemporary India,' *EPW* (31 January 1998), pp. 3–10. I am grateful to Vinay Bahl for bringing these critiques, to my attention.

historicization of history')? Does he really believe that science is merely a tool of authoritarianism, when he concedes that it once served as a source of criticism—and he himself freely draws on the findings of modern psychology to make his case? Is he a relativist when it comes to knowledge, when he states that 'cultural relativism...is acceptable only to the extent it accepts the universalism of some core values of humankind?[60] Does he really propose that all the evils in Indian society came with colonialism, when he concedes that this society also had a 'dark side'? Is he enough to think that the dark side of this civilization had nothing to do with its bright side, when he has a rather integrated view of societies? Does he really oppose secularism when the pluralism and tolerance he advocates is very much informed by a secular world-view? Is he unaware of the importance of political economy, when the critique of developmentalism is one of his major contributions to contemporary thinking? Finally, is he really unaware of the burden of history, when so much of what he has to say is post-historical?

Having gone through Nandy's works, and thought through them in the writing of this essay, my answer to all of these questions is negative. The questions remain, and must remain open, for Nandy as well as for many others on the contemporary intellectual scene (in India or abroad), who seek radical questions to comprehend the fundamental problems of our times; when earlier answers, and the questions that prompted them, no longer seem sufficient. The failure of earlier radical efforts to confront problems of modernity may have been beneficial to the extent that they now drive the search deeper for those problems. The way we think the world is obviously one of those fundamental problems. As I read Nandy, it seems to me that one thread runs through his work no matter what the question addressed: to recall what has been suppressed or erased by the teleologies of modernity, so that modernity itself may enrich its cultural repertoire, and recover once again the critical impulses that lay at its origins. Everything else is 'experimenting with truth'.

---

[60] 'Towards a Third World Utopia,' pp. 54–5.

14

Evasions of the Postmodern Desire

Roby Rajan

No idea in recent times has witnessed as precipitous a decline in its fortunes as that of modernity. From East and West, North and South, Left and Right, has poured forth such a torrent of critiques, deconstructions, and debunkings that surviving moderns might be pardoned for feeling hounded—driven into the ark with their binaries intact. Meanwhile, theorists of every stripe have reared their heads claiming to speak for the oppressed, the subaltern, the marginalized, the victimized. Complete with their schools, journals, lecture-circuits, and web-sites, the aggregate effect would seem to be one of a rising tide of the disenfranchised that is on the brink of overwhelming the structures of global cultural and economic domination.

Beyond the carnival milling around the guillotining block of modernity however, it is still possible to discern in the distance many of the same old faces, altogether unconcerned with the death sentence pronounced upon them. Indeed, one detects a new bounce in their gait having recently slain the dragon of communism, and confident they can turn a profit by inviting the anti-moderns to form their own theme-park complete with dramatizations of the trial, judgement, and execution of modernity. This prospect of finding oneself as a prop in a critical Disneyland must, I suspect, haunt every contemporary theorist no matter how earnest—and is a question to which I would like to return; for now let us begin with an overview of the great anti-modern wave.

ADIEU SCIENCE, ADIEU HISTORY

Its first casualty has been science, or rather the justification for science. Not that the research labs and funding agencies are on the verge of being shut down. On the contrary, there is a predictable chorus for 'more research' every time a problem surfaces in the social, psychological or natural domain. Nevertheless, it is now more or less a cliche that 'Science is discursive and rhetorical too', inducing a yawn even in the conference-going set. Indeed, to pronounce from the lectern that something or the other has been 'proven scientifically' is guaranteed to cause a ripple of twitters across the lecture hall. The correspondence theory of truth championed by the positivists has had to be hastily tossed overboard in favour of a narrative of changing 'paradigms' and 'research programmes' that provide criteria for theory choice and for what is or is not to count as acceptable evidence for theory. Science as a whole has had to come to terms with this humbler self-understanding as just another kind of narrative, and the imperialism of its claims has also had to be scaled back in proportion.

The second major casualty has been history. Again, not that university history departments are about to be disbanded. On the contrary, one is increasingly assaulted in the media by such platitudes as 'It has to be viewed in a historical perspective' or 'We must learn from the lessons of history.' Still, history has been vanquished at a number of different levels. The first—that there are 'historical laws' working their way through human societies—has been given a burial even by the most vulgar Marxists who would now rather speak of historical 'tendencies' and 'probabilities'. The second—the idea of history as the tale of Kings, Queens, and other eminences—has fallen prey to the democratizing trends of the times so that 'social histories', 'subaltern histories' and 'cultural histories' which purport to tell the stories of ordinary people leading ordinary lives are now *de rigueur*. The third—and perhaps fatal—blow to ye-olde-history has been a discrediting of the idea that the past is a gradual accretion of facts somewhat like—to use an ungainly metaphor—the waste dumps outside American towns where one layer is piled on top of the previous one and so on to form gently rising mountains of rubbish. No fact exists independent of interpretation, we are told, and interpretations are always multiple—so that we have as many histories as there are interpretations. This takes much of the punch out of history by reducing 'past reality' to the status of a 'text' open to multiple readings. As a result, various teleological ideas of the forward movement of history such as 'progress', 'growth', and 'development' now languish by the wayside.

As if all that wasn't enough, 'truth' itself has entered into crises. Nobody seems to know what the word means any more. Time was when there were distinct truths corresponding to the separate domains of fact and value: science and history supplied factual truth about nature and the past, and religious commandments or secular ethical principles furnished truth in the value domain. We have already touched upon the fates of science and history. The crisis in the value domain has, if anything, been deeper: whereas science and history could in practice still go about their usual business—albeit under altered conditions of legitimacy—with value, all bridges had been burnt. Having abandoned the gods for the somber voice of Reason, and then disrobing the latter to find a quivering false prophet has unleashed a massive hunt for substitutes that now appears to have culminated in the 'postmodern'.

THE NOUVEAU FOREIGN LEGION

The charge of the postmodern brigade has been led by Jean-Francois Lyotard who has achieved fame on the strength of his declaration that all 'grand narratives' have now come to a close, and by the following stirring call to arms: 'Let us wage a war on totality; let us be witnesses to the unpresentable; let us activate the differences and save the honor of the name.'[1] This apotheosis was first set in motion by a 'crisis of representation' said to be consequent upon the allegedly startling discovery by Ferdinand de Saussure that 'in language there are only differences without positive terms'[2]—by which is meant that the signs of language acquire meaning through their differential relationships with each other rather than a referential relationship with objects outside of language. The import of this 'finding' has been that since language cannot refer to a truth outside itself, everything expressed in language becomes a form of 'textuality'. But even this was too 'logocentric' for Jacques Derrida for whom language was not just a matter of difference but also of *differance*—by which he

---

[1] J. F. Lyotard, *The Postmodern Condition: A Report on Knowledge* (Minneapolis: University of Minnesota Press, 1984), p. 82.

[2] F. de Saussure, *Course in General Linguistics*, (trans.), W. Baskin (New York: McGraw Hill, 1966), p. 120.

means that every act of signification is riven by 'slippages' immanent in language itself. All representational authority is held to be undermined as a consequence; 'truth,' Derrida has famously declared, 'is plural'.[3] History, science, philosophy, are all at bottom linguistic practices, and being subject to *differance*, cannot serve as ground for truth. This is therefore held to be the most general economy: 'since there is no economy without *differance*, it is the most general structure of economy itself'.[4] The idea of 'general economy' here is meant to invoke associations with production, consumption, circulation and exchange—but of meanings rather than goods and services. This general economy of meanings is held to be characterized always by 'excess' in contrast to the 'restricted economy' of goods and services where the defining condition is that of scarcity.[5] A politics aimed at changing cultural representations in the general economy of meanings is said to supersede an earlier politics of struggle over surplus in the restricted economy.

Much of what goes by the name of postmodernism turns around this supplanting of an earlier (modern) semiotic in which signifier (word) was held to correspond to signified (concept) and whose evaluative categories were those of adequacy and accuracy; in declaring the freedom of signifier from signified, an 'excess' of meanings is thought to be released through the unending 'play' of signifiers that is set in motion by the lack of any referential authority. What then, one might ask, is 'society'? 'An ensemble of "language games"'[6] is Lyotard's answer—language games incommensurate with each other, each deriving its logic from its own immanent laws of signification. What of 'tradition' then? That, according to Lyotard, would amount to a coherent cultural meaning which is derisively labelled 'cultural policy', a form of 'totalizing' and therefore of authoritarianism. 'Politics' of the

---

[3] J. Derrida, *Spurs: Nietzsche's Styles*, (trans.), B. Harlow (Chicago: University of Chicago Press, 1978), p. 103.

[4] Derrida quoted in Irene Harvey, *Derrida and the Economy of Differance* (Bloomington: Indiana University Press, 1986), p. 205.

[5] J. Derrida, 'From Restricted to General Economy' *in Writing and Difference*, (trans.), Alan Bass (Chicago: University of Chicago Press, 1978), pp. 251–77.

[6] J. F. Lyotard and J. L. Thebaud, *Just Gaming*, (trans.), W. Godzich (Minneapolis: University of Minnesota Press, 1985), pp. 50–1.

anti-totalitarian variety is held to consist of 'games' of 'pastiche' and 'irony' through which the connection between signifier and signified is indefinitely deferred and the obviousness of collectively-held meanings is obscured by 'problematizing' any certainty about 'the real.' 'Pastiche' and 'irony' are thought to produce a 'radical' political effect by emptying all local contexts of ready-made meanings and opening the way for 'multiple truths'.

Here the Frenchmen are unexpectedly joined by their traditional Anglo-American antagonists in the person of Richard Rorty who after having shattered the 'mirror of nature' has discovered behind it the secret that now 'neither the religious nor the secular and liberal morality seems possible, and no third alternative has emerged'.[7] Rorty himself then boldly steps forward to fill this vacuum by proposing 'the aesthetic life' as the good life. This aesthetic life is to be one of 'private perfection' and 'self-creation', a life motivated by the 'desire to enlarge oneself', 'the desire to embrace more and more possibilities' and escape the limiting 'inherited descriptions' of oneself—a desire expressed in 'the aesthetic search for novel experiences and novel language'.[8] This quest for private perfection is coupled with a 'public morality' of liberal individualism which is to provide the necessary stable framework of social organization to pursue the good life. The aim of a just and free society is 'letting its citizens be as privatistic, irrationalist, and aestheticist as they please so long as they do it on their own time.'[9] The two moralities, private and public, are held to be separable and never to be confused with each other;[10] 'there is no reason why one cannot be a revolutionary activist on weekdays and a reader of John Ashberry on weekends,' Rorty assures us.[11] We are all then enjoined to make our lives 'works of

---

[7] Richard Rorty, 'Freud, Morality, and Hermeneutics', *New Literary History* 12 (1980), p. 180.

[8] Richard Rorty, 'Freud and Moral Reflection', in J. H. Smith and W. Kerrigan (eds), *Pragmatism's Freud: The Moral Disposition of Psychoanalysis* (Baltimore: Johns Hopkins University Press, 1986), pp. 11–5.

[9] Richard Rorty, *Contingency, Irony, and Solidarity* (Cambridge: Cambridge University Press, 1989), p. xiv.

[10] Rorty, ibid., pp. xii–xiv.

[11] Richard Rorty, 'Duties to the Self and to Others', *Salmagundi*, no. 111, (Summer 1996), p. 64.

art' on the model of the intellectual 'ironist' (presumably exemplified by Rorty himself) who revels in constantly changing self-descriptions and narrations.

In the modern West, this advocacy of the aesthetic life as the good life is at least as old as Oscar Wilde whose ideal aesthete 'will realize himself in many forms, and by a thousand different ways, and will be ever curious of new sensations and fresh points of view.'[12] But unlike Wilde who goes on to add that through constant change, the aesthete will find 'his true unity,' Rorty and other postmoderns proclaim 'fragmentation' as our enduring condition. After Freud, it is said, any conception of a unified self must be a chimera because a person is just 'a network of beliefs, desires, and emotions with nothing behind it',[13] or alternatively 'a combination of quasi-person composed of incompatible systems',[14] or yet again 'a random assemblage of contingent and idiosyncratic needs'.[15] This multiplication of selves outdoes Freud himself for whom the unconscious, although repressed, was nevertheless held together with the rest of the self in a provisional unity.

The idea that the subject lacked all unity comes not from Freud but from Jacques Lacan whose main contribution has been to integrate Saussure's idea of language as a differential system with the split subject of Freudian psychoanalysis. The self, in this theory, is held to be produced through language and therefore marked by the gaps and absences characteristic of language itself. This non-identity of the subject is the effect of its entry into 'the symbolic' (by the acquisition of language) from the secure realm of the 'imaginary' where the child is identical with itself and its mother. This separation of child from mother is the Oedipal crisis in which the unity and identity of the 'imaginary' is forever shattered—this time, not by the classic intervention of the biological father, but by the acquisition of language. Simultaneously, a 'primary repression' is said to occur: a repression of the desire for the mother—and this repression, Lacan has famously declared, structures the unconscious like a language. The desire to regain

[12] Oscar Wilde, *The Works of Oscar Wilde* (New York: Dutton, 1954), p. 934.

[13] Richard Rorty, 'Postmodernist Bourgeois Liberalism,' *Journal of Philosophy*, 80 (1983), pp. 583–9.

[14] Rorty, 'Freud and Moral Reflection,' p. 9.

[15] Rorty, ibid., p. 12.

identity with the mother is said to haunt the subject for the remainder of its life, and in all of life's activities, it seeks after the originary unity. This continual seeking which is all to no avail—because what the subject finds is never identical with what it seeks—is termed the 'lack' in the subject.

Lacan's decomposition of human subjectivity into a chain of signifiers was not quite enough for the duo of Deleuze and Guattari who were determined to blow into bits whatever little remained of the self. According to them, the problem with Lacanian psychoanalysis stems from its treating of desire as the unfillable lack that emerges between need and satisfaction. After dismissing this 'traditional logic of desire' as 'all wrong' because it is 'an idealistic conception',[16] they proceed to replace it with one in which desire is an autonomous primary force rather than a secondary function of needs. Desire, for Deleuze and Guattari, is 'production'—not lack—independent of either the imaginary or the symbolic, and being 'irreducible to any sort of unity', is able to resist socially imposed meanings.[17] The deployment of the economic metaphor of production is deliberate because what this duo wants to do is nothing short of a fusion of the Freudian and Marxian enterprises by denouncing the Oedipal structure as one of the primary modes of restricting desire in capitalist societies. After having 'deterritorialized' desire by subverting the beliefs of tradition, capitalism is said to 'reterritorialize' it by channelling all production into the commodity-form—a re-territorialization that this dream-team wants to smash. All conception of 'need' is subsequently thrown to the winds because need is just another version of 'lack' which is 'created, planned, and organized in and through social production'.[18] The Oedipus complex emerges as the villain of the piece because under capitalism, this is what re-territorializes desire within the Oedipal triangle of the nuclear family—with the result that only a residual is available for the larger social domain which therefore falls under the regulatory sway of capital. The heroes of this drama turn out to be

---

[16] G. Deleuze and F. Guattari, *Anti-Oedipus: Capitalism and Schizophrenia*, (trans.), R. Hurley *et al.* (Minneapolis: University of Minnesota Press, 1983), p. 25.

[17] Ibid., p. 42.

[18] Ibid., p. 28.

schizophrenics in whom Oedipalization has not taken, and who are able to perceive through pure 'difference' because they do not assign to signifiers any spatio-temporal points of outside reference—and therefore remain open to the ebb and flow of the flux of desire.

This version of liberation has even been taken up by some Marxists tired of waiting on the sidelines watching 'late capitalism' becoming later and later by successfully negotiating one 'crisis' after another and going from strength to strength. Determined not to set themselves up for disappointment yet again by clinging to the rusty doctrines of historical materialism, Marxists like Jameson have embraced postmodernism by trying to turn it into 'the cultural logic of late capitalism.[19] *Contra* Lyotard, Marxism is then re-installed as the psychohistorical master narrative of humankind: from, 'long-dead issues as the seasonal alteration of the economy of a primitive tribe...to passionate disputes about the nature of the Trinity,' all are folded back into 'the unity of a single great collective story...Marxism, the collective struggle to arrest a realm of freedom from a realm of Necessity'.[20] Marxism can then be made to function as humanity's 'political unconscious' and even to 'rewrite certain religious concepts—most notably Christian historicism and the concept of providence, but also the pre-theological systems of primitive magic—as anticipatory foreshadowings of historical materialism within precapitalist social formations in which scientific thinking is available as such'.[21] After much hermeneuticizing, psychoanalyzing, and postmodernizing, Jameson—still keeping faith with his Marxism—must eventually come home to its founding myth of the utopian future of industrialism, even when he despairs of finding any 'historical agent' to carry this programme forward in the land of the original 'information worker'.

Meanwhile, loud lamentations emanate from the other end of the spectrum about the sapping of cultural vitality by postmodern hedonism. Traditionalists like Daniel Bell worry that the entire project of modernity is being undermined by an antinomianism

[19] Fredric Jameson, *Postmodernism, or The Cultural Logic of Late Capitalism* (Durham: Duke University Press, 1991).

[20] Fredric Jameson, *The Political Unconscious: Narrative as a Socially Symbolic Act*, (Ithaca: Cornell University Press, 1981), pp. 19–20.

[21] Ibid., p. 285.

which served well in the battle with feudal authority but is now eroding the very culture it had ushered in. Artistic modernism, despite its contempt toward the bourgeoisie, was still in some relation with its cultural contexts because according to Bell, 'it ranged itself on the side of order and, implicitly, of a rationality of form if not of content'.[22] Indeed, it was from this tension between modernism and its bourgeois context that its most creative impulses are held to spring. 'Today', says Bell, 'modernism is exhausted. There is no tension. The creative impulses have gone slack. It has become an empty vessel. The impulse to rebellion has become institutionalized by the "culture mass" and its experimental forms have become the syntax and semiotics of advertising and *haute couture*.'[23] However, Bell has nothing to put in its place except nostalgia for the old bourgeois values of hard work and piety: 'The effort to find excitement and meaning in literature and art as a substitute for religion led to modernism as a cultural mode. Yet modernism is exhausted and the various kinds of postmodernism (in the psychedelic efforts to expand consciousness without boundaries) are simply the decomposition of the self in an effort to erase individual ego.'[24] This yearning for the trusty old 'individual ego' allied with a solid work ethic on the one hand and with traditional church authority on the other, coupled with the hasty dismissal of every 'effort to erase individual ego' as some 'psychedelic effort to expand consciousness' bespeaks Bell's fear that the current proliferation of alternative models of self and salvation in the West may finally deliver the death blow to a system vastly successful in the economic realm but for that very reason unable to contain its attendant 'cultural contradictions'.

POSTMODERN OMISSIONS

One notable absence from the various theories that litter the postmodern landscape is any mention of suffering—a concept seen as helplessly *arrière-garde* for the postmodern world of the fragment. Adorno's old fashioned insistence that 'the need to lend a

[22] Daniel Bell, *The Cultural Contradictions of Capitalism* (New York: Basic Books, 1982), pp. 28–9.

[23] Ibid., p. 20.

[24] Ibid., pp. 28–9.

voice to suffering is a condition of all truth'[25] is dismissed on the grounds that there is no 'truth' waiting to be spoken, and 'suffering' is in any case an appeal to 'experience' which is just 'discursively constructed' and therefore open to the deconstructor's demystifications. From here it is a small step to turning a deaf ear to the *logos* (speech) of the *pathein* (suffering) in pathologies such as schizophrenia and celebrating it as the new model for emancipation. It is well known among clinicians that many schizophrenias, especially in cases of paranoia, are characterized by rage, envy, vengefulness, and aggression, and tend to degenerate into irreversible catatonic depression, but these are connections we hear nothing about from the theorists of postmodern play, too busy writing paeans to schizophrenic dispersal. Meanwhile, the 'treatment' of schizophrenics is left to the devices of psychiatry, the science that may well be responsible for exacerbating the conditions it treats.[26] Madness is madness, but perhaps even madness is death only when it cannot be heard amidst the din of theory.

'Need' is also an unmentionable in postmodern theory because it is held to be merely derivative of the unmoved mover of desire. Since the demand for need fulfilment is, in Lacanian psychoanalysis, ultimately to no avail—because the subject will never find the originary identity it seeks—the self is fated to flit from one *objet petit* to desire to another, which sets off chains of imaginary substitutions *ad infinitum*. In this ingenious justification for unlimited consumption, desire always exceeds needs, generating ever wider circuits of desiring because of the 'excess' that is always said to lie beyond consumption. When Deleuze and Guattari subsequently advise that today's revolutionaries 'carry out their undertakings along the lines of the schizo process' by 'becoming caught up in a flux of desire that threatens the social order',[27] they do not seem to be aware that the global sex tourism industry has already been implementing this revolutionary programme for some years now with plane-loads of middle-aged German men arriving in Thailand as the revolutionary vanguard. This has

[25] Theodor Adorno, *Negative Dialectics*, (trans.), E. B. Ashton (New York: Continuum, 1992), pp. 17–8.

[26] See Roby Rajan, 'Pathological Rationality/Rational Pathologies,' *Alternatives*, 17 (1992), pp. 339–70.

[27] Quoted in David Harvey, *The Condition of Postmodernity* (Oxford: Basil Blackwell, 1990), p. 352.

occurred even as the site of Oedipal triangulation in the West—
the nuclear family—has been greatly enfeebled; the subsequent
unleashing of desire has resulted not in 'threatening the social
order' as anticipated by Deleuze and Guattari but its re-
territorialization—this time literally in the bodies of young girls
and boys of the Third World.

The weakening of the ego in postmodernism and the breakdown
of normative cultural codes has likewise culminated not in the
dramatic expansion of freedom as predicted by the theorists of
play, but in a greatly intensified consumption that has rushed in
to fill the void. Here the proper analogy is not with schizophrenia
but with the related condition of depression. It is common clinical
knowledge that depressions can take the form of restless, agitated,
and manic activity as well as a deadening of affect.[28] In such cases,
the activity functions as an expression of depressive rage and a
defence against the intensity of depressive experience. Perhaps
underlying the general economy of *differance* lies the even more
general economy of a collective *depression* for which the only
defence appears to be more and more *consommation*. But as
clinicians are well aware, all defensive behaviour ultimately serves
only to intensify the experience, driving the self from one addiction
to another. Lacking any unity of its own and extremely dependent
on the opinion of others and the image their reflection confirms
or casts in doubt, the postmodern self is filled with rage both for
itself and for those whose approval and admiration it craves,
throwing itself with ever greater fury into the vortex of a
narcotized consumption. Deleuze and Guattari had naively thought
that with the sluice gates opened, a massive wave of desire would
wash away the lowlands of capitalism; but the levees and channels
on the other side had already been prepared, ready to receive and
direct the flood toward the great sink hole of consumption.

The therapy that is now being prescribed for this condition is,
as we have seen with Rorty, to transform contemporary fragmentation into an aesthetic of continuous self-redescription. What these
doctors of postmodernism seem to be overlooking in their obitu-
aries of a unified self and proclamations of the 'de-centred' subject
are other traditions that have never considered the self to be either

[28] See Robert Jay Lifton, *The Life of the Self: Toward a New Psychology*
(New York: Basic Books, 1983).

entirely whole or completely fragmented. Rather, wholeness has been seen as something to be forged out of inherited fragments—fragments which however, unlike the morally blank fragments of postmodernism, were always informed by conceptions of wholeness. Nor have such traditions ever had much difficulty recognizing and venerating their saints, *pirs,* and *mahatmas* who have made themselves whole in the course of living their lives.

By delivering the injunction to 'create yourself' using an entirely new formula and become 'a self which your predecessors never knew was possible,'[29] Rorty wants to thumb his nose at all inherited conceptions of wholeness, and to wish himself and us back into the modernist *avant-garde.* Meanwhile, unbeknownst to him, the marketing and advertising departments have been at work for some decades now persuading us to make ourselves anew every few weeks, not be just a replica of the past, not be a mere copy of others, to be bold and different, to be our own person. The 'new' that Rorty proclaims as our postmodern salvation has already been produced, packaged, processed, and digested in the codes of fashion; once again the intellectual scales the steep sides of theory and reaches the summit only to find scribbled on rock the fading inscription: 'consumption was here'.

RETURN OF THE PAGAN

Rorty's fame on the lecture circuit derives from his persona as a vigorous proponent of what he terms 'the culture of liberalism' not hobbled by any 'search for foundations'. Here is how he sets it apart from 'older forms of cultural life':

The difference between a search for foundations and an attempt at redescription is emblematic of the difference between the culture of liberalism and older forms of cultural life. For in its ideal form, the culture of liberalism would be one which was enlightened, secular through and through. It would be one in which no trace of divinity remained, either in the form of a divinized world or a divinized self. Such a culture would have no room for the notion that there are nonhuman forces to which human beings should be responsible. It would drop, or drastically reinterpret, not only the idea of holiness but those of 'devotion to truth' and of 'fulfilment of the deepest needs of the spirit'. The process of de-divinization would, ideally, culminate in our no longer being able to see any use for

---

[29] Rorty, *Contingency, Irony, Solidarity,* p. 24.

the notion that finite, mortal, contingently existing human beings might derive the meanings of their lives from anything except other finite, mortal, contingently existing human beings. In such a culture, warnings of 'relativism', queries whether social institutions had become increasingly 'rational' in modern times, and doubts about whether the aims of liberal society were 'objective moral values' would seem merely quaint.[30]

In its eagerness to debunk divinity and elevate man as the measure of all things, it is Rorty's postmodern passage that has a distinctly quaint ring to it. Why, it might be asked, is Rorty still shaking his sword at divinity when Nietzsche had already announced that God was dead over a century ago, and consumerism has not only buried but recycled Him as a lifestyle choice? The answer lies in the constant postmodern need to reiterate its hatred of the referent.

While Rorty is busy scandalizing us with his gestures of throwing God overboard, Lyotard stands at the ready to hurl the fault of 'totalitarianism' at every invocation of tradition. Curiously though, Lyotard is anxious to describe his own postmodernism as a 'new paganism'; however we soon find out that this has nothing to do with the sacred invoked in pagan practices but is merely Lyotard's way of allowing performativity to act as narrative legitimation in the supposed manner of pagan story telling. He then ventures to offer us a sign to discern when 'people are not as pagan as they should be': 'that they believe in the signified of what they are saying, that they stick to this signified, and that they think that they are in the true'.[31] Despite the arrival of the scientists of *differance* however, the Cashinahua Indians—who Lyotard appears to have stumbled upon in the course of his anthropological readings and uses to demonstrate his theory—have always had available for their stories the signified of the sacred, bereft of which the stories would not signify at all. Lyotard's attempt to explain Cashinahua stories as purely performative, and to subsequently invest his own theory with the authority of 'paganism' tells us more about the signified of his own narrative—i.e. a secularism now emasculated—than about the lack of one for the Cashinahua.

Another way to put the matter would be to remind Lyotard that the signified of myth is not collapsible to the signified of either

---

[30] Ibid., p. 45.
[31] J. F. Lyotard and J. L. Thebaud, *Just Gaming*, p. 62.

science or history, because it lies beyond the pale of his entire theory of signification. To revel in the play of difference of his own texts is one thing, to treat entire cultures and their myths as versions of textuality and *differance* is quite another. Lyotard's own 'paganism' is not answerable to any referent other than secular intellectualism, but he should not by extension imagine that the rest of humankind have also lost their referents. His reduction of myth to separable instances of performativity by individual story-tellers altogether overlooks their continuity as what Ashis Nandy has called 'morality tales' informed by 'the principle of principled forgetfulness'.[32] Unlike the signified of history which has screened the past for traces of ethical content in the interests of accuracy, mythologization is not just a memorialization but a 'moralization' which remembers the past for meaning-making in the present. This often involves a collective forgetting because to remember 'accurately' can cleanse the past of moral contamination only at the expense of producing a history that one may look to for settling scores and exacting vendettas, but which cannot supply any vision save that of its own nihilistic certitude. The maxims of secular ethics that are sometimes brought to bear on historical facts to extract 'lessons' only operate as a tool of dissection on the cadaver of history, and lacking any links to collective ritual, memory, or utopia, remain a form of intellection with no social effectivity. Indeed, if it were simply a matter of blending historical fact with the proper dose of ethical maxim, the *Führer* would surely have lacked the appeal he had in the very birthplace of secular ethics and scientific history.

The postmodern avant-garde prides itself on having pried open the gap between signifier and signified to let a thousand truths bloom, but it is grievously mistaken in its conceit that it is the first to discover plurality in signification. Many traditional cultures have always worked with plural conceptions of their collective inheritance without waiting for Jacques Derrida to step ashore preaching the new gospel of the plurality of truths. The difference however is that while academic careers are now being built on the vexed question of how to marry an ethics to the new science of *differance*, the integrity of a moral vision informed by 'principled

---

[32] Ashis Nandy, 'History's Forgotten Doubles', *History and Theory*, (May 1993), p. 47.

forgetfulness' is a given in traditions and not a rider to be derived from the theorems of *differance*.

Myths, Ashis Nandy reminds us, can reconfigure the past and transcend it through creative improvisations—but not by releasing the past to pure textuality and *differance*. The past is still an authority but 'the nature of the authority is seen as shifting, amorphous and amenable to intervention'[33] within the broad constraints of a moral vision. The past remains open to intervention because it remains beholden to the moral urgency of the present; as Nandy puts it, the 'past is always open, whereas...(the) future is so only to the extent that it is a rediscovery or renewal.'[34] Unlike history which is tethered to its veracity, myths remain open to interpretation and reinterpretation, and the past is therefore continually remade by the tasks it is called to by the present and by its responsibility to always re-envision new and plural futures. Here, Nandy is not merely proposing an alternative hermeneutic applicable equally to myth and history; the hermeneutics of history must be practised in heroic signified-free isolation, whereas myth always has available to it the consolations of what Walter Benjamin has called the indestructibility of the aura of religion.

OF LEFT AND RIGHT

What sets Nandy apart from traditionalists of the West like Daniel Bell is an acute awareness of the ever-present dangers of reifying tradition:

Traditions too can objectify by drawing a line between a culture and those who live by that culture, by setting up some as the true interpreters of a culture and others as falsifiers, and by trying to defend the core of a culture from its periphery. Such uncritical commitment tends to undervalue folk as opposed to the classical, the contextual as opposed to the textual, the reinterpreted as opposed to the professionally interpreted, and the subsequent or interpolated as opposed to the original.[35]

---

[33] Ashis Nandy, *The Intimate Enemy* (Delhi: Oxford University Press, 1983) p. 57.

[34] Ibid., p. 58.

[35] Ashis Nandy, *Traditions, Tyranny and Utopias* (Delhi: Oxford University Press, 1987), p. 122.

Whereas Bell wants to banish the ghosts of postmodernism and rewind the spools of modernism so that it can be played back to us again, Nandy's is a past that must be activated through the exigencies of the present and recoverable only in the dialectical tensions that constitute it. This is why while Bell wants to summon the troops to wage war on the postmodern devil, Nandy's demand is the more modest one of opening up a space for dialogues between cultures, without any of them being forced to give up its frame of reference as a precondition. Like Jameson, Nandy too calls us to a Utopia but unlike Marxism's Utopia where industrialism's promise of wresting humankind away from the 'realm of necessity' into 'the realm of freedom' will be realized, Nandy's is not a Utopia where all traditional and non-secular frames have been cast away as the necessary trade for entry into 'the realm of freedom.' Rather, Nandy urges us on to a Utopia of maximal dialogue, exchange, and miscegenation between the universalisms emanating from widely divergent cultural frames, even frames as seemingly contradictory as myth and history, the sacred and the secular; the dystopia would be one frame reigning triumphant producing blueprints for the good life and proscribing any dissent deemed not up to snuff.

In Jameson's materialist dialectic, it is the unrealized potential within any mode of production which becomes a historical force for the development of humankind through specific forms of social and economic organization. Yet, Jameson is anxious to distance himself from any conception of the wholeness of the self or its alienation lest it be construed as 'essentialist.' But a Marxist like Marcuse was quite aware of the dangers of flirting with moral nihilism:

The immemorially acquired image of essence was formed in mankind's historical experience, which is preserved in the present form of reality, so that it can be remembered and refined to the status of essence. All historical struggles for a better organization of the impoverished conditions of existence, as well as all of suffering mankind's religious and ethical conceptions of a more just order of things, are preserved in the dialectical concept of the essence of man.[36]

Unlike Jameson who wants to jettison 'essentialism' but still salvage the Marxian programme through invocations of Utopia,

---

[36] Herbert Marcuse, *Negations: Essays in Critical Theory* (Boston: Beacon Press, 1968), p. 75.

Marcuse is explicit about the crucial links between 'the essence of man' and its realization in Utopia:

The positive concept of essence, culminating in the concept of the essence of man, which sustains all critical and polemical distinctions between essence and appearance as their guiding principle and model, is rooted in this potential structure...the essential relations represent the truth of the manifestations only insofar as the concepts which comprehend them already contain their own negation and transcendence.[37]

What Marcuse is saying here is that the 'truth of the manifestations' is not a purely epistemological question but must include critical and ethical elements as well. Marcuse's critique which contains both 'an accusation and an imperative' is rooted in the tension between essence and appearance—i.e. in the unrealized potential of the present. Although Marcuse's conception of the 'essence of man' and his Utopia make no room for alternative cultural frames and presumes upon the singularity of a universalism for all humankind, he does remain true to 'all of suffering mankind's religious and ethical conceptions' which is then distilled into his 'dialectical concept of man' for a critique rooted in the unrealized potential of humankind.

This is vastly more than can be said of Richard Rorty who imagines that all such conceptions of human essence and wholeness have become obsolete, and that we must all now live our lives on the model of the postmodern work of art. What is remarkable about this prescription is the complete and total absence of any form of the dialectic: 'fragmentation' is announced as our present condition in the manner of an objective description and 'aesthetic creation' is brought in *ex nihilo* as the solution. Traditions that have preserved plural conceptions of wholeness are instructed that they switch their models of 'moral reflection and sophistication' away from 'self-knowledge and purification' to 'self-creation and self-enlargement'.[38]

The struggle to simultaneously achieve ethical individuation and social reciprocity has been a perennial one in all cultures, and postmodernism is merely deluded if it thinks that it has bypassed it by clearly marking the private off from the public, or short-circuited it through the play of *differance*. The *modus operandi* of

[37] Ibid., p. 86.
[38] Richard Rorty, 'Freud and Moral Reflection,' pp. 11–12.

disciplinary separation has of course tried to efface this interpenetration of the projects of individuation and reciprocity: the theorists have neatly apportioned it into the specialist fields of individual psychology and social theory. The psychologists are busy offering us models of individual growth as if this growth did not call us to political tasks, and the political theorists are falling over each proclaiming their radicalism as if the oversocialized ego were automatically capable of an authentic politics. The psychoanalysts for their part have gone beyond ego psychology but have left us holding the ego's rubble with instructions to commence 'play' with our free-floating signifiers even before we have had occasion to mourn its disintegration. Here we are well advised to heed Erikson's warning that 'when the human being...loses an essential wholeness, he restructures himself and the world by taking recourse to what we may call totalism'.[39] We have now seen the face of this new totalism in the era of the postmodern—and its name is consumption.

OF CHILD AND MAN

Jurgen Habermas is among the few contemporary theorists who has recognized the significance of the relationship between the self and the social: 'The evolutionary learning processes of societies are dependent on the competencies of the individuals who belong to them. The latter, in turn, do not acquire their competences as isolated monads, but by growing into the symbolic structures of their life-world.'[40] But then Habermas, too beholden to the language of a steady evolutionism, brings in Lawrence Kohlberg's stage-wise model of ethical development that proceeds through 'pre-conventional' (obedience, conformity) and 'conventional' (interpersonal expectations, agreements, and contracts) stages to the 'post-conventional' stage in which the self understands its various rights and duties and is capable of procedural applications of universal ethical principles. This final stage modelled after the Kantian moral agent—autonomous, socially responsible, and

[39] Erik Erikson, *Identity, Youth and Crisis* (New York: Norton, 1968), p. 81.
[40] Jurgen Habermas, *Communication and the Evolution of Society* (Boston: Beacon, 1979), pp. 97–8.

possessing communicative competence—marks the outer limit of all such secular theories of individual evolution.

Childhood in such theories always appears as a stage to be overcome and cast off for good once the adult is in possession of the fullness of his maturity. Any return is only understood as a pathological regression to be treated by the psychological sciences. Such theories can make no sense of a figure like Gandhi, whose childlike comportment was the first thing that struck the visitor. Ashis Nandy describes it as follows: 'Not only did every Westerner and Westernized Indian who came in touch with Gandhi refer at least once to his child's smile; his admirers and detractors dutifully found him childlike and childish respectively.'[41] If this is to be diagnosed as regression by the psychologist, then perhaps he should dismiss all of Indian culture as regressive as well because no one in recent times has struck as deep and responsive a chord with the ordinary people of India as Gandhi did with his 'childishness'. That this lies altogether beyond the pale of the secular theories of human development ought to alert us to the possibility that try as it might to stretch and expand and tear at the boundaries of the ego by making it scale various peaks of socialization and universalization (or alternatively, by blowing it apart into scattered chains of signifiers), the ideology of the adult transcending once and for all his 'earlier stages' runs through them all and emasculates the self for subsequent colonization by consumption. To paraphrase Marcuse, postmodern theories of psychoanalysis that purport to have left the ego behind contain an accusation but no imperative. Of course the theorist is always ready to spout the tedious trope of 'play' at every seminar, but he has no inkling of what to do about the predicament of his own child, whose play has now fallen entirely under the purview and supervision of the adult's socializing technologies.

In his description of Gandhi, Nandy is suggesting that perhaps it is to childhood that we must look to counter the pathologies of oversocialization. Selfhood for Gandhi is a gift, the gift of an unrealized potential; but it is a potential that can never be brought to realization without the succour and assistance of the cultural conditions within which it must incubate. The self's potential to become whole no matter how 'fragmented' its present condition,

[41] Ashis Nandy, *The Intimate Enemy*, p. 56.

is also its moral claim to cultural conditions that will acknowledge this potential and enable its fulfilment—and is ultimately what motivates its political engagements. Beyond Freud's 'socialized ego', beyond Kohlberg's 'universal ethical principles', beyond Habermas's 'communicative competence' stands Gandhi of the childish smile asking us to undo our oversocialization and to retrieve from our childhoods a self that is capable both of individual spontaneity and of the social reciprocity necessary for authentic political engagement. Unlike Rorty's weekday revolutionary, responsibilities to self and society are inseparable for Gandhi; moreover, as Nandy says, such an emphasis is already 'built into the more sensitive traditional theories of self-in-society'.[42] This is Nandy's way of saying that we can always see in traditions possibilities for our individuation and reciprocation that no blinding flash of postmodern super-enlightenment and no schema to liberate us from dogma, ignorance, and superstition, can eclipse. This is asserted with the full awareness that every tradition is irremediably ambivalent—but this ambivalence is seen to be precisely its strength, the source of its tensions, and what makes for the possibility of it being turned and modified, its internal stresses played with, and its limits transgressed without leaping to a bold new platform of knowledge.

One of the reasons the postmodern self is at such risk today is that it is a self only in a formal sense: its selfhood is recognized in terms of its rights to maximize whatever satisfactions it chooses but when it looks to the culture for guidance as to what such satisfactions ought to be, all the culture can supply is the warning not to transgress upon the identical formal rights of others. The postmodern self thus finds itself socialized into an empty vessel waiting for adventitious filling which a grateful machinery of consumption is then happy to supply. Countering this is not simply a question of applying the right technologies of 'self-improvement' to oneself or taking up some arbitrary political cause in one's spare time as the postmoderns would have us do, but of the double struggle for simultaneous individuation and reciprocity. No sudden overcoming of the subject-object dichotomy or easy recovery of a sense of belonging is thereby guaranteed; but from

[42] Ashis Nandy, 'Cultural Frames for Social Transformation: A Credo,' *Alternatives*, 12, 1987, p. 120.

this vantage point, the ecstasy displayed by postmodern theorists when faced with the possibility of complete disintegration of self can also be put down to an affectation which need not detain us for very long. True, it has become rather difficult for increasing numbers of people to ignore them because the august halls of the Western academy are today peopled by this breed, and wherever one turns, pale shadows flit about mumbling the homilies of 'discourse', 'subjectivity', and 'sites of resistance'. But many early converts who had eagerly jumped onto the sparkling new wagon of postmodern speak have begun to get a sniff of the stench that has started to emanate from the carcass of its exhausted vocabulary. Future revolutionaries—post-postmoderns perhaps—are well advised to heed Seyla Benhabib's warning that 'the repression of internal and external nature has grown to such an unprecedented proportion that the rebellion against this repression itself becomes the object of new exploitation and manipulation.'[43]

Far from the thicket of postmodernism, stands Ashis Nandy as perhaps the only contemporary theorist with a positive vision of how the sacred can be reconciled with a commitment to cultural pluralism. Unlike the postmodernists—but like the tradition he is concerned to defend—one always already knows what he is going to say; yet every new encounter feels fresh as the morning dew.

Lyotard's Revenge

What, we may ask in conclusion, lies in store for Nandy's vision of intercultural dialogue? What, in other words, are the chances that we may push back the limits of the current imperialism so that traditions may be brought in for a mutual give and take with it? Why must consumption listen to us when it is already in total control, gently lifting us from the cradle and leading us by the hand all the way to our funeral casket? What hope does the sacred have against the shopping mall?

Here the prognosis is not good. The reason is that consumption craves plurality and has already mastered the technology of how to turn it into its opposite. Indeed it is willing to pay a premium for anything claiming origin in 'the margin', 'the different', 'the

[43] Seyla Benhabib, *Critique, Norm, and Utopia* (New York: Columbia University Press, 1986), p. 175.

other', 'the defiant', 'the resistant', so that it can multiply its niches. It has already disowned science and history for its legitimation; and whereas the shell of the nation state still remains, real authority is now vested in the marketing departments. As for dissent, that is precisely the diet it gorges itself on; the more 'radical' the dissent, the better—it may even hire the most radical dissenters as consultants for new product ideas. It is happy to fund proposals for cultural preservation and traditional rejuvenation because homogeneity is just what it dreads. It had already sung the requiem for the ideas of 'growth', 'progress', and 'development' long before the theorists; today it asks us to live in the here-and-now, to let go, be free. It is the first to denounce the destruction of the environment and is always in the vanguard to set up foundations for wilderness preservation. It despises the artificiality of polyester, plastic, and styrofoam, and urges that we go natural in every aspect of our lives. Its army of bluejeaned, earringed, long haired 'customer service representatives' now sells us its products urging us to break out of our shackles and express our dissent by individualizing our consumption patterns. It exhorts us to taste pure experience, live on the edge, smash all the codes, upset all the hiearchies. It processes all our fantasies into a convenient aesthetic, offering both Establishment and Revolution in one package. It looks to newer and newer forms of minoritarianism to expand its reach, and can even turn the guilt of the majority into market opportunity. Its surplus production of shock, outrage, and rebellion is limited only by a fear of market saturation, and its only recurring nightmare is that the scope for transgressions might get exhausted.

Lyotard of course would be happy to invite Nandy into this postmodern palace of language games. Nandy's quandary is that if he does not accept the invitation, then he must go unheard; but if he does accept it, he will most likely have to content himself with a room in the subsidized minoritarian wing with the attendant risk of waking up in the dungeon of cultural relativism. And there Lyotard's laughter may still reach him.

15

Ashis Nandy and Globalist Discourse

Frederick Buell

Recently, Malcolm Waters has argued that 'just as postmodernism was *the* concept of the 1980s, globalization may be *the* concept of the 1990s'. The mainstreaming of talk about the 'global economy' in the US over the last decade makes such a claim plausible, even though a look at the academic landscape in the west might make globalization seems but one participant in a carnival of discourses of crises and paradigm change. This carnival includes a wide variety of high-profile 'acts' ranging from deconstructionism to the multiplying 'posts-' (the postcolonial, the postmodern, the postindustrial, the postnational, the posthuman), from the end of ideology, nationalism, and nature to the advent of the third wave, the information age, and a host of other twenty-first centuryist movements. The profusion of discourses is, of course, suspicious: whether these are a succession of Lyotardian moves in the knowledge game, whether these testify to the commodification of knowledge into a succession of intellectual novelties to be consumed and discarded, or whether these testify more fundamentally to the anxieties and possibilities of a new phase of global reorganization, it is necessary to see this profusion of discourses as symptom rather than explanation, as part of a process, not simply a perspective on it.

A reader of Ashis Nandy will be grateful to him for providing an important way of doing just this. The more mainstream versions of this latter-day discursive millenarianism might well be regarded, ruefully through his eyes, as extensions of modernist logic into a 'global' age—an age in which the word 'global' signifies, from a critical perspective, a new assault on what lies outside of modernity and a new lowering of barriers (economic, societal, cultural, and geographical) to penetration by global consumer culture. The more oppositional—or, to use the word so fetishized these days, 'subversive'—of these movements would similarly need demystification, and Nandy's coolly incisive comment about postmodernism might apply to them all: they are part of 'a successful attempt to locate the world capital of dissent in the West' and a number of them operate 'by appropriating the available non-Western critiques of the West'.[1]

But, before we explore this, rather depressing view of the first-world knowledge industry and the process of globalization, I would like to argue that it masks what formerly were nearly equally prominent, and certainly more interesting possibilities. Today, as I have argued at length elsewhere, the language of the 'global'—which has had a strong Utopian element in it from the start—has undergone a neoliberal-corporate takeover, and thought about ongoing globalization has been inextricably linked, in mainstream US discourse, to visions of renewed American centrality in the world. Similarly, the most powerful contrarian views of globalization picture it as a new, still more inequitable phase of capitalism's domination of the world. In the process, however, the *faux*-Utopianism of first world visions of a new 'borderless' and 'global' economy has trumped a more genuine Utopianism—one expressed most powerfully in a vision of a world transforming itself thanks to a vastly improved and potentially transformative inter-cultural dialogue.[2]

The situation just a decade previous was quite different. Many in the United States were preoccupied with the apparent loss of US global hegemony to a dominant Japan and an empowered Pacific Rim and/or to a vision of the new, post-communist global system as post-imperial and centreless. The anxieties produced by this perception sponsored the growth of varieties of domestic US

[1] Ashis Nandy, 'State, History and Exile in South Asian Politics', *Emergences* 7–8 (1995–6), p. 125.

[2] See my 'Nationalist Postnationalism: Globalist Discourse in Contemporary American Culture,' *American Quarterly* 50: 3 (September, 1998), pp. 548–91.

fundamentalism, expressed most fashionably in conservative positions in the 'culture wars'. For others, however, this same situation meant promise, rather than crisis, and the terms 'global' and 'globalization' implied very different possible futures than restored US hegemony and the triumph of capitalism. It was here that the more genuine, alternative Utopia mentioned above was located.

In the eighties and early nineties, then, a number of alternative possibilities were quite publicly and robustly explored, possibilities which opened up considerable hope for a variety of forms of cultural activism and, at the same time, looked toward very different futures for the globalization process. Some versions of multiculturalism and postcolonialism, for example, looked forward not only to decentring and pluralizing metropolitan cultures; they also seemed to be operating in sync with a variety of global changes, from the vastly increased global mobility of peoples and information to the rising awareness that the world, in becoming one world rather than three, was becoming, possibly, a complex, interactive system, not a new imperium. Strains of postcolonialism and multiculturalism alike celebrated the transformation of previously external critiques of metropolitan cultures into internal ones, as with Edward Said's 'voyage in', and postcolonial and multicultural intellectuals were seen by a substantial number of cultural critics as key interpreters for metropolitan traditions. And commentators on cultural globalization, like Arjun Appadurai—along with many writers in the journal he and Carol Breakenridge started, *Public Culture*—proclaimed and studied in detail the startling polycentricity and interactiveness of the emerging world system, one in which money, ideas, technology, people, and cultural practices circulated in a vastly more rapid and cosmopolitan-hybrid fashion than ever before.[3]

Scholars who explored the alternative possibilities thus created came from a variety of disciplinary positions and theoretical commitments; for convenience, I will dub them postnationalist-globalists. As I have elsewhere argued, common themes in their work are the creative decomposition of the ethnically and culturally centred nation-state, on the one hand, and an attack on the

---

[3] See Edward Said, *Culture and Imperialism* (New York: Knopf, 1993) and Arjun Appadurai, *Modernity at Large: Cultural Dimensions of Globalization* (Minneapolis, University of Minnesota Press: 1996).

three worlds theory, the centred model for global order, on the other. If the three worlds theory divided the postwar global ecumene into separate 'worlds', ones distinguished and hierarchically ranked according to both geocultural-geopolitical distinctions (their distance from a geographical centre) and geo-temporal distinctions (distance from the full attainment of modernity), 'postnationalist-globalist' scholars argued that ongoing global reorganization was promoting the deconstruction of these boundaries. A similar process was at work in culturally and ethnically centred nation-states. The result was a world that looked more like (and looked on itself as) a complex, decentred, interactive synchronic system.[4] For societies and a world thus reshaped, intercultural dialogue was not just a goal to be pursued, but an essential and vitally active part of the restructuring in process.

In this opening, Nandy represented for me—as indeed he still does—one of the most cogent Utopian voices for the possibilities of a world still in play in its reorganization. Even more, for example, than Said did with his notion of the 'voyage in', Bill Ashcroft, Gareth Griffiths, and Helen Tiffin did with their portrayal of the empire writing back, or James Clifford attempted with his concept of polyphonic ethnography, Nandy, in analysing the psychological-cultural dimensions of colonial oppression and in elaborating what he called a 'third world utopia', articulated one of the fullest versions of the potential of intercultural dialogue—or, perhaps better, polylogue—to an era of global reorganization. Nandy's version was the most substantial for a number of reasons, not the least of which was his clear-sighted awareness of the complexities of such dialogue.

First, as Nandy along with many others recognized, today's intercultural dialogues do not take place between separate, autonomous, and equal partners. No: in the modern, colonial-postcolonial world, cultures have been anything but separate, autonomous, and equal; they have been inextricably entangled with each other for centuries. They have been 'intimate enemies'. But more important for the future, Nandy significantly adds, is the fact that, since 'there is always a continuity between the aggressor and his victim,...a liberation from oppressive structures outside has at the same time

---

[4] See Frederick Buell, *National Culture and the New Global System* (Baltimore: Johns Hopkins, 1994).

to mean freedom from an oppressive part of one's own self.'[5] After thus psychologizing liberation, Nandy makes a still more distinctive move: following Gandhi, he argues that full liberation means not only healing the oppressed, but also the oppressors of the consequences of their oppression. Nandy's project is thus not just to write 'on the continuity between winners and losers, seen from the losers' point of view', but to reveal how each of the cultural deformations colonialism creates is also 'a live problem in exactly those parts of the world which are commonly considered privileged'.[6]

Thus, a good portion of Nandy's *The Intimate Enemy*, his book best known in the West, is devoted to analysing the ways in which colonialism deformed the culture of England as well as the culture of India. Included in Nandy's list of problematic deformities in metropolitan culture—each of which involves he argues, the suppression of critical subtraditions in that culture by means of the hypertrophy of one particular cultural strain—are the deformation of manliness into 'aggression, achievement, control, competition and power' (9); the suppression of women; the marginalization of cultural repertoires associated with that of childhood and old age; the ideological privileging of male-adulthood as normative; the invidious division of cultures and societies into 'childlike' or primitive and adult or modern; and the reduction of the plural complexity of a culture into 'a false sense of cultural homogeneity' (32).[7] Similarly, Nandy's work emphasizes the ways in which official 'third world' nationalism has subtly replicated these deformities.

[5] Eric Wolf, *Europe and the People Without History* (Berkeley: University of California Press, 1982), provides an extended, demystifying analysis of the effects on the cultures of colonized peoples thanks to continuities between their cultures and those of their oppressors, but the work of Frantz Fanon is clearly Nandy's major influence in this analysis. Nandy goes well beyond this influence in his Gandhian emphasis on the equally deleterious effect on the culture of the colonizer of colonial relationships, and, in doing so, mines less well-known ground. Buell, *National Culture and the Global System*, pp. 133–7. The quotation from Nandy comes from 'Towards a Third World Utopia,' *Traditions, Tyranny and Utopias: Essays in the Politics of Awareness* (Delhi: Oxford University Press, 1987), p. 33.

[6] Ashis Nandy, 'Towards a Third World Utopia', p. 52.

[7] Ashis Nandy, *The Intimate Enemy: Loss and Recovery of Self under Colonialism* (Delhi: Oxford University Press, 1983), p. 9 and p. 32.

Most salient in this respect is Nandy's criticism of Frantz Fanon, whose advocacy of revolutionary violence 'ties the victim more deeply to the culture of oppression than any collaboration can'; it does so because 'cultural acceptance of the major technique of oppression in our times, organized violence, cannot but further socialize the victims to the basic values of his oppressors.'[8] More broadly still, Nandy has argued that the oppositional nationalism replicates the culture of its aggressors by cultivating an ideology of hypermasculinity and cultural reductivism in the name of an homogenous, manufactured, and thus modern 'tradition'; even more subtly, Nandy argues that this manufacture represents not simple absorption of metropolitan patterns, but a reinterpretation of tradition and the promotion of one of its subcultures of the colonized (in India, the idea of Kshatriyahood) to a position of dominance.[9]

I would like to underscore one element in this list of deformities: Nandy's critique of the ideal of cultural homogeneity as pathological and his constant awareness of the real pluralism of what we still call 'a' culture. Such a position involves, of course, a sharp rejection of one of the chief tenets of contemporary nationalism, which is, to my mind, one of Nandy's most important contributions to a genuinely alternative 'postnational-global' understanding of culture and modernity today. Today, for a culture to be an 'imagined community' and to have a 'common culture' seems to many especially inevitable and valuable, if that culture is to be healthy and survive; from the neo-fundamentalist position of the right in the US culture wars—vehemently lamenting the loss of a common culture as a means of stigmatizing the left—to even mandarin demystifications of nationalism by scholars like Benedict Anderson and Immanuel Wallerstein, a 'common culture' is still the attribute most associated with the attainment of power and legitimacy.[10] Correspondingly, the prospect of a weakening of national cultural consensus has evoked considerable anxiety, and sensational versions of non-metropolitan ethnic conflict have been

[8] Ashis Nandy, 'Towards a Third World Utopia', p. 34.

[9] Ashis Nandy, *The Intimate Enemy*, pp. 22–4.

[10] See Benedict Anderson, *Imagined Communities: Reflection on the Origin and Spread of Nationalism* (London: Verso, 1991) and the introduction to Immanuel Wallerstein, *The Modern World System* (New York: Academic Press, 1974).

foregrounded as the darker side of the new, global world order. The absence of common national cultures, coupled with ethnic strife, yields, to the metropolitan eyes, horrific 'pandaemonium'— to cite the title of a book by Daniel Patrick Moynihan.[11] Further, Samuel Huntington has enhanced these generalized fears with a more specific scenario for onrushing global conflict, one in which nations, no longer controlled by cold war ideological-political alignments, realign themselves and fiercely oppose each other in a wave of fundamentalist, civilizational consolidations. The result, according to Huntington, will be, internationally, a dispersal of violence and conflict about the globe and, domestically, it will be a severely threatened and much weakened, unhappily divided, multicultural United States.[12]

But, for a reader of Nandy, the passing of nationalism might yield less lament than opportunity, if one accepts his proposition that the very ideal of cultural homogeneity is aberration not norm. More important, one understands that it is a recent aberration, a product of colonialism and part of the culture of modernity. Nandy's vision is, in this regard, distinctive in being both majesterially civilizational, like William McNeill's in his *Polyethnicity and National Unity in World History*, and, unlike McNeill's, pointedly political. The decomposition of cultural homogeneity is not merely a vanguard condition, the revelation of an increasingly postnational world in formation; it is also an echo of the more foundational human past, an echo of practices, elaborated over millennia, of the 'premodern' world.[13] Though Nandy is not without metropolitan company in making this assertion, he is, as I shall argue below, distinctive and instructive in the degree of contemporary relevance he assigns to it.

This brings me to a second set of points to make about the subtlety of Nandy's vision of intercultural dialogue. If 'intercultural dialogue' is complicated by the fact that its partners have long been intimately connected with each other and share a history

[11] Daniel Patrick Moynihan, *Pandaemonium: Ethnicity in International Politics* (New York: Oxford University Press, 1993).

[12] Samuel P. Huntington, *The Clash of Civilizations and the Remaking of World Order* (New York: Simon and Schuster, 1996).

[13] William H. McNeill, *Polyethnicity and National Unity in World History* (Toronto: University of Toronto Press, 1985).

of deformation, contemporary dialogue cannot rely on existing spokespersons if it is to be therapeutic. Officially designated (or self-designated) conversation partners—spokespersons for a culture—should be highly suspect, being voices that are, first, constructed by the very pathological relationships one wants to undo and, second, part of the communication circuits produced by this pathological history. One needs beware of elite-official interpreters speaking in elite-official conversations on behalf of reified cultures, and to see them instead as symptoms of problems to be understood and faced. The truer dialogue partners are the 'cultures' themselves, and these, as well as the deeper conversations they sponsor, are, for several reasons, far more complex than official spokespersons allow them to be.

They are extremely complex, first and foremost, because 'cultures' are, as Nandy has argued, plural. Once the ideal of cultural homogeneity is revealed as an historical deformity not a foundational good, 'cultures' are revealed as multiple and even internally conflicting entities, containing a multitude of traditions and subtraditions. This means that 'dialogues' between them must be incredibly complex, taking place as they do between plural entities. Nor is the juxtaposition of these entities to be simplified in any way. Cultures are neither to be understood in a universalist or relativist frame; they are neither *au fond* the same nor completely different. Fetishizing cultural difference in a relativistic way others two cultures excessively. Were a 'third world' nationalist to pursue such an agenda, it would mean yielding to an 'imposed burden to be perfectly non-Western' and 'to stress only those parts of his culture which are recessive in the West and to underplay both those which his culture shares with the West and those which remain undefined by the West.'[14] On the other hand, this 'sharing' does not constitute universal humanism, as complex cultures have different Gestalts of dominant and recessive subtraditions, as well as both similar and dissimilar, shared and unshared components. If Nandy's sense of the complexity that results is unusual and elusive amid all the 'either-ors' of metropolitan debates, it would but prove one of his points: his thought here draws on the resources of non-modern cultures, resources scorned and ruled out as 'primitive' by the 'modern' West. Not

[14] Ashis Nandy, *The Intimate Enemy*, p. 73.

letting existing spokespersons and communication circuits govern dialogue allows Nandy the non-modern resource of thinking without recourse to the law of the excluded middle and to pursue, in his theory, a form of the non-dualism he has seen as characteristic of non-modern cultures generally.

A second problem in theorizing intercultural dialogue as an interaction between 'cultures' is that 'cultures' do not speak for themselves. They need interpreter-translators in order to enter into dialogue, and these, for Nandy, must be critical interpreter-translators who stand outside of, and see into, dominant ideologies. This requires a particular kind of critical, public, engaged intellectual, someone who can act as an enabler of complex dialogue. Being such a figure is, in my reading of Nandy, perhaps his deepest ambition. Though such a figure may sound like an elite official interpreter by yet another name—and such would indeed be a risk—s(he) is not, and it is interesting in this respect to contrast Nandy's conception with what Paul Ricoeur proposes as the mediator for creative encounters between cultures. Ricoeur's figure is not an official nationalist interpreter, but an artist 'who gives expression to his nation only if he does not intend it and if no one orders him to do it.'[15] The culture Ricoeur's mediator speaks for is ultimately unitary; the interpretation is not officially commissioned, but also without intentional critical engagement; and the interpreter, a creative genius, is clearly privileged over the interpreted, which would finally be nothing without him. Nandy's position as critical translator invokes, by comparison, a more modest and yet more specifically designated figure, a person with a number of unusual skills. These include, first of all, listening, with a psychologist's as well as sensitive critic's finely and professionally tuned ear, for complicated polyphonic voices, for culture as a multiplicity of often conflicting and critical subcultures, rather than a unity. Second, in listening to this disunity, the mediator must pay special attention to subcultures and subtraditions officially suppressed, such as non-modern and non-elite ones; third, the mediator needs be a skilled translator, capable of reformulating incompatible and/or incommensurate discourses, so that the integrity of neither is lost as communication is established. Fourth, the

---

[15] Paul Ricoeur, 'Universal Civilization and National Cultures', *History and Truth* (Evanston: Northwestern University Press, 1965), pp. 271–87.

mediator is committed to interpretation and translation as part of a therapeutic process of understanding and healing within and between cultures.

This latter point is perhaps the most important. A key feature of Nandy's intercultural dialogue is that it is, specifically, a therapeutic dialogue, one that changes and helps liberate both partners without, however, erasing their plural and complex different cultural repertoires. Nandy's exquisitely finely-tuned depiction of the process—for me, one of the most memorable moments in his work—makes the therapeutic complexity of the process clear:

The search for a civilization's utopia...needs not merely the ability to interpret and reinterpret one's own traditions, but also the ability to involve the often-recessive aspects of other civilizations as allies in one's struggle for cultural self-discovery, the willingness to become allies to other civilizations trying to discover their other faces, and the skills to give more centrality to these new readings of civilizations and civilizational concerns. This is the only form of a dialogue of cultures which can transcend the flourishing intercultural barters of our times.[16]

Old impositions, then, can be turned to positive use: the internalization, by formerly colonized lands, of the cultures of their oppressors enables a rich use of the 'often-recessive' features of those metropolitan cultures—metropolitan critical subtraditions repressed during the colonial era—in the process of their own self-discovery in the post-colonial period. It also encourages postcolonial intellectuals to become allies in metropolitan self-discovery. The other way round, however, the situation is more problematic. Though, in 1983, Nandy wrote that the West had not, probably, similarly incorporated India—and was, therefore, therapeutically less advantaged—a metropolitan 'postnationalist-globalist' might feel, perhaps, that some of that deficiency has been remedied by the 'voyage in' of postcolonial intellectuals and their becoming allies in an attempt at self-understanding by the culture of the metropolitan core. At any event, therapeutic change is both the rationale and goal of Nandy's Utopian theory, and, despite the results of the last decade of 'global' discourse—despite the foregrounding of the global economy over all other forms of

[16] Ashis Nandy, 'Towards a Third World Utopia', p. 55.

global exchange—Nandy's formulation stands as one of the most compelling visions of an alternative future for our time.

But, as I said at the outset, I have watched, as a metropolitan critic, the possibility of alternative futures shrink during the last decade, and I would now like to turn to the ways in which Nandy's work is helpful in supplying explanations for this disappointing development. Nandy states one side of the issue clearly when he contrasts the ideologies of the developmentalist present with those of the colonialist past. Whereas metropolitan faith in the superiority of its modern culture involved, under colonialism, the attempt to prove its cultural superiority to others, it also knew that it could not annihilate the others and that it had to live with them. There was still, Nandy argues, a sense of limits. But this, he continues,

has given away to a new form of totalism where even if you have developed the whole world, you are not happy unless you have developed the last person living in the Andamans, because even that survival of the non-developed world in some infinitesimally small pocket makes you insecure, makes you feel that there is another source of budding dissent that may come up against the fully-controlled world you have established.[17]

In short, globalization in the postcolonial, US-dominated period— the period from World War II to the present, from the commencement of US developmentalism to the rise of an American-style global consumerism—represents a much more complete attempt to recreate the earth's people; it involves the extension into a disturbing new phase of what Nandy has analysed, extensively and caustically, as modernist cultural totalism.

Nandy's critique of modernist cultural totalism is, though less well known in the West than his critique of colonialism, a crucial part of his thought, and it focuses frequently on the ways modernist culture—especially through its privileging of science and historiography—have helped rule the 'third world' or 'traditional cultures' out of global intercultural dialogue and subjected them

---

[17] Vinay Lal, 'The Defiance of Defiance and Liberation for the Victims of History: Ashis Nandy in Conversation with Vinay Lal,' *Emergences* 7–8 (1995–6), p. 65.

to a one-way process of continuing deformation and change. 'Modernity' has done this, Nandy shows, in several ways: by delegitimizing 'traditional' knowledges and relegating them to separate, premodern status, and by undertaking a variety of 'modernizing' social engineering projects that seek to regulate and ultimately eliminate the non-modern. These range from the organized violence of the colonial period to the sometimes subtler arrangements of the postwar period, and recent efforts to make the 'modern' into the only act available in the global village have been, Nandy argues, still more totalist in their ambitions than the policies and actions of the colonial period.

A look at the present reveals how contemporary metropolitan interests in the 'postmodern' represents, despite all its overt rejection of modernist totalism, in fact a general intensification, not diminution of this process. If 'modernity, like modern science, could live with everything except an attenuated status and a limited, non-proselytizing role' (102), the situation is far worse in the 'postmodern' era. The aftermath of postwar US-led developmentalism, coupled with the ratcheting of the world economy into a new global phase, has led to the attempt, in fact and especially in fantasy, to penetrate every last enclave of possible resistance, to use Fredric Jameson's terminology for describing the pre-conditions of postmodern culture. Jameson, a critic of postmodernism as the dominant cultural ideology of late capitalism, singles out two resistant enclaves as the last to go: Nature and the Unconscious. Or, as he puts it still more starkly, 'postmodernism is what you have when the modernization process is complete and nature is gone for good.'[18] To Jameson's short list of penetrated enclaves—Nature and the Unconscious—we could add, following Nandy, the idea of culture. Whereas terms like 'cultural relativism' and 'cultural pluralism' indicated that metropolitan cultures of their era were not committed to erasing cultural differences, but to restructuring them into diminished and more tightly regulated enclaves, postwar developmentalism coupled with contemporary global consumerism (or consumerism in its postmodern mode) seems bent on finding one or another method of erasing or incorporating them. As many have noted, if McDonaldization

---

[18] Fredric Jameson, *Postmodernism, Or, The Cultural Logic of Late Capitalism* (Durham: Duke University press, 1991), p. 49 and p. ix.

doesn't wipe out cultural difference wholesale, a new postmodern consumerism that thrives on difference—that scours the world's cultures for new material to utilize, commodify, and market globally—will only slightly more subtly do the trick.

For a global marketer to celebrate the completion of modernization and the arrival of a new, postmodern era of global capitalism as a kind of transcendence and fulfilment of former dreams is one thing. For a critic of these dreams, like Jameson, to make an assertion that modernization is now complete is much more serious, and it is a scary indication of how powerful the lure of the 'postmodern' is in metropolitan discourse. For to take the modernization process as complete in some fundamental sense—a claim which seems to me to be quite incorrect—is anything but a neutral historical position. I do agree that postmodernism and the global economy have placed us at the point where metropolitan intellectuals can imagine, futuristically, a completely penetrated and developed world. But I would add, significantly, that we are anything but there yet, and it takes a deaf ear to a whole area of 'global' discourse—the discourse of the global environmental crisis—to omit mentioning the lively possibility that overall global modernization is not ecologically possible. Worse, strong ideological pressure exists to entice us to take this fantasy as fact: so that accepting such an assertion, consciously or unconsciously, cheerfully or critically, means bringing some very disturbing agendas into play.

To state the matter most harshly, to assert the final triumph of modernization is to accept the most effective piece of propaganda of contemporary free market ideologues and the 'postmodern' corporate libertarians at face value: it means to accept a proposition that is disturbingly even more sweeping and fundamental than the well-publicized corporate and conservative buzzwords it resembles, such as the 'triumph of global capitalism', 'the end of ideology', and the transformative nature of the new 'information age'. It is also to disregard the fact that the totalist tenor of all of these propositions have had their (much less publicized) level-headed critics.[19] Though the acceptance of this kind of futurist

[19] The extent to which the new economy is really global and national economies subjected to it has been harshly styled, on the left and right, as 'globaloney'; the 'end of ideology' has been still more robustly debunked; and the transformative claims of the information age have also been countered.

timeline has an important kind of attractiveness, both stylistic and analytic—it enables those who accept it to write as part of an intellectual vanguard movement—it also allies them, however much they may belatedly criticize, with contemporary global capitalism, which has appropriated (particularly in the US, home of cyberlibertarianism and the global information industry) just this sort of avant-garde energy for itself.

All this is to point out little more than what others have underscored when they have observed the slippery way the subversions of 'postmodernism' seem uncomfortably to involve an acceptance of mainstream contemporary consumerism.[20] The result is that the most searching criticism of postmodernism as a de facto totalist movement, needs to work on two fronts: the exposure of the way that the new global-postmodern economy is totalist in its ambition to 'develop' everyone and the exposure of the way movements opposing it are often secret sharers of this very trait. If we begun this section by pointing out Nandy's critique of the former, the overt totalism of postmodernizing global capitalism, we need now to turn to his analysis of the latter, the covert totalism of the critical postmodern opposition—and therefore to his assertion, which I quoted at the beginning of this essay, that postmodernism is part of 'a successful attempt to locate the world capital of dissent in the West' and that it operates 'by appropriating the available non-western critiques of the West'.

If one believes Jameson's assertion that modernization is complete, and that this is the condition that must lie at the heart of contemporary critical analysis, the real action is back in the metropolis and metropolitan interest in 'third world' postcolonial intellectuals as allies in its struggle toward self-awareness is, in

---

On the former, see Steve Hanke, 'Globalization is Globaloney', *Fortune Magazine* (January 1, 1986), p. 56; Ellen Wood, '"Globalization" or "Globaloney"?' *Monthly Review* 48. 9 (Feb, 1997), pp. 21–33; and William Tabb, 'Globalization Is An Issue; the Power of Capital is The Issue', *Monthly Review* 49. 2 (June, 1997), pp. 20–31. On the latter, see the 'technorealist' manifesto at http://memex.org/meme4-02.html.

[20] For an acidly witty version of this wisdom coupled with an appreciation of Nandy, see Roby Rajan, 'Postmodernism's Hidden Economy', *Emergences* 7–8 (1995–6), pp. 187–206.

effect, over. A postmodern and anti-global-capitalist opposition would be seen as holding the keys to future dissent, not a postcolonial one. We find exactly this to be the explicitly the case among the neo-Marxian followers of Fredric Jameson who have written critically about the cultural effects of globalization. For them, postcolonial analyses not only miss the point of the new economic realities, they are also to be unmasked and discredited as part of its insidious commodification of cultural desires.[21] The result is that the key critical interpreters of the new global system are once again metropolitan insiders, and Nandy's suspicion seems to be accurate.

Less clear, but also perceptible, is the way that metropolitan thought specifically about cultural difference (particularly in its more 'postmodern' forms) has also attempted a repatriation of dissent. I do not want to be as sweeping here as Nandy is, for I would apply his remark about postmodernism less as outright delegitimization of metropolitan cultural activism than as an instructional and critical test to which it, for the most part, has not been submitted; in so doing, I would enlist Nandy's remark as an ally in metropolitan attempts at self-discovery.

In thinking about diversity, the metropolitan theory boom has sponsored a proliferation of movements based on a version of the very wisdom Nandy brought to the colonial and postcolonial situation. In the US in particular, the era in which cultural nationalism dominated discourse—a period running roughly from the 1965 proclamation of Black Power into the globalizing late 70s, one that paralleled the upsurge of anti-colonial nationalism world-wide—gave way to a second generation, a generation of what many call post-essentialist politics, which formed itself in critical dialogue with the first. This changing of the terms of cultural dispute was, like Nandy's critique of Fanon, frequently based on a sense that anticolonial and ethnic nationalism replicated features of the societies they resisted and had become therefore limiting and oppressive themselves. At the same time, post-essentialist politics called for the creation of a far fuller ecology of identity positions—or post-identities—under a greater variety of theoretical banners

---

[21] See Rob Wilson and Wimal Dissanayake, *Global/Local: Cultural Production and the Transnational Imaginary* (Durham: Duke University Press, 1996).

than nationalism or cultural nationalism had even begun to imagine.[22]

Any reader of contemporary cultural criticism in the US will realize that the ecology of critical possibilities in this era of post-identity positions and alliances is extremely full, and, like the diverse ecology of 'traditional' cultures that Nandy's 'critical traditionalism' explores, both the sheer number of, and the emphasis on hybridity and heterogeneity in, these positions is considerable. One can think of analyses and advocacy of the following types of 'post-identities': multi-cultural and postcolonial; hybrid, syncretic and heterogeneous; fluid and migratory; interruptive; decentred and marginalized; exilic and diasporic; gendered; gay and queer; global, immigrant, and third world cosmopolitan. One can further think of 'post-identities' based on women of colour, rainbow and other coalitions; on varieties of cultural boundary crossings; on residency in borderlands, literal and metaphoric; and on invented and imagined communities. Many, indeed most, of the theories on which these 'post-identity' positions are based, yoke overtly or covertly, emphasis on the importance and value of these positions to the problems and possibilities of an increasingly 'global' world; further, most see themselves, to one degree or another, as allies with and inheritors of postcolonial critiques of cultural domination.

But have two-way bridges really been built thereby between metropole and periphery? Or are there ways in which metropolitan discourse seeks to be the senior partner in such collaborations in today's 'global' world? One way of answering these questions is to ask what is most notably missing from this metropolitan list. I would argue that what is missing is inventiveness in bringing 'non-modern' and non-elite cultural positions into this postmodern play. The problem is that, like Jameson's postmodernism, much post-essentialist metropolitan cultural theory is written in a vanguardist or avant-garde atmosphere, the hidden logic of which is the logic of supersession, the logic of hypermodernity. Folks

---

[22] For an unusually lucid and engagingly written account of the process, see Elaine Kim, 'Introduction', *Charlie Chan Is Dead*, (ed.), Jessica Hagedorn (New York: Oxford University Press, 1987), pp. vii–xiv. I feel free to add to the terminological glut by calling the new era one of 'post-identity' politics, for, if you conceive of it as mobilizing 'identity positions' rather than 'identities', you have left the logic and politics of 'identity' a large step behind.

with transgressively heterogeneous identities are 'ahead' of folks who don't realize they have them or for whom heterogeneity is not a progressive transgression; this assumption is bolstered by postmodernism's desire to style these post-identity awarenesses as those of fully modernized/developed world. Compounding the problem is that folks advocating these post-identity positions tend to be located these days in universities or mandarin positions in cultural debates and thus tend to be urban elités as well as vanguards. Folks like these have interests very different than Nandy's, who focuses on the plurality of critical-traditional cultures that impinge particularly on the ordinary, non-modern, non-heroic person.

Vinay Lal's comment about Nandy's development in this regard is extremely illuminating:

In 'Cultural Frames for Social Transformation: A Credo' (1987), Nandy described himself as a *critical traditionalist*, an idea that upholders of reified notions of tradition, which appears to be the only way that both adherents and critics of tradition are prepared to view it, would find oxymoronic. Lately he would prefer to be known as an advocate of the view that we must be propelled towards the acceptance of an ecological plurality of knowledge systems and civilizations.[23]

Nandy's shift in formulation—from advocacy of critical traditionalism to ecological plurality—relocates his ideas from postcolonial critique to global Utopianism; but, in this, the past is still a crucial guide to the future, for, as Lal goes on to point out, Nandy finds 'the traditional world more post-modern, more comfortable with multiple and fluid identities, than the late twentieth century.' Nandy is not alone in asserting that postmodern heterogeneity is, in one way or another, deeply 'traditional'; this claim is, as mentioned above, the subject of one of William McNeill's books and also informs the work of other cultural historians, particularly those following in the wake of Martin Bernal's contested revision of the Western foundational past. Still, most dispute relegates, in good modern/postmodern fashion, this sort of heterogeneity, however it may be, to the past. Modernity has wiped it out. At best, it is remembered as something

---

[23] Vinay Lal, 'The Defiance of Defiance and Liberation for the Victims of History: Ashis Nandy in Conversation with Vinay Lal,' *Emergences* 7–8 (1995–6), p. 6.

the postmodern 'returns to' as it reveals itself. Multicultural theory is, for the most part, similarly fixed in the circumstances of the present and the possibilities of the future; it maintains this prospective focus in part due to its elite-theoretical commitment to social constructionism and in part due to its need to defend itself from conservative broadsides against ethnic revivalism as un-American, fundamentalist, separatist, and violent.[24]

Nandy himself comments acutely on one of the reasons for the skewed emphases of US cultural debate: America is, he argues, 'primarily a culture of the uprooted' and it seeks to deny that it is, in this, atypical, preferring

to see itself as a model for the rest of the world, a haven where the poor, the powerless and the discarded of other lands have come and remade their lives voluntarily and produced a culture that now makes transcultural sense. This preference is continuously endorsed by the élites of other countries, especially those of the third world, constantly talking of catching up with the United States in the distant future.[25]

In the comment is both sympathy for the particularism of US culture, but also a warning against its limitations—and particularly against the temptation to set up US cultural achievements as a model for the rest of the world. As a culture of exile, the US is, as Nandy argues, deeply implicated in the culture of modernity: 'while the over-stretched modern self offers us a wide range of choices as far as self-construction and self-expression go, it cannot adequately protect our self-consistency and self-continuity.[26]

Different visions of post-identity politics in the US need thus to be tested in several ways. First, they need to be queried about the extent to which they may be secretly implicated with their twin and yet opposite, global consumer culture. Thus, when David Rieff criticizes multiculturalism as a silent partner to the TNCs, as handmaiden of global capitalism's diversification and

[24] Roby Rajan gives a marvellous example of such postmodern antics in his description of Lyotard's use of the Cashinahua to advance his vision of postmodernism as a '*new* paganism' (my italics added); see 'Postmodernism's Hidden Economy,' p. 197. Nikil Pal Singh gives a rich historical contextualization to the ways in which the global horizons of contemporary multiculturalism are limited; see 'Culture/Wars: Recording Empire in an Age of Democracy,' *American Quarterly* 50: 3 (September, 1998), pp. 471–522.

[25] Ashis Nandy, 'State, History and Exile in South Asian Politics,' p. 114.

[26] Ashis Nandy, 'State, History and Exile in South Asian Politics,' p. 115.

extension of markets, not liberatory, 'multiculturalists' need to take his comments seriously. Rieff notes that 'cultural diversity', 'difference', and 'product diversity' are appropriate bedfellows, and an awareness of cultural diversity is essential to extending markets globally (in advertising, product development, and marketing strategies) in an ever more deeply penetrated world, as potential consumers become more global-multicultural.[27] Second, and more important, different versions of metropolitan post-identity politics need to be tested concerning whether they, overtly or covertly, seek to set themselves up as global models—as visions of the future that other nations should seek to develop towards. In so far as people within and outside the US come to believe, with Federico Mayor Zargosa, that 'America's main role in the new world order is not as a military superpower, but a multicultural superpower', a new form of imperialism, not a new era of global democracy will be the result.[28] The first of these critical tests has been invoked far more robustly than the second; indeed, blindness to the second possibility—and unconscious replication of the US exceptionalist/universalist ideology that runs from John Winthrop's sermon and revolutionary era nationalism to the present—has put some excellent cultural critics in difficulty.[29]

In voicing these criticisms, however, I do not mean to delegitimize US post-identity politics by undercutting from the left what so many more have tried to undercut from the right. Nandy's comments about the US and postmodernism should, I believe, work to make people see it, first of all, as a local-US discourse—one crafted to meet local needs, to serve the cause of anti-racism in the US—and, second, as one that, though it clearly responds to changes in the global environment, cannot and should not be exported uncritically as a model for others.[30] US theorists/practitioners

[27] David Rieff, 'Multiculturalism's Silent Partner,' *Harper's Magazine* (Aug. 1993), pp. 62–72.

[28] Quoted in Pico Iyer, 'The Global Village Finally Arrives,' *Time* 21 (Fall, 1993), p. 87.

[29] I think of Arjun Appadurai's uncomfortably nationalist vision of a postnational America in 'Patriotism and Its Futures,' *Public Culture* 2: 2(1993), pp. 411–30. See also Nikil Pal Singh, 'Culture/Wars: Recording Empire' for a history of conflations of American universalism and global reality.

[30] A vanguard position for ethnic cultural activism in the US draws on powerful (modern) notions enshrined in national identity (America as the place

should remember Nandy in their awareness of its limitations and specificities and also remember Nandy in remembering that, in so far as it is disseminated, it needs to be internalized and modified, not imitated, by other traditions in their attempts to own terms. Second, they should remember Nandy in their enrich their own discourses—they should use Nandy's outside criticisms as allies in their own self-discovery. To do this would mean a wide number of things, including the following: mounting a new critique of the appropriation of both 'postmodernism' and 'globalism' by a new wave of neo-imperialism and the effect of this, within US affairs, to suppress other possibilities and cooptation of cultural theory; exploring the ways in which metropolitan-based cultural dissent needs to continue to yoke external critiques to its own attempts at self-discovery; and exploring the benefits of non-elite, non-modern subtraditions that continue to exist in metropolitan society and that offer substantial criticism of modernity and its ideologies.

The latter project is perhaps the most difficult. Gertrude Stein quipped that the US is the oldest country in the world, because it entered the modern era first; critical non-modern subtraditions, in Nandy's sense, have been embattled in the US as nowhere else in the world. Still, non-modern subtraditions do continue to exist and to be of considerable value to a fuller, less flattened cultural activism in the US, in one area in particular. I mean the area Jameson asserted was gone for good from the postmodern era, one which, along with culture, gender, and modernity, has also been a enduring concern for Nandy: the discourse of nature. Far more than postmodern cultural activism, the discourse of nature displays the persistence in metropolitan society of recessive 'non-modern' cultural traditions and also the attempt, in the last several decades, to cancel and/or co-opt these in the name of postmodernity.

For the environment, too, the 1990s have been a 'global' decade. Widespread publicizing of the discovery of a global environmental crisis of great magnitude culminated in the 1992 Rio conference.

---

where a new race is being forged), even as it transgresses the (modern) stigmatization of non-northern European cultures as non-modern, and it promotes a form of ethnic politics for an era in which, on the one hand, a powerful right has vilified multicultural diversity as tribalist and regressive and, on the other hand, avant-garde identities have become part of mainstream chic.

There, North-South differences occasioned much dissension, but one area of agreement between first and third world elités emerged. Development was still possible if it became 'sustainable development.' Sustainable development turned, according to Jim MacNeill, Pieter Winsemius, and Taizo Yakushiji, the Club of Rome's picture of 'limits to growth'—characterized by Zbigniew Brezezinski as a 'pessimist manifesto'—into a realizable 'growth of limits', and it returned some optimism to the sense of pervading, perhaps even apocalyptic, crisis that Rio also propagated.[31] It sponsored, among other things, visions of new, environmental friendly technologies deployed in global development projects, benefiting third world recipients and new first world environmental industries.

On the one hand, 'sustainable development' has a certain postmodern flavour to it, erecting itself, as it does, out of the acknowledgment of the failure of the modern idea of overcoming nature and promising, as it does, a replacement of modernism's sharp distinction between nature and culture with a newly-found synergistic relationship between them. On the other hand, it seems suspiciously like an ideological bandaid, something that covers up, while it continues into a supposedly 'new' era, the ills of modernity. In either reading, the widespread propagation of 'sustainable development' has restored legitimacy to the idea and ideals of postwar developmentalism, and helped hold a crisis at bay while collaborating in the contemporary sort of totalism Nandy decries. It has, on the one hand, revitalized developmentalism, despite mounting concern that development has not mitigated but, in fact, exacerbated the differences between the global rich and poor. On the other hand, it has returned environmental activism and dissent to metropolitan control: as Wolfgang Sachs argues, the idea of sustainable development promoted at Rio, successfully relegitimized the very national corporate and governmental elités who put us in this position in the first place; helped co-opt environmental NGOs; and helped hive off and delegitimize the 'radical' environmentalist opposition committed to voicing a fundamentally non-modern idea—the criticism of growth.[32]

[31] Jim MacNeill, Peter Winsemius, Taizo Yakushiji, *Beyond Interdependence: The Meshing of the World's Economy and the Earth's Ecology* (New York: Oxford University Press, 1991), pp. v., 29.

[32] Wolfgang Sachs, (ed.), *Global Ecology: A New Arena of Political Conflict* (London, Zed Books, 1993).

But, while those in favour of 'sustainable development' sought to legitimize their position by means of modernist science—by research, data accumulation, and reliance on technological development—other, more explicitly postmodern voices showed little or no such restraint. In this camp, we would have to include a variety of wings of the contemporary libertarian corporate avant-garde, from gadflies like Julian Simon to exponents of 'post-scarcity' economics and prophets of new technologies, including information publicists, nanotechnology visionaries and genetic engineering pr people. For them, 'nature' in the old sense as an 'other' to man was over, and the dropping of this barrier was styled as part of a new era of technological innovation and capitalist development—one that would lead to an earth made both capitalist-rich and post-industrially green. A similar metropolitan attempt to appropriate activism on behalf of nature has come, as eco-critics have pointed out, from postmodern cultural criticism devoted to seeing social constructionism everywhere, even in nature—in ideas of 'nature' and in 'nature' itself—and to dismissing much of the environmentalist legacy in the process.[33]

If the 'non-modern' environmental opposition, locally and also globally, has suffered from a severe frontal assault, on the one hand, and co-optation on the other, there has been some attempt to reformulate an environmental opposition that draws, in a more sophisticated way than before, on non-modern attitudes and lore. For example, there has been a growing attempt to bring a variety of formerly-excluded players and perspectives into metropolitan environmental debates—to effect, in short, a kind of 'voyage in' to environmental debates by advocates of multicultural and postcolonial perspectives. This has occurred robustly in the

[33] Some sharp eco-critical judgments on postmodernism and contemporary cultural theory can be found in Lawrence Buell, *The Environmental Imagination: Thoreau, Nature Writing, and the Formation of American Culture* (Cambridge: Harvard University Press, 1995) and Cheryl Glotfelty, 'Introduction,' *The Ecocriticism Reader* (Athens: University of Georgia Press, 1996). On the deconstruction of 'nature' and the attempt to style nature itself as social constructionist, see William Cronon, *Uncommon Ground: Rethinking the Human Place in Nature* (New York: W. W. Norton, 1996) on the former, and Kevin Kelly, *Out of Control: The New Biology of Machines, Social Systems, and the Economic World* (Reading: Addison-Wesley, 1994) for an exuberant cyberlibertarian version of the latter.

environmental justice movement in the US and also in postcolonial environmentalism and the biodiversity movement globally.[34] There are, however, a number of indications that, just as in the area of cultural studies, co-optation, as much as dialogue may be the result, and that metropolitan intellectuals again need to make 'non-modern' and 'third world' figures allies in their self-discovery.

When one reads about metropolitan acknowledgement of the environmental knowledges of pre-modern peoples, it becomes extremely important to ask whether this means appropriation of their knowledge, or extension of actual environmental stewardship to them. The truth is that it almost always does not mean the latter. One worries when the shaman Don Antonio Montero Pisco collaborates with the ethnobotanist James Duke, in exploring and preserving the pharmacopeia of the Amazon; as Don Antonio says, 'My country doesn't support herbal medicine. Young people view it as *basura*—garbage. It's foreigners who value my knowledge.' One worries even more when Arran Gare, in his *Postmodernism and the Environmental Crisis*, argues that 'the best example of postmodern politics in action is the Chipko movement of Northern India which has succeeded in putting a stop to logging and other environmentally destructive activities in the Garwhal Himalaya.'[35] Is this adoption of the Chipko movement as the prime example of localist activism, as theorized by Deleuze and Guattari, an appropriation by the postmodern, rather than an attempt to find an ally in the first world's struggle to utilize suppressed traditions for its own self-realization? Is the attempt to patent genetic material in third world crops or peoples not an appropriation by the postmodern? Aren't these re-stylings, along with increased taboos

---

[34] See, for example, on the ecojustice movement, Giovanna Di Chiro, 'Nature as Community: The Convergence of Environment and Social Justice,' *Uncommon Ground*, pp. 298–320; for a postcolonial criticism of the US wilderness tradition, see Ramachandra Guha, 'Radical American Environmentalism and Wilderness Preservation: A Third World Critique,' *Environmental Ethics* 11 (Spring, 1989), pp. 71–83 and Frédérique Apffel Marglin and Purna Chandra Mishra, 'Sacred Grovers: Regenerating the Body, the Land, and the Community,' *Global Ecology*, pp. 197–207.

[35] Arran E. Gare, *Postmodernism and the Environmental Crisis* (New York: Routledge, 1995), p. 96.

in the US against cultivating non-modern resistance to growth, disturbing in both their local and global consequences?

I think the loss of the alternative future imaginable in the late 1980s and early 1990s represents a definite flattening of the ecology of metropolitan cultural repertoires—be they in the area of cultural diversity or environmental consciousness and activism—and thus a loss in appreciation for what Nandy values and advocates. But I would be repeating the very error I criticized above if I suggested that the ecosystem of alternative knowledges had completely crashed, that postmodernization, like Jameson's modernization, was now complete.

Just how far the world as a whole is from such a state emerges from one of the great disconnects in the conversation about globalization in the US academy. Whereas Jamesonian theorists of global capitalism have tried to claim fundamental global modernization by emphasizing shocking facts like the number of TNCs whose annual budgets exceed the GNPs of large countries and asserting the global penetration of American-style consumerism, conservatives like Samuel Huntington have magisterially ignored them by arguing that the culture so many feel has taken over the world is actually weak, confined to at most a mere 1 per cent of the global population and more probably only 1 per cent. In 1994, CNN reaches just 1 per cent, and 'its president predicted that its English broadcasts might eventually appeal to 2 to 4 per cent of the market.'[36] Moreover, English itself is only spoken by roughly 7 per cent of the world's population (compared to 16 per cent for Mandarin)—a figure that has actually declined since 1958.

In a sense, one needs to say 'a plague on both your houses.' One needs to fault Huntington for his sensationalizing, fundamentalist, rabble-rousing conclusions and to fault critics of US-led global capitalism for their monomaniacal erasure of the non-modern legacies still alive in the world. Ashis Nandy, in emphasizing the living complexity of non-modern and non-western cultures, and in trying to bring to metropolitan attention the importance of the cultural repertoires of the ordinary, non-modern peoples of the non-western world, doesn't simply steer between these extremes.

---

[36] Samuel Huntington, *The Clash of Civilizations and the Remaking of World Order*, p. 59.

Instead, he tries to make metropolitan intellectuals take seriously, the full cultural complexity of the lifeworlds of the majority of people now alive on the planet. He refuses to rule out all who are not yet thoroughly modernized, or reduce them into membership in homogenous cultures, or claim they are all reshaped by global consumerism and free-market ideology, or distance them as part of an undifferentiable mass of the new global poor yearning to be developed, or portray them as in an inherently fundamentalist-separate opposition to the West. Nandy opposes these attempts to standardize, manage, distance and exclude their complexity. Equally important, his depiction of the complex intercultural dialogue that they and their repertoires need to be part of challenges the newly 'global' era to live up to its promises, while his comments about the postmodern warn us that even metropolitan good (i.e. critical) intentions have still (as they have had in the past) the capacity to subordinate the perspectives of most of the world's population.

16

Cricket and Modernity

Peter Wollen

Ashis Nandy's extraordinary book, *The Tao Of Cricket*, begins with the following first sentence: 'Cricket is an Indian game accidentally discovered by the English.' He goes on to argue that cricket in its pristine and pure form is essentially 'Indian' in the sense that it corresponds to deep cultural (and indeed spiritual) impulses within Indian life, impulses which have sadly become alien to the English, a people who lost touch with a crucial element of their own past and became (belatedly) enslaved to a deceptive idea of 'modernity'. Cricket, Nandy argues, is a pagan game, a privileged enclave of childhood fantasy and age-old magic which challenges the modern ethos of aggressive competition, instant excitement, relentless nationalism and rationalized efficiency. No wonder that the Americans utterly fail to comprehend cricket, as they seek to induct us all into the soulless norms of the 'global economy'.

Perhaps I am exaggerating a little. Nandy is well aware of the need for balanced professionalism and the national importance of the proud moment in Indian history when Indians showed they were able to outplay the English at their own game. But he feels that this trend within the game should not be developed too far, towards what he calls 'clenched-teeth cricket', in case it damages the other, sweeter, more enlightened values of cricket—the ones which relate to its slowness (five days for a single match), its arbitrariness (changes in the weather can change the whole course of a game), its reliance on gullibility and guile and its unique aesthetic qualities (the idiosyncratic harnessing of nimble footwork, exquisite hand-eye co-ordination and split-second timing to create a personal style). He dreads the day when cricket is finally simplified for television, reduced to action-bites, with all the emphasis placed on violent confrontation, concentrated excitement and rapid results.

I was brought up, on my mother's side, in a cricketing family. My uncle, 'Tiny' Waterman, played for his county, Essex, as an unpaid amateur (a 'Gentleman', rather than a paid 'Player', in the old-fashioned parlance) and went on afterwards to become a selector for the M.C.C., picking the England team. As you might expect, he was an all-rounder, middle of the order, a useful bat who could be counted on to take the odd wicket as a change bowler. In a way, he exemplified many of the old-fashioned virtues which Nandy extols. Being English, however, I tend to look back on his cricketing days now with wry amusement rather than family pride. His kind of cricket, after all, has come to stand for a bygone age of English history.

Cricket in England is culturally weighed down by the residues of an unlamented age of snobbery and class distinction, the last days of the Empire, the amateur approach to making money and running the country, and the weird mixture of Victorian athleticism with 'muscular Christianity' which produced such ancient saws as 'Keep a straight bat,' 'Play up, play up and play the game' and, of course, 'It isn't cricket!' The English are shame-faced about cricket. It is a striking fact, but not so strange when you think about it, that the two best books on cricket, the two most vivid and the most thoughtful, should have been written by an Indian, Ashis Nandy, and by a Trinidadian, C. L. R. James, author of *Beyond a Boundary*. (I might add that the best account of the early history of English cricket, *Cricket and the Victorians*, was by a Canadian, Keith Sandiford).

In effect, Ashis Nandy's book is about the pressure every culture feels towards 'modernity' and 'modernization' and how the game of cricket reminds us of the good reasons why we should reject their will o'the wisp allure. England, since those fabled days of yore when the sound of leather on willow rang throughout the land, has finally been dragged, so it seems, into its own insular preoc-cupation with modernity. Nandy argues that India, on the other hand, still retains a reservoir of values which, properly appreciated, subtly understood, should enable it to make the necessary com-promises and live within the global economy, with just a modicum of aggression and competitiveness but without fully submitting to its norms. His argument for cricket runs parallel to the argument he developed in his earlier work, *The Intimate Enemy*, for the importance of the Gandhian legacy, so corrupted and neglected in current Indian politics.

Implicitly, at least, Nandy sees cricket itself as a game founded on a historic English compromise, between rationality and magic, professionalism and play, serious effort and festivity, which was sealed by the great Victorian cricketer, W. G. Grace, who flourished for forty years at the end of the last century. Grace, a gentlemen, dominated the game while he was active on the field, brought great crowds flocking to see him perform and gave credibility to the idea of the amateur. Grace, unprecedentedly effective as a batsman, played the game, it seemed, for reasons of personal enjoyment and civic spirit. He embodied the cricketer's code of accepting defeat without rancour, never questioning the umpire's decision, doing the decent thing rather than living by the letter of the rules. Yet, at the same time, Grace was also a ruthless run-machine, piling up unprecendentedly high scores for his team and something of a 'shamateur,' a gentleman who made more money out of the game than any professional player of his time.

For Nandy, despite all his shortcomings, Grace still represents a spirit of childlike irresponsibility—naughty rather than wicked. He sees Grace as incarnating, paradoxically, two quite different approaches to the game—the Christian/professional, with its emphasis on utilitarian values, winning at any cost, etc., and the pagan/amateur, with its emphasis on gusto and fun.

The magic of cricket, one can say, comes from the interplay of two different kinds of magic: (1) the magic of the pre-industrial, pagan world, living with the concepts of an active, powerful nature and a mostly inscrutable destiny shaping human performance and (2) the magic of the expiatory Christian virtues, such as stoicism, hard work and fierce concentration, which serve to undo one's openness to the first kind of magic.

In Grace's cricket, the two kinds of magic were both strongly present, locked in an unending conflict.

Nandy sees the same conflict re-enacted in Ranjitsinhji, the Indian prince who conquered English cricket in the late nineteenth century, eventually (in 1896) beating Grace's record of runs scored in a season, and then going on to outdo himself with further great feats of batsmanship. In England, Ranji attributed his success to the scientific approach, to diligence and concentration. In India, he was a westernizer, pro-English, relatively frugal in his personal princely expenditures, building a port and railways, reforming education, bringing Edwin Lutyens to Jamnagar as a city planner in an effort to rebuild the old disease-ridden state capital. The English, however, saw him as an oriental magician, slight in build but wielding his bat like an enchanted wand, as a genius, a juggler, an intuitive artist.

Obviously, there is an element of condescension mingled with admiration in this type of description, but it reminds me also of the Bloomsbury enthusiasm for the orientalism of Diaghilev's Ballet Russe and Nijinsky's dancing (about which I have written in my book *Raiding The Icebox*) on to which they projected an ambiguous aesthetic which had been suppressed in their own culture. Nandy too writes appreciatively about Bloomsbury, its anti-Victorianism and its anti-imperialism, in the pages of *The Intimate Enemy*. (As a footnote to this, it was Leonard and Virginia Woolf, at the Hogarth Press, who published the first book by C. L. R. James.) Ranjitsinhji, like Grace, can be seen as embodying once again the split between artist and scientist, virtuoso and utilitarian, amateur (Ranji, of course, was a gentleman) and professional that marks the whole history of cricket. For Nandy, the aristocratic aesthetic, represented by Ranjitsinhji, was supplemented within the Indian game by a lower-class plebian ethos of street (or *maidan*) cricket. For the poor, cricket was a path of upward social mobility—but it favoured the gifted rather than the well-trained or the scientifically correct. The plebeian tradition brought with it its own contradictory qualities—a drive towards professionalism but also a vernacular brio and spontaneity. In a similar spirit, James linked Caribbean cricket to carnival and calypso.

If we look back at the history of cricket in England, we can see how the historic compromise that Nandy admires was struck even before the time of Grace. Grace was able emblematically to create modern cricket on the basis of the reforms cricket had already undergone in the previous decades, roughly following, as it happened, Queen Victoria's accession to the throne in 1837. This Victorian re-structuring of cricket is sketched out schematically in lucidly attractive terms by C. L. R. James in the chapter of *Beyond a Boundary* entitled 'Prolegomena to W. G.' James's thesis is that:

in all essentials the modern game was formed and shaped between 1778, when Hazlitt was born, and 1830, when he died. It was created by the yeoman farmer, the gamekeeper, the potter, the tinker, the Nottingham coal-miner, the Yorkshire factory-hand. These artisans made it, men of hand and eye. Rich and idle young noblemen and some substantial city people contributed money, organization and prestige. Between them, by 1837 they had evolved a highly complicated game with all the characteristics of a genuinely national art form: founded on elements long present in the nation, profoundly popular in origin, yet attracting to it disinterested elements of the leisured and educated classes.

James goes on to argue that, after 1837—after the First Reform Bill of 1832, after the Repeal of the Corn Laws in 1846—the Victorian middle class began to exert political power, a class strongly marked by the tradition of puritanism, appearing now in the form of evangelical Christianity. It was this evangelical middle class which re-shaped cricket through the medium of the 'public school' system—the reform of the fee-paying boarding school for the education of the upper classes—symbolized for James by the changes instituted by Thomas Arnold at Rugby school in the 1850s and memorialized in 1857 by Thomas Hughes's novel, *Tom Brown's Schooldays*, a book which left a lasting mark on British culture.

These were the founding years of what others have called 'Muscular Christianity', an attempt to retain the aristocratic virtues of public service and outdoor sport, while getting rid of the aristocratic penchant for violence and vice, and to emphasize instead the middle-class virtues of hard work and moral commitment, while de-emphasizing utilitarianism and commercialism. Essentially, their project was that of building a historic compromise between the aristocracy and the bourgeoisie as political classes. The creation of a common public school culture would provide the basis for co-operation, now that the historic Reform and Corn Law battles were settled. Cricket was a key element in this social pact.

For James and, in another way, for Nandy, this pact provided the foundation for the development of cricket as a game which, paradoxically, can be seen as both modern and pre-modern, protestant and pagan, utilitarian and ludic, professional and amateur, occidental and oriental, urban and rural, British and Indian (or West Indian)—the cascade of paradoxes which fascinates them both, albeit with different emphases at certain points. For an English student of the game, it looks, perhaps, a little different, though it also provokes many of the same questions. In the last analysis, this is because the discourse of 'modernity' is necessarily rather different in India or Trinidad from what it is in England. For the ex-colonial country, the idea of modernity has always been bound up with the idea of independence, of emancipation from tutelage, of building a nation, of catching up with the West.

Both Nandy and James rightly recognize the significance of the moments when Indian or West Indian cricketers proved themselves to be as good as, or better than, English cricketers—first by the individual achievements of a Ranjitsinhji or a Constantine, then by victories against the English national team in Test Matches, first in single games, then in an entire series. These were the symbolic moments when the nation entered into modernity through sport. At the same time, India and the West Indies remained, politically and economically, peripheral and, so to speak, backward—or, if you prefer the equally unilinear euphemisms, 'developing' or 'emerging'. The path forward to modernization became a crucial priority—one which was naturally seen in terms of learning from the already 'developed' world, of emulating its established definition of what it meant to be modern.

In England, the debate over modernization took a very different form. Instead of how to catch up, the issue became how to explain why England had already been caught up and overtaken, and how to reverse this trend, how to avoid a reverse slide into backwardness. Although the writing had long been legible on the wall, this debate did not really get under way until after the period of decolonization and the end of empire, on the one hand, and, on the other hand, the undeniable ascent of the United States as the world's leading political, economic and military power in the post-World War II era. Both of these developments had a particular impact on the English perception of cricket. First because cricket, above all others, had been the game played and encouraged by the imperial ruling class—from the Governor-General downward—and had played a central role in the construction of the imperial image. Second, because Britain's competitors—the United States, Western Europe, Japan, etc, did not play cricket at all, but favoured other sports instead. For these reasons, cricket in England could easily appear as too closely tied to a bygone age and an outmoded world-view.

The most recent Tory prime minister, John Major, expressed his patriotic vision of old England, as opposed to modern Europe, by appealing to the time-honoured scene of cricket played on the rustic village green—but everybody understood that he was putting the fantasy world of cricket forward in order to appease a trend in his own party towards a backward-looking 'Little Englandism', mired in heritage and mythology. Forward-looking Europe would never understand cricket, so why would we want to submerge our precious national identity into their multi-national conglomerate? Who wouldn't prefer our cricket to their globalism and rationalism and modernity? Obviously, this kind of praise was virtually a death-knell for cricket.

Whereas Nandy—and to some extent James—are able to hold on to cricket as a pointer towards an alternative path of modernization, in Britain it looks much more straightforwardly anachronistic. Support for an unmodernized cricket simply looks nostalgic. Yet, reading Nandy's book, I found myself beginning to question this kind of obvious ideological assumption, not by rethinking my attitude towards cricket, but rather by rethinking he value of modernity. In particular, I went to look once again at the so-called Nairn-Anderson theses, published in *New Left Review* in the 1960s—a series of essays which, together with Martin Wiener's *English Culture and the Decline of the Industrial Spirit*, had once shaped my own ideas on this subject, particularly through Perry Anderson's 1965 essay 'Origins of the Present Crisis', reprinted in his recent collection, *English Questions*.

Essentially, Anderson argued that the 'historic bloc' constituted by the alliance of aristocracy and bourgeoisie in the nineteenth century proved fatal to England's development in the twentieth century. It enabled the old aristocracy to extend its hold on power, politically and culturally, right up to the 1960s, in continued alliance with a supine bourgeoisie long acclimatized to its norms. As a result, in Anderson's words, chronic entropy had set in and 'the ruling order now, in the main, realizes that it must change once again. The international pressures of contemporary capitalism require a radical adaptation. The unfinished work of 1640 and 1832 must be taken up where it was left off.' That is to say, the First Reform Bill fell painfully short of a full assumption of power by the bourgeoisie and the time had finally come, over a hundred years later, to rid the country of the historic compromise between aristocrat and capitalist. In cricket terms, as we have seen, this would mean full-scale reform of the game, following, for instance, the lead of the Australian entrepreneur Kerry Packer, by introducing shorter and speedier one-day matches, revision of the rules to streamline the game, alliances with the media and liberalization of the wage structure to create an elite of highly-paid super-stars.

In political terms, of course, this meant Thatcherism. In January 1987, Anderson reconsidered his earlier call for modernization in a reflective new essay, 'The Figures of Desent', also published in the *New Left Review*. Anderson reiterated his indictment of 'the archaic nature of a ruling stratum whose personnel and traditions stretched back to an agrarian and aristocratic past that had been unbroken for centuries by civil commotion or foreign defeat.' This ruling stratum, as we have seen, was essentially a cricket-playing stratum and cricket indeed played a crucial role in the establishment of its hegemony. After discussing the failure of a series of Labour governments to disturb an unyielding status quo and dismantle the 'historic compromise' that had dominated English politics, he turns to discuss the role of Thatcherism and the 'radical right' which came to power in 1979 (and remains there, in modified form, at the time of writing).

Anderson concluded that Thatcherism too had failed to reverse the decline of Britain by reviving manufacturing industry. In fact, by the time Thatcher won her electoral victory it was already too late to reach this goal, because the power of the nation state itself had been fatally undermined by the arrival of a new trans-national phase of capitalism. Henceforth, structural changes in British society would come in response to pressure from without rather than within, from the global money market, the global labour market and the vicissitudes of world trading patterns. It may seem that I have strayed rather far from the question of cricket. But, in fact, the advent of the global economy forces us, once again, to re-think the whole question of modernity. Perhaps the epoch in which 'modernization' was a pressing preoccupation of national states has now passed. The concept of 'modernity' itself has mutated along with the world economy.

Recently, in *New Formations* 28, Peter Osborne has emphasized that, while we are rightly conscious that a certain period of modernity has now come to an end, we should resist the temptation to think that something else must naturally replace it, such as a newly established 'postmodernity'. What we actually have, in Osborne's words, is 'a still open period of transition', in which a persistent modernity is being erratically transformed. Discussing Ulrich Beck's thesis that we are embarking reflexively on a transition from one form of modernity to another, from what he calls 'industrial society' to a new genre of 'risk society', Osborne argues that this kind of transition, as described by its own advocates, can be characterized as 'conservative modernization', a way of managing change within modernity, in contrast to the 'reactionary radicalism' of the New Right, which breaks with ongoing modernization in order to resurrect a mythical past.

In their schematic histories of cricket, both James and Nandy identify a crucial turning-point when they distance themselves from the radical 'Bodyline' tactics of the English team led by Douglas Jardine in the 1930s, whose aggressive fast bowlers deliberately targeted the batsman rather than the wicket, although batsmen are properly dismissed only when the wicket they are defending is hit by the ball. Jardine and his attacking bowlers sought instead to intimidate or even physically disable the batsman and thus achieve their goal more bluntly and effectively, in a way which many felt was alien to the sporting spirit of the game. Hence the reproachful cry from James and Nandy of 'It's not cricket!'

Both writers see Jardine's bodyline strategy in a similar political way, as analogous to fascism or to ultra-imperialism—nationalism plus violence plus aggression. Their approach implies that Jardine was a 'reactionary radical', seeking to do away with Victorian compromise and re-instate an aristocratic aggressiveness and will-to-win. Jardine's vision of cricket was typical of a mythical warrior mentality, harking back both to his own experience in World War I and to the ruthless pre-Victorian days when the English aristocracy played cricket aggressively for enormously high gambling stakes. He wanted to overthrow the Victorian compromise and return to the uncontrolled violence of earlier times, when winning counted for more than playing the game. (In the pure Victorian view of the world, as Nandy points out, a 'grand defeat' was always preferable to an 'inglorious victory'.)

For Nandy, Jardine's approach prefigured the changes which nationalism and commodification seek to impose on cricket today—'a tougher spirit of competition, a more developed work ethic, greater masculinity, ruthless organization, instantaneousness, media-sensitivity, technicism and greater achievement concerns.' In Nandy's view, 'the sportsman, as a folk hero, then gradually begins to symbolize the idea of a hard-working, innocent, patriotic, law-abiding citizen whose exhibitionist narcissism, instrumental view of other human beings, and conventionality are justified by his conformity to the dominant social norms represented by "the rules of the game".' In such an over-professionalized model, not only is the playful aspect of sport lost, but also its folkways, the area which is governed, so to speak, by common law rather than statutory law, oral tradition rather than written authority. Cricket has always left such unregulated, customary areas.

Nandy's stand against clenched-teeth modernization can be seen, perhaps, as another version of radicalism—one which stresses, not the ruthlessness of the warrior, but the playfulness of the child. Nandy persistently stresses the role of nature in cricket—the way in which the vicissitudes of weather can affect the outcome of a game and tip the balance from one side to another, irrespective of their skill and effort. There is a sense in which Nandy's nature-oriented view of cricket echoes many 'Green' and feminist critiques of modernity, with their stress on the destructive effects of permanent modernization as it spreads across the whole surface of the globe. Recently, discussing India with a friend, we came up jokingly with the idea of 'futurist luddism' as one we could both support. Nandy's view of Indian cricket contains the same paradox—a rejection of modernity combined with a commitment to a transformed future. As Nandy argues, history is not unilinear, as the rhetoric of modernization brusquely assumes. Let's hope that cricket continues to pursues its path down devious byways, finessing the relentlessly forward trajectory of modernity. Like other art-forms it holds out a Utopian promise which we discard at our peril.

Select Bibliography, 1979–98 of the Writings of Ashis Nandy[*]

Vinay Lal

The following abbreviations have been used in the bibliography:

AEP   *At the Edge of Psychology* (1980)

TTU   *Traditions, Tyranny, and Utopias* (1987)

SF   *The Savage Freud* (1995)

'Emancipating Science', in *Science and Technology and Future*, edited by
   Buchholz and Wolfgange Gmelin. (Munchen: K. G. Saur, 1979). Also
   in *Seminar*, no. 238 (June 1979), pp. 33–6.

'Herbert Marcuse: Metapsychologist—A Tribute'. *Alternatives* 5, 3 (November 1979).

Alternative Sciences: Creativity and Authenticity in Two Indian Scientists.
   (New Delhi: Allied Publishers, 1980; new edn, New Delhi: Oxford
   University Press, 1995).

At the Edge of Psychology: Essays in Politics and Culture. (Delhi: Oxford
   University Press, 1980); paperback edn published as Oxford India
   Paperback, 1990. Includes the following essays: 'Sati: A Nineteenth
   Century Tale of Women, Violence and Protest', pp. 1–31; 'Woman
   versus Womanliness in India: An Essay in Cultural and Political
   Psychology', pp. 32–46; 'The Making and Unmaking of Political

* Since pieces appearing in the special double issue of *Emergences*, nos 7–8
(1995–6), entitled *Plural Worlds, Multiple Selves: Ashis Nandy and the Post-
Columbian Future*, have been reproduced in this volume, they are not mentioned in this bibliography, unless they have also been published, in the same
or different version, elsewhere.

Cultures in India', pp. 47–69; 'Final Encounter: The Politics of the Assassination of Gandhi', pp. 70–98; 'Adorno in India: Revisiting the Psychology of Fascism', pp. 99–111; and 'Indira Gandhi and the Culture of Indian Politics', pp. 112–30.**

'Woman Versus Womanliness', in *Indian Women: From Purdah to Modernity*, (ed.), B. R. Nanda. (New Delhi: Vikas Publishing House, 1976), pp. 146–60. Also published in AEP, pp. 32–47.

'The Popular Hindi Film: Ideology and First Principles'. *India International Centre Quarterly* 8, 1 (1980), pp. 89–96; reprinted as 'The Supermarket of Dreams', *The Illustrated Weekly of India* (16 March 1986), pp. 48, 50–1.

'A Post-colonial View of the East and the West'. *Alternatives* 8, 1 (March 1982), pp. 25–48.

'Science for the Unafraid'. *Deccan Herald* (30 May 1982); also in *Mainstream*, 26 June 1982; translated into Tamil by K. Manoharan, in *Vinayana Manobhava* (Madras: Lokayan, 1982).

The Intimate Enemy: Loss and Recovery of Self Under Colonialism. (New Delhi: Oxford University Press, 1983); paperback edn, 1988; translated into Gujarati as *Anatarang Ari,* (trans.), Tridip S. Dave (Ahmedabad: Behavioural Sciences Centre, 1991), and into Hindi as *Antaranga Shatru,* (trans.), Pawan Agarwal, forthcoming.

'Towards an Alternative Politics of Psychology'. *International Social Science Journal* 35, 2 (1983): pp. 323–38.

'Culture, State and the Rediscovery of Indian Politics'. *EPW* 19, 49 (8 Dec. 1984): pp. 2078–83.

'Reconstructing Childhood: A Critique of the Ideology of Adulthood'. *Alternatives* 10, 3 (Sept. 1984) pp. 359–75; revised version published in TTU, pp. 56–76. Earlier and briefer versions published in *The Times of India*, 2–4 February 1982.

'An anti-secularist manifesto'. *Seminar*, no. 314 (October 1985), pp. 1–12.

'The Bomb'. *Illustrated Weekly of India* (4 August 1985).

'The Shadow State'. *Illustrated Weekly of India* (24 February 1985) pp. 20–3.

'The Idea of Development: The Experience of Modern Psychology as a Cautionary Tale', in *Human Development in Its Social Context: A Collective Exploration*, (eds), Carlos Malmann and Oscar Nudler.

** Reviewed by Veena Das, 'Studies in Power and Authority', *Indian Express* (3 May 1981); also, vol. 22, no. 3 of the *Journal of Commonwealth & Comparative Politics* (November 1984), with contributions by Franklin A. Presler, Lucian W. Pye, Arun Bose, Sanjukta Gupta, Richard Gombich, and G. Morris Carstairs, and a response by Ashis Nandy, 'Cultures of Politics and Politics of Cultures', is devoted to a discussion of *At the Edge of Psychology*.

(London: Hodder and Stoughton, 1986). Earlier and shorter version first published in *The Times of India*, July 5 and 6, 1983.

'Ranji, Cricket and Nationalism'. *The Sunday Statesman Miscellany* (16 February 1986), pp. 1–4.

'The Sociology of Sati.' *Indian Express* (5 October 1987).

'An Intelligent Critic's Guide to Indian Cinema'. *Deep Focus*, Pt. I, 'The Cultural Matrix of the Popular Film', 1, 1 (December 1987): pp. 68–72; Pt. II, 1, 2 (June 1988): pp. 53–60; Pt. III, 'The Double in Commercial Films', 1, 3 (November 1988): 58–61; all parts published together in SF, pp. 196–236.

'Cultural Frames for Social Transformation: A Credo'. *Alternatives* 12 (1987): pp. 113–23. Also published in *Political Discourse: Explorations in Indian and Western Political Thought*, (eds), Bhikhu Parekh and Thomas Pantham (New Delhi: Sage, 1987), and as 'Winners and Victims' in *Development*, no. 1(1987). Earlier version published as 'Cultural Frames for Social Intervention: A Personal Credo', *Indian Philosophical Quarterly* 11, no. 4 (October 1984).

'Development and Authoritarianism: An Epitaph on Social Engineering'. *Lokayan Bulletin* 5, 1 (1987): pp. 39–50; also published in *Journal fur Entwicklungspolitik* 1 (1987).

Traditions, Tyranny and Utopias: Essays in the Politics of Awareness. (New Delhi: Oxford University Press, 1987); paperback edn, 1992. Includes the following essays: 'Evaluating Utopias: Considerations for a Dialogue of Cultures and Faiths', pp. 1–19; 'Towards a Third World Utopia', pp. 20–55; 'Reconstructing Childhood: A Critique of the Ideology of Adulthood', pp. 56–76l; 'The Traditions of Technology', pp. 77–94; 'Science, Authoritarianism and Culture: On the Scope and Limits of Isolation Outside and Clinic', pp. 95–126; and 'From Outside the Imperium: Gandhi's Cultural Critique of the West', pp. 127–62.

'The Human Factor'. *The Illustrated Weekly of India* (17 January 1988): pp. 20–3.

'Science in Utopia: Equity, Plurality and Openness', in *Social Reality: Perspectives and Understanding*, Janak Pandey (ed.), (New Delhi: Concept, 1988) Earlier version in *Indian International Centre Quarterly* 10, 1 (1983).

'After the Raj'. *Seminar*, no. 361 (Sept. 1989): pp. 26–31.

'The Home and the World'. *The Illustrated Weekly of India* (30 July 1989): pp. 48–51.

'Collapse of a World-View'. *Indian Express* (29 July 1989).

'The Political Culture of the Indian State'. *Daedalus* (Fall 1989): pp. 1–26.

'Shamans, Savages and the Wilderness: On the Audibility of Dissent and the Future of Civilizations'. *Alternatives* 14 (1989): pp. 263–77; portions published as 'Liberation for Those who do not Speak the

Language of Liberation', in *The Theory and Practice of Liberation at the End of the Twentieth Century*. (Brussels: The Lelio Basso Foundation for the Rights and the Liberation of Peoples, 1988).

The Tao of Cricket: On Games of Destiny and the Destiny of Games. (New Delhi: Viking and Penguin, 1989).

'The Discreet Chams of Indian Terrorism'. *The Journal of Commonwealth and Comparative Politics* 12 (1990): pp. 25–43. Also published in SF, pp. 1–31.

'Dialogue and the Diaspora'. Interview with Nikos Papastergiadis. *Third Text* 11 (Summer 1990).

'The Politics of Secularism and the Recovery of Religious Tolerance', in *Mirrors of Violence: Communities, Riots and Survivors in South Asia*, pp. 69–93. (ed.), Veena Das. (Delhi: Oxford University Press, 1990) Also reprinted in *The Book Review* 14, 6 (November–December 1990): pp. 23–9; in *Sovereignty in the World System: Contending Conceptions in Changing Global Order* (Boulder, Colorado: Lynne Rienner, 1989); and as a publication of the Rajiv Gandhi Institute for Contemporary Studies, New Delhi, Paper No. 29 (1995), with a response by Akeel Bilgrami. Earlier version published as 'The Fate of Secularism', in *Forum Gazette*, 1 and 16 July 1986, and in *The Illustrated Weekly of India* (20 July 1986).

'Satyajit Ray's Secret Guide to Exquisite Murders: Creativity, Social Criticism, and the Partitioning of the Self'. *East-West Film Journal* 4, 2 (1990): pp. 14–37. Also published in SF, pp. 237–66.

'Hinduism versus Hindutva: The Inevitability of a Confrontation'. *The Times of India* (18 February 1991).

'The Remembered City'. *Seminar*, no. 379 (March 1991), pp. 43–7.

'Terrorism Indian Style'. *Indian Express (Sunday) Magazine* (7 April 1991: 1ff. Longer version published as 'Terrorism—Indian Style', *Seminar*, no. 401 (January 1993), pp. 35–41, and in the series 'Hull Papers in Politics' (University of Hull, 1992).

'Images of the Indian State', in *The State in Crisis: Dr Mohan Sinha Mehta Memorial Lectures*, (ed.), P. S. Sundaram. (Bombay: Somaiya Publications, 1992).

'Irresistibly of Crime Fiction'. *Hindu Sunday Magazine* (5 July 1992), p. xiv.

'Irrationally Yours'. *The Sunday Observer Colour Magazine* (15–21 November 1992), 'Life' Section, p. 1.

'In the Name of God'. *The Sunday Observer Colour Magazine* (6–12 December 1992), 'Life' Section, p. 1.

'The Other Within: The Strange Case of Radhabinod Pal's Judgment on Culpability'. *New Literary History* 23, 1 (Winter 1992): pp. 45–67. Also published in SF, pp. 53–80.

'Secularism'. *Seminar*, no. 394 (June 1992): pp. 29–30.

'State', in *The Development Dictionary: A Guide of Knowledge and Power*, (ed.), Wolfgang Sachs (London: Zed Books, 1992), pp. 264–74.

'Why Is sport no longer cricket?' *The Hindu* (6 December 1992).

'Oh! What a Lovely Science'. *Z Papers* 11, no. 4 (July–October 1993).

'Trialogue as a Foreword', foreword to Makarand Paranjape, *Decolonization and Development: Hind Svaraj Revisioned* (New Delhi: Sage Publications, 1993): pp. 7–13.

'Culture, Voice and Development: A Primer for the Unsuspecting'. *Thesis Eleven*, no. 39 (1994): pp. 1–18.

The Illegitimacy of Nationalism: Rabindranath Tagore and the Politics of Self. (New Delhi: Oxford University Press, 1994), portion previously published as 'The Fear of Nationalism', *Yatra* 2, edn Alok Bhalla (New Delhi: Harper Collins, 1994): pp. 3–18.

'Sati as Profit Versus Sati as a Spectacle: The Public Debate on Roop Kanwar's Death'. In *Sati, the Blessing and the Curse: The Burning of Wives in India*, (ed.), John Stratton Hawley (New York: Oxford University Press, 1994): pp. 13–159. Also published as 'Sati in Kali Yuga: The Public Debate on Roop Kanwar's Death', in SF, pp. 32–52.

'The Fear of Gandhi: Nathuram Godse and His Successors'. *The Times of India* (27 April 1994).

'Sudden Death'. *Sunday Times of India* (10 July 1994), p. 16.

'Sugar in History: An Obituary of the Humble Jaggery'. *The Times of India* (16 July 1994).

'Philosophy of Coca-Cola: The Simple Joy of Living'. *The Times of India* (27 August 1994).

'Value of Politics: The Greedy Road to Success'. *The Times of India* (10 September 1994).

'Fear in the Air: The Inner Demons of Society'. *The Times of India* (14 October 1994).

'Violence in Our Times: In Search of Total Control'. *The Times of India* (29 October 1994).

'Culture as Resistance: Violence, Victimhood and Voice'. *The Times of India* (10 December 1994).

'Human Rights Today: View from the West and East'. *The Times of India* (28 December 1994).

'Development and Violence [pamphlet]'. Trier: Zentrum fur europaische Studien, Universitat Trier, 1995.

'History's Forgotten Doubles' *History and Theory*, Theme Issue 34: World Historians and their Critics (1995): pp. 44–66; reprinted in Philip Pomper, Richard H. Elphick, and Richard T. Vann, (eds), *World History; Ideologies, Structures, and Identities* (Oxford: Basil Blackwell, 1998), pp. 159–78.

Ashis Nandy: A Reader, (ed.), D. R. Nagaraj (in Kannada). (Heggodu, Karnataka: Akshara Prakashana, 1995) *Akshara Chintana* series.

The Savage Freud and Other Essays in Possible and Retrievable Selves. (New Delhi: Oxford University Press, 1995; Princeton: Princeton University Press, 1995); Includes the essays: 'The Discreet Charms of Indian Terrorism', pp. 1–31; 'Sati in Kali Yuga: The Public Debate on Roop Kanwar's Death', pp. 32–51; 'The Other Within: The Strange Case of Radhabinod Pal's Judgement on Culpability', pp. 53–80; 'The Savage Freud: The First Non-Western Psychoanalyst and the Politics of Secret Selves in Colonial India', pp. 81–144; 'Moern Medicine and Its Nonmodern Critics: A Study in Discourse', pp. 145–95; 'An Intelligent Critic's Guide to Indian Cinema', pp. 196–236; and 'Satyajit Ray's Secret Guide to Exquisite Murders: Creativity, Social Criticism, and the Partioning of the Self', pp. 237–66.

'Popular Cinema: A Slum's Eye View of Indian Politics'. *The Times of India* (9 January 1995).

'The Future University'. *Seminar*, no. 425 (January 1995): pp. 95–6.

'And just how evil is our neighbour?', *Sunday Times of India* (29 January 1995), 'Insight', p. 3.

'Popular Cinema: The Politics of Triviality'. *The Times of India* (2 February 1995).

'Culture of Consumerism: Targeting the Lonely Individual'. *The Times of India* (6 March 1995).

'Responses to Development: Dissent and Cultural Destruction'. *The Times of India* (15 April 1995).

'Depressing Prognosis: Redefining the Indian State'. *The Times of India* (15 May 1995).

'Emergency Remembered: Standing up to be Counted'. *The Times of India* (22 June 1995).

'Hindi Cinema and Half-Forgotten Dialects: An Interview with Ashis Nandy.' By Christopher Pinney. *Visual Anthropology Review* 11, no. 2 (Fall 1995): pp. 7–16.

'Future of Poverty: Development and Destitution'. *The Times of India* (16 February 1996).

'Bearing Witness to the Future'. *Futures* 28, nos 6–7 (August– September 1996): pp. 636–9; shorter version published as 'Can future studies create opportunities for dissent?' *Futures Bulletin* 22, no. 3 (September 1996): 1, 15–6.

'Bashiruddin Ahmed: A Scholar of Indian Democracy [Obituary]'. *The Times of India* (14 September 1996).

'Satyajit Ray's India'. *Deep Focus: A Film Quarterly* (Bangalore) 6 (1996): pp. 32–8.

'Modern Science and Authoritarianism: From Objectivity to Objectification'. *Bulletin Sci. Tech. Soc.* 17, no. 1 (1997): pp. 8–12.

'The Twilight of Certitudes: Secularism, Hindu Nationalism, and Other Masks of Deculturation'. *Alternatives* 22, no. 2 (April–June 1997): pp. 157–76.

'A Report on the Present State of Health of the Gods and Goddesses in South Asia.' *Manushi*, no. 99 (March–April 1997): pp. 5–9.

'The Fantastic India–Pakistan Battle'. *Futures* 29, no. 10 (December 1997): pp. 909–18.

'The Future of Dissent'. *Seminar*, no. 460 (December 1997): pp. 42–5.

'Consumerism: Its Hidden Beauties and Politics'. *Development* 41, no. 1 (1998): pp. 58–60.

Exiled at Home: Comprising *At the Edge of Psychology, The Intimate Enemy,* and *Creating a Nationality.* [Omnibus Volume.] Introduction by D. R. Nagaraj. (Delhi: Oxford University Press, 1998).

'The Epidemic of Nuclearism: A Clinical Profile of the Genocidal Mentality'. *WFSF* [World Futures Studies Federation] *Bulletin* 24, no. 3 (September 1998): pp. 12–3.

(Ed.) *Science, Hegemony and Violence: A Requiem for Modernity.* (Tokyo: United Nations University; New Delhi: Oxford University Press, 1988); paperback (edn), 1990. Includes 'Introduction: Science as a Reason of State', pp. 1–23. [Review by T. G. Vaidyanathan in *Lokayan Bulletin* 7, 1 (January–February 1989): 71–6].

(Ed.) *The Secret Politics of Our Desires: Innocence, Culpability and Indian Popular Cinema.* (London: Zed Press, and New Delhi: Oxford University Press, 1998). Includes 'Introduction: Indian Popular Cinema as a Slum's Eye View of Politics', pp. 1–18.

(Ed. with D. L. Sheth). *The Multiverse of Democracy: Essays in Honour of Rajni Kothari.* (New Delhi: Sage Publications, 1996).

Comparative Electoral Systems: Report of a Non-Governmental Group on Bangladesh (with Fakruddin Ahmed, Yadunath Khanal, Izlal Haider Zaidi, and Jeevan Thiagarajah). (Colombo: International Centre for Ethnic Studies, 1990).

'A New Kind of Rioting' (with Veena Das). *The Illustrated Weekly of India* (23 December 1984).

'Violence, Victimhood, and the Language of Silence' (with Veena Das). *Contributions to Indian Sociology* 19, 1 (January–June 1985): pp. 177–95. Reprinted in *The Word and the World: Fantasy, Symbol and Record,* (ed.), Veena Das. (New Delhi: Sage, 1986).

'Only Widows and Orphans Left' (with Veena Das, R. K. Das, and Manoranjan Mohanty). *Indian Express* (16 November 1984); also published in Hindi in *Jansatta* (19 November 1984).

'Culture and Personality in India' (with Sudhir Kakar). In *A Survey of Research in Psychology,* 1971–6, (ed.), Udai Pareekh. (Bombay: Popular Prakashan, 1980).

The Blinded Eye: 500 Years of Christopher Columbus (with Ziauddin Sardar,

Claude Alvares, and Merryl Wyn Davies). (Goa: The Other Press; New York: Apex Press, 1993); another version (with Ziauddin Sardar and Merryl Wyn Davies) published as *Barbaric Others: A Manifesto on Western Racism*. (London: Pluto Press; New York: Westview Press, 1993).

Report of the SAARC-NGO Observer Mission to National Assembly Elections, Pakistan—1990 (with Dorab Patel, K. Subhan, and others). (Colombo: International Centre for Ethnic Studies, 1992).

Creating a Nationality: The Ramjanmabhumi Movement and Fear of the Self (with Shikha Trivedy, Achut Yagnik and Shail Mayaram). (New Delhi: Oxford University Press, 1995).

Modern Medicine and Its Non-Modern Critics: A Study in Discourse' (with Shiv Viswanathan). In *Dominating Knowledges*, (eds), Frederique A. and Steve Marglin (Oxford: Clarendon Press, 1990), pp. 145–84.